Clarken well

X   X

D1134179

...gate Street

Bartholomew Close

Holborn

St. Bride's Churchyard

T H A M E S

A S.t Margarets	E Palace Gates	I S.t Mary Reunited	N Strand Bridge	R Walks along the R...
B Fountain	F Gates	K Spring Garden	O S.t Dunstans	S Snow hill
C Clock Tower	G Cock Pit	L S.t Martins	P Temple Gate	T Smith field
D Parliament Ho.	H Queens Garden	M S.t Giles's	Q Bridwell Palace	V V V. City Walls.

JOHN MILTON

MAN · POET · POLEMIST

JOHN MILTON

MAN · POET · POLEMIST

By EMILE SAILLENS

AGRÉGÉ DE L'UNIVERSITÉ

(Prize of the French Academy)

BASIL BLACKWELL

OXFORD

1964

John Milton, poète combattant was published in 1959
by Librairie Gallimard; this English version was
first printed in 1964

Printed in Great Britain for BASIL BLACKWELL & MOTT, LTD.
by A. R. MOWBRAY & Co. LIMITED in the City of Oxford
and bound at the KEMP HALL BINDERY

PREFACE

THIS is a version of my *John Milton, poète combattant*, written by a Frenchman for the general French reader.

Over three hundred years we vied with our English neighbours in their cult of Milton; our capital city boasts a 'rue Milton'; yet very few of us to-day are aware that two books of Milton against absolute power were burnt at Paris and Toulouse many years before we heard of Shakespeare. Mirabeau translated *Areopagitica*, Marie-Antoinette read *Paradise Regained*, but both works are unknown to our public to-day.

I deeply regretted this eclipse. Individual values being threatened to-day as much as ever, it would be greatly to our advantage to keep in mind the arguments of their mighty advocate, or to witness at the very least how nobly a true love of liberty can shape the life of a man. But the last biography of Milton in French was written by De Guerle in 1868, under Napoleon III; it has long been superseded in most respects. I decided then to tell Milton's life as we know it to-day as clearly as I could, examining impartially his writings year by year; mapping out with some precision his chaotic battle-field, but barely mentioning, if at all, the side issues that appeal only to the specialist. It seemed to me that such a record, unadorned and impersonal, would best serve Milton's memory. The spectacle of a great man playing a great rôle at the greatest moment of a great nation must suffice to win for him the admiration and respect of my French readers and might induce some of them to read Milton himself.

I was greatly encouraged by the fact that French scholarship is still interested in Milton. Men like Saurat, Thomas, Delattre, Legouis, or the historian E. G. Léonard, have helped us to understand him better. Other workers are carrying on the task. The response to their efforts is perceptible and is bound to increase.

Indeed such efforts plead in our favour more effectually than the excuse that the indifference of the French public is no exception. An English critic wrote to me: 'A sympathetic understanding of Milton's character and genius is in general sadly to seek in his own country', and he laid the blame for this on Dr. Johnson's 'caricature' of Milton the man. In fact, France and England are involved in the world-wide eclipse foreseen by Macaulay. 'The decline of Milton's fame', declares C. S. Lewis, 'marks a stage in the rebellion of "civilization" against civility.' Granted, but we have here an explanation, not an absolution. On the contrary, since 'une redoutable pan-Béotie' (Renan's phrase) and a Milton are antagonistic, a return to Milton is doubly necessary.

Professor B. A. Wright, in the preface to his *Milton's 'Paradise Lost'*, recognizes the general situation, but refuses to lose heart: 'Swimming against the tide, I do not expect to get anywhere, but tides turn'. The publisher responsible for this English edition also believes that they do. Surely Milton cannot be ignored or misunderstood for ever among the English-speaking nations who owe so much to his genius and his sacrifice.

I wish to express my gratitude to Miss K. Pond for her aid in making the translation, to Mr. R. W. Gibson for compiling the Bibliography, to Miss S. Burchardt for making the Index, to Miss E. Halliday for making a fair copy of the transcript for the press, and to Professor Hugh Trevor Roper for reading it and saving me from historical errors. I have no less pleasure in thanking for their encouragements, researches, and constructive criticisms, Professors Jacques Blondel (Univ. Clermont-Ferrand), Merritt Y. Hughes (Univ. Wisconsin), Pierre Legouis (Univ. Lyon), Jean Loiseau (Univ. Bordeaux), Olivier Lutaud (Sorbonne), Howard C. Rice Jr. (Univ. Princeton), Sir Douglas Savory (Univ. Belfast), and last, not least, the kindly and painstaking publisher of these pages, Sir Basil Blackwell.

EMILE SAILLENS

1964

References

The ENGLISH POEMS are quoted from 'The Poetical Works of J. M.', in the *Oxford Standard Authors,* the LATIN and ITALIAN POEMS from the translations edited by E. H. Visiak for the *Nonesuch Library* (thanks are due to the respective publishers for courteously granting permission for their use);

the CHIEF PROSE WORKS, from the easily accessible St. John edition, published in *Bohn's Library* (B);

the COLLEGE EXERCISES, the STATE LETTERS, and some other pieces, from *Masson's* 'Life of Milton' (M);

Pascal's PENSÉES, from the Brunschvicg edition published by *Nelson,* 1955;

the quotations from the BIBLE follow the *Authorized Version.*

The extracts from *Milton* by John Bailey and from *John Milton* by Professor Kenneth Muir are quoted by the gracious permission respectively of the Oxford University Press and Messrs. Longmans, Green & Co. Ltd.

CONTENTS

'UP . . . INTO THE HEAVEN OF HEAVENS'

ILLUSTRATIONS

The end papers are reproduced from Agas's Map of London,
1563 circa. The names of streets and places associated with
Milton have been enlarged.

'What can be more noble
or more useful in human affairs
than the vindication of liberty?'
MILTON TO OLDENBURG.

'Peu d'hommes ont fait
autant d'honneur à l'homme.'
TAINE.

INTRODUCTION

'MILTON fait liberté de tout, et prêche l'indépendance de l'homme sous quelque rapport que ce soit.' So Chateaubriand.[1]

What did Milton understand by 'liberty'? The material and moral possibility of obeying the law within us; not to be dependent on either a police force, or our own follies. Liberty thus conceived implies the supremacy of reason, a watchful personal discipline, the responsibility of the individual in all respects. Laws indeed are necessary, but insufficient: 'the intention of laws is to check the commission of vice; but liberty is the best school of virtue'.[2]

At the call of events, Milton fought for various liberties, then thrice he sang liberty itself.

Our primary sources of information are himself, his nephew Edward Phillips, his friends Aubrey and Ellwood, and an anonymous witness who was probably his former pupil, Skinner. In the next generation, Toland and Richardson collected together a few reminiscences. Then the image was blurred by legends. Over the years 1859 to 1894, David Masson published a biography in seven volumes, but problems remained and research continues.

'Not a defect in the whole of his body', Aubrey noted— 'his harmonical and noble soul did lodge in a beautiful and well-proportioned body'. He had a pale, long-shaped face, a broad forehead, large dark grey eyes which kept their brilliancy even when he became blind, a long, firm nose, the lower lip rather full, the chin resolute. He rolled his R's in Elizabethan fashion ('a certain sign of a satirical wit', declared Dryden). His light brown hair, long like that of his Adam, brushed his shoulders. His stature was somewhat short, his gestures lively, his step quick. According to the anonymous witness 'his gait was erect and manly, bespeaking courage and undauntedness (or a *nil conscire*)'. He seemed ten years younger than his age. He

---

[1] *Essai sur la Littérature anglaise*, 1836. [2] *Second Defence*, Bohn I, 294.

was sober and careful in his attire. He wore a small sword with silver hilt, and boasted that he did not fear an assailant stronger than himself. His ear was very sensitive; he had a 'delicate tuneful voice' (Aubrey), and played the organ and the bass-viol. His memory was all the more ready because he was in the habit of classifying his reading. 'He was of a very cheerful humour . . . and extremely pleasant in conversation . . . but satirical' (Aubrey). 'His deportment was sweet and affable' (Anon. W.).

He has often been accused of pride. His masters at Cambridge already observed that he was 'not ignorant of his own parts', and we should look in vain in his work for the humility of the sonnets of Michelangelo. But must we condemn what Descartes calls 'la vraie générosité qui fait qu'un homme s'estime au plus haut point qu'il se peut légitimement estimer'? Was Péguy wrong in writing to Lotte—'J'ai un office, j'ai des responsabilités énormes. Au fond, c'est une renaissance du catholicisme qui se fait par moi'? Milton also was persuaded that he had an office and responsibilities. The world would be very poor if the creators among us were not sustained by an awareness of their own value. Milton, however, never called for a reform in his interest alone. He did not regard himself as an exceptional being—hence the insistence of his demands.

What must be regretted both in him and his work is that he reacted badly to the shocks of reality. Very sensitive in his youth, he hardened his will, steeled it with reason. Virtue and liberty, one conditioning the other, seemed to him a matter of clear-sightedness and energy. His Samson asserted: 'All wickedness is weakness'. This is more or less the thought of Vauvenargues—'La raison et la liberté sont incompatibles avec la faiblesse'. Vauvenargues, however, said elsewhere—'Il est triste que la bonté n'accompagne pas toujours la force'.

It is not easy to follow the footsteps of a great poet wholly engaged in a revolution. Wholly, for in Milton everything is linked together—personal life, religious faith, patriotism, learning, prose and poetry. No dictionary can explain the most limpid of his sonnets. Every revolution presupposes undercurrents and compromises. How can an inflexible personality collaborate in such circumstances? It fell to Milton, because he remained true to himself, to oppose the very men whom he had just defended. People speak of 'Milton, the great Puritan poet'. A convenient cliché, but nothing more. Certainly, no one fought more ardently for the Puritan ideal, but what we might call the Puritan people branched off into very different tribes, and Milton belonged to none of them. Not only so; he had nearly all the Puritans of that time as his opponents. If we want to understand what he did and said, we must begin by throwing a glance at the religious and political aspects of the England of his time.

Many of the lords and almost all the gentry followed Charles I only with reluctance, for his absolutism cut across their age-old rights. On the other hand, as the merchant class grew richer, it became more impatient of arbitrary taxation. The various manifestations of discontent, however, would have remained fruitless if the Puritans had not set up against the religious and logical doctrine of the divine right of kings a doctrine no less religious and no less logical.

Since the time of Henry VIII the sovereign had appointed the bishops, and the latter enjoined on the people 'passive obedience' to King and Church. To subject the clergy themselves to the Crown was in conformity with the teachings of Luther. Henry VIII may indeed have refuted the theology of the monk of Erfurt, but his policy suited him perfectly. Luther said 'The world is the world and will never change'. The terrible drama it presents has been staged by God himself. Every member of the social body, prince or bourgeois, merchant or rough soldier, must faithfully play the part that Providence has assigned him. As a member of the church, he will nevertheless live in spirit 'in this kingdom of Christ where, wholly concerned with our salvation, we should practise charity, and the higher virtues which have no concern with this world here

B

below'.[1] Since nations are composed of actual or virtual criminals, they must have stern and undisputed masters.[2] God makes use of bad kings as necessary scourges. *Everyman, Herr Omnes*, has only one right—the right to be silent. The main tenets of the Puritans, however, hardly differed from those of Calvin.[3] Against the despairing conception of the 'jovial' Luther, the 'stern' Calvin set the optimism of the Renaissance. The world can and must change for the better. It is sufficient that 'the elect' should keep to the unadulterated Gospel, give the example of a pure life and, if circumstances will permit, subject the city to the divine law. Every man can know this law, if he listens to the Bible and his conscience. All the elect, therefore, are equal in dignity. A Calvinist parish was governed then, as to-day, by ministers and laymen chosen or accepted by itself. The ministers, equal among themselves, conformed to the decisions of elected assemblies (local, regional, or national) formed of ministers and laymen. Therefore, in any given country, the Calvinists formed an elective federation in which the authority emanated from the faithful. In Calvinist territory the prince could not, as in a Lutheran country or in England, be the *head* of the national church, but only its *arm*.[4] In fact, since the spiritual authority must always prevail, the Calvinist countries fell under the yoke of their clergy. Yet, in the name of the egalitarian principle, Castellion had already risen against Calvin. The doctrine ended by producing its fruit, despite the inconsequences of man. Faith in the autonomy of conscience was to justify the multiplication of the sects, which would render mutual tolerance necessary.

Thus the rôle of the Puritans stands out clearly. Consciously or not, indifferent or not to political problems, they undermined the theory of absolute monarchy by right

[1] See Lucien Febvre, *Martin Luther*, 1945, p. 249. Cf. Père Didon (*Les Allemands*, 1864) on 'bicephalous Germany'. Similarly, F. W. Foerster (*Erlebte Weltgeschichte*, 1954): 'the Leibnitz-Bach-Goethe brain invariably capitulates before the Ludendorff-Haushofer-Hitler brain'.
[2] See below, p. 202.
[3] See W. Haller, *The Rise of Puritanism*, New York, 1938, p. 3.
[4] Calvin, however, recognized the duties of a French subject, and French kings could rely on their Huguenots. Milton has drawn an argument from this—see p. 93.

divine. When they were powerful, Charles had to give way, or disappear. In 1638, the Puritans of Scotland took up arms against him. He was defeated ten years later by the Puritans of England.

Here a first cleavage in the Calvinist ranks becomes apparent. The struggle was so long because the Scottish Puritans and those of England fought amongst themselves. Now national jealousy played its part, of course, but it was not the only factor. Two ecclesiastical conceptions were in opposition.

In England, compromise had followed compromise. After the 'national-Catholicism' of Henry VIII, who reconciled Rome and Luther, the clergy of Edward VI had juxtaposed Luther and Zwingli. Once Mary Tudor was dead, Elizabeth restored this hybrid creed. 'In her reign', says Sir Maurice Powicke,[1] 'the Church had a medieval constitution, and a comprehensive liturgy, in which ancient, medieval, Lutheran and Zwinglian elements were welded together in beautiful English.' But she severely repressed unadulterated Calvinism as dangerous for monarchs. By some irony of history, it had entered Great Britain thanks to the violence of Mary Tudor and her Spanish husband. The English refugees in Germany, Holland and Switzerland had been able to compare Lutherans with Calvinists. Many had listened to Calvin in person. John Knox the Scotsman, former chaplain to Edward VI, had even founded an English and Calvinist Church in what was known as 'anti-Rome', Geneva to wit.

When Elizabeth came to the throne the exiles returned armed with precise ideas, and determined, according to Milton's expression, on 'the reforming of reformation itself' (B. II, 91). Elizabeth was crowned in 1558. The word 'Puritan' appears for the first time in a document in 1564, the year in which Shakespeare was born. It was then four years since the Scottish Parliament, under the impulsion of Knox, had bound Scotland to the discipline of Geneva. It is worth noting that Elizabeth, by sending a supply of

[1] *The Reformation in England*, Oxford Paperback, 1961, p. 125.

troops, had helped forward a conversion which must weaken her neighbour.

Scotland had thus passed directly and *en masse* from Catholicism to integral Calvinism, and the Kirk was kept on the right road by the iron hand of its 'presbyters'. In England there had been a gradual progression and a process of splitting up.

The progression had been only gradual because the authorities persecuted the Puritans for their lack of docility, and because worldlings jeered at them for their rigorism. (Shakespeare let fly more than one barb against these Utopians.) None the less, there was a progression; the memory of Wycliffe was still alive when the Bibles of the exiled Tyndale arrived from Germany. These were succeeded in turn by the small Geneva Bibles. Rome was detested for her many plots against the national autonomy; and it was just these Puritans who condemned the slightest recall of Papistical worship.

'The theology most prevalent among the ministers was Calvinist' (Powicke), but they seldom preached, to avoid disturbing men's minds. Many minds were thus open to the liberating message which the Puritans carried from house to house.[1] Lastly, the thousands of Huguenots who had taken refuge in England, for the most part first-class artisans, were very much listened to by the people. In 1587, Parliament would have followed them and 'reformed the Reformation', if the Queen had not opposed her veto.

Thus it happened that Puritanism at its apogee drew to itself nine Englishmen out of ten. This meant that it included the necessary number of fools, madmen and profiteers to discredit it.[2] It also followed that it was

---

[1] Burghley wrote to Elizabeth: 'The Puritans are oversqueamish and nice, yet with their careful catechising and diligent preaching, they bring forth that fruit which Your Most Excellent Majesty is to desire and wish, namely the lessening and diminishing of the papistical numbers'.

[2] This reference might well suffice, since everyone knows the English Puritans of that time. In France they are known from Taine's *Littérature anglaise* or from Hugo's *Cromwell*. The comparison, however, suggests a question. Is it not true that Hugo's exaggerations correspond better to the common conception than Taine's impartial picture? The merits of the Puritans are less familiar to us than their ridiculous side, a ridiculousness which is pardonable and which others have shared (Chaucer's Lady Prioress 'entuned in her nose ful semely' and the French Capuchins

divided. Many Anglicans who were more or less Puritans, such as Milton's parents and their son in his youth, relied on God and time. Others justified themselves by the promise of Christ, to be present wherever two or three should assemble in his name. Their clandestine groups considered themselves as so many autonomous churches, free to ally themselves or otherwise with similar communities. These 'Independents' appeared as early as 1582 and soon broke into sects. The Baptists, for instance, formed about 1608, reserved baptism for candidates of the age of reason. One of them, Busher, published his plea for complete toleration as early as 1614. An immediate and severe repression forced thousands of these dissidents to leave the country. At the time of the Great Rebellion many returned from Holland or even from America, to fight in the front rank. One of them supported Milton.

Among the dissidents of modest condition, spiritual egalitarianism was often expressed in social claims. The Levellers, among others, who have usually been calumniated, demanded a single Chamber elected by a wider suffrage and the abolition of hereditary privileges. Cromwell detested their leaders, for though he himself was an Independent and recruited from all the sects, he intended to change nothing of the social order of things.

In short, these small islands, with their seven million souls, were already harbouring as many confessions as the English-speaking world does to-day.

Mother Church was the only comforter of the Irish, downtrodden as they were by thirty thousand Anglican and Presbyterian colonists. In England and Scotland about three hundred powerful families had succeeded in remaining Catholic, but the Old Religion seemed to have disappeared from the countryside. A bare handful of old people still stammered out some syllables of the Latin of the Mass.

were still singing nasally under Louis XV), but a censor without indulgence discourages indulgence. Moreover, if he uses force, he can become odious. A single example will suffice. The Puritans preached that the Christian feasts were for the most part pagan in origin, in which they were hardly mistaken. So they refused to keep them, and this was their right. But to forbid Merry England to eat plum pudding on Christmas Day—there was an aberration all the more unpardonable as the new inquisitors called themselves individualists. See later, pp. 130 and 193.

Yet in 1642, suddenly, one half of Yorkshire declared itself
Catholic and strengthened the royal army. For the Catholics,
even in Ireland, or under Elizabeth even when excom-
municated, invariably supported the throne.

The High Church, Anglican, ritualistic, and well endowed, included the prelates, the great families, Oxford
and Cambridge; it served four thousand parishes out of
nine thousand.

Nearly all the gentry and upper middle class professed
Anglicanism of Puritan tendencies, or Broad Churchman-
ship. They saw in the episcopate a purely human institution, but a useful one, which it was sufficient to hold in
respect. Very loyal to the throne, all they regretted was
that the King was surrounded by evil counsellors. Among
other eminent men, the Broad Church counted the scholar
Usher, primate of Ireland; the lawyer Selden, no less
scholarly, a resolute anti-clerical whose motto was 'Above
all things Liberty', jailed for a pamphlet against absolutism;
Robert Greville, second Lord Brooke, who refused to fight
for Charles, wrote in favour of toleration, and fell before
Lichfield; the great Commoner, Sir John Eliot, who died
in prison; Hampden, who risked the loss of his fortune and
was killed in the firing line; the incorruptible and infallible
'King Pym', buried at Westminster in 1643, and thrown
into the common ditch in 1661.

The Presbyterians meant Scotland apart from the High-
lands and the Episcopalian Northeast, and also the City of
London, which they over-ran on the coming of James
Stuart. One of these integral Calvinists was Milton's
tutor.

As to the dissidents, it would take several pages merely
to enumerate those sects which pullulated under the
Commonwealth.

It was into this confused and stubborn conflict between
men who spoke the same language and invoked the same
Bible that a man enamoured of solitude and poetry deliberately plunged, and almost lost his life, after losing therein
both sight and reputation.

THE WINGS

A PURITAN CHILDHOOD

1608–1625

IN the heart of the City of London stands a small church, formerly known as *Sancta Maria de Arcubus* and to-day as St. Mary-le-Bow, or Bow Church for short, whose bells the true Cockney must hear from his cradle. Their peal rang out through Bread Street, a narrow but very busy thoroughfare of only sixteen houses, where John, son of John Milton, scrivener, was born on December 9th, 1608.

It was only five years since Mary Stuart's son had begun to reign, and the Age of Elizabeth was still something more than a memory. At the Mermaid tavern, situated in Bread Street itself, Ben Jonson and Shakespeare still used to meet. Neither *The Tempest*, *A Winter's Tale* nor *Cymbeline* were yet written.

The City, with its lath and plaster houses leaning close together over murky gutters, was an invitation both to plague and to fire. Yet a new spirit was at work there. Twenty years earlier, the miraculous defeat of the Armada had thrown open to the English untold treasures across the seas. Two hundred London traders were sending out sailors by the thousand on far-flung adventures. Already seven times more active than all other English ports put together, before the end of the century London was to increase from two hundred thousand souls to half a million.

Consequently the outskirts of the great capital saw the trees falling and the houses going up. The scriveners, the 'escrivains publics' of Norman times, now become dealers in property and money-lenders (sometimes lampooned as usurers), were thus doing excellent business. The father of the new-born child was one of the most prosperous. The City thought highly of his diligence, his common sense, his good nature and, above all, his utter honesty (*integerrimo patre*, his son declared). Under the emblem of his corporation—a spread eagle holding an ink-stand in its beak and a register in its claws—he built up the fortune which was to enable the poet to be his own master.

To understand Milton we must not look to heredity. His own brother lived as a royalist and died a Catholic. We should rather turn to the influence of early impressions. For instance, the individualism of the man doubtless derived largely from the time when the child used to listen to the story of his grandfather Richard.

In the time of good Queen Bess the scrivener's father, Richard Milton, was a landowner cultivating a modest estate near Oxford in the village of Stanton St. John. He was a figure of some importance in the neighbourhood, for he was a keeper of the royal forest of Shotover. Moreover, as a yeoman he depended directly on the Crown. The majority of the nobles might well have envied him his independence. A convinced Catholic, but respecting the new laws, he attended the Church of England services though he wished that God would bring them to an end. Most probably, when the cause of Rome seemed to right itself, he would laughingly warn his schismatical neighbours in the current phrase: 'The price of faggots will go up, my friends!'

In 1571, however, the Pope forbade this double allegiance. From then onwards the faithful Catholics worshipped at home. Yet Richard changed his habits so little that in 1582 he was appointed churchwarden. At that time his son was up at Oxford, reading music perhaps, and allowed himself to be won over to the baneful Puritan ideas—so much so that in the vacation of 1585 Richard saw a Bible on John's table. He immediately threatened to cut off his allowance and disinherit him. John left his studies and set out for London with his flute as his sole possession. He was twenty-two.

Fifteen years later—Elizabeth being still on the throne—the Anglican clergy sought to suppress the Catholic recusants. Every subject of the Queen must attend the

Anglican service, under penalty of a fine of twenty pounds for each month's absence (more than £200 at present-day values). Richard was a man of honour and did not again set foot in church. So in July 1601 he had to pay sixty pounds over to the Treasury. Three months later another such fine brought him to ruin. John thus found himself without an inheritance in a way that his father had never foreseen.

The boy, however, had made his way. He first of all lived by his skill as a musician, then found employment with a scrivener. In 1600, he was admitted to the corporation. The following year he married the daughter of a City tailor, and in 1603 set up for himself in Bread Street as owner of a house of more than fifteen rooms. When in 1634, however, his colleagues offered him the mastership of the scriveners' corporation, he refused. 'He would not make himself wholly a slave to the world' (Phillips). To the professional emblem he preferred his own coat of arms—argent, an eagle with wings displayed, two-headed gules, beaked and legged sable. In the evenings, in his large room on the first floor, the reluctant man of business gathered his friends around him—John Lane, the poet, who railed against the vices of the Elizabethans, Thomas Morley, the organist of St. Paul's—to listen to each other's poetry (the elder Milton was a poet) and play music, sometimes of their own composing. The scrivener had some reputation as a composer; he enriched the Psalter with several tunes. He had an organ. The very year in which Richard was ruined there appeared a collection of musical madrigals—*The Triumphes of Oriana* (i.e. Elizabeth)—in which his son had collaborated. The madrigal was not, indeed, an austere type of music—the opera derived from it—but a Puritan was not necessarily a Philistine, he could denounce Rome without breaking with her sons. The scrivener was not a little proud of a certain gold medal (complete with its chain) bestowed upon him by a Polish prince in gratitude for an *In Nomine* in forty parts.

Such was the father of the abettor of regicides; of his mother, Sarah Jeffrey, we know next to nothing. Milton

merely tells us that she was highly esteemed in the neighbourhood for her almsgiving. Edward Phillips pronounces
her 'incomparable in virtue and kindness'. She had very weak
sight, whereas her husband could read without spectacles
at the age of eighty. It was, then, to his mother that Milton
owed his poor sight. She doubtless had no part in the
formation of his mind. At that time there was no schooling
for girls in England. Daughters of high-born families had
tutors and might be very cultured, but the Englishwoman
of the common people and of the lower classes was very
ignorant. The illiteracy of Shakespeare's daughters was
perfectly normal.

The scrivener had had two daughters, one of whom had
died in infancy, before John's birth; after John came two
more girls who did not survive, then a boy, Christopher.

The case of a well-to-do family like this losing three
children out of six was not uncommon. Milton himself
was to lose two children out of five, his daughter Deborah
seven out of ten. Hygiene was rudimentary. Careful people
once or twice a year burned in the street the straw which had
served them as carpet, whilst a perfumer 'smoked the musty
rooms' by burning herbs.[1] After this the fleas frolicked about
again in the fresh straw. Ladies would go out of a Crown
minister's house with their skirts full of these pests. England
was primitive in other respects too—in fanaticism, in the
passion for rhythm, and in cruelty.

Religious feeling ran so high that King James sometimes went to try to convert a heretic in his dungeon
before sending him to the scaffold. 'Theology is paramount
here', declared Grotius in 1603. Casaubon, at about the same
time, deplored the fact that both king and people were
incapable of interesting themselves in literary matters 'since
all their thoughts were given to controversy'. Families
were divided by insoluble problems which were discussed
in the open street, and all the more hotly since books were
lacking. Only London, Oxford and Cambridge were
authorized to print books and they brought out a bare
hundred and fifty titles a year.

---

[1] *Much Ado,* I, iii.

In an Elizabethan comedy one of the characters says to his friend: 'Thou art like a barber's zither—the first comer can draw what music he likes from thee', for among the barbers of that time musical instruments were in use to help customers to wait patiently. Men of all walks of life sang, played the viola and the mandola, fiddlers went from one baronial hall to another. In the poorest villages, musicians would offer their services to travellers, who were astonished to be awakened by a choir of peasants.

Yet cock-fights and bear-baitings were popular, and the hand of justice was heavy. We shall come across the pillory, the lash, the red-hot iron and other niceties again. Here is what was meant by the classic formula 'hanged, drawn and quartered', describing the punishment of traitors. From the stench of his cell (which forced the judge always to keep sweet-smelling herbs on his table) the wretched man was dragged on a hurdle or at a horse's tail to the gibbet of Tyburn. There he was hanged for an instant, then taken down and . . . mutilated. The executioner then disembowelled him, struck him in the face with his still throbbing heart, and burnt his entrails before his eyes. Finally the victim was decapitated and cut into four.[1] The head, impregnated with a red substance which repelled the birds and preserved the tissues, would remain exposed at the entrance to London Bridge; the quarters, similarly prepared, would ornament the gates of important cities.

All this explains many a contrast in the literature of the time and in Milton himself.

According to Aubrey, at the time when his father had the boy's portrait painted, his master was 'a Puritan in Essex who cut his hair short'.[2] This portrait is dated 1618. The master in question was Thomas Young, a thirty-year-old pastor, whose father, a Scottish minister, had been persecuted for his Presbyterian beliefs. The son, then, could have had no kindly feelings towards the episcopalian system. After subsisting on temporary posts and on giving lessons in the provinces and on the outskirts of London,

[1] See Brewer's Dictionary of Phrase and Fable, sub voce 'Draw'.
[2] Aubrey probably meant that the master was a Roundhead. But, as we shall see, Young did not wish to go on to perfection without his pupil.

he was appointed to a London parish in this very year, 1618.
Now Milton has told us that Young was his first master,
and surely the child's education must have begun before
he was ten years old. Milton was never robust, his complexion was strikingly pale, he had been delicate throughout
his childhood. Unless we are to take no account of Aubrey's
reference 'in Essex', must we not suppose that John lived
for some time far from 'the populous city . . . where Houses
thick and Sewers annoy the Aire' (P.L. IX, 446), learning
the rudiments of Latin from the young pastor of a country
parish, and that he returned to London when his master
was appointed there? Had the father no hand in this appointment? About 1620 John was admitted to St. Paul's School,
but Young continued to supervise his work.

It should be noted in passing that Thomas Young
belonged to the Anglican clergy, and that his case was by
no means exceptional. The Archbishop of Canterbury
himself was a declared Calvinist. King James relied on the
Puritans to keep the Romanizers in check. All he asked of
them was not to demonstrate against the Established Church.

St. Paul's continues to be one of England's leading public
schools. Field-Marshal Montgomery was educated there.
In Milton's time there was no better school in England.
It had been founded in 1512 by John Colet, the Greek
scholar and precursor of the reformers, the friend of
Erasmus and of Thomas More, for the free education of
poor men's children without distinction of nation. An
endowment from Colet made it possible to accept at St.
Paul's 'as many holders of bursaries as the miraculous
draught of fishes had brought in large fish', to wit, one
hundred and fifty-three.

In a vast hall there were eight classes, arranged on eight
benches. There were no backs to the benches, and no desks.
The injunction, *Aut doce, aut disce, aut discede*, 'Teach, learn
or depart', was repeated in the stained-glass of every window.
The entire staff consisted only of Doctor Gill, an assistant
and the chaplain. Gill, the best pedagogue of his time despite
his 'whipping fits', was known for his great work on the
Trinity, his learned and ingenious English grammar,

Logonomia Anglica, and for his talent as a lute player. He
was a patriot, having lived through the defeat of the
Armada. He could have said like his predecessor Mulcaster,
'I honour Latin, but worship English'. He blamed Chaucer
for his borrowings from the French and put Spenser above
Homer.

The boys learnt their Latin in the manuals of Erasmus and
Colet. The first headmaster, Lilly, had left them his famous
Latin grammar quoted by Shakespeare, the only one used
in England for two hundred years. After four years of
Latin, Greek was tackled. At the end of their studies they
learnt to read the *Psalms* in the original Hebrew. Inevitably
the curriculum included the history and geography of
classical countries and the Holy Land, mythology and even
Church history. Lactantius, Prudentius, and Sabellius who
denied the Trinity, were expounded to them. Ovid was the
favourite poet; his *Metamorphoses* obviously derived from
Genesis, and his faultless and graceful versification lent
itself to imitation. To know how to turn out Latin verse
was the seal of a liberal education, and made it possible
to make one's mark in any country in Europe. As for the
sciences, in those days at St. Paul's as in other schools they
were content with the propositions of Euclid, and the
astronomy of Holywood, known as Sacrobosco, who
flourished in the reign of Edward I.

Fine scholarship demands hard work. Lessons went on
from 7 o'clock in the morning until 11, and from 1 o'clock
until 5. John, however, did not limit himself to the ordinary
curriculum. Private tutors taught him French, Italian, and
the bass-viol, while his father made 'an accomplished
organist' of him (Aubrey). In 1654 he was to write:

> From twelve years of age, I hardly ever left my studies,
> or went to bed before midnight. This primarily led to my loss
> of sight. My eyes were naturally weak, and I was subject to
> frequent head-aches; which, however, could not chill the ardour
> of my curiosity, or retard the progress of my improvement.[1]

Milton judges the universities of his country very severely,
but shows nothing but gratitude in speaking of his school.

[1] *Second Defence*, Bohn I, 254.

It was the school which had 'formed him to the best and elegantest authors of the learned tongues'. His motto was always that written over the gate of St. Paul's—*Fide et Bonis Literis*. Gill had inculcated in him the religion of England and of Spenser. He never forgot that before condemning Sabellius one must have read him. Finally, St. Paul's brought him two friendships.

The headmaster's assistant was Doctor Gill's own son, eleven years older than Milton; he wrote Greek and Latin poetry with ease. He and Milton exchanged what they wrote, the younger eager for the criticisms of the elder. A deeper understanding grew up between Milton and Charles Diodati, the son of a well-known doctor, nephew of a theologian of Geneva and grandson of a refugee from Lucca. Charles, gay, teasing and warm-hearted, and the serious John, whom he understood and admired, were complementary to each other. They were of the same age, but the Italian was precocious. He went up to Oxford in 1623, two years before Milton was ready for Cambridge.

'He sat up very late', says Aubrey, 'and his father ordered the maid to sit up for him.' This remark suggests a picture of the young lad still at work when the household was asleep, finding study all the harder because of his weak eyes; and it also shows the solicitude of his parents. As a child Milton was made much of, like the youthful Montaigne. The prudent *paterfamilias* did not neglect his other children —Anne would have a generous dowry, Christopher was to be a judge—but a daughter could not provide opportunity for the two-headed eagle to spread its wings in full flight, and Christopher was without talent and shared neither the tastes nor the ideas of his father. John, on the contrary, had begun to sing as soon as he could speak, appreciated poetry, had a true Puritan heart. It was of his own childhood he would be thinking when he put on the lips of Christ:

> When I was yet a child, no childish play
> To me was pleasing, all my mind was set
> Serious to learn and know, and thence to do

JOHN MILTON AT THE AGE OF 10

What might be publick good; myself I thought
Born to that end, born to promote all truth,
All righteous things: therefore above my years,
The Law of God I red, and found it sweet. . . .[1]

This 'serious' child—an epithet dear to Milton—was
destined by his parents for the Church, and their wish was
his too.

The portrait of 1618, mentioned above (page 7), shows
us a small, fair-haired aristocratic child, with thoughtful
eyes and pointed face.[2] An element of contrast gives us the
impression that the Milton household, or at any rate the
mother, must have found the tutor too severe: the boy's
hair is close-cropped, but the doublet is of brocade and the
collar of rich lace—foreshadowings of the twofold allegiance
characteristic of the life and work to come.

Two events at least in this year 1618 must have struck
John's imagination. He who was so frequently to sing the
praises of the heavens and of light saw the comet which
made Europe tremble and which was, in fact, followed by
the Thirty Years' War.

The other unforgettable incident was the execution of
Sir Walter Raleigh, Elizabeth's former page, soldier, cour-
tier, explorer, conspirator, colonizer, historian, poet and,
moreover, sworn enemy of Spain. Condemned to death
for a conspiracy in 1603, his sentence had been commuted to
life imprisonment. In 1617 the King had him brought out of
prison to send him to find gold in America, but all Raleigh
had brought back was a bitter quarrel with Spain, and
Madrid had demanded his death. James, who was seeking to obtain the hand of a Spanish princess for his son,
had the sentence of 1603 carried out. None of his faults
gave greater offence to his subjects; Elizabeth would never
have disregarded national feeling to this extent.

In 1619 a sordid business which has left its mark in
history was set on foot. At the beginning of the reign
some Puritans had taken refuge in the Low Countries,
where many of them were unhappy. Moreover, the King's

---

[1] *Paradise Regained*, I, 201 seqq.
[2] A tradition recently exploded attributed the portrait to a Dutch artist, Janssen.

C

new favourite, Buckingham, had set out to persecute even
the moderate English Puritans. The London Virginia
Company offered to establish the dissatisfied refugees from
Holland in Virginia, as indented servants, a condition
amounting to quasi-serfdom, which even to-day makes
American schoolboys indignant.[1]

In 1620 a few dauntless Puritans were brought from
Holland to Southampton in a dilapidated tub; they then
trans-shipped into an 180-ton three-master, the *Mayflower*,
which put in at Plymouth. At these two ports they were
joined by a few Puritans from England. The 'Pilgrim
Fathers', as history has named them, set sail for the New
World on September 16th. They were forty-one men,
accompanied by about sixty women and children.

News of them was brought in the spring of 1621, when
the captain of the *Mayflower* got back to London. He confessed that he had accepted one hundred pounds from a rival
company to land the emigrants not, as agreed, in Virginia,
where fellow-countrymen were awaiting them, but in the
region of the Hudson River still unknown to the white man,
and then a storm had driven the ship to the north coast of
Cape Cod. The distress of the victims had touched the
captain, who told them the whole truth, and helped them to
establish themselves. When spring came, however, half the
colonists had perished.

Such was the origin of New England, 'dont l'austérité
et l'énergie devaient être comme le sel de la grande terre
à créer et à maintenir d'un océan à l'autre' (J. Canu).

This pitiable exodus certainly escaped the attention of the
majority of Englishmen, but Cromwell must have known
about it; it was in 1620 that he came to study in London
and there married the daughter of the provost of the
merchants. John likewise could not but be aware of it, for
his father knew everything that was brewing among the
City men. Expatriations for reasons of conscience were to

---

[1] 'En échange de leur passage, les colons travailleraient pendant sept ans, tous
les jours sauf le dimanche, au profit de leurs transporteurs. Après quoi, les profits
de la colonisation iraient à une société par actions, dans laquelle les capitalistes
entreraient en proportion de leurs avances, et les colons de leur nombre et de leur
âge.' J. Canu, *Histoire de la nation américaine*, Paris, 1947.

follow one another until the day when Charles I, less prudent than his father, forbade them. It was the royal police who were to prevent Cromwell from embarking. Milton in 1642 was to write:

> What numbers of faithful and freeborn Englishmen, and good Christians, have been constrained to forsake their dearest home, their friends and kindred, whom nothing but the wide ocean, and the savage deserts of America, could hide and shelter from the fury of the bishops. . . . Let the astrologer be dismayed at the portentous blaze of comets, and impressions in the air, as foretelling troubles and changes to states: I shall believe there cannot be a more ill-boding sign to a nation (God turn the omen from us!) than when the inhabitants, to avoid insufferable grievances at home, are enforced by heaps to forsake their native country.[1]

King James got on badly with his Parliaments. A serious clash occurred in 1621. In 1620, at the White Mountain near Prague, the Imperial troops had crushed Frederick V, Elector Palatine, King of Bohemia, leader of the Evangelical Union and son-in-law of King James. The Bavarians occupied the Palatinate. On November 14th, 1621, the Parliament unanimously voted for war with Spain, 'the chief support of the Catholic cause'. James was anxious to have the friendship of Spain and vaunted his prerogatives. The Commons reminded him of their indefeasible rights (December 18th). Whereupon the King had the register of the minutes brought to him and tore out the offending pages. This unprecedented sacrilege was the talk of the entire kingdom. John certainly heard his father and his tutor debating this question, which was to recur so often in his writings—'in what do kings differ from tyrants?'

That same year Buckingham struck a direct blow at the peace of the Bread Street household—Thomas Young was deprived of his living and had to go and live with his wife and children in Hamburg, where the English merchants adhered to the discipline of Geneva. John's indignation was profound. He was thirteen, an age when injustice is intolerable. Five years later, in his *Fourth Elegy*, addressed to his master, he exclaimed:

[1] *Of Reformation in England*, Bohn II, 399.

O Mother Land, inhospitable Home. . .
Why ruthlessly exile
(O Iron-heart!) sons that are void of guile . . .[1]

And he then compared Young to the prophet Elias, to
St. Paul, to Jesus himself, all forced to flee for reasons of
religion.
We have from Aubrey that 'Anno Domini 1619, he was
ten years old and was then a poet'. A child has nothing to
say, but he can have a style. Milton asserts that this was his
own case.

> . . . it was found that whether aught was imposed me by
> them that had the overlooking, or betaken to of mine own
> choice in English, or other tongue, prosing or versing, but
> chiefly by this latter, the style, by certain vital signs it had, was
> likely to live.[2]

All Milton cared to save of his schoolboy's verses was the
paraphrase of *Psalms* 114 and 136. These early efforts
interest the French because they show the influence of
Guillaume de Salluste, sieur du Bartas, a Huguenot and a
Gascon. In 1578 du Bartas had given an account of the
Creation, *La Première Semaine*, which was so well received
by Protestant Europe that it was reprinted thirty times in
six years. This was the first sacred epic; mythology was
rigorously excluded from it; the author was careful to write
only 'verse that a maid can read without a blush'.[3]
For over three hundred years now the French have found
du Bartas unreadable, but the Elizabethans feared neither
disconnectedness, over-emphasis nor confusion of style.
Their poets drew largely from the Gascon epic as soon
as Sylvester had translated it for them.[4] He reproduced
all its singularities in well-turned verse. In particular they
adopted the compound epithet taken from the Greeks by
the Pléiade. Du Bartas abused it,[5] but it has never ceased to

---

[1] Tr. Skeat, Nonesuch, p. 778.
[2] *Reason of Church Government*, Bohn II, 477.
[3] 'Des vers que sans rougir la vierge puisse lire.'
[4] Sylvester's title is *Devine Weekes and Workes*.
[5]   . . . O terre porte-grains,
            Porte-or, porte-santé, porte-habits, porte-humains,
            Porte-fruits, porte-tours! . . .

proliferate among men of English speech. If Milton in his psalms avoided an inflated style, he none the less used the compound epithet and his rhythm followed Sylvester. The manly forcefulness of the Gascon and his translator were just what pleased him. And, above all, the sacred text read day by day in his home, so beautiful in the 1611 version (that is, the 'Authorized version' or 'Bible of King James') seemed to require but a few more touches to become true verse. Milton was to turn towards many other and better masters—he has not even named du Bartas—but when in his turn he put *Genesis* into verse, he revived, among other inventions of du Bartas, the heavenly Muse Urania.[1]

We have seen that Doctor Gill greatly admired Spenser. At the end of his life Milton was to declare to Dryden that Spenser had been *his* master. What he appreciated in him above all was the moralist. In the *Areopagitica* he writes: 'Our sage and serious poet Spenser (whom I dare be known to think a better teacher than Scotus or Aquinas)'. Sir Guyon of *The Faerie Queene* was already Milton's hero.

It has sometimes been claimed that Milton had too much the sense of his own worth to be subject to the influence of a man of moderate gifts like Thomas Young. But Young had won over the serious child by his affection, his knowledge, his sincere piety, all the solid qualities which had marked him out for the parents' choice.

Now, if John worked without respite, it was not only through 'curiosity'—he had the persistent conviction that God would demand of him a rigorous account, and it is difficult to think that this tragic sense of life can have come to him from the Gills or from the parents of Diodati, or even from his own parents. All these people were 'wise unto sobriety'.[2] It was Young, the Scotsman, the Calvinist, the minister, who in the first place engraved on the child's conscience the formidable parable of the talents. Milton himself has given evidence of this in the first of his letters which we have.

[1] See George C. Taylor, *Milton's Use of Du Bartas*, Cambridge, 1944.
[2] Cf. Molière, *Le Misanthrope* I, i:
    La parfaite raison fuit toute extrêmité
    Et veut que l'on soit *sage avec sobriété*.

In March 1627, returning from Cambridge to spend the Easter vacation with his parents, he learnt that the Imperial troops were besieging Hamburg. He had owed Young a letter for a long time. In point of fact he owed him a letter of thanks for a Hebrew Bible which his tutor had sent him when he went up to the university. Filled with anxiety and remorse, he atoned for his negligence first of all by a letter, then by the *Fourth Elegy* quoted above. The elegy, written in Cambridge, grandiloquent and learned, does not contain the revealing word. It is to be found in the letter previously written in London, 'without the help of books' (*non libris, ut soleo, circumseptus*), blurted out under the blow of the news (B. III, 487):

> Though I had determined, my excellent tutor, to write you an epistle in verse, yet I could not satisfy myself without sending also another in prose, for the emotions of my gratitude, which your services so justly inspire, are too expansive and too warm to be expressed in the confined limits of poetical metre; they demand the unconstrained freedom of prose, or rather the exuberant richness of Asiatic phraseology: though it would far exceed my power accurately to describe how much I am obliged to you. . . . Heaven knows that I regard you as a father.

We do not regard a man as our father because he has drummed our declensions into us or repeatedly told us not to stoop. Such an expression, from the pen of a boy like Milton at twenty, is decisive. It was indeed to Young that he owed a rule of life, of which we can think what we please, but which he followed right to the end.

II

CAMBRIDGE
1625–1632

MILTON took his leave of Doctor Gill before the end of 1624, but his going up to Cambridge was postponed on account of a family celebration. His sister Anne had married a clerk of the Crown Office in Chancery, Phillips by name, and their first child, Anne, was baptized in January 1625.

In February, young Milton went up to matriculate in company with another St. Paul's boy, Pory; he then returned to spend the rest of the winter at home. The five or six days that this double journey took gave the young Cockney a lesson in country humour, thanks to the University carrier, old Hobson. Although he was at the time over eighty and one of the richest citizens of Cambridge, he still drove his great wain with its team of eight horses every week from Cambridge to the Bull Inn and back. In the four corners of the kingdom, grave clergymen and sober judges, when they recalled their youth, smiled at the memory of the shrewd, burly carrier whose humour has enriched the language with the phrase 'Hobson's choice'.

At the beginning of April, Hobson drove John away for good.

At that time Cambridge contained only six thousand permanent inhabitants and the three thousand students and masters of its dozen colleges. The plague, however, broke out there as often as in London. Milton was a member of Christ's College, founded in 1515, whose gardens led out into meadow-land. On the first floor of the north wing the visitor can still see the room in which the boy was to achieve lasting fame. The furniture consisted of three or four beds, roughly-made chairs, and an ink-stained table. The first time he went out, the exile's heart must have sunk. In this bitter time of the year before Easter, on those Fens later to be made famous by Cromwell, reeds and bulrushes waved to and fro as far as the eye could see.

Of Milton's relations with the fourteen masters of Christ's or with those of the other colleges, scarcely anything is known. His fellow students lost no time in furnishing him with a nickname that suited him to perfection. He looked like a girl (as is proved by a portrait), he was well-behaved, and boasted of it, he was particular in his dress, and reserved—they called him 'Domina'—the Lady of Christ's. This hurt his vanity, but his pride came to terms with it. He had no temptation to emulate those who were making fun of him. The majority were destined to fill the ranks of the clergy, but many of them lodged in inns despite the regulations, and some of them found themselves forced to marry mine host's daughter. To keep up with the tone of the Court they swore and strutted about in extravagant ruffs, with the love-lock and buckled shoes complete with spurs. Some of them boasted of atheism, or practised debauchery, on principle. In honour of important visitors, of Rubens, for instance, or of the King himself, these future ministers of religion acted plays, sometimes anything but decorous, with pointed mimicry.

> . . . so many of the young divines, and those in next aptitude to divinity, have been seen so often upon the stage, writhing and unboning their clergy limbs to all the antic and dishonest gestures of Trinculoes, buffoons and bawds; prostituting the shame of that ministry, which either they had, or were nigh having, to the eyes of courtiers and court ladies, with their grooms and mademoiselles. There, while they acted and over-acted, among other young scholars, I was a spectator; they thought themselves gallant men, and I thought them fools; they made sport, and I laughed; they mispronounced, and I misliked; and, to make up the atticism, they were out, and I hissed.[1]

Such extravagances were calculated to wound the Puritan students. They were fairly numerous in Cambridge, where the spirit of schism had been active in the previous reign. For their part these anti-Papists made a point of eating meat in Lent.

More serious than this guerilla warfare was the general idleness. With the certainty that their noble patron would

[1] *Apology for Smectymnuus*, Bohn III, 114.

find them a parish, the future ministers learnt no more than was indispensable. Three years after his arrival, Milton wrote to Doctor Gill's son:

> Truly, amongst us here, as far as I know, there are hardly one or two that do not fly off unfeathered to Theology while all but rude and unitiated in either Philology or Philosophy,— content also with the slightest possible touch of Theology it- self, just as much as may suffice for sticking together a little sermon anyhow, and stitching it over with worn patches obtained promiscuously. . . . For myself, finding almost no real companions in study here, I should certainly be looking straight back to London, were I not meditating a retirement during this summer vacation into a deeply literary leisure. . . . [1]

In curriculum and methods St. Paul's was ahead of Cambridge, essentially a training ground for the clergy. There, under cover of Aristotle, the medieval syllogism was still cultivated, and despite Bacon, Erasmus and Peter Ramus, research was concerned with words rather than things. In conformity with Bacon's wish, a lectureship in History was founded by Lord Brooke in 1627. The follow- ing year Laud had it suspended—the lecturer, Dr. Izaac Dorislaus of Leyden, had 'spoken too much of the rights of the people' in connection with Tacitus. The group of the moderns was weak and suspect. To this group Milton belonged.

The college time-table was suited to a hard-working student. Rising at five, he attended chapel at six, followed by breakfast; from eight to twelve there were lectures and examinations in the several colleges; dinner was at noon, then an hour or two was spent in inter-collegiate exercises; at seven o'clock there were evening prayers and supper; lights out at eleven. Four years of this régime produced a Bachelor of Arts, three additional years, an M.A.

All-important were the *prolusions*.[2] Under the presidency of a Master of Arts, the future Bachelors spoke before their fellow-students and masters on philosophical-literary subjects—'On the Music of the Spheres', 'The Platonic Idea

[1] *Letter to Alexander Gill*, July 2nd, 1628, Masson I, 194, or Bohn III, 490.
[2] The Roman *prolusio* was a sham fight between gladiators, preceding the mortal combat.

in Aristotle', 'Is Day more excellent than Night?', 'Does the Destruction of a Substance involve a Resolution into first Matter?' (a problem met with in alchemy). A debate usually followed. The thesis could be imposed. On the day when Milton defended the statement that 'Knowledge makes men happier than Ignorance', he was bold enough to let his audience know that he had asked to prove the contrary, but had been ordered to do otherwise.

Milton complained more than once to his academic audience that 'he was snatched away from his studies for idle dissertations' that were devoid of facts, devoid of personal reactions, easily put together with a little Latin and a little reading. He declared publicly:

> What is logic? The queen, truly, of arts, if treated according to her worth. But alas! What madness there is in reason! Here it is not men that live, but only finches feeding on thistles and thorns.[1]

One day he put before his fellow-students the notion that instead of poring over folios, young men ought

> to see places trodden by the ancient heroes, to traverse regions ennobled by wars, triumphs, and even the fables of illustrious poets . . . to observe the manners of men and the fairly ordered states in which nations have arranged themselves . . . and from these again to direct the mind downward to the secret virtues of stones and plants. Nor hesitate, my hearers, even to soar into the heavens . . .[2]

It is none the less true that such contests could fashion orators. Milton's pamphlets are the spoken word and his great poems abound in dissertations. 'L'éloquence', Chateaubriand has said, 'forme une des qualités essentielles du talent de l'auteur; les discours prononcés par ses personnages sont souvent des modèles d'adresse et d'énergie'. 'Energy' is not a strong enough word. Milton has been justly blamed for his violence in controversy. It would seem that he sought not so much to refute the theory as to crush the man, and for this Cambridge was largely responsible. Modern sportsmen have their challenges, the Middle Ages made the defence of a thesis into a kind of joust.

---

[1] *Exercise* VII, Masson I, 361–2.   [2] *Prolusion* III, Masson I, 282.

Luther's gesture in nailing his theses to a church-door is
like that of Cervantes' knights nailing their challenges to
the trees. In Milton's time, indeed, people still loved
public discussions 'to the utterance'. In 1615, for instance,
precisely in Cambridge, when King James came to satisfy
himself as to the advance of learning, the University put on
for his entertainment a disputation between two masters,
one defending the Reformation, the other the Roman faith
(both, naturally, were good Anglicans). The pseudo-papist
was so severely harassed, badgered and pounded that in
the end he swooned. Whereupon James replaced him,
only to be beaten in his turn. It so happened that ten years
later, the victor, Chappell the rhetorician, was to become
young Milton's tutor.

In this year, 1625, when the youthful captive was growing
used to his cage, London was preparing for him his strange
destiny. Charles had been king since March. In May he
had married the sister of Louis XIII. Two years earlier,
at the news that the Spanish marriage had come to nothing,
the English people had lighted bonfires for joy. Was the
French marriage much better? Richelieu had laid down his
conditions; Henrietta was bringing with her a small papist
court, and the royal households would hear mass as in
the time of Mary Tudor. What would be the fate of the
Puritans? To eliminate them was the dearest desire of
William Laud, the holder of a Welsh bishopric, entrusted
with ecclesiastical affairs by Buckingham.

Laud was then fifty-two. He was a small man, high-
coloured, with close-cropped hair, lavishly provided with
all the qualities of a great religious leader—piety, learning, activity, courage, disinterestedness, tenacity. Unfortunately he was obsessed by a chimera. His policy of
'Thorough' sought to impose upon both Englishmen and
Scots a single dogma that excluded predestination; one
and the same episcopal hierarchy under an absolute monarch;
a single solemn and pompous ceremonial. Now, as Laud
and his followers had adopted many of the religious senti-

ments prevailing in the fourth and fifth centuries, their ideas and practices inevitably gave the impression that they were leading back the English by gradual steps to the religion of their immediate ancestors, Roman Catholicism. In fact, the Laudians believed that Rome, because it had divinely appointed bishops, was a true church, but that it had departed from the purity of the early times. Yet the impression they gave was so strong that it led moderate Anglicans to join the Puritans, and deceived even the Vatican. On two occasions, in order to encourage the supposed good intentions of Laud, a cardinal's hat was offered him in private. But he twice refused to accept it. 'Something dwelt within him', he said, 'which would not suffer his compliance, till Rome were other than it is'. When Anglican courtiers, thinking to please the Queen, became Catholics, he called such conversions, perversions. Charles was to make him Bishop of London in 1628, Chancellor of Oxford in 1630, First Minister in 1632, Archbishop of Canterbury in 1633. At the beginning of the reign, he had shown the King a report on the state of the clergy in which the Laudians were marked with an O (orthodox) and the others with a P (Puritan).

Charles meant well, and was the most cultured king England had ever had. To his undoing he paid too much attention to the Queen, Buckingham and Laud; the Queen was surrounded by three hundred French Catholics, who constituted a political party. The simple solution—a uniform religion under an absolute prince, held a fascination for Charles. As early as 1625 he antagonized Parliament by asking for subsidies without deigning to indicate their purpose. Closely linked with France through his marriage, he dared, despite his people, to send the fleet out to attack La Rochelle. One of his ministers saved the situation at the eleventh hour by contriving a mutiny of the crews, but the reign was beginning badly. In August 1625, Sir Robert Phelips solemnly warned the Commons: 'England is the last monarchy that yet retains her liberties. Let them not perish now!' The drama had begun.

Some of its consequences affected the Cambridge student in his very modest sphere. Chappell, his tutor, was severe, opposed to any reform of the curriculum, and . . . Laudian. In 1626—it is not known for what offence—he had his pupil rusticated. Aubrey had it on the authority of Milton's brother that he whipped him. It is more than likely that the offence was a refusal to obey, or some other impulse of individualism. According to the *Elegia prima*, which reached Diodati at Oxford, the rebel felt no regret at all for the swamps of Cambridge, 'so little favourable to the servants of Phoebus'. For two months—April and May—he read at leisure the poets of the day, in particular Giles and Phineas Fletcher, frequented theatres and concerts, and wandered around the outskirts of London which were frequented also by 'choirs of maidens' (*virgineos choros*). The sight of them enraptured the naive youth, convinced that the maids neither of Greece nor of Rome in former times, nor those of foreign lands to-day, could match Britain's daughters. To reassure Diodati, who was also a good-living man, Milton was careful to specify that he had 'fled false Circe's halls'.

Back in the fold once more, he was assigned, contrary to custom, to another master. Tovey was an understanding tutor. Perhaps encouraged by him or more probably by Joseph Meade,[1] the greatest of the tutors in Milton's time there, Milton displayed his talent by composing in Latin the funeral panegyric of four friends or members of the University, and then an epic fragment, again in Latin verse, on the Gunpowder Plot. Choice of subject, eloquence, learning, patriotism—nothing was lacking. In this year, 1626, Cambridge woke up to the fact that she was nursing one poet more.

In the following year at Easter, Milton learnt of the siege of Hamburg, and we have seen what he wrote to his second father on that occasion. Shortly afterwards, he addressed his *Seventh Elegy* to Diodati under a quite different inspiration. In London he had encountered a staggeringly beautiful

---

[1] Meade seems to have been the 'old Damaetas' mentioned in *Lycidas* (l. 36). See Marjorie Nicolson, *Modern Language Notes*, XLI (1926) and Merritt Y. Hughes, *John Milton Complete Poems and Major Prose*, p. 121, n. 36.

daughter of Eve, had pursued her for a moment or two and seen her disappear. The poem ended with a request which was never to be granted:

> Now, O son of Venus . . .
> So prosper thou this single orison:
> Whatever Fair be destin'd mine to be
> One shaft may pierce both hearts, and make us one.[1]

This very fine poem is the only one of Milton's in which the passion of desire breaks out. Twenty years later, when publishing the verse he wrote in youth, he hesitated. Now that he had become a doctor in Israel, ought he to place before the public such a fervid effusion? On the other hand it seemed a pity that a page worthy of Catullus should perish. He thought he could overcome the difficulty by adding ten lines to disavow 'these vain trophies of idleness', unworthy of a Platonist.

Soon after this incident the student became involved, perhaps without knowing it, in his father's affairs. In June, a man named Powell, a squire and justice of the peace, came to borrow from the scrivener three hundred pounds for the purchase of land. The lender stipulated that if payment were not forthcoming within six months, 'John Milton of Cambridge' should hold a mortgage of five hundred pounds on the estate of Richard Powell. It was common practice for the real lender to bring a supposititious lender into the contract. We shall have occasion, however, to speak of this transaction again.

Twice in 1628 Milton at last gave expression to his personal feelings in English verse. His sister having lost her little girl, Anne, he wanted to show her his sympathy, and as she had no knowledge of Latin, he composed a dozen stanzas in English which remained unpublished until 1673. Soon after this private and personal beginning, Cambridge in assembly heard the 'Lady of Christ's' proclaim himself a poet, first of all in Latin and then in his mother tongue.

A fellow of Milton's college, whose name has not come down to us, presented himself for a degree in philosophy.

[1] Tr. Skeat, Nonesuch, p. 783.

His thesis, less shallow than it seems, was that 'Nature does not grow old'—*Naturam non pati senium*. Custom required that on the defence of a thesis the audience should be presented with a piece of Latin verse, and as the candidate had 'long neglected such trifles' (as explained by Milton to Gill's son), he begged Milton to compose the verse for him. Milton was delighted to accept. He was entirely of the opinion that the Moderns could equal the Ancients. Followers of Bacon and the Puritans believed in progress. The defence of the thesis was to take place in July. Back in the spring Milton began on his hexameters:

> Still too the Sea-King cleaves Sicilian
> Pelorus' foot; still, o'er wide waters, swell
> The hollow roarings of his herald's shell . . .
> Nor is thy primal age's vigour flown,
> O Earth,—his fragrance yet Narcissus keeps;—
> Yet he whom Phoebus weeps,
> And Venus' favourite comely are as aye!
> Ne'er too did shamefast Earth more treasures hold—
> Gems under sea, 'neath hills her baneful gold!
> Thus changeless shall endure, most justly true
> This Order of the World, time's end unto—
> Then the Last Day's conflagrance Earth shall waste,
> From Pole to Pole, with Heav'ns huge vault embrac'd,
> And all the Universal Frame entire
> Flame, as on one stupendous funeral Pyre.[1]

In other words, Doctor Gill was right: England could breed a second Homer. According to custom, copies of the text were distributed to the audience. For the first time, Milton saw himself in print. He duly sent a copy to the younger Gill.

A few days later, the end of the year celebrations enabled the student to establish his candidature for glory openly and in English. The celebrations included an absurd colloquy, the participants in which represented characters taken from Aristotle—Ens (Being), and his sons, the Attributes. The part of Ens was played by Milton. He protested against his nickname of Domina, asking:

> Why seem I to them too little of a man? . . . Is it because I

[1] *Nature not Impaired by Time*, Tr. Skeat, Nonesuch, pp. 785–6.

have never been able to quaff huge tankards lustily . . . or
because I have never, like a seven years' herdsman, laid myself
down and snored at midday; in fine, perchance, because I have
never proved my manhood in the same way as those debauched
blackguards?[1]

This was the end of the 'Lady of Christ's'. Moreover,
Milton now had three years seniority and the hostility of
the early days was giving place to friendship and kindness.
Encouraged by this change in attitude, Ens emerged from
the wearisome Latin colloquy to exclaim in English verse:

> Hail native Language! . . .
> Here I salute thee and thy pardon ask: . . .
> That now I use thee in my latter task:
> The daintiest dishes shall be serv'd up last.
> I pray thee then deny me not thy aide
> For this same small neglect that I have made:
> But haste thee strait to do me once a Pleasure,
> And from thy wardrope bring thy chiefest treasure;
> Not those new fangled toys . . .
> But cull those richest Robes, and gay'st attire
> Which deepest Spirits, and choicest Wits desire:
> I have some naked thoughts that rove about
> And loudly knock to have their passage out;
> And wearie of their place do only stay
> Till thou hast deck't them in thy best aray:
> That so they may without suspect or fears
> Fly swiftly to this fair Assembly's ears;
> Yet I had rather if I were to chuse,
> Thy service in some graver subject use,
> Such as may make thee search thy coffers round,
> Before thou cloath my fancy in fit sound:
> Such where the deep transported mind may soare
> Above the wheeling poles, and at Heav'ns dore
> Look in, and see each blissful Deitie . . .
> Then passing through the Spheres of watchful fire,
> And mistie Regions of wide air next under,
> And hills of Snow and lofts of piled Thunder,
> May tell at length how green-ey'd Naptune raves . . .
> Then sing of secret things that came to pass
> When Beldam Nature in her cradle was;
> And last of Kings and Queens and *Hero's* old,

[1] *Vacation Exercise*, Masson I, 292.

JOHN MILTON AT THE AGE OF 21

Such as the wise *Demodocus* once told
In solemn Songs at King *Alcinous* feast,
While sad *Ulisses* soul and all the rest
Are held with his melodious harmonie
In willing chains and sweet captivitie.
But fie my wandring Muse how thou dost stray![1]

Thus Milton at nineteen dreamed of singing the secrets of the gods, the origin of the world, and heroism. There was to be much of all three in his epic. Moreover, he suffered from not having sufficient confidence in the English language to carry through so vast a work. This difficulty was to hold him back for a long time and perhaps he never quite mastered it.[2]

He was disquieted on another head: for an Englishman of his time, to write in his own language was to cut himself off from Europe. Bacon composed in English for his convenience, and then translated into Latin for his reputation's sake. It was against his wish that his famous essays appeared in their English dress. He complained that modern languages would be the ruin of letters.[3] A hundred years later, Addison was to call *Paradise Lost* a divine poem although written in English, like a palace built of brick.

While Milton was gradually becoming aware of his poetic gift, Cromwell was beginning his career in the Commons, Alford in the House was quoting to his colleagues Bodin's question: 'Who is the sovereign?', and Charles was acquiescing in the Petition of Rights, while secretly resolved to evade this man-made engagement rather than renounce his prerogatives of divine right. Since war had broken out between England and France, and Buckingham had failed before La Rochelle, a new expedition was decided upon. Buckingham was on the point of setting out once more

---

[1] *At a Vacation Exercise*, 1–53.
[2] 'Our language sunk under him and was unequal to that greatness of soul which furnished him with such glorious conceptions.'—Addison.
[3] Cf. Chateaubriand, 'Cette division des langues qui s'oppose chez les Modernes aux renommées universelles'.—*Essai sur la littérature anglaise.*

D

when he was stabbed, in August 1628.[1] La Rochelle fell in October. Soon afterwards Laud was to break off all relations with continental Protestantism. The breach between Charles and his subjects was growing wider. In March 1629, Milton took his degree, and Charles's third parliament was dissolved without having yielded anything or obtained anything. The country was to live without a parliament for eleven long years.

If we are to believe the *Fifth Elegy*—one hundred and forty passionate lines—the spring of 1629 was exceptionally fine, even at Cambridge. In the language of Ovid the new Bachelor expressed his wonder and admiration at the sight—'wanton Earth' offering herself to the Sun's caress, sighing out her love, while Pan makes august Cybele blush and the mountain nymph is careful not to shun too quickly the amorous Faun. Another theme, however, appears—'the poet is a seer, a prophet'.

> Hot grows my heart, stirr'd by a force unseen,
> And hallow'd sounds impel my raptur'd mind.
> Apollo comes—Behold those locks entwin'd
> With Daphnian bays—'tis Phoebus' self I see![2]

His spirit was as disturbed as his fatherland. Sometimes, with a book or a friend, he walked up and down a certain avenue of the college gardens (known to-day as Milton's Walk), at others he went out into the country to commune with the earth and the trees. He declared (Masson, I, 297–8) that he had never found anything more fruitful for his genius than studious and liberal leisures. . . . He called to witness the woods, the rivers and the dear elms of the English villages, under which, the previous year, if he were allowed to betray the secrets of the goddesses, he remembered having so delightfully enjoyed the company of the Muses. 'Amid rural scenes and sequestered glades, I seemed as if I could have vegetated through a hidden eternity.'

---

[1] Doctor Gill's son was arrested for having spoken in favour of the assassin in a tavern and for having spoken of the King with the utmost disrespect. His father managed to get him off with two years' imprisonment. He was to live down this lapse and to be Head of St. Paul's in his turn. We have no evidence that Milton withdrew his friendship from him. (See below, p. 44.)

[2] *On the Approach of Spring*, tr. Skeat, Nonesuch, p. 788.

There was the same feeling for the cosmos in his verses on *The Platonic Idea as understood by Aristotle*:

> Declare, O mighty Goddess Powers,
> Presiding o'er the Sacred Bowers,
> And thou (yclept Mnemosyne)
> Blest Mother of the Deity
> Ninefold, and thou who in some deep
> Far Cave, reclin'd at ease, dost keep
> Jove's Records and his fix'd Decrees,
> Archives and high solemnities—
> (Thou who art hight 'Eternity'!)
> Declare, who First of All was he
> Whom skilful Nature chose as Plan
> And Pattern for the race of Man.
>   Eterne—Unwasting—with the Skies
> Coeval—and (by contraries)
> One—Universal—he, 'tis said,
> In God's similitude was made! . . .
> Chance he may rove the ten-spher'd heights,
> Companion of the Eternal Lights,
> Or in yon orbed Moon abide
> That sticks so close our Earth beside;
> Or on forgetful Lethe's banks
> Sit listlessly amid the ranks
> Of souls that wait imbodiment—
> Or whether (if 'tis rather meant!)
> Some far sequester'd shore upon
> Of this our World, he stalks alone,
> Man's archetype, with Titan stride
> And head upheav'd, as who defied
> The gods—of more majestick size
> Than Atlas, Shoulderer of the Skies.[1]

The analogies with Shelley are unquestionable, and Milton could have written a new version of Lucretius. Higher than the elm-trees of the villages, however, loomed Ely's cathedral, rising above the fens like Chartres above the Beauce. From its towers the call of Christendom floated down, answered by the cry of Sir John Eliot to his colleagues as the King's soldiers were taking him away: 'The Gospel! That is the truth that made this kingdom blessed.'

[1] Tr. Skeat, Nonesuch, pp. 786–7.

In this same spring of 1629 Milton saw his master Young
once more. He had somehow or other obtained a living at
Stowmarket, a village situated about forty-five miles east
of Cambridge. A mulberry-tree which Milton is said to
have planted is still to be seen there.

On Christmas morning, 1629, Milton began the *Ode to
the Nativity*, perhaps the finest in the English language,
according to Hallam. 'Il y a là', declared Emile Legouis, 'ce
que nul autre ne possède autant que Milton, une perfection
absolue dans le choix des mots et des sonorités. . . . Il
peut paraître incroyable aujourd'hui que la surprenante
beauté de cette ode à la fois si imaginative et si classique
n'ait pas saisi les contemporains par sa sublime perfection.'[1]
Indeed, a never-failing afflatus runs through it, controlled in
every detail and embracing every tone; the work comprises
three movements—the fixing of the event in time and space;
the song of the angels; the fall of paganism. The scholar
can be recognized in it from the echoes of Plato, Virgil
and fifty others. The novice is revealed by the *concetti*.
A strong but tender piety is present everywhere. The poet
will develop his technique, but we shall never again find
such an inspiration straight from the heart. That day, with
his whole soul, he dedicated himself.

It may be asked why Milton, who had so little confidence
in his use of English, did not celebrate the Nativity in Latin.
The explanation is to be found in the *Sixth Elegy*. Milton
wrote this for Diodati around New Year's Day, when he
was still working at his ode. He told his friend that he
wanted to offer Christ on his birthday a gift he had received
himself with the earliest rays of the dawn. As he awoke the
English lines made music within him and he followed their
inspiration.

The principal merit of this *Sixth Elegy* is that it shows us
Milton already prepared to pay the price of greatness.

Diodati was neither frivolous nor lazy—he occasionally
wrote to Milton in Greek—but he knew how to work with
measure. In 1626 he declared to his friend, writing in
Greek:

[1] *Histoire de la littérature anglaise*, p. 561.

I who am inferior to you in everything yet surpass you on one point—I can work with measure. Live then! Laugh and enjoy your youth.[1]

At the close of this year, 1629, he sent Milton his greetings, but his Latin verse showed signs of haste, and he apologized for it—he was invited everywhere and on all sides there was nothing but feasting and carousing. The essence of Milton's reply, that is of the *Elegia Sexta*, can be reduced to this: 'You are a writer of elegies, a mere writer of elegies, you are therefore right in having a good time, but I . . .'

> Bacchus to Song, Song is to Bacchus wed; . . .
> But who chaunts wars, and climes that brook control
> Of full-grown Jove, or chiefs above the span
> Of human, or devote Heroic soul,
> Or the Eternal gods' Celestial Plan,
> Or Hell's deep worlds aw'd by that baying Hound—
> Austere as Samos' sage his life should be:
> His harmless banquet herbs, and on the ground
> Hard by, upfill'd from the wave translucent, stand
> His dish of beechen tree;
> The clear crystalline Spring
> Alone his cup's abstemious plenishing.
> To these add youth unstain'd and pure of sin,
> Steel'd and unspotted both of heart and hand;
> So risest thou, O holy Augur, dight
> In robes of glistering white,
> With lustral waters' sluice, to enter in
> Before the throne of anger'd Deity!
> After this sort Tiresias liv'd (they write)—
> Tiresias, wiser for his banish'd sight;[2]
> So Linos, bard of Thebes in time gone by;
> Seer Calchas thus unhom'd
> Fled his doom'd hearth; so aged Orpheus roam'd
> Who oft in desert cave the savage beast
> Tamed; and he, too, that liv'd on nature's least—
> Brook-drinking Homer, . . .
> For sure to heav'n the Bard is dedicate,
> And is the gods' high-priest,
> To breathe the hidden Jove from lips and breast.[3]

[1] Masson I, 163.
[2] Milton, while he still had the gift of sight, more than once mentioned the case of Tiresias. [3] Tr. Skeat, Nonesuch, p. 793-5.

Michelangelo, who never forgot Savonarola, spoke in much the same vein in his *Dialogue on Painting in the City of Rome*:

> Good painting draws near to God and is linked with him ... Therefore it is not sufficient for the painter that he be a great and skilful master. I think rather that his life should be as pure and holy as possible, in order that the Holy Spirit may direct his thoughts.

Milton praised the sanctity of marriage, but outside marriage he admitted only continence. To simple abstention he finally gave a positive value.[1] He saw in it a kind of magic means of obtaining access to the supreme truths. In the same way in our own times Vivekananda has declared that it is only by continence and chastity that it is possible to realize the *brahman* (union with the absolute). When Milton, publicly accused of bad morals, had to defend himself publicly, he related in the *Apology for Smectymnuus* how, by constant reading he had been brought gradually to a religious respect for woman.

After the orators and historians, the young student began upon the elegiac poets. He found them delightful and easy to imitate. He noticed that the more worthy their beloved the more highly they esteemed themselves. If, then, he himself knew how to choose the object of his praise with more wisdom than they and more love of virtue, he could at least equal them. But he deplored their offences against chastity ('Their art I still applauded, but the men I deplored') and rejoiced when he came in contact with Dante and Petrarch.

> And long it was not after, when I was confirmed in this opinion, that he who would not be frustrate of his hope to write well hereafter in laudable things, ought himself to be a true poem; that is, a composition and pattern of the best and honourablest things; not presuming to sing high praises of heroic men, or famous cities, unless he have in himself the experience and the practice of all that which is praise-worthy. These reasonings, together with a certain niceness of nature, an honest haughtiness, and self-esteem either of what I was,

---

[1] See Saurat, *Milton, Man and Thinker*, Dent, 1946.

or what I might be (which let envy call pride), and lastly that modesty, whereof, though not in the title-page, yet here I may be excused to make some beseeming profession; ...[1]

He then plunged into chivalry. Every knight swore to defend the honour of women even at the risk of his life.

Then I learned what a noble virtue chastity sure must be ... Only this my mind gave me, that every free and gentle spirit, without that oath, ought to be born a knight, nor needed to expect the gilt spur, or the laying of a sword upon his shoulder to stir him up both by his counsel and his arms, to secure and protect the weakness of any attempted chastity.[2]

From 'the laureate fraternity of the poets' the young reader was led to Plato and Xenophon. They taught him that 'the first and chief office of love begins and ends in the soul'.

But having had the doctrine of holy scripture unfolding those chaste and high mysteries, with timeliest care infused, that 'the body is for the Lord and the Lord for the body'; thus also I argued to myself, that if unchastity in a woman, whom St. Paul terms the glory of man, be such a scandal and dishonour, then certainly in a man, who is both the image and glory of God, it must, though commonly not so thought, be much more deflouring and dishonourable; in that he sins both against his own body, which is the perfecter sex, and his own glory, which is in the woman; and, that which is worst, against the image and glory of God, which is in himself.[3]

At the beginning of 1630, Milton wanted to write a sequel to his *Nativity Ode* by singing the Passion of Christ, but he had to limit himself to eight glittering stanzas. When he eventually published this fragment, he explained that the subject had seemed to him beyond his years. It is certain that he never returned to it.

The plague swept over Cambridge in April 1630. The University closed its doors and old Hobson fell ill from inactivity. It is possible that Milton saw Young again at Stowmarket. His *Song on May Morning*, generally dated 1630, very short, but so full of joy and substance, was surely not inspired by Cambridge in mourning, or by London.

[1] *Smectymnuus*, Bohn III, 117–18.   [2] Ibid., 118–19.   [3] Ibid., 122.

He did not find Diodati again in London, for at that time he was studying theology with his uncle in Geneva. It was probably that summer, however, that Milton met, either at the Diodati's, or in their circle, a young Italian girl who spoke several languages, had eyes like fire and sang like a siren. The man with the beechwood cup was dazzled, but Emilia was a flirt. An English sonnet *To the Nightingale* was found inadequate; was not the language of love Italian? The unhappy youth opened his Petrarch again and constructed three fine sonnets and a *canzone* (in addition to a sonnet to inform Diodati). Emilia may have found her poet too serious, or perhaps too short of stature.[1] In a final Italian sonnet, like Corneille scorned by the Marquise, he told her what she was losing:

> A modest youth, in love a simpleton,
> When to escape myself I seek and shift,
> Lady, I of my heart the humble gift
> Vow unto thee. In trials many a one,
> True, brave, it has been, firm to things begun,
> By gracious, prudent, worthy thoughts uplift.
> When roars the great world, in the thunder-rift,
> Its own self, armour adamant, it will don,
> From chance and envy as securely barred,
> From hopes and fears that still the crowd abuse,
> As inward gifts and high worth coveting,
> And the resounding lyre, and every Muse.
> There only wilt thou find it not so hard
> Where Love hath fixed his ever cureless sting.[2]

A very accurate self-portrait, the conclusion of which, above all, we must keep in mind. It is woman who will be the danger for Milton and for his heroes. Once this has been said, there is no need for us to waste our pity over a young man who was so pleased with himself. Besides, poetry had relieved him.

During this vacation which lasted six months, he could have met all the rhymesters of London, but he most likely

---

[1] This Emilia seems to reappear as Aegle in *Epitaphium Damonis*:
'Mistress of measures and the lutist's art
Aegle—consumed, alas! by pride of heart'.
(Nonesuch, p. 810.)

[2] Tr. G. MacDonald, Nonesuch, p. 822.

avoided the 'amorists', such as Suckling or Carew, or even Davenant, who was too worldly. On the other hand, he probably saw Spenser's disciple, Willian Browne, author of *Britannia's Pastorals*, his elder by seven years, whom he had read closely and by whom he was influenced. And everything leads us to credit a very curious encounter between the young ascetic and the kindly old Bohemian, Ben Jonson, poet laureate.

The second folio of Shakespeare, published in 1632, contains epigraphs by Ben Jonson, Milton and various young poets of London. It is surprising, when we think of it, that out of five or six thousand students Milton alone, as yet unknown, should have had the privilege of praising the author of *Hamlet* in company with the author of *Volpone*. If we put together certain facts the problem will appear less obscure.

Milton's verse was inserted by Jonson, since it was Jonson who prepared the edition. Moreover, this verse he had not merely accepted but solicited, since Milton only signed it with his initials, being unwilling to acknowledge such a trifle publicly. (But it is a trifle which eclipses the rest of the page—sixteen lines on a *concetto* of Jonson himself: Shakespeare has no need of a monument, his hearers are 'petrified' with admiration.) There was then debate and compromise. As to the date—when Milton, in 1645, published this epigraph under his full name, he dated it 1630.

The hypothesis of a meeting presents no difficulty. Milton admired the poet laureate for his virile style and his learning. Jonson influenced his verse for a period, and there is something of him in the song *On May Morning*. Moreover, Ben Jonson encouraged the young, and as an old Cambridge man he was particularly interested in her poets. One of them, Randolph, he counted among his 'sons'. Again, he was a good Latin scholar, and the quality of Milton's Latin verse must have attracted his attention if he had come across a sample of it. Now we have seen that some hundreds of copies of the poem *Naturam non pati senium* had been printed, and all Cambridge knew who was the true author of it.

Two facts at least are beyond question—the veteran's gesture of welcome and the reticence of the beginner. Milton aimed very high. He admired Spenser, but not the Spenserian stanza, because a fixed form must always hamper, more or less, the movement of thought. He esteemed Browne, but soon rejected his couplets. The robust Jonson was too formal and not musical enough. How were liberty of spirit and the refinements of music to be reconciled with that indispensable element in poetry—a cadence which the ear expects? Perhaps the solution came to him in 1630; in any case before 1634. We shall refer to this again.

While the poet meditated, Laud was pressing the Puritans harder. As archbishop and as enjoying the favour of the supreme governor of the Church, that is the King, he forced the bishops to sweep their dioceses clean. The case of Dr. Leighton caused a sensation. Formerly a Presbyterian minister, he had become a physician in order to make a living. He was arrested in February 1630 and committed to prison for a tract that was two years old. In November an attempt to escape earned him the pillory, the loss of his ears, branding with a red-hot iron, and then close imprisonment for the rest of his days.

Milton was still in London when a fellowship fell vacant in his college. He applied, his only rival being another student of Christ's, Edward King. King was five years younger, but his father was Secretary for Ireland, and his uncle held the Irish bishopric of Elphin. When Milton returned to Cambridge in November he learnt that by the King's order the appointment had gone to his fellow-student. It was not against the latter that he bore a grudge.

In February 1631, Christopher Milton joined his brother at Christ's, and was entrusted to Tovey. In the autumn Anne Phillips lost her husband. A few widely differing poems appeared at intervals throughout the year.

For Hobson, who had died in January, Milton composed in verse not one epitaph but two—the one macabre, the other pitted with puns. In the latter he quoted the insatiable carrier's last words: 'More weight!'

In April, a good friend of literature, the Marchioness of Winchester, died quite young. Jonson, Davenant and others celebrated her memory. Milton associated himself with them in an *Epitaph* of a hundred or so eight-syllable lines, unadorned, subdued in tone, in which Browne's influence can be recognized.

It was, it seems, three months later, in the course of the ceremony at the close of the academic year, that he read in the presence of the whole University two short poems composed, like the preceding *Epitaph*, in octosyllabic couplets. They were *L' Allegro* and *Il Penseroso*. Never have three hundred lines of poetry breathed out so many appeals to the imagination. Burke regarded *Il Penseroso* as the finest poem in English. The titles seem to evoke music itself, Handel was to adopt them. The poet lacked the exact words to delineate the man who seeks experience of delights and the man who meditates rather than he observes. These two characters, after all, are but two aspects of Milton and of all of us.

The merry man begins his day with the lark, spends it among the labours of the field, and ends it either at the theatre or a concert, or in a cottage where he will listen to the tales around the fire, and then be lulled to sleep by whispering winds. To the theatre Milton gives four lines, three of which set the learned Jonson in contrast with Shakespeare and his spontaneity. To music, however, he devotes sixteen lines.

The meditative man comes out at nightfall when the nightingale ('most musical, most melancholy!') amid perfect silence deigns to chant Even-Song. The wandering moon seems to seek her path in the immensity of night. From a height the solitary walker listens to the curfew ringing out mournfully over some remote sea-shore. In bad weather, before the glowing embers that 'teach light to counterfeit a gloom', he hears the cricket on the hearth or the drowsy refrain of the night-watchman. In a high and lonely tower, at the hour of midnight, he will read Plato, Hermes

Trismegistus, treatises on demonology, gorgeous tragedies, romances full of tourneys and enchanted forests. Thus he will see the dawn appear 'kerchief'd in a comely Cloud'. Fearing the heat of the day, he will go and sleep near a stream under 'a monumental Oak'.[1] He is visited by 'some strange mysterious dream', then awakes to the music sent by the unseen Genius of the Wood. Reaching the 'studious cloisters pale' he sees under 'the high embowed roof' the storied windows cast 'a dim religious light', while organ and choir 'dissolve him into ecstasies and bring all Heav'n before his eyes'. Meditation, however, best befits old men. The *Penseroso* will end his days in a hermitage where he will study 'every star' and 'every herb' till he attains to 'something like prophetic strain'.

Literary reminiscences are naturally abundant here. Thanks to Burton melancholy had been in fashion for the past ten years. The setting, however, was new. No one had yet evoked the gentle English countryside in its various aspects, noting what nature could suggest to a man who had 'read all the books' but was unacquainted with 'the sadness of the flesh'.[2] The walker gives his preference to melancholy, but for him melancholy does not mean the bitterness of a life frustrated. She is a 'Goddess, sage and holy whose saintly visage is too bright to hit the Sense of human sight'; 'a pensive nun, devout and pure', with her long dark habit. She is the heavenly Counseller of a mind seeking to draw near to the power of prophecy.

The 'twin poems' help us to measure Milton's literary influence. Racine has written nothing more restrained than these three hundred and twenty-eight lines. Yet the themes they outline—rustic life, folklore, chivalry, sea, moon, magic, dream, music and many others—had been dear to the Elizabethans and were to nourish the romanticism of Europe. Milton is classical, but none the less cherishes every portion of his English heritage. If the people of England took pleasure for a time in abstractions, it was mainly under

---

[1] A good example of Milton's complexity of expression. Three simultaneous meanings—'colossal', 'witness to the past', and 'apt for construction'. Chaucer and Spenser contented themselves with 'builder oak'.

[2] Mallarmé: 'La chair est triste, hélas! et j'ai lu tous les livres'.

the influence of France. They soon returned to their emotional and realistic tradition, and it was Milton who in a great measure helped them to do so. To him Keats owed his finest verse. James Thomson worshipped Milton. The first of his *Seasons*, 'Winter', published in 1726, was drawn from Nature, but the *Saisons* of Saint-Lambert, which did not appear before 1769, were still entirely derived from books.

At the end of 1631, on the threshold of his twenty-fourth year, Milton was concerned that he had written nothing that was worthy of him. Diodati had already given up theology, to establish himself as a doctor. In Cambridge, on frequent occasions, very youthful fellow-students would show their brilliancy before distinguished visitors. In this same year, 1631, in the month of March, the royal couple had applauded Randolph and Hausted for two plays which were printed immediately. Milton certainly did not envy their success. To please the King did not tempt him at all. In November, when the Cambridge poets had celebrated the birth of Princess Mary, Milton had stood aside. Still, while younger men proved their worth, he remained sterile. Would his hour never come? The well-known sonnet which on internal evidence must be dated 1631, shows that he resigned himself to the care of One who was wiser than himself:

> How soon hath time the suttle theef of youth,
>   Stoln on his wing my three and twentith yeer!
>   My hasting dayes flie on with full career,
>   But my late spring no bud or blossom shew'th.
> Perhaps my semblance might deceive the truth,
>   That I to manhood am arriv'd so near,
>   And inward ripenes doth much less appear,
>   That som more timely-happy spirits indu'th.
> Yet be it less or more, or soon or slow,
>   It shall be still in strictest measure eev'n,
>   To that same lot, however mean, or high,
> Toward which Time leads me, and the will of Heav'n;
>   All is, if I have grace to use it so,
>   As ever in my great task-Masters eye.

Despite its brevity this piece is doubly paradoxical.

Under its Christian aspect, it follows the *Fourth Nemean Ode* of Pindar. Then, although its author deplores his sterility, he is reviving a literary genre.

The sonnet, brought from Italy by Wyatt in 1527, had swiftly degenerated under the English sky. In Shakespeare it was no more than three quatrains followed by a distich. Moreover, contrary to Italian custom, the English sonnet spoke only of love. It had fallen into disuse when Milton studied Petrarch and Della Casa. In a letter which will be referred to later, he spoke of 'the Petrarchian stanza', since the English word 'sonnet' would have been misleading if applied to an authentic sonnet on the Italian model. Now 'Emilia's Garland', this sonnet of 1631, and those which were to follow, restored to the neglected form both its strictness and its varied use. Wordsworth, converted to the sonnet by reading Milton, was to write:

> Scorn not the Sonnet . . .
> . . . when a damp
> Fell round the path of Milton, in his hand
> The thing became a trumpet, whence he blew
> Soul-animating strains—alas, too few!

Keats, Shelley, Rossetti, the two Brownings, Meredith and many others have shed lustre on the student's 'Petrarchian stanza'.

The first half of 1632 was taken up with preparation for finals. On July 3rd, Milton was admitted Master of Arts with honours. Then he left to rejoin his parents, who had been living in retirement in the country since their second son had gone up to Cambridge.

III

THE VIGIL-AT-ARMS
1632–1639

HAMMERSMITH to-day is nothing but a junction of bus routes: at that time it was a village. There it seems began a vigil-at-arms of more than seven years—three years in Hammersmith,[1] the same at Horton near Windsor, the rest in Italy.

The elder Milton was nearly seventy. He was dismayed when his Master of Arts son explained to him that this fine-sounding title was valueless for him, John, in the England of Laud. In May 1632, a sermon against popery and freewill had resulted for its preacher, Nathaniel Barnard, in a fine of a thousand pounds, excommunication and imprisonment. One could hide in a village like Young, but one had to be sure of one's bishop and serve out to country bumpkins the official fare. Moreover now, though this was of recent date, no one any longer could take orders unless he swore obedience to the present and future directives of the bench of bishops. How was it possible to subscribe in advance to the injunctions of a hierarchy which was itself enslaved? Milton declared in 1641 (B. II, 482): 'I have been church-outed by the prelates'.

For the same reasons the teaching profession was closed to him. His masters in Cambridge had just offered him a Fellowship (B. III, 111), but it was impossible to teach without having taken orders, and Laud kept a close watch on both Universities. No sooner was he appointed Chancellor of Oxford than he re-cast the statutes and dismissed three professors. In Cambridge, the Chancellor, Lord Holland, was a great friend of the Queen and of Buckingham, and certain of the Masters sent reports about their colleagues to Laud.

[1] See Harris Fletcher, *Journal of English and German Philology*, 1952.

Should be become a lawyer like Christopher, who was going to begin his law in London that year? Milton could not resign himself to invoking 'Publick Law sore-wrenched too oft' (*Ad Patrem*), to sullying his mind with the black deeds of clients and the quibbles of pettifoggers.

It was necessary, then, to wait, to prepare oneself by concentrated efforts, that is by untrammelled study, for the tasks which might present or impose themselves . . . for the writing of a great poem, perhaps. The old scrivener felt himself disarmed before a young man so learned, so eloquent, so obstinate, and so tenderly loved.

Some unknown person intervened, perhaps a London minister. John had often received advice from him, and with deference. He saw John without obtaining a definite reply. Next day John wrote to him confirming his resolution to devote himself to study. His letter was an examination of conscience. Two drafts of it are extant, the substance of which is as follows:

In sundry respects each of our meetings has been of profit to me, and I am grateful to you for warning me, like a faithful night-watchman, that the hours of my night are flying away (for such I call my life, as yet obscure and unserviceable to mankind), and the day is drawing near for me, wherein Christ commands all to labour while there is light. . . . You regret that I waste my years dreaming. But my love of study must proceed from a principle, good, bad, or natural. If it were bad, other bad desires—love of gain, pride, ambition, would call me more powerfully than a poor, regardless and unprofitable sin of curiosity, whereby a man cuts himself off from all action and becomes the most helpless, pusillanimous, and unweaponed creature in the world. If its origin were natural, other natural inclinations would prevail over it—I should first desire to found a family, I should take up early some honourable employment, and I should even try to achieve immortal fame—the normal wish of every true Scholar—by hastening to publish as others have done. My thirst for learning is, then, the pursuit of something good. It leaves aside the shadows and notions, to tend to the supreme good known and presented, to the solid good flowing from due and timely obedience to that command in the Gospel set out by the terrible judgement of him that hid the talent. If I remain as it were in suspense, it is through duty, it is to make my talent produce the most I can. The workers of the eleventh hour received the same wages as the others.

Yet, that you may see that I am something suspicious of myself, and do take notice of a certain belatedness in me, I am the bolder to send you some of my nightward thoughts some while since, because they come in not altogether unfitly, made up in a Petrarchian stanza, which I told you of.[1]

The sonnet *How soon hath Time* followed. This fine plea omitted the essential point—the secret and irresistible urge to equal the greatest poets.

The elder Milton resigned himself. To thank and reassure him, the son addressed to him the glowing epistle *Ad Patrem*,[2] in which he glorified the magic power and sacred character of song, *carmen*, the incantation. After this he began upon personal arguments: 'To a musician father, a poet son. Moreover, you have not shown me the well-trodden path of lucre, nor assigned me to the study of law and the disgustful cries of the courts. Far from the noise of the town, you have allowed me to learn Latin, Greek, French, Italian, Hebrew. Thanks to you, I have caught a glimpse of the mysteries of knowledge. Now that it offers itself to me, must I shun it?'

> Hence I, although but least of the scholars' throng,
> Shall sit 'mid ivy-crowns and laurels proud;
> Nor mix obscure the idle rout among,
> But may, from eyes profane, my footsteps shroud . . .
> O Verses, pastime of my youthful days,[3]
> If ye dare hope eternally to live
> And see the light, and thus your lord survive
> (So dark Oblivion drive you not to dwell
> In gloom Tartarean), haply will this praise
> Of mine uptreasure well,
> And that dear Parent's name which was so long
> The burden of my song,
> To unborn ages as Example tell.[4]

[1] Masson I, 324–5.
[2] Critics disagree over the dating of *Ad Patrem*. On account of its style, Tillyard (*Milton*, 384) assigns it to 'the period round *Lycidas*'. I prefer to follow Masson I, 334 and Hanford, *Youth of Milton*, 130–1.
[3] *Et vos, O nostri, juvenilia carmina, lusus.*
[4] Tr. Skeat, Nonesuch, 799–800.

E

Milton himself has summed up what his life was at that time.

> I enjoyed an interval of uninterrupted leisure, which I entirely devoted to the perusal of the Greek and Latin classics; though I occasionally visited the metropolis, either for the sake of purchasing books, or of learning something new in mathematics or in music, in which I, at that time, found a source of pleasure and amusement.[1]

'Entirely devoted' is a generalization. True, for Milton as for his age the treasure of Antiquity surpassed all. The Elizabethans had had a glimpse of it; Milton wanted to master it. According to Bentley, the great scholar of the eighteenth century, he must have known Homer by heart. In 1634, he sent to Doctor Gill's son an 'ode in Greek composed in bed before daybreak on I know not what impulse' (B. III, 491).

Yet he disdained erudition in itself, philology for its own sake. He was to declare in 1652:

> From my very youth, I have been bent extremely upon such sort of studies, as inclined me, if not to do great things myself, at least to celebrate those that did.[2]

Similarly in Cambridge, praising learning:

> And what additional pleasure it is to the mind to wing its way through all the histories and local sites of nations . . . This is nothing less . . . than to be present as if living in every age, and have been born as it were coeval with Time herself; verily, while for the glory of our name we look forward into the future, this will be to extend and outstretch life backward from the womb, and to extort from unwilling fate a certain foregone immortality. I omit that with which what can be counted equivalent? To be the oracle of many nations; to have one's house a kind of temple; to be such as kings and commonwealths invite to come to them, such as neighbours and foreigners flock to visit, such as to have even once seen shall be boasted of by others as something meritorious.[3]

'To be the oracle and poet of the gods', he wrote to Diodati in 1629, 'to be the oracle of many nations', to come

[1] *Second Defence*, Bohn I, 255.
[2] *First Defence*, Bohn I 5; and see below, pp. 120 and 196.
[3] *Exercise VII*, Masson I, 300-1.

down from the mount with one's hands full of truths, that was what mattered to him, he had no wish to compete with those he called 'the grammarians', the herd of annotators, commentators, translators and biographers.

In 1874, in the attics of an English mansion, a commonplace book of Milton's was discovered, in which during more than thirty years he and his amanuenses had jotted down passages from his reading. The pages are entitled *Rex*, *Matrimonium*, *Libertas*, etc., and indexed under the main headings of Ethics, Politics and Economics. Since the poet's handwriting changed a little after Italy (the small e, for instance, is very different), we can make out that as far back as the years 1632–38 he had studied the ancient Fathers, and also Machiavelli, Bodin and Ochino. He had followed methodically the history of the Greeks, of the Romans, of the Middle Ages, of the free cities. There we can see that he was a republican by temperament, and that it was not by chance that he noted down: 'Sulpicius Severus declares that the very name of a king was always very odious among a free-born people'. In his *Index Oeconomicus* he records works on the fiscal systems of the Ancients. His notes on marriage come from a mind without prejudice. He studies the distinction between the civil and the ecclesiastical power. A reference to an *Index Theologicus* which has been lost proves that he had begun to 'scrutinize and ascertain for himself the several points of his religious belief'.[1]

Thus was formed the polemist capable of denouncing without hesitation an error of the Talmudists, of quoting a score of authorities on the same page, or of comparing *currente calamo* the laws of several countries. His poetry, too, was to show the variety of his reading. Professor Tillotson writes:

And so one goes through Milton hearing, or is it dreaming one hears? the voice of Greek, Latin and older English poets chiming like boys and men into the counterpoint . . . only

---

[1] *De Doctrina Christiana*, preface. Bohn IV, 2.

Milton could appreciate Milton comprehensively and with minutest delicacy. And the more closely our commonplace books tally with his, the farther his utterance will range and rove in our minds, the longer the echoes that it will strike from the scooped stone.[1]

In his long retreat Milton acquired a reserve of strength, 'unlimited power', says Pattison.

He was far, however, from overrating study. He understood so well the necessity of inspiration that inspiration in the secular sense of the word seemed to him inadequate. In a revealing passage in which he promised the people of England that he would enrich their literature, he was to declare:

> A work not to be raised from the heat of youth, or the vapours of wine; like that which flows at waste from the pen of some vulgar amourist, or the trencher fury of a rhyming parasite; nor to be obtained by the invocation of Dame Memory and her siren daughters, but by devout prayer to that eternal Spirit, who can enrich with all utterance and knowledge, and sends out his seraphim, with the hallowed fire of his altar, to touch and purify the lips of whom he pleases: to this must be added industrious and select reading, steady observation, insight into all seemly and generous arts and affairs.[2]

Prayer should thus come before work. Both profit by solitude.

> . . . And Wisdoms self
> Oft seeks to sweet retired Solitude,
> Where with her best nurse Contemplation
> She plumes her feathers, and lets grow her wings
> That in the various bussle of resort
> Were all to ruffl'd, and somtimes impair'd.[3]

This period, like the previous one, has left us only a very few poems, but they are of exceptional quality.

When the love of music called him to London, there Milton met Henry Lawes, musician of the King's Chapel, and the best composer of the time. He knew everyone at

---

[1] *Essays in Criticism and Research*, Cambridge, 1942, p. 177.
[2] *Reason of Church Government*, Bohn II, 481.
[3] *Comus*, 374–9.

Court and taught music in noble families, in particular in that of John Egerton, Earl of Bridgewater, Viscount Brackley, member of the Privy Council, Lord President of Wales, and son-in-law of the Dowager-Countess of Derby. This very great lady had been praised for her beauty and her wit by the 'singing birds' of the Golden Age. Queen Bess had deigned to stay in her mansion of Harefield, about ten miles to the north of Horton. The Egertons lived fifteen miles away, and frequently visited her.

In 1633, in the Queen's Avenue, the grandchildren of Spenser's Amaryllis performed for her a miniature masque, *Arcades*, in which Lawes and Milton had collaborated. The libretto runs to no more than a hundred and nine lines. The plot is simplicity itself. A few young shepherds and shepherdesses seek their queen, discover her in the person of the countess, and dance and sing in her honour. This trifle was played one summer's night, under 'branching elms star-proof'. A little girl sang. Then the Genius of the Wood told of the mysterious life of the trees and the 'sweet compulsion' of the music of the spheres, 'which none can hear of human mould with gross unpurged ear'. A short song followed, to which a chorus replied. Shakespeare wrote nothing more light and airy. Spenser's cousin was able to live over again her own Arcardia.

Trinity College, Cambridge, possesses a precious note-book begun by Milton about 1641, in which he wrote several poems and projects for poems. The order followed is not always chronological, but in default of other indications, we must hold to the fact that immediately after *Arcades* he has placed three short poems: *At a Solemn Music*, then *On Time, set on a Clock-Case*, and then *Upon the Circumcision*. Two of them show a technical progress similar to that of Beethoven inaugurating his third manner.

We have seen that Milton wanted a better scheme than the stanza or the rhymed couplet which, in Bergson's phrase, are no better than 'du mécanique plaqué sur du vivant'. If Milton left *The Passion* unfinished, it was partly because he had begun it in stanzas. Here we have the first examples of the Miltonian verse-paragraph, suggested perhaps by Spenser's *Epithalamium* or the Italian *canzone*: a group of lines (sometimes unequal, but linked by the rhymes and the run-on line) which corresponds in length and rhythm to the exigences of the thought and sensibility. *On Time* is composed of two of these microcosms. *At a Solemn Music* is the surge of a breaker of twenty-four lines, followed by a surf of four.

In the year of the *Arcades*, Bridgewater was still governing Wales from London. In 1634, he went to take up his residence at Ludlow Castle,[1] near the River Severn. The event called for a celebration, Lawes was invited to contribute to it and called upon Milton. This time what was wanted was a real masque, one of those plays, half-comedy, half-ballet, which were performed by amateurs at Court and at great houses. The genre included an interlude—the anti-masque—often burlesque, and left to professionals. The libretto was considered of slight importance, of which Jonson complained. What was demanded primarily was music, scenery, costumes, graceful or whimsical dances. Imported from Italy long before Spenser, the masque had reached its culmination under King James with Jonson and the scene-painter Inigo Jones; then it had gone out of fashion. In this very year, 1634, however, it regained favour.

Milton's text could be entitled 'Temptation repelled', or 'Heaven watches over virtue'. John Dalton called it *Comus* in 1738. Milton, leaving his disreputable hero in the background, always contented himself with the title *A Maske*.

The performance was given at Ludlow Castle in 1634 on Michaelmas night. The principal actors were Alice, a daughter of the Earl, not yet fifteen, two younger brothers, Lawes in the part of an Attendant Spirit, and two more participants, not identified yet, who played Comus and the goddess Sabrina.

---

[1] Built by a companion of the Conqueror, Roger de Montgomery.

Alice and her two brothers have lost their way at night in
a forest inhabited by the enchanter Comus, as dangerous
as his mother Circe. Lady Alice becomes separated from
her brothers, meets Comus and allows herself to be guided
by him. When they arrive at his palace he offers her an
enchanted seat, from which she is unable to move. To the
sound of sweet music, before a table loaded with delicious
food, he offers the girl magic potions. She refuses, for she
has seen at the back of the hall some of the sorcerer's victims,
beasts who were formerly human beings. (This is the anti-
masque.) He then begins a eulogy of pleasure in which the
cynicism of a profligate alternates with the majesty of a great
poet of Nature. It is Hugo's Satyr[1] carrying out the trial
of 'the lean and sallow Abstinence'.

> . . . if all the world
> Should in a pet of temperance feed on Pulse,
> Drink the clear stream, and nothing wear but Freize,
> Th'all-giver would be unthank't, would be unprais'd   719-22

Nature would be 'strangled with her waste fertility'. Beauty
is Nature's coin and must be current.

> . . . coarse complexions
> And cheeks of sorry grain will serve to ply
> The sampler, and to teize the huswifes wooll.
> What need of vermeil-tinctur'd lip for that,
> Love-darting eyes, or tresses like the Morn?   748-52

Alice refutes the sophist, although he is 'not fit to hear
himself convinc't' (791). Her brothers talk of her under
the trees. The younger is anxious, the elder reassures him:
virtue can rely on the help of heaven. In fact, a protecting
Spirit comes forward, disguised as a shepherd, and guides the
children to Comus's palace where they enter with swords
raised. Comus, however, has disappeared. Since Alice is
still bound by the spell, the Spirit has recourse to the goddess
Sabrina. She touches Alice with her pure fresh hands—
Alice is free. The Spirit brings the children back to their
parents. Country-dancers and the children 'triumph in
victorious dance o're sensual Folly and Intemperance'.

[1] *Légende des Siècles*, III, Prologue.

Before flying back to 'the broad fields of the sky' the Spirit proclaims:

> Mortals that would follow me,
> Love vertue, she alone is free,
> She can teach ye how to clime
> Higher then the Spheary chime;
> Or if Vertue feeble were,
> Heav'n it self would stoop to her.

An exact judgment was passed on *Comus* in 1638 by the Provost of Eton, Sir Henry Wotton, a former diplomat, a distinguished man of letters and himself a poet. He wrote to his young neighbour: 'I should much commend the tragical part, if the lyrical did not ravish me with a certain Doric delicacy in your songs and odes; whereunto I must plainly confess to have seen yet nothing parallel in our language. *Ipsa mollities.*'

He could not have insinuated more delicately that the substance was not of the same value as the form. The former secretary to the Earl of Essex had discovered anew with delight the exuberant style of the Elizabethans and congratulated Milton on his light and accurate touch, but the action gave place too easily to dialogue and even to didactic monologue. The characters lacked the depth of reality. Fictitious or childish, they were scarcely more than the mouth-pieces of the author. Sir Henry felt all this, and we are assured of it. Comus puts forward temptations which the anchorite rejected. It is the Lady of Christ's who is here defending 'the sage and serious doctrine of Virginity'. The two young boys discuss chastity as seriously as if they were budding Miltons. In prose or verse, Milton would never weary of repeating the precept of the good spirit: 'Love virtue, she alone is free'. As to Sabrina, 'a Virgin pure', who frees the soul paralysed by the tempter and whose victory is celebrated by a dance, she clearly represents the Severn and the fresh English countryside, but how much more also divine grace, associated with 'most innocent nature',[1] the world as God created it. Plato asserts in the *Timaeus*: 'He was good. . . . Being without

---

[1] 'Impostor do not charge most innocent nature.' *Comus,* 761.

envy, he willed that all things should be born as much as possible like to him' (29 e). Similarly *Genesis*: 'And God saw all that he had made, and behold, it was very good' (1. 31). And likewise St. Augustine, quoting Plato (*De Civ. Dei* XI, 21). Divine grace purifies man, frees him, re-establishes him in the 'enormous bliss' of the garden of Eden. And nature in her turn is ready to help pure hearts. Virtue, in a word, is for Milton nature regained, an idea frequently expressed by him, and always to be read between the lines, which Voltaire discerns in *Paradise Lost*: 'Milton ne s'élève pas au-dessus de la nature humaine, mais au-dessus de la nature corrompue'.[1]

Essentially, *Comus* is a confession, in the sense in which St. Augustine used the word. If we needed further proof of this, we should find it in the lyricism that 'ravished' Wotton. It saves everything, transforms everything. Saintsbury preferred *Comus* to *Paradise Lost*. Taine inclined to the same view ('peut-être son chef d'oeuvre . . . le sublime adoré sur un autel de fleurs'). From beginning to end, in fact, the same voice is lifted, touched with emotion, beyond compare.

Here we are faced with a paradoxical fact—the poet would not acknowledge publicly this inordinately personal work until he inserted it in his first volume of poems of 1645, i.e. eleven years after the performance. Several among the President's guests wanted to possess the delightful libretto. Whose was it? It was impossible to know. Recourse was then had to Lawes, the friend of everybody. Although very busy at the time, composing ballets for the Court with Carew and Davenant, he obligingly furnished copies but without revealing the author's name, since this indirect procedure went on for three years. Clearly, then, the Egerton family must have kept complete silence about Milton and he himself must have attached considerable importance to the incognito. Only in 1637 did the musician, 'his pen being weary', obtain from the poet the permission— grudgingly given—to publish. Milton did not sign his work and emphasized his refusal by a bitter motto.

[1] *Essai sur la poésie épique*, 1728.

Is it to be thought that the 'idle Achilles' was ashamed of this 'mere amusement'?[1] But *Comus* was no mere apprentice's effort plucked from deserved oblivion by an over-zealous friend. The President, his wife, and three of their children performed in the play. It had been written for them, their London guests and the notabilities living round about, that is for connoisseurs. Milton had surely endeavoured to satisfy them and one cannot produce a *Comus* without a certain capacity for self-criticism. The demands for the libretto must have removed the last shred of doubt.

An American Milton scholar, Harris Fletcher, has pointed out that during his retreat in the country Milton's sentiments underwent a substantial change, and he hints at some 'unfortunate experience' with the Egerton family.[2] This supposition would appear to have some foundation and becomes more definite when we try to link together certain facts that are either safely assumed or generally admitted. Moral certainties then emerge which we shall insert between square brackets.

Lady Derby had taken back into her household her widowed daughter, Lady Chandos, with her ten children, two of them girls. A sister of Lady Chandos, Lady Huntingdon, had left two sons and two daughters when she died. As to the Egertons, they had two daughters married and five unmarried daughters were still living with them besides Alice. The eldest of these Egerton girls, Elizabeth, was twenty-five; the next one, Mary, was an exceptionally gifted singer. We know this from Lawes himself who, in 1653, dedicated to her a collection of his melodies.

---

[1] Racine, *Iphigénie en Aulide*, I, ii.
  ... de si nobles succès! ...
  De toute autre valeur éternels monuments,
  Ne sont d'Achille oisif que les amusements.

[2] *The Life and Times of John Milton*, Boston, 1941, introducing a revision of Moody's edition of the *Complete Poetical Works*. Page 14—'His biographers generally have made of the whole period at Horton a sort of idyllic pastoral. ... It was actually a period in which something happened that completely changed Milton's life but which cannot be exactly determined except by its results'. Page 16—'But how did he first meet them [the Egertons], and why did the connection terminate so suddenly with the writing of *Comus*? The Egertons were Royalists and Anglicans: and, while Milton had as yet exhibited none of the intense resentment of priests and prelates, does his association with the Egertons mean that the bitter attack on the corruptions of the clergy, found in the next poem he wrote after *Comus*, grew out of an unfortunate experience with the Egertons?'

The performance of *Arcades* was necessarily preceded by rehearsals. [The writer of the libretto must have met his interpreters and their cousins at least once.] Between the performance of this play and the first rehearsals for *Comus*, a year at least, perhaps more than two, elapsed. [During this interval did not the poet sometimes revisit Harefield?] Spenser was Milton's model, *Comus* is of the same texture as *The Faerie Queene*. Now Lady Derby and her sisters had been celebrated in their youth by Spenser, who was their kinsman. [If Milton was received at Harefield once, he was so ten times. An Amaryllis of seventy-three wanted nothing better than to speak of her poet to a poet. Among the young ladies who animated Harefield House, one or other surely must sometimes have taken pleasure in listening to her grandmother chatting with the youthful author of *Arcades*.]

The rehearsals of *Comus* required more time than those of *Arcades*. [Milton must have seen his interpreters several times.] When Alice or the unknown lady who played Sabrina rehearsed one of the songs, Lawes judged and advised. [Are we to believe that he was always the only judge? It seems more likely that a small concert sometimes took place spontaneously, Milton accompanying on the bassviol, and one or other of Alice's sisters taking up the tune in turn.]

All five sisters were musicians. Masson assures us (I, 589) that several, whose portraits he had seen, have been 'very handsome'. As to Milton, in 1634 he was an elegant young gentleman of twenty-five with a nobly chiselled face, weak but large and luminous eyes, a delicate complexion, somewhat short in stature, but well set up, very alert, a skilful fencer. He was passionately devoted to music, sang as naturally as he breathed, played the organ in a masterly manner, was deeply moved at the sound of a beautiful feminine voice. He knew Latin, of course, and Greek, and what not, but above all he wrote poetry in Italian. He was gentle and pleasant, very gay, and the essence of politeness, as great poets usually are. In short, sooner or later, between him and some noble listener the spark of love was inevitable unless a miracle occurred. [The miracle did not happen. We are irresistibly reminded of Tasso, of Schubert with the Esterhazys, of many another Ruy Blas, without forgetting those of our own days.]

When Lawes and/or the family asked Milton for a masque, he composed a kind of symphony 'd'une originalité entière, d'une élévation de style extraordinaire' (Taine), on themes which haunted this virginal man—temptation of the flesh, the power of reason and will, the necessity of grace, the conquest of liberty and joy by virtue. [Was it only for the benefit of the Earl's guests that he expressed himself so passionately? In whatever circumstance one wills, the unknown girl or he himself imparts the secret or allows it to transpire. All is over.] The masque was performed on the day appointed. [Was the author present, however? In any case he disappears from the magic circle and his very name, if only to spare him, will no longer be mentioned.]

We know nothing of the details, but these broad lines are sufficient. A text, however, would be welcome. Let us refer, then, to the motto on the title page of 1637. Milton could have said with Poussin that he had 'neglected nothing': his very epigraphs should be read closely. The following is drawn from the *Second Bucolic*, where Corydon laments:

> Eheu quid volui misero mihi! Floribus austrum
> Perditus . . .

> Alas! What have I been about in my folly? On my flowers I have let in the sirocco, unfortunate that I am (Verity).

This cry has always been interpreted as the alarmed protest of a young writer: 'I am going to be condemned on a premature publication'. But Milton excelled at counterpoint. Perhaps we have here not a poet's, but a man's complaint: 'These avowals have destroyed me!' If we consult Virgil, we find that 'to let in the sirocco on one's flowers' was a simple proverbial saying meaning to make one's own misfortune. After *perditus* comes another expression, less graceful but with the same meaning: 'I have let loose the wild boars in the fountain'. Now in what did Corydon's blunder consist? He does not reproach himself with a *premature* gesture, but with a *presumptuous* gesture.

Alexis comes from the town, and his master is rich. When he rejects Corydon's rustic gifts, the latter attributes his ill-success to his own social inferiority. He says to himself: *Rusticus es*—'Thou art a peasant'. We may perhaps venture to interpret: 'You live in a cottage at the expense of a retired scrivener. You should have thought of that.' It is curious that in 1637, the year in which Lawes printed *Comus*, as if this new presentation to the public and the preparatory revision had reawakened the solitary's humiliation, he told Diodati that he was weary of living 'in obscurity and in a cramped manner'. A few weeks later he complained, for the only time in his life, that poets were scorned.[1]

In any event, it is not to be thought that Milton realized too late that a Puritan should hold the theatre in abhorrence. He was not so foolish and the question is not so simple.

The English stage had been brutal before Shakespeare's time. Afterwards it relapsed into its brutality. The Commonwealth was to close the theatres, but already for twenty years they had been playing only for the populace and the libertines of the fashionable world. The middle classes stayed at home, and in the great families masques were performed among friends. Moreover, when Queen Henrietta had wanted to revive the stage and, among other measures, had called in French actresses, Puritans and jingoists had rebelled. In 1632, a Presbyterian lawyer, the intrepid pamphleteer Prynne, exploded. His *Histriomastix* inevitably offended the Queen. During his trial, the 'Friends of the King', courtiers, lawyers and university men, reacted in favour of the theatre and, going for the easiest thing, revived the masque. The legal fraternity of London disbursed the incredible sum of twenty-one thousand pounds to present in February 1634 the astounding *Triumph of Peace*, the Court almost as much to give a fortnight later the *Coelum Britannicum* in which Charles played a part.

---

[1] See, p. 60. Other indications of an unhappy love-affair will be found in my article 'Une hypothèse à propos de Comus', *Études anglaises*, April–June 1959. A disappointment of this nature would best explain the three years of silence between *Comus* and *Lycidas*, at least in part the journey to Italy, and above all the fatal marriage.

Lawes had collaborated in both masques. Christopher
Milton, a law student and a Royalist, surely must have
marched through the streets of London with the company
performing the *Triumph of Peace*. In June, Prynne was
condemned to perpetual imprisonment and a fine of five
thousand pounds. The executioner cut off one of his ears
at Westminster and the other at Cheapside, and while he
was in the pillory, the smoke from his pamphlets almost
stifled him.

At this date Milton had begun to write *Comus*. He had
always been convinced that the theatre could do much
to improve morals. In 1641, in his *Reason of Church Government*, he was to praise it and claim state patronage for it.
Comus, two years earlier than Corneille's *Le Cid*, brought to
the stage 'une action morale et intérieure dans son principe'.[1]
The Ludlow masque implicitly suggested to the extremists
in both camps a solution of their debate, i.e. a synthesis, the
purifying theatre exemplified by the Greeks, which Milton
himself was to defend in his preface to *Samson Agonistes*.

The year 1637 in which *Comus* was printed is to be
reckoned among the most important in the religious and
political history of Great Britain.

For eight years now, Charles had been filling his coffers
by means of decrees and expedients. To satisfy the grave
and urgent needs of his navy, he had revived a war-tax,
known as ship-money, which first of all was levied in the
counties bordering the sea, then extended to the country
as a whole, and finally declared permanent by decree. In
itself the tax was justifiable, but the tax-payer had not been
consulted. Hampden's gesture is well known. This cousin
of Cromwell, a very rich landowner, had already suffered
imprisonment in 1626 rather than subscribe to a forced
loan. Rather than hand over twenty shillings ship-money,
he began a law-suit which cost him a fortune. The whole
country was on his side. In 1637 he was at last condemned,
under government pressure, and borne through London in
triumph.

[1] Lanson, in connection with 'Le Cid' in *Hist. de la Litt. française,* p. 425.

That same year a lawyer, a minister and a doctor, already under lock and key for having spoken ill of the ruling power, issued new tracts against Laud's abuses from the recesses of their prison. They were condemned to the loss of their ears, life imprisonment, and a fine of five thousand pounds. The lawyer was Prynne; the executioner had to sever certain muscles. Moreover he slit his nostrils and branded him on the cheek with the letters S.L., Seditious Libeller. As the two men were taken through the streets, Londoners threw flowers, wept for pity, or howled with rage.

Again in 1637, an incident occurred in Scotland, the consequences of which were to be fatal to Charles Stuart. His father had been clever enough to graft bishops on to the Presbyterian system. This compromise was workable, but Laud resolved to put an end to it. One Sunday in July, in the principal church in Edinburgh, when the Anglican dean, surrounded by the ecclesiastical and civil authorities, began the liturgy specially drawn up by Laud, an old woman Calvinist, Jenny Geddes, threw a stool at his head, crying out that it was popery. The disturbance immediately spread through the town and shortly afterwards through the whole of Scotland. In March 1638, the Presbyterians were to renew their Covenant of 1581,[1] their pact with God to defend their faith until death.

Milton could not approve taxation by decree (B. II, 95), but what offended him above all were the spiritual and moral consequences of Laud's policy. Laud had too quickly replaced his Puritan personnel by 'orthodox' men or men supposedly orthodox, though often ignorant or mercenary. Milton, however, could not imitate Prynne. Good taste, the shyness of the scholar, proper pride, counselled him against this. Did he even think of it? We wonder when we read his long confidence to Diodati of 23rd September, 1637, in Latin interspersed with Greek, which Chateaubriand called 'une lettre sublime'.[2]

[1] An old French word (see Littré). 'Dieu a un covenant avec les hommes', said Calvin. In 1581, James VI of Scotland, the future James I of England, asked the Scots to swear a covenant with him when he saw himself threatened by a league of Catholic lords supported by Spain.
[2] Bohn III, 493–5, or Masson I, 643–6. The italics show the passages in Greek.

Lest you should threaten too much, know that it is impossible for me not to love men like you. What besides God has resolved concerning me I know not, but this at least: *He has instilled into me, if into anyone, a vehement love of the beautiful.* Not with so much labour, as the fables have it, is Ceres said to have sought her daughter Proserpina as it is my habit day and night to seek for this *idea of the beautiful*, as for a certain image of supreme beauty, through all the forms and faces of things (*for many are the shapes of things divine*) and to follow it as it leads me on by some sure traces which I seem to recognize. Hence it is that, when anyone scorns what the vulgar opine in their depraved estimation of things, and dares to feel and speak and be that which the highest wisdom throughout all ages has taught to be the best, to that man I attach myself forthwith by a kind of real necessity, wherever I find him.[1] If, whether by nature or by fate, I am so circumstanced that by no effort and labour of mine can I myself rise to such an honour and elevation, yet that I should always worship and look up to those who have attained that glory, or happily aspire to it, neither gods nor men, I reckon, have bidden nay.

But now I know you wish to have your curiosity satisfied. You make many anxious enquiries, even as to what I am at present thinking of. Hearken, Theodotus, but let it be in your private ear, lest I blush; and allow me for a little to use big language with you. You ask me what I am thinking of? So may the good Deity help me, of immortality! And what am I doing? *Growing my wings* and meditating flight; but as yet our Pegasus raises himself on very tender pinions. Let us be lowly wise![2]

I will now tell you seriously what I am thinking of. I am thinking of migrating into some Inn of the Lawyers where I can find a pleasant and shady walking-ground, because there I shall have both a more convenient habitation among a number of companions if I wish to remain at home, and more *suitable headquarters* if I choose to make excursions in any direction.

---

[1] Cf. Michelangelo to Gianotti (*Dialoghi*): 'When I see a man who possesses some talent, some gift of the mind, a man who knows how to do something better than the rest of the world, I am constrained to become fond of him, and then I give myself to him so completely that I no longer belong to myself'.

[2] 'Quid agitem quaeris; ita me, bonus Deus, immortalitatem. Quid agem vero?— Πτεροφυῶ et volare meditor; sed tenellis admodum adhuc pennis evehit noster Pegasus. Humile sapiemus!' The *pterophuô* comes from Plato. 'The soul, in presence of the beautiful, recalls its fatherland; the man trembles, he has fever, he feels an irritation because he is growing wings for his soul.' *Phaedrus*, 251 c.

Where I am now, as you know, I live obscurely and in a cramped manner. You shall also have information respecting my studies. I have by continuous reading brought down the affairs of the Greeks as far as to the time when they ceased to be Greeks. I have been long engaged in the obscure business of the state of Italians under the Longobards, the Franks and the Germans, down to the time when liberty was granted them by Rodolph, King of Germany: from that period it will be better to read separately what each City did by its own wars. But what are *you* doing? . . . Meanwhile, if it can be done without trouble to you, I beg you to send me Justiniani, the historian of the Venetians . . . London: Septemb. 23, 1637.

There in full light is a Platonist poet, intoxicated with his young strength, a methodical explorer of the past, and a hermit who can endure his hermitage no longer. But not a word, either in these lines or in the rest of the letter, on the situation of the country. A fortnight later, however, the occasion presented itself to protest to some purpose; Milton took it.

In October his College informed him that Edward King, on his way to Ireland, had been shipwrecked and drowned. Cambridge was preparing a memorial volume of verse. Could they count on Milton?

On the eve of the shipwreck, 9th August, Jonson's remains had been brought to Westminster. What a contrast between the glorious dead and King who was scarcely known! King was not without talent. His piety, his morals, his desire to be of service had ensured him the esteem and affection of all. His untimely death made Milton tremble, and all the more so since that year many had died of the plague in Horton. Might not John Milton also leave this world without having known fame! Would at least a poet be found to tell of the promise he had given? To deserve this homage Milton himself would bring his own tribute to poor King. As King had been destined for the Church, an allusion to the reign of 'Thorough' would be easy. Since University publications were exempt from censorship, he must seize the opportunity and write in English in order to reach more readers. *Lycidas* was finished in November 1637. The volume appeared a month or two afterwards—

F

twenty-three poems in Latin or Greek, then thirteen in
English, one of which, extravagant in tone, was by the
future satirist, Cleveland. The last one bore the initials J.M.

There is no need to inquire what the work owes to
Striggio, to Landi, to Phineas Fletcher and many others.
As to its beauty, here are three testimonies—'The touch-
stone of poetic taste' (Tennyson); 'The high-water mark
of English poesy, and of Milton's own production' (Pattison); 'The first five lines are the most musical in all the
known realms of verse' (Swinburne).[1]

Milton called *Lycidas* a 'monody'—a solo without accom-
paniment. In less than two hundred lines, a shepherd
mourns the death of his friend. He first of all apologizes
for offering him laurels and myrtles culled before their
season. But how can one refuse a song to Lycidas, who
has died before coming to the age of man? He recalls
their common occupations and the merits of the dead man.
Alas! the Muse who sent Orpheus into the world could do
nothing to save her son. Is the pursuit of glory then vain?
It would be so if true glory were an earthly thing.

> Alas! What boots it with uncessant care
> To tend the homely slighted Shepherds trade,
> And strictly meditate the thankles Muse,
> Were it not better don as others use,
> To sport with *Amaryllis* in the shade,
> Or with the tangles of *Neaera's* hair?
> *Fame* is the spur that the clear spirit doth raise
> (That last infirmity of Noble mind)
> To scorn delights, and live laborious dayes;
> But the fair Guerdon when we hope to find,
> And think to burst out into sudden blaze,[2]
> Comes the blind *Fury* with th' abhorred shears,

[1] The five lines are:
> Yet once more, O ye Laurels, and once more
> Ye Myrtles brown, with Ivy never-sear,
> I come to pluck your Berries harsh and crude,
> And with forc'd fingers rude,
> Shatter your leaves before the mellowing year.

[2] 'Burst out into sudden blaze'—It is the cry of the Cid—'Mes pareils à deux fois
ne se font point connaître / Et pour leurs coups d'essai veulent des coups de maître'
(Corneille, *Le Cid*, II, ii). Milton is so moved that his secret escapes him. When a
particular circumstance made him throw on the gaming-table one of his gold pieces,
he did not deign to pick up his winnings. What he wanted was to stake all on a
number and break the bank.

And slits the thin-spun life. But not the praise,
Phoebus repli'd, and touch'd my trembling ears;
Fame is no plant that grows on mortal soil,
Nor in the glistering foil
Set off to th' world, nor in broad rumour lies,
But lives and spreds aloft by those pure eyes,
And perfet witnes of all-judging Jove;
As he pronounces lastly on each deed,
Of so much fame in Heav'n expect thy meed.   64-84

We then return to Lycidas. It was by water that he
perished. In succession appear an envoy of Neptune, the
god of the river Cam, and finally 'the Pilot of the Galilean
Lake', the apostle Peter, head of the Church:

How well could I have spar'd for thee young swain,
Anow of such as for their bellies sake,
Creep and intrude, and climb into the fold?
Of other care they little reck'ning make,
Than how to scramble at the shearers feast,
And shove away the worthy bidden guest;
Blind mouthes! that scarce themselves know how to hold
A Sheep-hook, or have learn'd ought els the least
That to the faithfull Herdsmans art belongs!
What recks it them? What need they? They are sped;
And when they list, their lean and flashy songs
Grate on their scrannel Pipes of wretched straw,
The hungry Sheep look up, and are not fed,
But swoln with wind, and the rank mist they draw,
Rot inwardly, and foul contagion spread:
Besides what the grim Woolf with privy paw
Daily devours apace, and nothing sed,
But that two-handed engine at the door,
Stands ready to smite once, and smite no more.   113-31

The elegy continues. All the flowers of the *Anthology* are
summoned. But where is the sheaf to be laid? Perhaps at
this moment Lycidas 'beyond the stormy Hebrides visits
the bottom of the monstrous world',[1] or else slumbers off
the Cornish coast . . . Oh no, 'he hears the unexpressive
nuptial Song in the blest Kingdoms meek of joy and love'
. . . Twilight comes down, the shepherd must depart:

[1] I.e. peopled with monsters; cf. Hugo: 'il chanta la terre monstrueuse' (*Légende des Siècles*, III, 'Le Satyre', ii).

At last he rose, and twitch'd his Mantle blew:
To morrow to fresh Woods, and Pastures new.

This last line has not given up its secret. Was it a farewell to minor poetry, a return to the land of the living, or did it refer to the journey to Italy? Is there perhaps a link between the preceding line and the political situation? If the mantle is blue, it is certainly not because 'blew' rhymed with 'pastures new'. Milton was not that kind of writer. The Covenanters had adopted blue, whereas the Royalists' colour was red. The tribe of the predestinate applied to itself the order given by God to Moses (*Numbers* 15, 38–39): 'Speak unto the children of Israel, and bid them that they make them fringes in the border of their garments . . . and that they put upon the fringe of the border a ribband of blue . . . that ye may look upon it and remember all the commandments of the Lord'.

Young's former pupil must have approved the Scottish rising which was in full swing while he was composing *Lycidas*. Is it possible that he foresaw the consequences of the event? His threat would lead us to think so. A score of explanations of the 'two-handed engine at the door' have been proposed. The most probable is that the Puritans were looking forward to the time when Charles would have to summon the two Houses. Milton may have been referring, as well, to the two-handed Sword of Justice alluded to in *The Tenure of Kings* (B. II, 8)—'be he king or tyrant, or emperor, the Sword of Justice is above him . . .'.

A further allusion to the followers of Laud, also veiled, is, however, unmistakable. Asking himself whether the dead body of Lycidas had drifted towards Cornwall (why Cornwall?), Milton wrote:

> Or whether thou to our moist vows deny'd,
> Sleep'st by the fable of *Bellerus* old,
> Where the great vision of the guarded Mount
> Looks towards *Namancos* and *Bayona's* hold.   159–62

For his contemporaries, the meaning was clear. The Romans had called Land's End *Bolerium* or *Bellerium*. Hence the legendary Bellerus, protector of Cornwall.

The 'guarded Mount', therefore, was the Penzance St. Michael's Mount, and the 'great vision' that of the archangel who had one day appeared to some fishermen of those parts. Namancos and Bayona are places in Spanish Finisterre shown in the English atlas. Consequently, the plain meaning was: 'Thou art perhaps slumbering off Cornwall, near St. Michael's Mount, whence the protecting archangel keeps watch over the country of the Armada'. But it was no longer Spain which threatened the liberty of conscience of the English. So Milton continues: 'Look homeward Angel now, and melt with ruth'. The Armada of Milton's day was Laud's clergy.

Lycidas marks the decisive stage in the twofold destiny of the poet and polemist. Milton points out here that literary glory is often illusory, always precarious and of secondary importance. We shall be judged on our deeds (*on each deed*, 83). Deeds first and last, write in order to act. *Lycidas* is an act, the first gesture of the polemist, his first step towards a goal of which he is yet unaware.

Milton perhaps had his departure for Italy in mind when he wrote to Diodati in September 1637 that he lived obscure and cramped for space.

His mother had died in May. Christopher was going to be called to the Bar, and had taken a wife. The young couple would take care of the father while the elder son, 'with his father's consent and assistance' (Phillips), would seek 'the traces of beauty' in classical lands. He would cure himself of that restlessness which is so evident, better even than in a London school of law. The expedition was to last perhaps two years and would cost at least five hundred pounds.

The traveller obtained letters of introduction from several people. Lawes procured a passport for him. Wotton, who had already read *Comus* without knowing who was the author, then received the poet and his poem and sent him in April 1638, with the appreciation we have already seen, an itinerary, a letter for the embassy in Paris, others for Italians, and this advice which he himself had received from a prudent Florentine: 'Pensieri stretti ed il viso sciolto', 'thoughts kept to oneself and an open face enable one to travel safely the whole world through'.

Shortly after the receipt of this letter Milton set off, 'with a servant'. Later a political opponent was to remind him sourly that having travelled with so small a suite, he ought not to sing quite so loud. For in those spacious times, the burlesque poet Charles d'Assouci, when he left for Italy, 'although he was neither count nor marquis did not fail to have a retinue of two pages'.

IV

THE JOURNEY TO ITALY
1638–1639

Arrived in Paris, Milton presented himself to the English ambassador, Lord Scudamore, a protégé of Laud who disavowed the French Protestants and kept an eye on the English dissidents who had taken refuge in France. Not having read *Lycidas*, he received Wotton's friend 'very courteously'. Through him, the traveller could have had the entrée everywhere, but he stayed only 'a few days' in Paris.

There was some excuse for his haste—the Grand Siècle was still in its infancy. Corneille and Descartes were but beginning their careers, the Academy had been in existence a brief three years, Bossuet was a boy of eleven. In a word—the Sun-King would not be born until five months after Milton's visit. Italy, on the other hand, was 'the seat of civilization and the hospitable domicile of every species of erudition'.[1]

It is legitimate to think, however, that political feeling had something to do with it. France had four times the population of England and a master of genius. Her growing strength made Englishmen uneasy. It was the naval policy of Richelieu that had determined Charles to demand ship-money by decree. The jealousy that was to prompt so many crimes against Europe was born. To avoid admitting it, English people persuaded themselves that William of Normandy had deprived them of time-honoured liberties and they took pleasure in belittling the sons of their oppressors. The vivacity of France they called frivolity, her frankness cynicism, her politeness affectation, her refinements self-indulgence. True, God had given her Calvin, but Calvin she had expelled. Now Milton shared these prejudices—from which Cromwell managed to keep himself

---

[1] *Second Defence*, Bohn I, 252.

free. We can find the plumed France of d'Artagnan attractive if we like; Milton, who saw the musketeers on cavalcade, sneered at the 'monsieurs of Paris'.[1] One of them, however, the frivolous Cyrano, in this very year 1638,[2] received his first wound in that war with the Habsburgs in which Puritan England never sacrificed a man or a shilling.

It is morally certain that the traveller introduced himself to his friend's relative, Elie Diodati, an advocate at the High Court of Paris. This little-known but very active personage, a friend of Gassendi, of Campanella, and of Peiresc, interested himself in all victims of intolerance in Catholic lands. He had seen Galileo several times and translated several of his works into Latin. When Milton passed through Paris, Elie Diodati had just published a translation of the *Dialoghi*. A few months later, in a letter dated 14th August, Galileo thanked him for having served his interests with the Estates General of the Low Countries. It is highly probable that the advocate entrusted Milton with some discreet mission.

The only reminiscence of Paris mentioned by Milton was an interview with a Dutchman. It is true that the Dutchman in question was the eminent European Grotius, jurist, diplomat, exegete, and even dramatic author—it was after his example that Corneille was to 'risk' *Polyeucte*. Wotton was a friend of his. In 1638 he was representing Sweden in Paris and at the instigation of a Presbyterian minister, John Durie, son of a Scottish refugee in Holland, whom we shall meet again, he worked for a closer understanding between Swedish Lutherans and the half-Lutheran Anglicans. He expected that the Danes, and then the French Protestants, would follow suit. Through Scudamore, he tried to persuade Laud, but Laud turned a deaf ear.

Wotton had recommended to his young friend one of the usual itineraries—in Paris, embark at the port of St. Paul,[4] then travel up the Seine and up the Yonne as far as Auxerre. From there he would reach Chalon-sur-Saône by road, and

---

[1] See below p. 122.
[2] Cyrano de Bergerac (1614–55), soldier, poet, dramatist, and author of a *Journey to the Planets*.
[3] Corneille, *Examen de 'Polyeucte'*.
[4] Still in operation along the Quai des Célestins, opposite the Ile St. Louis.

there re-embark for Lyons and Avignon. He would take the road again as far as Marseilles, whence boats left for Genoa daily.

Doubtless Milton could scarcely wait to hear Italian spoken—from Avignon he turned aside by the former Roman road, the 'Via Aurelia',[1] to Nice, where he took ship for Genoa. Then, via Leghorn and Pisa, he finally reached Florence in August, three months after his departure from Horton. His paradise was to continue without a cloud until the following May. Yet while he enjoyed the sweetness of Florence, an epidemic carried off Diodati. At such distances, however, private people could only correspond through sailors and merchants. The traveller had already left Italy when he heard of his loss.

Before accompanying Milton further, it may be well to sum up his general impressions and reactions.

As the barge carrying him slipped down the mighty Rhone, he had the revelation of light. Tuscany in the month of August, completed his initiation. The man born and bred under hazy skies caught at last the full meaning of that brief word 'light' and all the translations of it that he had ever known. Similarly, he found that in certain countries beauty flowered spontaneously. Many a time he was to express his regret at having been born 'too near to the Pole'.[2] Nevertheless, much of the miracle of the Mediterranean escaped him completely.

Goethe once remarked to Eckermann: 'We have eyes and ears only for what we know'. We may prove this by comparing Goethe and Milton in the presence of the treasures of Italy. Goethe wanted to see everything and to understand what he saw. He climbed Vesuvius twice, frequented museums and ruins, drew, painted and modelled, investigated the rocks, the plants and the fossils. Milton was of another century and another race. England understood nothing of the plastic arts and blamed the Dutch for 'cluttering themselves up with rubbishy pictures'. Every

[1] Now part of the *Route Nationale* 7.
[2] *Mansus*, 18; *Areopagitica* (Bohn II, 53); *Of Education* (Bohn III, 468); *Paradise Lost*, IX, 44.

young Englishman of good family went on his Italian tour, but no travel diary of this period even mentions Raphael. Not a word from Milton proves that he saw the Sistine Chapel.

On the other hand, he did enjoy the pleasures that Italy offered to his ear. Latin pronounced in the Roman way seemed to him so beautiful that from that time he ceased to speak Latin, and would not listen to it, deformed in the English way. As to Italian music, it was to be one of the great consolations of the lonely polemist.

The Italian musicians were the best in Europe. In Rome, Frescobaldi, 'father of organists' and creator of the fugue, was playing in St. Peter's; Carissimi, the creator of the oratorio, was in charge of the music at the German College. In Venice, a city which possessed three opera houses, Monteverdi was teaching and proving that in the expression of the emotions, music 'goes further' than words. Moreover, during the forty years that had elapsed since Italy had created opera, she had brought it to perfection and the genre included these essential new features: the conformity of the melody to the text and the replacement of polyphony by harmony. Milton agreed strongly that the music should follow the pattern of the verse. Lawes, who had studied under an Italianized Englishman,[1] practised the *aria parlante*, intermediary between the recitative and the song. His fellow-musicians blamed him for it. Milton now fully understood his merit. In 1646 he was to congratulate him in exact terms:

> *Harry* whose tuneful and well measur'd Song
> First taught our English Musick how to span
> Words with just note and accent, not to scan
> With *Midas* Ears, committing short and long; . . .
> To after-age thou shalt be writ the man
> That with smooth aire couldst humor best our tongue . . .
> *Dante* shall give Fame leave to set thee higher
> Then his *Casella*, whom he woo'd to sing
> Met in the milder shades of Purgatory.

Literary Italy exercised on the traveller a still more marked influence. Certainly the Golden Age was over,

---

[1] Giovanni Coperario, to wit, or plain John Cooper.

Tasso had been dead for forty years, Tassoni, Marini, decadent poets, had themselves disappeared. But a 'demi-monde littéraire' (to use Lamartine's expression in connection with a salon where, however, he had met Balzac), made up for the master minds. About 1638, Rome alone counted some five hundred poetasters, and each town one or two academies where patricians discussed grammar and prosody, presented the latest-born offspring of their Muse and exchanged plaudits and quips. Milton had the privilege of sitting as a confrère among the academicians of Florence, Rome and Venice. This dapper fresh-faced Englishman who knew so much, seemed to them a prodigy. They could teach him nothing, but he owed them other benefits.

Nature had not intended Milton for the crudities of a revolution. The sensitivity of *Il Penseroso* required at one time solitude, at another understanding friendship. When scores of cultured Italians displayed to the traveller the sympathy that the Italian Diodati had shown him, his heart expanded.

In the same way he found pleasure and profit in exchanging ideas with people who never put forward an opinion but with a smile. The sessions of the Italian academies did not take place in the same climate as the Cambridge prolusions and *combats de pachydermes* (Taine). If there is remarkable urbanity in many dialogues of *Paradise Lost*, it is partly due to the young patricians of Italy.

Above all, Milton owed to them the certain knowledge of his strength. The encouragements of Jonson or of Wotton had their value, but to be praised in the language of Tasso in the land of Virgil banished diffidence.

But much latelier in the private academies of Italy, whither I was favoured to resort, perceiving that some trifles which I had in memory, composed at under twenty or thereabout (for the manner is that every one must give some proof of his wit and reading there), met with acceptance above what was looked for; and other things which I had shifted in scarcity of books and conveniences to patch up amongst them, were received with written encomiums, which the Italian is not forward to bestow on men on this side the Alps; I began thus far to assent

both to them and divers of my friends here at home, and not
less to an inward prompting which now grew daily upon me,
that by labour and intense study (which I take to be my portion
in this life), joined with the strong propensity of nature, I might
perhaps leave something so written to aftertimes, as they
should not willingly let it die. . . . I applied myself to that
resolution, which Ariosto followed against the persuasions of
Bembo, to fix all the industry and art I could unite to the
adorning of my native tongue. . . .[1]

Milton was to remain deeply grateful to his Italian
friends.

No time will ever abolish the agreeable recollections which
I cherish of Jacopo Gaddi, Carlo Dati, Frescobaldi, Coltellini,
Buommattei, Chimentelli, Francini, and many others.[2]

Eighty years after Milton's death there was discovered
in England a manuscript collection of fifty Italian sonnets
composed by a Florentine named Malatesti and dedicated
by him to Milton. This collection had certainly crossed
the Channel in the poet's luggage. Yet it was a series of
ribald equivocations in connection with an Italian girl, la
Tina. But—what a dedication! *All'Illmo. Signore et Padrone
Oss^{mo} Signor Giovanni Milton, nobile Inghlese.* Malatesti, a bon
vivant in his forties, had doubtless meant to tease this little
Englishman whose virtue got on his nerves.

Here emerges a question at which we can smile, but which
Milton has answered in all seriousness. Did his virtue
never yield to the temptations of Italy? Volcanic Naples,
'beneath the lidless eye of heaven', out of three hundred
thousand inhabitants counted thirty thousand courtesans.
One day an adversary would argue that if Milton was blind,
it was through having looked at the Italian girls too closely.
Milton was to answer him:

[I] call the Deity to witness, that in all those places in which
vice meets with so little discouragement, and is practised with
so little shame, I never once deviated from the paths of integrity
and virtue, and perpetually reflected that, though my conduct
might escape the notice of men, it could not elude the inspection
of God.[3]

---

[1] *Church Government*, Bohn II, 477–8.   [2] *Second Defence*, Bohn I, 255–6.
[3] *Second Defence*, Bohn I, 257.

This is a far cry from Goethe taking an Italian mistress to complete his documentation. But Milton was not lying. A year before his protest, in 1653, a Dutch scholar, Heinsius, wrote from Venice to his friend Vossius:

> I had believed Milton dead. . . . What Saumaise says about Milton's conduct in Italy is mere calumny. . . . I wish his own cheeks were as safe from his wife's nails as Milton is from that imputation. That Englishman was even disliked by the Italians among whom he lived a long time, on account of his too severe morals.[1]

In one regard, however, this man in love with glory could not come off unscathed. There is always more or less of flattery and unreality in the relationships of a traveller with his hosts. His very visit is a compliment and pre-disposes them in his favour. Quarrels of ideas, of factions, or of persons, bypass the foreigner who will be gone to-morrow. During his stay in Italy, Milton met only people who were happy to please him. In his own interest, then, they should not have called this little man with the resolute step, proud of his eagle and his sword, 'Illustrious Lord and Patron'. One day he thought himself marked out for attention by a cardinal, and at once became devoted to him. He was to return to his own country less pleased with it and better pleased with himself.

It is time to come to the various stages of his journey: Florence (two months), Rome (the same), Naples (a month), Rome (two months), Florence (the same), Venice (a month).

In Florence, thanks to Sir Henry, Milton was received 'immediately' (*statim*) as a friend in the best families and as a confrère by the Accademia degli Svogliati (the Disgusted). He attached himself principally to Carlo Dati, who has been mentioned earlier. A pupil of Galileo, he was to become at twenty-two, in 1640, secretary of the Accademia della Crusca, then to teach Greek at the University, to publish works on mathematics, the history of art, archaeology, philology, and eventually to be honoured with a pension by Louis XIV.

[1] Masson IV, 475.

On 10th September Milton wrote at length to Father Buommattei, who was preparing a Tuscan grammar, to point out to him the desiderata of the foreign reader. He assured him that he was writing to him in Latin out of respect for the incomparable Tuscan tongue. Six days later, according to the register of the Svogliati, 'il Giovanni Miltone, Inglese' was reading to them 'a Latin poem in very erudite hexameters.'

Long afterwards the monks of Vallombrosa showed visitors several souvenirs of Milton's visit. He had played on their organ. One aspect of the site has found a place in *Paradise Lost*:

> Nathless he so endur'd, till on the Beach
> Of that inflamed Sea, he stood and calld
> His Legions, Angel Forms, who lay intranst
> Thick as Autumnal Leaves that strow the Brooks
> In *Vallombrosa*, where th' *Etrurian* shades
> High overarcht imbowr;[1]

The excursion took place therefore at the end of the first stay. A visit to Galileo should be assigned to the same period. Milton must have been eager to see this man who was the talk of learned Europe and might die any day.

He was living near the Porta S. Giorgio in a very fine villa, which the Inquisitor of Venice had forbidden him to leave, even to consult a doctor. Yet Galileo was then seventy-four, nearly blind, and so weakened by a hernia that he seldom left his bed, and could scarcely speak. He received letters, but the Inquisitor had refused the *imprimatur* to 'any writing of his, past or future'. In principle he was to receive nobody; in fact, visitors were fairly numerous.[2]

Six years later, pleading for the suppression of the censorship, Milton was to write:

> There it was I found and visited the famous Galileo, grown old, a prisoner to the Inquisition, for thinking in astronomy otherwise then the Franciscan and Dominican licensers thought.[3]

[1] I, 299 sqq.   [2] Aubanel, *Le Génie sous la tiare, Urbain VIII et Galilée*, 1929.
[3] *Areopagitica*, Bohn II, 82.

Thrice his epic makes allusion to the father of modern science (I, 288; III, 590; V, 262). No other contemporary appears in it.

Milton has asserted (B. I, 256) that he visited 'the antiquities of Rome'. He has never mentioned any one of them in particular. Papal Rome, active, brilliant, fresher for him than that of the Caesars, offered him many and keen enjoyments. For example, he there heard Leonora Baroni, the first singer of Europe. Three short Latin poems gave expression to Milton's delight. One of them recalled that Tasso had lost his reason through love for a Leonora and declared that if he had heard Leonora Baroni, her heavenly voice would have cured him.

Milton has not breathed a word of a very different incident (M. I, 800). The visitors' book of the English Jesuit College records that on 30th October, 1638; the Fathers entertained at dinner four Englishmen of distinction, among them '*Dominus Miltonus, cum famulo*'—with his servant.

In the passage in which Milton speaks of the Roman antiquities, he declares that he was 'very pleasantly received by Lucas Holstein and other men of knowledge and talent'. Holstein was one of the Librarians of the Vatican, the 'other men of knowledge and talent' are unknown to us. Rome possessed nine academies. It was Cherubini, one of the *Umoristi*, a young scholar now forgotten, who introduced Milton to Holstein. Moreover, two obscure poets put Milton on a level with Homer and Virgil; when one of them fell ill, Milton offered him his sympathy in about fifty lines of verse, absurdly dithyrambic. We should prefer to ignore this exchange of flummery, but Milton himself made a point of having the extravagances of Salvaggi and Salzelli printed with the poems of his youth.

His relations with Holstein do him greater credit. This German by birth had been a Lutheran. Finding that the young heretic was worthy of it, he showed him his rare books and precious manuscripts 'impatient to spring into life'. Like Montaigne sixty years earlier, Milton was allowed to handle the Latin treatise of Henry VIII against Luther, signed by the author and bearing this distich also from his royal hand:

> *Anglorum rex Henricus, Leo decime, mittit*
> *Hoc opus, et fidei testem et amicitiae.*

Henry, King of the English, sends thee, Leo X, this work, as a pledge both of his faith and friendship.

Holstein was so pleased with his English visitor that he made him a present of two of his works and asked him to undertake some research for him.

In November, Milton left Rome for Naples, where he intended to embark for Greece. He travelled with a 'recluse' who, when they entered Naples, took him to the man who could interest him most—the wealthy octogenarian Manso, Marquis of Villa, a former patron of Tasso and his devoted biographer. Tasso had dedicated to him his *Dialogue of Friendship*, and given the name of Manso to one of the 'magnanimous and courteous knights' of his *Jerusalem Delivered*. Manso and Milton took to each other immediately. The old marquis came and talked with the young poet in his inn. He conducted him round the city, and to the palace of the Spanish viceroy. None of the sights of Naples has found a place in Milton's work.

In Scotland the storm was rising. In the month of November the Presbyterian Assembly had dared to sit, despite Charles's prohibition. It deposed the bishops appointed by Laud and suppressed the episcopacy in Scotland. The King could not brook this defiance; war was certain. When 'the melancholy news' reached Naples, Milton gave up the projected journey to Greece:

> I thought it base to be travelling for amusement abroad, while my fellow citizens were fighting for liberty at home.[1]

He then took leave of the 'magnanimous and courteous' Manso, who handed him two of his writings, 'gravely apologizing for not having been able to show him more

---

[1] *Second Defence*, Bohn I, 256.

civility because he had spoken of religious matters with so little reserve'. Milton thanked him lavishly in one hundred lines of Latin verse, to which the marquis replied by repeating the play on words of Gregory the Great: 'In thee, mind, form, grace, countenance and morals are beyond reproach. If but thy faith were also, thou wouldst not be an Angle but an angel.'

Milton's epistle *Mansus* contains a lengthy confidence:

Hence, Manso, I who thee as sire revere,
In Clio's and great Phoebus' name present
Prayers for thy health through many a happy year.
Although, of years unripe, my steps I bent
From Hyperborean zone to sojourn here,
Thou of thy noble mind wilt ne'er refuse
For too remote, my Muse,
Which sparely nurtur'd 'neath the freezing Bear,
Hath fear'd not (overbold, perchance) to fly
Throughout the cities of thine Italy.

We, too, have swans that on our River's breast
Ourselves through night's dark watches fluting seem
To have heard where Thames, drawing his silver stream
From urns crystalline, with effusion wide
Inbathes his sea-green locks in ocean's tide ...

Should I recall, to grace the songs I sing,
Britain's old kings and Arthur marshalling wars
Ev'n in the World Beneath—should e'er I tell
Of the Table's Fellowship invincible:
Heroes great-soul'd—should I with Britain's Mars
(So but the Muse due inspiration give!)
The imbattled Saxon squares to havock rive—[1]

Milton was about to leave Naples when some English merchants warned him that the Jesuits in Rome were planning to have him arrested if he passed through their city again, because he spoke too freely of religion. Therein lay the marquis's justification. Heinsius also said in the letter quoted above: 'The Italians say that he hit out strongly against the Pope on any occasion'. In fact, instead of following Wotton's advice: 'Thoughts secret, countenance open', Milton had made this rule for himself:

[1] Tr. Skeat, Nonesuch, p. 804–6.

G

'Never to be the first to speak of religion, but if [he] were asked about [his] faith, to declare it without any reserve or fear'. He would not condescend either to avoid Rome on the return journey or to modify this practice.

> . . . for about the space of two months I again openly defended, as I had done before, the reformed religion in the very metropolis of popery.[1]

Was he really in danger? He must have thought so, for Englishmen did not travel through Italy without a certain apprehension. Their guide-books recommended them to take various precautions—such as to change their rooms frequently. Milton himself has declared, however, that he was always listened to with the greatest kindness. No one disturbed him in any way. He none the less became convinced that the Italians were less fortunate than he.

> I have sat among their learned men (for that honour I had), and been counted happy to be born in such a place of philosophic freedom, as they supposed England was, while themselves did nothing but bemoan the servile condition into which learning amongst them was brought; that this was it which had damped the glory of Italian wits; that nothing had been there written now these many years but flattery and fustian.[2]

Similarly, in regard to the Jesuits:

> . . . the Jesuits, who are indeed the only corrupters of youth and good learning: and I have heard many wise and learned men in Italy say as much.[3]

He went away reluctantly. He doubtless learnt in Rome that the situation of his country did not demand his immediate return. He was back again in the Eternal City in January 1639, but did not tear himself away from it until the beginning of March, overwhelmed with unforgettable delights.

Urban VIII was a poet. He and his nephews Cardinals Francesco and Antonio Barberini were generous patrons of the arts and literature.

Francesco Barberini, although scarcely past forty, could

---

[1] *Second Defence*, Bohn I, 256.   [2] *Areopagitica*, Bohn II, 82.
[3] *Of Reformation in England*, Bohn II, 400.

do almost anything in Rome, since he was both the Pope's favourite and the idol of the Romans. His modesty was as great as his culture. An intimate friend of Galileo, he had not signed the condemnation of 1633. He was good. 'While I am alive', he liked to say, 'I will not allow Protestants to be troubled in any way'. He was specially charged with the interests of the Church in Great Britain. On the recommendation of Holstein, he wished to see Milton; charmed in his turn, he invited the traveller to a performance given in his palace.

Neither London nor Paris offered anything approaching the splendours of the Casa Barberini, recently completed by Bernini—marble halls adorned with ancient statues, a gallery of masters, colonnades, a library not unworthy of the Vatican, a theatre seating more than three thousand people, vast gardens graced by a temple going back to the time of King Numa. The lavishness of the Barberini made the populace murmur, but Milton enjoyed what he himself called 'this truly Roman magnificence'.

It was in this setting that he heard, on 27th February, a comic opera in three acts, *Chi soffre, speri* (He who suffers, should hope). Rospigliosi, the future pope, had written it, the music was by two well-known composers, the scenery by Bernini. The festivities lasted five hours. Between the acts the public walked through the gardens amid the tents, shows and stalls of a festive fair.

Next day Milton went to thank his host. A few weeks later, from Florence, he wrote to Holstein among other things:

> He [Cardinal Francisco Berberini] waited for me at the door, sought me out among the crowd, took my by the hand, and introduced me into the palace with every mark of the most flattering distinction. When I went the next day to render him my acknowledgments for this his gracious condescension, it was you who obtained me an interview, in which I experienced a degree of civility and kindness greater than I had any reason to expect from a person of his high dignity and character. . . . I add that you will lay me under new obligations if you will express my warmest acknowledgments, and my most respectful compliments, to the most noble Cardinal, whose great virtues,

and whose honest zeal, so favourable to the encouragement of all the liberal arts, are the constant objects of my admiration. Nor can I look without reverence on that mild, and if I may so speak, that lowly, loftiness of mind, which is exalted by its own humiliation, and to which we may apply a verse in the Ceres of Callimaehus:

ἴθματα μὲν χέρσῳ, κεφαλὰ δέ οἱ ἄψατ' 'Ολύμπῳ

On th'earth he treads, but to the heavens he soars.

His conduct may serve to shew other princes that a forbidding superciliousness and a dazzling parade of power are quite incompatible with real magnanimity. Nor do I think that while he lives any one will regret the loss of the Esti, the Farnese, or the Medici, who formerly espoused with so much zeal the patronage of literature. *Florence*, March 30th, 1639.[1]

On his return to the City of Flowers, Milton had been received as if he were returning to his fatherland. After a visit to Lucca, the native place of the Diodati, he resumed his journey in the middle of April. The route of his return passed through Ferrara where Ariosto's house and Tasso's prison were to be seen. In Venice he lingered a month, attracted by the 'curiosities' of the city, the music of Monteverdi, the civilities of the *Incogniti*, and the shipment of several cases of musical scores and of 'fine or rare' books.

Then, while Charles Stuart was marching against the Covenanters, Milton passed through Verona, Milan, the valley of Aosta, the Great St. Bernard, and came down to Geneva, where he stayed a fortnight.

There he conversed 'every day' with one of the leading citizens of the town, Giovanni Diodati, doctor of theology, and uncle of Charles.

At their first meeting Milton was distressed. The doctor thought he had learnt that Charles was dead! . . . The details, however, were lacking, the news was perhaps false, they must hope.[2]

Dr. Diodati was known for his Italian translation of the Bible, his French eloquence, his publications in Italian and

[1] Bohn III, 499–500.
[2] See *Epitaphium Damonis*, *Argumentum*: 'when he returned home, the news was confirmed to him'.

in French. He taught Hebrew at the University and directed the studies of a few young men who lodged in his large house by the lake.[1] One of his boarders was the heir to the Swedish throne, Charles Gustavus.

His example proved to Milton that a man devoted to study could at the same time maintain himself, pursue his personal work, and exercise a lasting influence on future leaders.

It was not about these matters, however, that the minister and his guest could 'hold daily conferences' for a fortnight on end. Their common passion was the future of Protestantism. Milton had discussed this with Grotius. Sir Henry Wotton and Doctor Diodati were both striving to revive the Reformation in Venice. The confidences and complaints that Milton had received 'from several Italians of good judgement' must of necessity have interested Giovanni Diodati in Geneva no less than they did his namesake in Paris, who was particularly preoccupied with the lot of the secret Protestants. On his side the Genevan professor was a mine of information. Geneva had already become an excellent observation post. It was perhaps there, between one of the Diodati, and Milton, that a plan was outlined, similar to that of Grotius, which Milton put forward in 1641 (ten years before Cromwell nearly succeeded in realizing it)—to put England at the head of European Protestantism.

From Lyons the poet returned by the route of his outward journey and was home again at the beginning of August 1639.

There had been bloodshed. Charles, after a defeat, had made a treaty with the Scots in June, but the Second 'Bishops' War' was to follow. There would still be bloodshed for the next ten years and more.

With the Italian sky, the marble palaces, the voice of Leonora, the applause of Florence, Milton had left behind him the last joys of his protracted and unfettered youth.

[1] In this villa Byron was to finish *Childe Harold*, and Madame Hanska received Balzac.

IN THE FRAY

V

AGAINST THE BISHOPS
1641–1642

In this month of August 1639, when the Scots are thanking God for their victory, the Milton family meet together at Horton to welcome John back and reorganize themselves. Christopher has been appointed to the Bench in Reading, his father will follow him there. It is three years since Anne married a colleague of her first husband, Thomas Agar. Since John wants to establish himself as a pedagogue, the Agars entrust to his care Phillips' sons, Edward and John. Edward is nine, John seven.

As the war was driving hundreds of families to London, at first Milton had to lodge with a tailor, opposite St. Bride's Churchyard, near Fleet Street. Only at the end of 1640 could he at last establish himself, 'with his books' and his nephews on the northern edge of the City in silent Aldersgate Street. There, at the end of a passage, was a 'spacious house with a large garden'.

> . . . where I again with rapture renewed my literary pursuits, and where I calmly awaited the issue of the contest, which I trusted to the wise conduct of Providence, and to the courage of the people.[1]

Charles having promised an indemnity to the victors, he had to call a Parliament, the first for eleven years. The Commons assembled in April 1640. Prompted by Pym, they laid down their conditions. The King dismissed them after eighteen days, without making any concession to them or obtaining a penny from them. The country remained on the 'alert; Pym took care that it should. The King attacked Scotland again, was again beaten, and recalled Parliament on 3rd November, 1640.[2]

[1] *Second Defence*, Bohn I, 257.
[2] The previous assembly is known as the Short Parliament. This, the famous Long Parliament, was not regularly dissolved, i.e. by the Crown, until 1660. The assemblies convened by Cromwell were not true parliaments.

This time England 'expected a new world', the Puritan emigration ceased and so many petitions flowed into Westminster that forty committees had to be created to examine them. Suddenly, led by Pym, the House attacked Strafford, Laud, the King, the Queen, and the bishops. Strafford tried to arrest the leaders, but was not quick enough and was himself imprisoned on 11th November. The following month Laud was kept under supervision and the Puritans demanded the abolition of the episcopate.

One of the poet's first duties was to compose a funeral elegy for Diodati. The *Lament for Damon*, partly outlined during those anxious weeks on the roads and rivers that stretched from Geneva to Boulogne, was completed in the lodgings opposite St. Bride's Churchyard, and printed in a small edition at the author's expense.[1]

Because it is in Latin, we may fail to realize that this second *Lycidas* excels the first in depth of feeling and variety of themes. Diodati, ranged among the saints and invoked as such (203–210), is associated with the joys of the traveller and the ambitions of the poet. The beginning is sheer regret:

> Alas, what gadding folly drew me astray
> To traverse shores I knew not of, and tread
> Peaks hung aloft in heav'n, and Alpine snow?
> Was there such need to see Rome's grave (although
> Rome were as Tityrus saw her when he left
> His flocks, his fields?)—to mourn of thee bereft
> Who wast so pleasant, friend! How could I dream,
> Twixt thee and me so many a deep to spread—
> Woods, rocks—so many a range and roaring stream?
> Ah, at the end I could have else compos'd
> Thy dying eyes, thy hand in mine have clos'd,
> That last farewell to say:
> 'Think of me still upon thy starward way!'[2]

There follows the remembrance of the happiness of Italy:

> Yet never (be ye sure) shall I repine,
> O Tuscan swains, for memories of you,

---

[1] The date may be inferred from the text: 'Twice with green ear the rising stalk 'gan swell, / The granges twice their golden harvests tell, / Since that predestined morn . . .' Diodati died in late August, 1638.

[2] Tr. Skeat, Nonesuch, p. 811–14.

Dear Youths who offer at the Muses' Shrine.
Here 'Grace' and 'Wit' were and (a Tuscan too)
Thou Damon, thou whose house her founder drew
From that old city of the Lucumo.[1]
O, how transported was my mind, when I
Diffus'd beside cool Arno's whispering flow,
In poplar glade, where tenderer grass doth grow,
Could violets pluck—pluck myrtles as they bend—
Hear with Menalcas Lycidas contend!
I, too, dar'd try, nor all displeas'd your mood,
Methinks, for here your gifts beside me lie—
Baskets, and wax-bound pipes and wine-cups rare.

Milton then thanks 'Datis' and 'Francinus' for their
praise, and sighs that he can never now show Damon the
gifts of Manso. Alas! he had hoped also to hear his friend
speak to him of healing herbs. He would have told him in
return of a recent disappointment and of his resolutions.

But I—(to reckon since the eleventh night
Is one more day), when some sublimer flight
My oat was sounding, scarce had laid my lip
To these new pipes, when they apart did slip,
Snapping their band; whereafter they no more
Their loftier tones could pour.
Ev'n now, misgives me lest, perchance, my lay
Presumptuously should soar.
Nay, I will tell it! Woodland Songs, give way!
Home, lambs, unfed; grief tasks your herdman now!

Of Trojan ships that rode of Richboro's strand[2]
I'd sing, and of this ancient royal Isle
Of Inogen, daughter of King Pandrasus;
Antique Belin, Dukes Bran, Arviragus:
Then, of new Britain in Armoric land;[3]
Next, of Igraine, who was by fatal wile
Of Arthur's birth expectant, with the guile
Of that false Gorlois' looks and armour ta'en,
Merlin's untruth. O last, should life remain,
On yon old pine, my Reed, thou'lt hang again—
How much forgot—or for thy native Muse

---

[1] The reference is to Lucca, which is, of course, in Tuscany.
[2] According to a legend of the Middle Ages, the Bretons or Brittons had come
from Troy, led by Brut, or Brutus.   [3] See p. 93.

The shrilling sound of Britain's war-pipe chuse.
But what? Too much for one all things to be,
Or hope—'twere guerdon quite enough for me,
Fame great enough: henceforth unknown I'll bide,
Inglorious quite to all the world beside,
If fair-hair'd Ouse, and all who Alan drink,
All Severn's whirlpools—Trent's tree-bosom'd brink—
Thou, chief, my Thames—and Tamar's ore-stain'd urn—
And utmost Orkney's waves of me may learn.
Home, lambs, unfed; grief tasks your herdman now!

Thus in 1640, Milton was still envisaging, as in Naples, an epic on the origins of his race, and in English. He admitted to having made an unsuccessful attempt, but from now onwards finally renounced Latin verse.

The Trinity MS. shows that in the following year he was thinking of other possibilities. The document contains, in fact, in addition to poems written before 1641, ninety-nine titles or rough outlines, two-thirds of which relate to Scripture and one-third to the history of England. All the themes are dramatic and the English subjects do not date further back than the Roman occupation. His unsuccessful attempt in 1640 had then persuaded Milton that he must fall back on drama and give up legends. Moreover, history itself seemed to him much less likely than the Bible to supply him with a subject.

Once installed in his spacious and silent house in Aldersgate, Milton had made a thorough examination of the chroniclers—Nennius, Malory, Holinshed, Gildas, Speed. . . . They disappointed him. On the eve of the Conquest, the 'free Saxons' were imitating France, speaking French, writing to one another in French, for pleasure—we should say through snobbery. 'They deserved their bondage', declared Milton. Similarly, this Arthur who had so valiantly decimated the Saxons was Romanized. And then, had he really existed? Was not Merlin a folk myth? The English knew their past very badly. The first lectureship in Old English was founded in Cambridge in the year 1638. Holinshed's *Chronicles* on which Shakespeare had drawn were a mass of legends and anecdotes. A reader of Sallust and Thucydides, Milton refused to build on hear-say. He wanted his work to be of service and lasting. Rather than illustrate legends, he must rid history of such accretions. This task was to occupy him for years to come.

Besides, after all, what can history itself offer the poet? Péguy has compared reality to a rose window, 'la rose réelle de fleurs de rose infiniment fouillées', and history to the 'pauvres carreaux de plâtre que nous mettons en leur lieu'. He despaired of Clio and sang of Eve.[1]

The spectacles of persecution and flight had taught Milton that true heroism goes further than sword-thrusts. He came back to this theme over and over again.

For all these reasons, he had already envisaged, in the Trinity note-book, three possible dramas on Samson and four on the Fall. His objective was taking shape, but nothing more. He continued to read, to make notes, to debate with himself. We cannot blame his circumspection. He already saw Shakespeare, the 'facile' Shakespeare, almost forgotten. All the epics of his day have come to grief. In France the *Alarics* and the *Charlemagnes* fared no better than the *Pucelle* of Chapelain. Milton saw the birth of Davenant's *Gondibert* in 1651, Benlowe's *Theophilus* in 1652, Cowley's *Davideis* in 1656, Chamberlayne's *Pharonnida* in 1659. And he lived to see all these marvels provide 'winding-sheets in Lent for pilchers'.

About his habits at this time, Edward Phillips gives us with a smile an unexpected piece of information.

> Once in three weeks or a month, he would drop into the society of some young sparks of his acquaintance, the chief whereof were Mr. Alphrey and Mr. Miller, two gentlemen of Gray's Inn, the beaux of those times, but nothing near so bad as those of now-a-days; with these gentlemen he would so far make bold with his body as now and then to keep a gawdy-day.

Milton has said himself that he was careful to keep the balance of his faculties.

> Those morning haunts are where they should be, at home; not sleeping, or concocting the surfeits of an irregular feast,

[1] *Clio* and *Eve* are the titles of two of his works.

but up and stirring, in winter often ere the sound of any bell
awake men to labour, or to devotion; in summer as oft with
the bird that first rouses, or not much tardier, to read good
authors, or cause them to be read, till the attention be weary, or
memory have its full fraught: then with useful and generous[1]
labours preserving the body's health and hardiness to render
lightsome, clear and not lumpish obedience to the mind, to
the cause of religion, and our country's liberty, when it shall
require firm hearts in sound bodies to stand and cover their
stations, rather than to see the ruin of our protestation, and the
inforcement of a slavish life.[2]

While Milton divided his time between his books, his
pupils, and physical exercises, public events followed their
course, imperious, swift, unfavourable to all poetry.
Strafford, the rampart of the throne, abandoned by his
king, was beheaded in May 1641, to the delirious joy of the
crowd. Two camps were forming, two labels appeared,
Cavaliers and Roundheads. In June the Star Chamber was
abolished, the press was virtually free. At once pamphlets
pullulated. The writers revised them on the press-stone,
the public read them while the printer's ink was still wet.
In twenty years, thirty thousand of such pamphlets were
to see the light. Even in the heart of the country, humble
people were eager to get hold of them. The King, who
wanted to read everything, paid twenty pounds for a tract.
Now, in the words of Milton:

> As soon as the liberty of speech was no longer subject to
> control, all mouths began to be opened against the bishops.[3]

The outcry is chiefly to be explained by the abuses from
which even hamlets suffered. They would not have happened had Laud not maintained that his bishops were *jure
divino*, like the King. He had good authority behind him.
Hincmar, bishop of Rheims in the ninth century, had said:
'Priests are the throne of God and he judges through their
mouths'; St. Ambrose: 'The glory of princes is to that of
the bishops as the brilliance of lead is to that of gold';
and Pope Gelasus: 'Priests are paramount in authority,

---

[1] 'Generous'—i.e. worthy of a man well-born: i.e., the noble art of fencing.
[2] *Apology for Smectymnuus*, Bohn III, 112–13.
[3] *Second Defence*, Bohn I, 257.

since on the Last Day it is they who will answer for the kings themselves'. Laud's prelates no longer judged, then, in the ecclesiastical courts, by royal delegation, but in their own name. They thus foisted themselves into many civil affairs from which they made large profits. The Puritans were not the only ones to condemn their methods. Many Royalists realized that the followers of Laud were harming the King's cause.

While tracts, pamphlets, and manifestos were raging, someone touched the poet's elbow as he leant over his books and showed him where his duty lay by requesting his help. He was Thomas Young.

The rising in Scotland had pleased the English Calvinists, including those Anglican clergymen whom Laud had marked with a P. Laymen or clerics, many Englishmen judged that the episcopal upas-tree should not be pruned, but destroyed 'root and branch'. Cromwell was among these 'radicals'; Young too. They were so numerous that the Commons, in February 1641, almost gave them satisfaction. The establishment, however, had good defenders. Hall, bishop of Exeter, known both for his verse and prose, had Laud's confidence. In 1640 he had published *Episcopacy by Divine Right Asserted*, and repeated it in January 1641 in his *Humble Remonstrance*. Five ministers, of whom Thomas Young was one, tried to confute him in a small book with an interminable title, signed 'Smectymnuus', a name made up of their initials, SM representing Stephen Marshall, EC Edmund Calamy, TY Thomas Young, etc. But Smectymnuus wrote less well than Hall, and knew it. Hence Young's visit to his learned former pupil.

Milton did more than revise the manuscript and enrich it by twenty pages. Like Pascal fifteen years later,[1] he himself pleaded for his friends. It cost him much, however (we know it from his *Reason of Church Government*) to 'leave a calm and pleasing solitariness . . . to embark in a troubled sea of noises and hoarse disputes', to play the part of a Tiresias 'who bemoaned that he knew more than other men', to be 'the displeaser and molester of thousands', instead of

[1] It was in defence of the Jansenists of Port-Royal that he wrote the *Provinciales*.

being 'the messenger of gladness and contentment to all mankind', to treat unwelcome subjects and to treat them in haste, renouncing 'all the curious touches of art which make the picture perfect', finally, to write in prose, 'wherein I have the use, as I may account, but of my left hand'.

But when God commands to take the trumpet, and blow a dolorous or a jarring blast, it lies not in man's will what he shall say, or what he shall conceal.[1]

But this I foresee, that should the church be brought under heavy oppression, and God have given me ability the while to reason against that man that should be the author of so foul a deed; or should she, by blessing from above on the industry and courage of faithful men, change this her distracted estate into better days, without the least furtherance or contribution of those few talents, which God at that present had lent me; I foresee what stories I should hear within myself, all my life after, of discourage and reproach. Timorous and ungrateful, the church of God is now again at the foot of her insulting enemies, and thou bewailest. What matters it for thee or thy bewailing? When time was, thou coulds't not find a syllable of all that thou hast read, or studied, to utter in her behalf. Yet ease and leisure was given thee for thy retired thoughts, out of the sweat of other men. Thou hast the diligence, the parts, the language of a man, if a vain subject were to be adorned or beautified; but when the cause of God and his church was to be pleaded, for which purpose that tongue was given thee which thou hast, God listened if he could hear thy voice among his zealous servants, but thou wert dumb as a beast; from henceforward be that which thine own brutish silence hath made thee.[2]

But were it the meanest under-service, if God by his secretary conscience enjoin it, it were sad for me if I should draw back; for me especially . . . thus church-outed by the prelates.[3]

In ten months, Milton published five works. *Smectymnuus* came out in March 1641. Milton then published *Of Reformation in England* (May or June, anonymous, a eulogy of the Presbyterian system); *Of Prelatical Episcopacy* (June, anonymous, a courteous reply to Usher); *Animadversions* (July, anonymous, a savage retort to Hall); *The Reason of Church Government urged against Prelaty* (February 1642,

---

[1] *Reason of Church Government*, Bohn II, 474.   [2] Ibid., 475.   [3] Ibid., 482.

signed, a refutation of seven treatises published by Usher and two other prelates); lastly, *Apology for Smectymnuus* (March 1642), in which Milton defended his friends and refuted the calumnies of Hall and his son. At this date Laud had been in the Tower a year, and for the past three months ten bishops, including Hall, had been there with him. For nearly twenty years the Anglican hierarchy was to remain on the fringe of history.

Milton was writing too quickly to avoid prolixity, repetitions and digressions. The crowd of facts and ideas that he brought into play may be grouped under three heads:

1. *Our episcopal system must go.* God has a predilection for England, since he has given her Wycliffe, and yet to-day she is nearer to Rome than the Reformed peoples on the Continent. The reason for this is that Henry VIII was obeying purely political motives, so that our Church, by his fault, has remained a Catholicism without a Pope, 'a pyramid without a point'. Thus our clergy hankers after Rome. Moreover, all State-clergy are oppressive and rapacious, and ours are no exception . . .

> Tell me, ye priests, wherefore this gold, wherefore these robes and surplices over the gospel? . . . Ye think by these gaudy glisterings to stir up the devotion of the rude multitude. . . . If the multitude be rude, the lips of the preacher must give knowledge, and not ceremonies, And although some Christians be new-born babes comparatively to some that are stronger, yet in respect of ceremony, which is but a rudiment of the Law, the weakest Christian hath thrown off the robes of his minority, and is a perfect man, as to legal rites.[1]

These despots are also ignoramuses. Oppression and ignorance signify obscurantism. Wealth and folly signify ostentation.

> They would request us to endure still the rustling of their silken cassocks, and that we would burst our midriffs, rather than laugh to see them under sail in all their lawn and sarcenet, their shrouds and tackle, with a geometrical rhomboides upon their heads.[2]

[1] *The Reason of Church Government*, Bohn II, 485.
[2] *Of Reform. in Engl.*, Bohn II, 416. Cf. Pascal—'Si les médecins avaient le vrai art de guérir, ils n'auraient que faire de bonnets carrés'—*Pensées*, Brunschvicg, 82.

H

Bishops openly affirm: 'No bishop, no king'. In fact, the bishops will bring us a revolution.

What more baneful to monarchy than a popular commotion? for the dissolution of monarchy slides aptest into a democracy; what stirs the Englishman, as our wisest writers have observed, sooner to rebellion, than violent and heavy hands upon their goods and purses?[1]

The bishops claim that they spare us schisms. But the first schism was precisely the institution of an absolute clergy.

The prelates, as they would have it thought, are the only mauls of schism. Forsooth, if they be put down, a deluge of innumerable sects will follow; . . . Do they keep away schism? If to bring a numb and chill stupidity of soul, an unactive blindness of mind, upon the people by their leaden doctrine, or no doctrine at all; if to persecute all knowing and zealous Christians by the violence of their courts, be to keep away schism, they keep schism away indeed. . . . With as good a plea might the dead palsy boast to a man, It is I that free you from stitches and pains, and the troublesome feeling of cold and heat, of wounds and strokes: if I were gone, all these would molest you. The winter might as well vaunt itself against the spring, I destroy all noisome and rank weeds, I keep down all pestilent vapours; yes, and all wholesome herbs, and all fresh dews, by your violent and hide-bound frost: but when the gentle west winds shall open the fruitful bosom of the earth, thus overgirded by your imprisonment, then the flowers put forth and spring, and then the sun shall scatter the mists, and the manuring hand of the tiller shall root up all that burdens the soil without thank to your bondage.[2]

2. *A discipline, however, is essential for us.*

He that hath read with judgment of nations and common-wealths, of cities and camps, of peace and war, sea and land, will readily agree that the flourishing and decaying of all civil societies, all the moments and turnings for human occasions, are moved to and fro as upon the axle of discipline.[3]

Milton discovered this law of societies even in the life of plants:

O Adam, one Almightie is, from whom
All things proceed, and up to him return,

---

[1] *Of Reformation* . . . Bohn II, 404.   [2] *Church Government*, Bohn II, 462–3.
[3] Ibid., 441–2.

If not deprav'd from good, created all
Such to perfection, one first matter all,
Indu'd with various forms, various degrees
Of substance, and in things that live, of life;
But more refin'd, more spiritous, and pure,
As neerer to him plac't or neerer tending
Each in their several active Sphears assigned,
Till body up to spirit work, in bounds
Proportion'd to each kind. So from the root
Springs lighter the green stalk, from thence the leaves
More aerie, last the bright consummate floure
Spirits odorous breathes.[1]

3. *Let us adopt the Presbyterian organization*. It can be reconciled with liberty, it is in conformity with the Gospel, it has stood its test, kings have nothing to fear from it —witness the Protestants of France (B. II, 415).

Moreover its adoption will ensure for us total union with Scotland, the friendship of the Protestants on the Continent, and even that of its Catholics, for they aspire to liberty.

. . . we had ere this seen our old conquerors, and afterwards liegemen, the Normans, together with the Britains, our proper colony,[2] and all the Gascoins that are the rightful dowry of our ancient kings, come with cap and knee, desiring the shadow of the English sceptre to defend them from the hot persecutions and taxes of the French.[3]

This sad mixture of religion and imperialism is only too well known to us. The plea is at fault on many other points. It condemns *en bloc* a hierarchy that was for the most part tolerant and upright (Milton himself treated Usher with deference). To ward off the dangers of anarchy, was it necessary to rely on the 'west winds' or adopt another national system? Could Milton really believe that a Calvinist clergy, once master of the country, would not become oppressive and greedy, according to his own rule? He advocated the Genevan organization, but was silent on the doctrine of Calvin, which he rejected in great part. Yet, if

[1] *Paradise Lost*, V, 469–82.
[2] The version then current of the fact that in the fifth century many insular Britons crossed the Channel to flee from the ferocity of another portion of the elect people—the Saxons.
[3] *Of Reformation in England*, Bohn II, 400.

the organization were installed, it would impose the doctrine. These difficulties and others Milton refused to see. Ardent and naive, he confined himself to his *Delenda Carthago*.

Let us see once and for all how he used his left hand. Chateaubriand has proclaimed him as great a writer in prose as in verse, but he exaggerated. It is better to believe some English critic—for instance, Professor Kenneth Muir:

> If Milton had never written a line of verse he would still be numbered among the great English writers. Yet his prose has often been adversely criticized. It is complained that his style is modelled on that of Cicero and that it is un-English in structure and vocabulary; that his sentences are so long that the reader loses his way before he reaches the end; that he is apt to be turgid. . . . But it is impossible to dispose of Milton as a prose stylist by generalizations of this kind, because he had not one style but several. . . . In his last period he wrote prose as plain and direct as that demanded by the anti-imaginative members of the Royal Society. . . . The early pamphlets had been written to persuade the leaders of opinion; the later ones appealed over the heads of the leaders to the ordinary citizens. . . . It may be, too, that he simplified his style because the later pamphlets had to be dictated.
>
> *John Milton*, pp. 99–100.

The dominant feature in Milton as a prose writer is authority. He means to be, as he had wished, the oracle of a nation, Moses at the foot of Mount Sinai. Others are ignorant or waver; he knows. Yet the style varies according to the Milton who is speaking. For he speaks; he has not the time to write.

There is the didactic Milton, whose subordinate clauses follow each other like waves that exhaust the swimmer. *Of Reformation in England* begins with a sentence of fourteen lines; the next contains thirty-seven. Those who mocked at his breathless leaps Milton called broken-winded. The vertigo we experience is aggravated by what he called 'paroxysms of citations'. As we go through his pages we admire an epithet, an image, an apt neologism, or some pithy sentence, worthy of Bacon or La Bruyère ('What the

prelates admire and have not, others have and admire not.'[1]—
'How hard it is when a man meets a fool to keep his tongue
from folly!'[2]—'Liberty of speaking, than which nothing is
more sweet to man'[3]), but the whole is beyond us and we
find it wearisome.

There is Milton the polemist, arrogant, impatient, sometimes as brutal as Swift, if not more so.[4] In this respect
there is little resemblance between the Puritan of the *Animadversions* and the Jansenist who wrote the *Provinciales*.
Both have recourse to dialogue, but Pascal *relates* a conversation between well-bred people ('I asked him . . . he
answered me . . .'). In the *Cinquième Lettre*, in connection
with a cynical *distinguo*, Pascal merely says: 'Oh how amusing
that is!' Milton reproduces verbatim a supposed conversation between the 'Remonstrant' Hall, a distinguished bishop
of seventy whom he quotes literally, and the young and
unknown pedagogue, John Milton.

> *Remonst.* No one clergy in the whole Christian world yields
> so many eminent scholars, learned preachers, grave, holy
> and accomplished divines, as this Church of England doth
> at this day.
>
> *Answer.* Ha! Ha! Ha![5]

Milton's uncouthness and insolence are not to be im-
puted solely to the times in which he lived. Men like
Chillingworth, Taylor, Usher, Selden, Fuller, Andrewes, all
Anglicans and firm as to their principles, showed themselves polite and even charitable. But Milton had two excuses
at least: the attitude of his adversaries and the importance
he attached to the contest. Bishop Hall or his son dared to
write: 'You that love Christ and know this miscreant
wretch, stone him to death, lest you smart for his impunity!'
(B. III, 124). In the second place, to be so deeply engaged
in a quarrel so paltry in itself could only enrage him, yet
fight he must, and fight to victory, because the miserable
encounter was part of the gigantic battle that dominated his

---

[1] *Apology for Smectymnuus*, Bohn III, 101.   [2] Ibid., 152.
[3] *Animadversions*, Bohn III, 47.
[4] On the odour of Hall's socks, see *Animadversions*, Bohn III, 91. See also below,
p. 98, n. 2.
[5] *Animadversions*, Bohn III, 87.

soul and inspired all his writings: the fight between matter and spirit, between order and liberty.

Finally there is the poet who from time to time soars above this conflict, which is so degrading for him. For instance, right in the middle of his horrible dialogue with Hall he makes his escape in a prayer of two pages:

> O thou the ever-begotten Light and perfect Image of the Father! . . . Come therefore, O thou that hast the seven stars in thy right hand . . . put on the visible robes of thy imperial majesty, take up that unlimited sceptre which thy Almighty Father hath bequeathed thee; for now the voice of thy bride calls thee, and all creatures sigh to be renewed.[1]

The poet helps the polemist to terminate *On Reformation in England* by an invocation of three pages in which Milton's imagination hovers over land and sea, joins itself to the angelic choirs and plunges into Hell with the Laudians.

> But they contrary, that by the impairing and diminution of the true faith, the distresses and servitude of their country, aspire to high dignity, rule, and promotion here, after a shameful end in this life (which God grant them), shall be thrown down eternally into the darkest and deepest gulf of hell, where, under the despiteful control, the trample and spurn of all the other damned, that in the anguish of their torture, shall have no other ease than to exercise a raving and bestial tyranny over them as their slaves and negroes, they shall remain in that plight for ever, the basest, the lowermost, the most dejected, most underfoot, and downtrodden vassals of perdition.[2]

This frenzied imprecation makes us tremble for the man that proffered it. But it also makes us appreciate what he suffered in silence when peaceful people had to flee to America, or Young to go into exile in Hamburg.

Moreover, in comparing this outburst with the discreet 'two-handed engine' of *Lycidas*, we can measure to what point poetry for Milton meant discipline and concentration.

[1] Bohn III, 71–2.   [2] *Of Reformation in England*, Bohn II, 419.

MARY POWELL

1642

THE impatience of the poet now bogged down in controversy had found more definite expression than a few passionate parentheses. In his last treatise he had promised the English people some poem worthy of them and of him.

> Time serves not now, and perhaps I might seem too profuse to give any certain account of what the mind at home, in the spacious circuits of her musing, hath liberty to propose to herself though of highest hope and hardest attempting; whether that epic form whereof the two poems of Homer, and those other two of Virgil and Tasso, are a diffuse, and the book of Job a brief model: or whether the rules of Aristotle herein are strictly to be kept, or nature to be followed, which in them that know art, and use judgment, is no transgression, but an enriching of art: and lastly, what king or knight, before the Conquest, might be chosen in whom to lay the pattern of a Christian hero. . . . The scripture also affords us a divine pastoral drama in the Song of Solomon, consisting of two persons, and a double chorus, as Origen rightly judges. And the Apocalypse of St. John is the majestic image of a high and stately tragedy. . . .[1]

Thus Milton was still hesitating on many points, but at least he now definitely thrust aside non-religious themes. If he was to sing of an English hero, he would be a Christian hero. A little further on he was explicit.

> These abilities, wheresoever they be found, are the inspired gift of God, rarely bestowed, but yet to some (though most abuse) in every nation; and are of power, beside the office of a pulpit, to imbreed and cherish in a great people the seeds of virtue and public civility, to allay the perturbations of the mind, and set the affections in right tune; to celebrate in glorious and lofty hymns the throne and equipage of God's almightiness,

---

[1] *The Reason of Church Government*, Bohn II, 478–9.

and what he works, and what he suffers to be wrought with
high providence in his church, to sing victorious agonies of
martyrs and saints, the deeds and triumphs of just and pious
nations, doing valiantly through faith against the enemies of
Christ; to deplore the general relapses of kingdoms and states
from justice and God's true worship.[1]

He had never spoken so clearly. During these ten months
he had received hard blows. Hall or his son had publicly
accused him of frequenting disreputable houses and of
advocating the system of Geneva because he wanted a
rich Presbyterian widow to marry him. They even fired
off this pretty remark: 'He was vomited out from Cambridge University into a suburb-sink of London which
since his coming up, has groaned under two evils—him
and the plague'. But at least he had been able to retort insult
for insult.[2] He pitied the silent victims, Sir John Eliot
who died of exhaustion in his dungeon, and those thousands
of obscure men who were, month after month, crossing the
sea.

Besides, after two years of civil war, his contempt for
military glory had increased. It was to become deeply
rooted. In 1656 he wrote to his former pupil, the future
Earl of Ranelagh:

> I would not have you lavish your admiration on . . . things
> of that nature in which force is of most avail . . . Do you
> learn to esteem great characters, not by the quantity of their
> animal strength, but by the habitual justice and temperance of
> their conduct.[3]

Ten years later in *Paradise Lost* he was to write ironically:

> . . . Sad task, yet argument
> Not less but more Heroic than the wrauth
> Of stern *Achilles* on his Foe pursu'd
> Thrice fugitive about *Troy* Wall;[4]
> Not sedulous by Nature to indite

---

[1] *Church Government*, Bohn II, 479.
[2] For instance, in *Apology for Smectymnuus* (Bohn III, 112): 'In the meantime that
suburb sink, as this rude scavenger calls it, and more than scurrilously taunts it with
the plague, having a worse plague in his middle entrail, that suburb wherein I
dwell shall be in my account a more honourable place than his university'.
[3] Bohn III, 511.   [4] *P.L.* IX, 13–16.

Warrs, hitherto the onely Argument
Heroic deemd, chief maistrie to dissect
With long and tedious havoc fabl'd Knights
In Battels feignd: the better fortitude
Of Patience and Heroic Martyrdom
Unsung;[1]

This option for deep tragedy, which is the combat of man with himself, must have followed shortly after the promise quoted above, for as early as 1642 Edward was shown the first version of the famous apostrophe of Satan to the sun which we read to-day in the epic of the Fall.

O thou that with surpassing Glory crownd,
Look'st from thy sole Dominion like the God
Of this new World; at whose sight all the Starrs
Hide thir diminisht heads; to thee I call,
But with no friendly voice, and add thy name
O Sun, to tell thee how I hate thy beams
That bring to my remembrance from what state
I fell, how glorious once above thy Spheare;
Till Pride and worse Ambition threw me down
Warring in Heav'n against Heav'ns matchless King:
Ah wherefore?[2]

These lines, however, were to serve as the opening of a tragedy, or perhaps an oratorio. In 1639 Davenant had asked for the authorization to build an opera hall, and Lawes was concerned in the project. We shall never know what would have been written instead of the epic we actually have, if in 1642, 'the accident' in the poet's life had not occurred. It was a situation such as Corneille conjured up in this very year 1642 in *Le Menteur*, II, ii:

Cette chaîne, qui dure autant que notre vie,
Et qui devrait donner plus de peur que d'envie,
Si l'on n'y prend bien garde, attache assez souvent
Le contraire au contraire, et le mort au vivant.

Milton was to write in 1643:

Nay, instead of being one flesh, they will be rather two carcasses chained unnaturally together or, as it may happen, a living soul bound to a dead corpse.[3]

[1] *P.L.* IX, 27–33.   [2] *P.L.* IV, 32–42.
[3] *The Doctrine and Discipline of Divorce*, Bohn III, 249.

What had happened? Edward Phillips gives us some idea of it:

> About Whitsuntide it was, or a little after, that he took a journey into the country; nobody about him certainly knowing the reason, or that it was any more than a journey of recreation; after a month's stay home he returns a married man, that went out a bachelor; his wife being Mary, the eldest daughter of Mr. Richard Powell, then a justice of peace, of Forrest Hill, near Shotover in Oxfordshire, some few of her nearest relations accompanying the bride to her new habitation; which by reason the father nor any body else were yet come, was able to receive them: where the feasting held for some days in celebration of the nuptials and for entertainment of the bride's friends. At length they took their leave and returning to Forrest Hill left the sister behind, probably not much to her satisfaction as appeared by the sequel.

Phillips was noting down what he remembered at a distance of fifty years, and he was not always exact. Moreover, what he said was incomplete. The two families had known each other for a long time past, for the village of the grandfather, Richard Milton, Stanton St. John, was within a mile of Forest Hill. The reader will remember that in 1627 Powell had borrowed three hundred pounds from the scrivener under promise to repay within six months, in default of which 'John Milton of Cambridge' would have a mortgage of five hundred pounds on the property of the borrower.[1] This contract, in appearance usurious, is a good example of the wisdom of the elder Milton. He knew Powell too well to refuse him a loan, but too well also not to keep him on a short rein.

This Richard Powell, in fact, was an intrepid optimist. Lord of the manor and Justice of the Peace, he exercised a hospitality that was all the more generous as he was a Royalist and a man who enjoyed the good things of life. Yet his revenues were modest and he had eleven children. With the three hundred pounds he had indeed bought land, but to borrow upon it immediately. In 1641, his manor was burdened with mortgages amounting to fourteen hundred pounds. It is doubtful, however, whether he

[1] See above, p. 24.

realized this. When this forerunner of Mr. Micawber made his will, he inserted in it properties which were imaginary or already sold.

Now at Whitsun, 1642, war was imminent between the King and the Parliament. After Strafford's execution Charles had continued to scheme first with England and then with Scotland, exploiting their political and religious differences. In November 1641, Pym had succeeded in getting the Great Remonstrance voted by a majority of eleven. On January 3rd following, Charles had himself tried to arrest, in full session, the five leaders of the Commons, but 'the birds had flown' in time. Parliament had then given itself a militia and the sovereign had left London. At Whitsuntide Charles was waiting at York for the arms which the Queen had gone to procure in Holland by selling the Crown jewels. Already communications were becoming less easy, commerce was lethargic, money owing was slow in coming in. The Powell debt, overdue for years now, was a particularly bad one, and the free and easy Richard Powell did not even reply to letters. This was a good reason for paying a visit to Forest Hill.

Or a good pretext, perhaps? Had not Milton already seen Mary? To the insinuation that he was courting a rich widow, he had replied:

> I think with them who, both in prudence and elegance of spirit, would choose a virgin of mean fortunes honestly bred, before the wealthiest widow.[1]

But if he had met the girl, he had not had the opportunity of judging her mind:

> ... and who knows not that the bashful muteness of a virgin may ofttimes hide all the unliveliness and natural sloth which is really unfit for conversation? Nor is there that freedom of access granted or presumed, as may suffice to a perfect discerning till too late; and where any indisposition is suspected, what more usual than the persuasion of friends that the acquaintance, as it increases, will amend all? And lastly, it is not strange though many, who have spent their youth chastely, are in some things not so quick-sighted, while they haste too eagerly to light the nuptial torch; nor is it, therefore, that for a modest

[1] *Apology for Smectymnuus*, Bohn III, 151.

error a man should forfeit so great a happiness, and no charitable means to release him, since they who have lived most loosely by reason of their bold accustoming, prove most successful in their matches, because their wild affections unsettling at will, have been as so many divorces to teach them experience. Whenas the sober man honouring the appearance of modesty, and hoping well of every social virtue under that veil, may easily chance to meet, if not with a body impenetrable, yet often with a mind to all other due conversation inaccessible, and to all the more estimable and superior purposes of matrimony useless and almost lifeless; and what a solace, what a fit help such a consort would be through the whole life of a man, is less pain to conjecture than to have experience.[1]

The word 'experience' ends the chapter. It is clear that Milton is speaking of his own misadventure. During his visit to the Powells, he had perhaps 'suspected some indisposition', but 'relatives and friends' had deluded him. He may have fallen in love at first sight, but there was certainly a conspiracy. If the lord of the manor had a generous imagination, Mrs. Powell knew how to calculate. Young Milton would be rich one day. Meanwhile with this sorry King who was liquidating his diamonds one had to expect the worst. For a royalist family the alliance with a champion of the Presbyterians would be a safeguard.

The said champion was assailed by a threefold temptation—'hunger, the occasion, the tender grass'.[2] He betrayed his hunger in the *Lament for Damon*: 'Twice luckless who has loved o'erlate'.[3] The occasion was the month of May amid the clash of arms: Mars and Venus have always worked reciprocally. As to the 'tender grass'—he was thirty-three, she sixteen.

Of Mary herself we know almost nothing. Not a fragment of a letter, a remark, an anecdote, or a vestige of description has come down to us in regard to her. She must have been pretty for Milton always to have spoken so bitterly of the power of seduction of women. Most probably she was

[1] *The Doctrine and Discipline of Divorce*, Bohn III, 190.
[2] Allusion to a famous line of La Fontaine (*Fables*, VII, 1). The Ass accuses himself of having brought the plague upon the animals by cropping a few blades of grass in a friar's meadow. 'La faim, l'occasion, l'herbe tendre, et, je pense / Quelque diable aussi me poussant . . .'
[3] ' . . . bis ille miser qui serus amavit' (85).

lacking in intelligence; he never reproached her with anything else. She has remained a shadow, a symbol, the unintentional snare. It is difficult not to imagine her as Milton first saw her in the faded splendour of the Powells' drawing-room, carefully dressed up for the occasion by her mother, indoctrinated by her father, lowering her eyes and not knowing what to say to the fine gentleman from London, herself the while transfigured in the eyes of him who would piously justify his courses and who was persuaded that Providence was putting an angel in his path.

The marriage was hurried through somewhere or other. The registers, whether at Forest Hill or in Oxford, have revealed nothing. Powell congratulated himself. He had promised a dowry of a thousand pounds, but . . . we should see later.

Thus ended the first act of this tragi-comedy. Milton Marprelate had been hoodwinked like a child. Act II, outlined by Phillips, followed:

> By that time she had for a month or thereabout led a philosophical life (after having been used to a great house, and much company and joviality), her friends, possibly incited by her own desire, made earnest suit by letter to have her company the remaining part of the summer, which was granted, on condition of her return at the time appointed, Michaelmas, or thereabout . . . Michaelmas being come, and no news of his wife's return, he sent for her by letter; and receiving no answer, sent several other letters, which were also unanswered; so that at last he dispatched down a foot messenger with a letter, desiring her return. But the messenger came back not only without an answer, at least a satisfactory one, but to the best of my remembrance, reported that he was dismissed with some sort of contempt.

The King's affairs were in fact now taking on a more favourable aspect. In October he had occupied Reading. Received with enthusiasm in Oxford, he had fixed his headquarters there. The Court was thus only about three miles away from Forest Hill. Now several of the Powells belonged to the royal army and, moreover, according to Phillips again, 'they began to repent them of having matched the eldest daughter of the family to a person so contrary

to them in opinion; and thought it would be a blot in their
escutcheon whenever that court should come to flourish
again'.

Let us try to elucidate Milton's case. It is common
enough for a man to be misunderstood by his wife or his
mistress, but he very seldom allows the fact to upset him.
Goethe loved and respected his housekeeper, Catherine, and
reserved for other women his confidences as a poet. The
French poet Gérard de Nerval did not blame Jenny Colon,
but himself: 'J'ai pris au sérieux les inventions des poètes,
et me suis fait une Laure ou une Béatrice d'une personne
ordinaire du siècle'.[1] Milton, too, as we have seen, had
taken the inventions of the poets seriously, dreaming of
Laura and of Beatrice, but he lacked Nerval's suppleness.
There may have been a violent scene when he realized
that he was dealing with 'an ordinary person of this world',
since he let the summer go by without writing and did not
go to Forest Hill in person.

His state of mind is partially revealed to us by a curious
incident. At the beginning of November, that is a good
month after Michaelmas, London was very nearly captured
by the Royalists. Only in the nick of time were they
repulsed by a mass sortie from the City. Milton was not
actively engaged, judging that 'his head was worth more
than his arm'. He was indeed so proud of his head that to
escape pillage, he deemed it sufficient to make himself
known. It is said that Raphael showed his absent friends
that he had called by tracing a perfect circle on their doors
with a single stroke of his chalk. The poet affixed to his a
splendid extravagant sonnet, the gist of which was: 'Soldier,
spare the house of a poet, Alexander spared that of Pindar,
and Sparta respected the city of Euripides'. We admire the
calmness of this abandoned husband, not less than the self-
assurance of a mere polemist comparing himself with
Euripides. He must have been in the ardour of composition,
wholly given up to the pleasure of seeing his drama
advance. The idea did not cross his mind that there might
be some connection between the royalist successes and

_____
[1] *Aurélia*, Première Partie, I.

Mary's absence. His masculine self-complacency, moreover, excluded any anxiety; the little goose would surely be back any day. Mary's absence, however, was to last three years.

When, a few weeks or months after the attack on London, Milton saw his messenger return crestfallen, he was 'incensed', said Phillips, who recalled some gesture or other, or some remark. But a child of twelve could not have any idea of the anguish and perturbation of his uncle. Milton, the chaste Milton, was to write: 'Those who have lived most loosely, by reason of their bold accustoming, prove most successful in their matches'. And this again, of which *incensed* gives no idea:

> And yet there follows upon this a worse temptation: for if he be such as hath spent his youth unblameably, and laid up his chiefest earthly comforts in the enjoyments of a contented marriage, nor did neglect that furtherance which was to be obtained therein by constant prayers; when he shall find himself bound fast to an uncomplying discord of nature, or, as it oft happens, to an image of earth and phlegm, with whom he looked to be the copartner of a sweet and gladsome society, and sees withal that his bondage is now inevitable; though he be almost the strongest Christian, he will be ready to despair in virtue, and mutiny against Divine Providence . . . Therefore when human frailty surcharged is at such a loss, charity ought to venture much, and use bold physic, lest an overtossed faith endanger to shipwreck.[1]

God could thus remain deaf to the 'constant prayers' of a just man! But was he a just man? Had he not taken a wife among the Philistines? The thoughts which tormented him 'like a deadly swarm of hornets'[2] were to have repercussions on the whole of the rest of his life.

If only he had been able to free himself! But the law only authorized divorce for adultery or impotence. A cruel law! Like King Lear in the storm, having compassion for 'the houseless heads', Milton thought of the thousands of divided households, above all of those, so numerous

---

[1] *The Doctrine and Discipline of Divorce*, Bohn III, 194.
[2] *Samson Agonistes*, 19 and 623.

then, where one of the partners had denounced the other to the military authorities.

Several months had elapsed since the return of the messenger when Milton at last saw the possibility of acting. In June 1643, Parliament convened an assembly of theologians to help it in reorganizing the Church. Ten lords were appointed, with twenty members of Parliament and about a hundred churchmen. The Presbyterians dominated (Young was among them), but the Parliament had also invited certain moderate prelates, including Usher. The prelates did not accept, and the Puritans had a clear field. This synod held its first session on July 1st at Westminster. On August 1st its members and the members of Parliament received an anonymous pamphlet of about fifty pages entitled *The Doctrine and Discipline of Divorce.* In order to be understood by the lay members, Milton had avoided the use of Latin. Never before had the problem been treated in English. The work was sold out at once; it was attacked, and Milton returned to the charge.

In February 1644, he published a second edition of his pamphlet, revised, considerably enlarged, and signed. In July he brought forward a weighty testimony—*The Judgment of Martin Bucer concerning Divorce.* It was the essence of the *De Regno Christi* in which Calvin's master and friend reassured Edward VI as to the validity of his father's re-marriage. In March 1645 came a third edition of the *Doctrine,* then *Tetrachordon*—a searching commentary on four biblical texts—and *Colasterion,* a slashing retort to a nameless objector.

Milton, of course, put forward a score of arguments, with the remarkable omission of any mention of the case of desertion. Nothing he wrote in prose is so human as his treatises on divorce. They are secular in tone, despite his constant recourse to the Bible. Milton knew how to cancel out one verse of Scripture by another. He went so far as to declare in *Tetrachordon* (B. III, 354): 'As no ordinance, so no covenant, no, not between God and man, much less between man and man, being, as all are, intended to the good of both parties, can hold to the deluding or making miserable of them both'. The following is the essence of the argument.

Institutions appear in their purity at their origin. In the beginning God declared: 'It is not good that the man should be alone. I will make him a help meet for him.' Thus marriage is primarily a conversation. To perpetuate the species is a law of nature, but truly human union implies a communion. What would Plato say of our coarse conception of marriage? Adultery is less serious than incompatibility of minds. These 'mixtures of minds that cannot unite' (B. III, 206) degrade both parties in the marriage, and there is a danger of the children being abnormal.[1] Divorce is a duty between a living being and a dead one; the soul has not the right to accept corruption. Moses allowed the husband to repudiate his wife for a physical defect. Now discord between souls is worse, and the law of Jesus is even more human than that of Moses. He has uttered this inexhaustible saying: 'The Sabbath was made for man, not man for the Sabbath'. The Fathers approved of the Christian separating from his or her pagan partner to safeguard the faith. The Reformers on the Continent have shown us the way. What are we waiting for? 'Let not England forget her precedence in teaching nations how to live' (B. III, 178). And then, when all has been said, the supreme law is charity.

> Yet now a civil, an indifferent, a sometime dissuaded law of marriage, must be forced upon us to fulfil, not only without charity, but against her. No place in heaven or earth, except hell, where charity may not enter . . .[2]
>
> Yet when I remember the little that our Saviour could prevail about this doctrine of charity against the crabbed textuists of his time, I make no wonder, but rest confident, that whoso prefers either matrimony or other ordinance before the good of man and the plain exigence of charity, let him profess papist, or protestant, or what he will, he is no better than a pharisee, and understands not the gospel . . .[3]
>
> God the Son hath put all other things under his own feet, but his commandments he hath left all under the feet of charity.[4]

---

[1] See pp. 139 and 248; also *Paradise Lost* III, 455-75, XI, 675-88.
[2] *Doctrine . . . of Divorce*, B. III, 176.   [3] Ibid., 179.   [4] Ibid., 273.

I

Milton found people to approve him among the cultured
Parliamentarians, but those 'crabbed textuists', the Westminster divines, protested, his friends the Presbyterians
above all. He was astounded and never forgave them.
Young preached against his theory; it does not appear
that Milton ever saw him again.

It must be admitted that his 'Doctrine' passed over the
rights of the woman partner too quickly. As to his 'Discipline' (the way of procedure), it was bound to shock. After
an attempt at conciliation by a minister of public worship,
the husband would simply notify his decision to the
magistrate. Milton explained—one would thus avoid
publicizing 'the unpleasingness and other concealments' of
a woman (B. III, 266), and moreover, even admitting
that the repudiation was unjustified, the wife must congratulate herself on being rid of a dishonest man (B. III,
268). What an opening for Hall! From his prison he
protested: 'Woe is me! What will all the Christian Churches
through the world think of our woeful degeneration?'
Prynne, who had passed from prison to Parliament, wrote
with his usual vigour: 'The man is a libertine, that thinketh
his wife a manacle, and his very garters shackles and fetters
to him; after the manner of the Independents, he is willing
to submit neither to God nor to man'. His pamphlet was
entitled *Divorce at Pleasure*. Another Presbyterian, Mr.
Palmer, preaching before both Houses on August 13th,
a day of Solemn Fast and Extraordinary Humiliation,
denounced 'a wicked book that was abroad and uncensured,
though deserving to be burnt' (M. III, 263). The Westminster divines tried to have Milton condemned by
Parliament. They did not succeed, but he was punished
in a different way.

In using English he had allowed his seed to fall upon
thorny ground rank with wild sects. It was to no purpose
that he thundered, at the beginning of his second edition,
against 'the brood of Belial, the draff of men, to whom no
liberty is pleasing, but unbridled and vagabond lust', [. . .
and who] 'will laugh broad perhaps, to see so great a strength

of scripture mustering up in favour, as they suppose, of their debaucheries' (B. III, 173). The harm was done.

In 1655, when the Hanseatic ambassador, Aitzema, wanted to have the *Doctrine* translated into Dutch, Milton warned him that he would prefer a Latin translation, because his books had made him 'experience how the vulgar are wont to receive opinions which are not agreeable to vulgar prejudices' (B. III, 509). In 1645, Milton 'experienced'. The Presbyterian minister, Edwards, published that year *Gangraena*, a catalogue of no less than 176 *Errors, Heresies, Blasphemies and Pernicious Practices of the Sectaries of this time* (M. III, 141). There he noted under No. 154 the sect of the Divorcers or Miltonists. He had made up a file, quoted facts and names. For instance (M. III, 189–92), a Mrs. Attaway, lace-maker and woman preacher, persuaded herself, after reading Milton, that she was bound in conscience to abjure her husband who 'did not walk in the way of Sion, nor speak the language of Canaan'. It is true that he was in the army and that she appreciated the fervour of a Baptist preacher called Jenney. Jenney was married, but his wife was closed to the things from on high. The twin souls ran away together. Edwards had the couple's letters and reproduced them.

In short, through the flight of a child, the strange England of that day had seen two groups of clergy and three assemblies disturbed, the whole kingdom scandalized and the emergence of an additional sect.

Milton, filled with pride at having roared so well, forgot the bars of his cage. Moreover, he had other worries than controversy and other pleasures too. In April 1643, the Parliamentary troops having retaken Reading, Christopher had to take refuge in Exeter, and his father had thus come to live with John. In 1644 the latter had published two treatises on subjects other than divorce, which will be discussed later. Moreover, according to Phillips, 'being a single man again, he made it his chief diversion now and then in an evening, to visit the lady Margaret Ley . . . a woman of great wit and ingenuity, who had a particular honour for him and took much delight in his company, as likewise her husband, Captain Hobson, a very accomplished gentleman'.

To those pleasant evenings away from Rev. Edwards and Mrs. Attaway, we are indebted for as noble a sonnet as Milton ever wrote, in praise of Lady Margaret Ley, her late father, and liberty. 'That good earl, once President of England's Council and her Treasury' under King James, disgraced by Charles, had been 'broken' by 'the sad breaking' of the Short Parliament,

> as that dishonest victory
> At *Chæronéa*, fatal to liberty
> Kill'd with report that Old man eloquent . . .

Milton had then, as we shall see, special reasons for thinking of Isocrates.

It seems that the unwilling celibate, dazed by the swift interruption of his initiation, carried his regrets from one friend's house to another. According to Phillips, 'he had a design of marrying one of Dr. Davis's daughters, a very handsome and witty gentlewoman'. But a girl of intelligence could not be tempted to enter into bigamy. For whom did Milton compose the sonnet beginning 'Lady that in the prime . . .'? Who was that 'Virgin wise and pure' who 'filled her odorous lamp with deeds of light'? We do not know. This period in Milton's life is a dark and troubled one. It is in no way astonishing that he later declared polygamy permissible. He would doubtless have ended by imitating the patriarchs as best he could if the war had not brought his fugitive back to him.

This First Civil War was fought out between three armies representing four religious persuasions. The royal army was composed of Anglicans and Catholics, that of the Parliament of Presbyterians and Independents, that of Scotland was Presbyterian. Between the two English armies, the victory was doubtful. At the beginning the Scots looked on: they had achieved their purpose, it was for the English to achieve theirs. Yet, if the King prevailed, the future of the Kirk would be dark indeed. They would intervene, therefore, if necessary, but under the guarantee that their religious liberty would be definitely assured. The soldiers of the Parliament were more often than not mercenaries and, above all, the commanders too often lacked conviction, or competence.[1] Parliament was compelled to call for reinforcements from Scotland. The Scots promised a force of twenty thousand men (a considerable number for the times), but on condition that England swore to the Covenant. The matter was in course of negotiation when Milton presented his address (August 1643). In September, Parliament accepted the deal and asked the country to sign the Covenant. Whereupon Charles enrolled Irishmen. They had no military value, however, and it was rumoured that their compatriots, in their rebellion of 1641, had massacred two hundred thousand of their English masters in Ulster alone.[2] These recruits cost the King many of his followers.

The tender of the Covenant showed that the Independents, who were opposed to any State Church, had become numerous. These individualists, among whom exiles returning from Holland or America were conspicuous, were energetically opposed by certain 'commissioners' who had rushed up from Edinburgh 'with the Holy Spirit in their bags' to see to it that the Scottish system was applied to England in all its rigour. Their impatience did not stop at flooding the ranks of the English clergy with Scotsmen. A scramble was beginning. The Independents were the obstacle; these people who were clamouring for toleration must be crushed. It was against them and not expressly against Milton that Palmer had declaimed. Setting forth the baneful results of toleration, he had cited among other examples 'a wicked book . . . abroad and uncensured'.

Palmer felt in a strong position. In the previous month (July 1644) the Scots had helped Cromwell to defeat Charles at Marston Moor. The cause of toleration, however, was not yet lost. Marston Moor had not been decisive. The

---

[1] In many cases discipline and honesty must have been insufficient; see below, p. 122.

[2] Modern estimates: about four thousand massacred for all Ireland, and six thousand dead of exposure and starvation.

two following encounters (in Cornwall in September, at
Newbury in October) were not decisive either. Obviously
it was costing the Scots too much to fight against their own
Stuart in the interests of the English, while the English
generals had too much respect for the throne to exploit
an advantage to the full.

Cromwell hit upon the solution. He proved to Parliament that the Scottish aid was superfluous. The religious
zeal of the Independents was equal to that of the Covenanters
or the old military honour of the Cavaliers. He undertook
to form an army of fifty thousand and to give them leaders
resolved to conquer. As early as September, Parliament
stopped prosecutions against the Independants. The
creation of the New Model was voted by the Commons in
January 1645 and ratified by the Lords in April. Without
waiting for the outcome of the debates, Cromwell had
acted. In June, at Naseby, his New Model inflicted on the
Royalists an irreparable defeat.

And at the same moment Milton found Mary again.
The Powell family, sensing that the King's defeat was
coming, had enquired about the poet's movements. His
attentions to Miss Davis or others made them uneasy.
On their side the Agars and various friends feared the
worst. 'All engines were set on work', says Phillips. 'At
last this device was pitched upon. There dwelt in the lane
of St. Martin's le Grand, which was hard by, a relation of
our author's, one Blackborough, whom it was known he
often visited. One time above the rest, he making his usual
visit, the wife was ready in another room, and on a sudden
he was surprised to see one whom he expected never to
see again, making submission and begging pardon on her
knees before him.' It was her mother, she said, who had
done it all. She wept, those present implored, Milton forgave.

> She ended weeping, and her lowlie plight,
> Immoveable till peace obtaind from fault
> Acknowledg'd and deplor'd, in *Adam* wraught
> Commiseration; soon his heart relented
> Towards her, his life so late and sole delight,
> Now at his feet submissive in distress . . .[1]

[1] *Paradise Lost*, X, 937–42.

According to the best informed witnesses, the couple lived henceforward without a clash. Mary was to die at twenty-seven in giving birth to her fourth child.

We have just seen that Milton seemed to reserve to the husband the right to divorce. Man, he said, is 'the master of the family'; he founds it, he dissolves it. This is an example of what has been called Milton's misogyny. Is the term exact?

Milton was thrice married (which hardly suggests rabid misogyny) and Mary's flight was the only discordant note in his married life. Towards his daughters, as we shall see, he did his duty, and more. He enjoyed the respectful admiration of Lady Margaret Ley; another great lady was to vow to him an inalienable friendship. If he was careful to remain chaste, we know that it was largely through reverènce for 'the glory of man'. Contempt for woman-kind, calm and complete, will be found in a Delille,[1] who laughed with his friends over the fact that Madame Delille had never read a line of what he wrote. Milton, on the contrary, had expected Mary Powell to be for him 'a sweet and gladsome partner . . . an intimate and speaking help, a ready and reviving associate . . . a fit conversing soul' (B. III, 191).

And yet. There is no smoke without fire. The clue to the enigma is that we can religiously admire woman and yet set man higher still. Eve herself said to her husband:

> . . . with that thy gentle hand
> Seisd mine, I yeilded, and from that time see
> How beauty is excelld by manly grace
> And wisdom, which alone is truly fair.[2]

Elsewhere it is Milton who declares:

> For contemplation hee and valour formd,
> For softness shee and sweet attractive grace,
> Hee for God onely, shee for God in him:
> His fair large Front and Eye sublime declar'd
> Absolute rule;[3]

---

[1] 1738–1813. Famous in his day; a translator of *Paradise Lost*.
[2] *Paradise Lost*, IV, 489–91.   [3] Ibid., 297–301.

The doctrine of the 'divorcer' doubtless underwent certain modifications to bring it into line with the realities of daily life. For instance, in *Tetrachordon*, after quoting several passages from St. Paul's Epistles, Milton declares:

> Nevertheless man is not to hold her as a servant, but receives her into a part of that empire which God proclaims him to, though not equally, yet largely, as his own image and glory; for it is no small glory to him, that a creature so like him should be made subject to him. Not but that particular exceptions may have place, if she exceed her husband in prudence and dexterity, and he contentedly yield: for then a superior and more natural law comes in, that the wiser should govern the less wise, whether male or female.[1]

The exception, however, proves the rule, and the rule, Milton was firmly persuaded, is that every creature owes obedience to another, except the human male, who takes his orders straight from the Creator. Woman can maintain and increase, she does not create. Instituted and inspired by God, man, king by right divine, must not divest himself of his prerogative—'nor from that right to part an hour'.[2] If he weakens, society degenerates. After the Fall, the Voice which walked in the first garden declares to the first man that he is alone responsible:

> To whom the sovran Presence thus repli'd.
> Was shee thy God, that her thou didst obey
> Before his voice, or was shee made thy guide,
> Superior, or but equal, that to her
> Thou didst resign thy Manhood, and the Place
> Wherein God set thee above her made of thee,
> And for thee, whose perfection farr excelld
> Hers in all real dignitie: Adornd
> She was indeed, and lovely to attract
> Thy love, not thy Subjection, and her Gifts
> Were such as under Government well seemd,
> Unseemly to beare rule, which was thy part
> And person, hadst thou known thy self aright.[3]

---

[1] Bohn III, 325.
[2] *Samson Agonistes*, 1056. A striking feature of the Puritan movement was the rôle assumed by the women. See John Earle, *Microcosmography*, 1628.
[3] *Paradise Lost*, X, 144–56.

The greater the value of woman, then, the more man should fear her. All desire is sorrow, says the Orient. 'Though terror be in love and beauty', cries Lucifer, subjugated for a moment by the beauty of the first woman (*P.L.*, IX, 490). A perfect woman, even if she loves us, can still be a source of suffering to us, since life can refuse her to us. Milton asks himself why God created woman:

> O why did God,
> Creator wise, that peopl'd highest Heav'n
> With Spirits Masculine, create at last
> This noveltie on Earth, this fair defect
> Of Nature, and not fill the World at once
> With Men as Angels without Feminine,
> Or find some other way to generate
> Mankind?[1]

Then follows an enumeration of the disorders and disappointments without which we should have neither tragedies nor *opera bouffe*.

> . . .: for either
> He never shall find out fit Mate, but such
> As some misfortune brings him, or mistake,
> Or whom he wishes most shall seldom gain
> Through her perversness, but shall see her gaind
> By a farr worse, or if she love, withheld
> By Parents, or his happiest choice too late
> Shall meet, alreadie linkt and Wedlock-bound
> To a fell Adversarie, his hate or shame:
> Which infinite calamitie shall cause
> To Human life, and houshold peace confound.[2]

Ageless, universal recriminations, or mere statements of what can never change. The term misogynist could no more be applied to Milton than to the Code Napoleon or to Homer. It is true that he does not make provision for the lot of the child; he was of his time, and the child is absent from his work. What marks him out is his frankness and the ingenuousness of his complaint. He should be praised all the more for having spoken so well of love, of smiles, of marriage, of woman. 'True love', says Raphael to Adam, 'does not consist in passion':

---

[1] *Paradise Lost*, X, 888–95.   [2] Ibid., 899–908.

                  . . .; Love refines
The thoughts, and heart enlarges, hath his seat
In Reason, and is judicious, is the scale
By which to heav'nly Love thou maist ascend,
Not sunk in carnal pleasure, for which cause
Among the Beasts no Mate for thee was found.
          To whom thus half abasht *Adam* repli'd.
Neither her out-side formd so fair, nor aught
In procreation common to all kindes
(Though higher of the genial Bed by farr,
And with mysterious reverence I deem)
So much delights me, as those graceful acts,
Those thousand decencies that daily flow
From all her words and actions, mixt with Love
And sweet compliance, which declare unfeignd
Union of Mind, or in us both one Soule;
Harmonie to behold in wedded pair
More grateful than harmonious sound to the eare.[1]

Therefore Adam will say to Eve:

Yet not so strictly hath our Lord impos'd
Labour, as to debarr us when we need
Refreshment, whether food, or talk between,
Food of the mind, or this sweet intercourse
Of looks and smiles, for smiles from Reason flow,
To brute deni'd, and are of Love the food,
Love not the lowest end of human life.
For not to irksome toile, but to delight
He made us, and delight to Reason joind.[2]

St. Paul saw in marriage a last resource, Tertullian called
it the gate of the devil, *janua diaboli*. The 'divorcer' is more
human:

Haile wedded Love, mysterious Law, true sourse
Of human ofspring, sole proprietie
In Paradise of all things common else.
By thee adulterous lust was driv'n from men
Among the bestial herds to raunge, by thee
Founded in Reason, Loyal, Just, and Pure,
Relations dear, and all the Charities
Of Father, Son, and Brother first were known.

---

[1] *Paradise Lost*, VIII, 589–606.   [2] Ibid., IX, 235–43.

Farr be it, that I should write thee sin or blame,
Or think thee unbefitting holiest place,
Perpetual Fountain of Domestic sweets,
Whose Bed is undefil'd and chast pronounc't,
Present, or past, as Saints and Patriarchs us'd.
Here Love his gold'n shafts imploies, here lights
His constant Lamp, and waves his purple wings,
Reigns here and revels;[1]

As to woman, which of her worshippers has ever rendered her homage as deep as this, in *Paradise Lost* again?

Grace was in all her steps, Heav'n in her Eye,
In every gesture dignitie and love.

. . . .

For well I understand in the prime end
Of Nature her th'inferiour, in the mind
And inward Faculties, which most excell,

. . . .

         . . . yet when I approach
Her loveliness, so absolute she seems
And in her self compleat, so well to know
Her own, that what she wills to do or say,
Seems wisest, vertuousest, discreetest, best;
All higher knowledge in her presence falls
Degraded, Wisdom in discourse with her
Looses discount'nanc't, and like folly shewes;
Autoritie and Reason on her waite,
As one intended first, not after made
Occasionally; and to consummate all,
Greatness of mind and nobleness thir seat
Build in her loveliest, and create an awe
About her, as a guard Angelic plac't.[2]

Alas! Poor Mary!

[1] *Paradise Lost*, IV, 750-64.   [2] Ibid., VIII, 488-559.

VII

SCHOOLS AND THE PRESS
1644

'OF EDUCATION'

MILTON had no difficulty in finding the few pupils who would provide him with a sufficiency.

His father's connection with the City, that of his brother-in-law with the Public Servants, and that of Lawes with the Court, would have enabled him to find enough pupils for a school. About 1644 he was teaching five ancient languages,[1] Italian, history, morals and many other things, to about ten young men, with a success which Phillips has vouched for. He sang with his pupils and prayed with them. On Sundays he made them read the Bible in Greek or Hebrew, commented upon it, then gave them a course in theology.

Even more than this school in embryo, the master's ideas keenly interested a certain merchant, Samuel Hartlib, the son of a man from the Baltic States and an English-woman. Hartlib had two passions—the gathering together of the Protestants of Europe, and the progress of knowledge. On the first point, his activities were guided by that John Durie who was in touch with Grotius. In the interests of knowledge, Hartlib ruined himself by giving endowments to students, inventors and scholars, he published, translated, urged people to write, corresponded with the Continent. In matters of pedagogy he swore by Comenius. This incomparable Moravian had come to London in 1642, at the request of Parliament, to create a 'universal College' there. The approach of the Civil War, however, had broken off this project, and Comenius had gone to organize the schools in Sweden.[2]

---

[1] Phillips: '. . . the Greek and Latin tongues . . . the chief oriental languages, viz., the Hebrew, Chaldee and Syriac.'

[2] See A. F. Young, *Comenius in England*, London, 1932; G. H. Turnbull, *Hartlib, Dury and Comenius*, London, 1947; Léonard, *Histoire générale du Protestantisme*, Paris, 1961, vol. II, pp. 182–5.

Hartlib had often urged Milton to impart to the public his views on education. In consequence there appeared in June 1644 an open letter—*Of Education, to Master Samuel Hartlib*.

We have seen what was lacking in Cambridge. The other universities of Europe were also primarily seminaries. Men such as Bacon, Galileo, Leibnitz, worked outside and apart from them. Neither Descartes, Spinoza nor Hobbes had had a chair. Gassendi and Pascal had followed the conferences which were held at the Baron de Montmor's. In London, on the initiative of Hartlib and of Robert Boyle, the chemist, the germ of the Royal Society[1] was to come into being in 1645. Since the first purpose of the schools was to feed the universities, they were not very numerous. Moreover, they were reserved for boys, and had not sufficient openings on to secular life. It was frequent in England for a rich squire not to be able to read, whereas his younger brother, a churchman, would have been to Oxford.

To form a quick appreciation of Milton's syllabus, we may compare it with that of Comenius. In his *Didactica magna* Comenius envisaged in every country, and in every village, 'nursery' and 'vernacular' schools for both sexes, mixed 'Latin' schools in the towns, then up-to-date universities and travel. The majority of the pupils would have become skilled workmen, an élite would have devoted themselves to research under the directives of the *Pansophia* (anticipating Unesco), which would co-ordinate for the whole of Europe not only the research of specialists but the curricula and the school text-books. Comenius was overflowing with ingenious systems. His guiding principle was respect for the real: it was essential to start from the concrete (even in the study of ancient languages), and proceed from the general to the particular, so as to terminate on a level with man's active life.

His works, some of which Hartlib had translated, had been known in England since 1631. Milton was wrong in

---

[1] The connection between the Royal Society and 'the invisible college' has yet to be established by the historians.

speaking contemptuously of them in this letter; he perhaps
owed a good deal to them. He, too, wished to start from
the concrete, to go at the pupil's pace and make a useful
citizen of him. He emphasized the futility of languages.

> And though a linguist should pride himself to have all the
> tongues that Babel cleft the world into, yet if he have not
> studied the solid things in them, as well as the words and
> lexicons, he were nothing so much to be esteemed a learned
> man, as any yeoman or tradesman competently wise in his
> mother dialect only.[1]

The learned tongues would not, however, be sacrificed,
but the pupils would learn them 'easily and delightfully',
because the difficulties would be wisely graded. As a start,
for instance, they would read from the text Cato the Elder,
who would speak to them of agriculture, and when they
were of an age to study morals, they would be able to read
Xenophon at sight. At no matter what moment in their
studies the meaning would leap to their eyes. There should
be no more than this. Translations from Latin or Greek
in writing are superfluous. Into Latin or Greek they are
worse: they implant solecisms (B. III, 465).

In the meantime men with a trade—shepherds, sailors,
huntsmen, apothecaries even, would come and explain
their various methods to the pupils, who would also travel
in a group and on horseback under chosen guides over the
whole countryside for purposes of study. They would be
initiated into all the sciences and their applications—
astronomy, military science, architecture, anatomy. They
would peruse the laws of Moses, of the Greeks, of the
Romans and of the Saxons, before coming to English
Common Law. It is needless to add that their religious
instruction would be highly developed.

At about the age of nineteen, having at last a general
notion of the world, they would embark upon English
dissertation and Latin or Greek verse.

They would practise wrestling and fencing, the organ,
the lute, and singing. And 'as they may have easily learnt

---

[1] *Of Education*, Bohn III, 464.

Italian at any odd hour' they will be able to amuse themselves by performing Latin, Greek, or Italian comedies in the original, and tragedies such as *Alcestis* or *The Trachiniae*.

> These ways would try all their peculiar gifts of nature; and if there were any secret excellence among them would fetch it out, and give it fair opportunities to advance itself by ... [1]

An all-important contrast between Comenius and Milton becomes immediately apparent. Comenius, driven from country to country by persecution and war, was a European. As a follower of the Gospel, he wanted to raise the people, including women. Milton was insular and an aristocrat. His chief preoccupation was that the new England lacked leaders. He wanted to create leaders for her without delay. For the want of this reform, he said, 'this nation perishes' (B. III, 462). 'That which I have to say, assuredly this nation hath extreme need should be done sooner than spoken' (463–4). What he envisaged was therefore the Aldersgate school completed and nationalized. In 'every city throughout the land' he wanted an establishment that should be 'both school and university'. Its system would be that of the boarding-school, 'which saves time and inculcates good habits'. The powers of the headmaster would be absolute. The pupils, admitted at the age of twelve, would have no need to study elsewhere (except those who must practise Medicine or Law) to embark, on their attaining their majority, upon the trade or profession of their choice, including the military profession.

In this year 1644 in which Parliament was in despair over its army, Milton offered a solution. His school would lodge one hundred and fifty persons of whom about twenty might be tutors and attendants. 'This number will allow us to form a foot company or two troops of cavalry.' Milton described the exercises and evolutions of his pupil-officers on the drill-ground with which the school would be obligatorily provided, and he envisaged their visiting fortified places, arsenals and the fleet. Convinced that his pupils would know how to 'fulfil all their duties, in peace as

---

[1] *Of Education*, Bohn III, 478.

in war, with justice, competence and magnanimity', he saw them as army leaders:

> They would not then, if they were trusted with fair and hope-ful armies, suffer them, for want of just and wise discipline, to shed away from about them like sick feathers, though they be never so oft supplied; they would not suffer their empty and unrecruitable colonels of twenty men in a company, to quaff out or convey into secret hoards, the wages of a delusive list, and a miserable remnant;[1]

Similarly, the new school, like those of Pythagoras and Isocrates, would form philosophers, historians and orators:

> Or whether they be to speak in parliament or council, honour and attention would be waiting on their lips. There would then also appear in pulpits other visage, other gestures, and stuff otherwise wrought than what we now sit under, oft-times to as great a trial of our patience as any other that they preach to us.[2]

In short, if people had listened to Milton, Oxford and Cambridge could have closed their doors. With the excep-tion of the doctors and lawyers, all those filling the higher posts of the nation would have come from these 'upper-grade high schools'. He even undertook to form a clergy (independent, doubtless). But his ambition did not go beyond this. Comenius, generous and far-sighted, en-visaged courses for all ages and all conditions, on an inter-national model. Milton limited himself to making provision for the English middle-class. Europe would follow if she wished to do so.

> Nor, [if my method is followed,] shall we then need the monsieurs of Paris to take our hopeful youth into their slight and prodigal custodies, and send them over, back again, trans-formed into mimics, apes and kickshaws.[3] But if they desire to see other countries at three or four and twenty years of age, . . . they will by that time be such as shall deserve the regard and honour of all men where they pass, and the society and friendship of those in all places who are best and most

---

[1] *Of Education*, Bohn III, 477.   [2] Ibid., 474.
[3] *Kickshaws*—cf. Usher's *Annals of the World*—'all the Asian comicks and kick-shaws crept into the Court'. The original meaning is a fancy dish, a French 'petit plat' or 'petit quelque chose' as in *Animadversions* (Bohn III, 55).

A MASKE

PRESENTED

At Ludlow Caſtle,

1 6 3 4 :

On Michaelmaſſe night *, before the*
RIGHT HONORABLE,

IOHN *Earle of Bridgewater ,* Vicount BRACKLY,
Lord Preſident *of* WALES *, And one of*
His MAIESTIES moſt honorable
Privie Counſell.

Eheu quid volui miſero mihi ! floribus auſtrum
Perditus ————

LONDON,

Printed for HVMPHREY ROBINSON,
at the ſigne of the *Three Pidgeons* in
Pauls Church-yard. 1 6 3 7. ſɛ

TITLE PAGE OF *COMUS*, 1637

eminent. And, perhaps, then other nations will be glad to visit us for their breeding, or else to imitate us in their own country.[1]

The plan has other defects. Pedagogues will always make the mistake of being born before their pupils.[2] How could Milton dare to teach the astronomy of Sacrobosco, when he had seen Galileo? Did he really think that his pupils would perform *The Trachiniae* in Greek for their recreation? *The New Atlantis*, which he did not even mention, would have been for them what Jules Verne is for us. Milton's syllabus was too literary and, moreover, as overloaded as that of Rabelais' Ponocrates, who kept Gargantua under such strict discipline that he had no spare hour in the day.

The thirst for knowing everything and experiencing everything brings Milton close to Rabelais. Rabelais' impetus can be recognized in a sentence like this:

...; that having in sport, but with much exactness and daily muster, served out the rudiments of their soldiership, in all the skill of embattling, marching, encamping, fortifying, besieging, and battering with all the helps of ancient and modern stratagems, tactics, and warlike maxims, they may as it were out of a long war come forth renowned and perfect commanders in the service of their country.[3]

Rabelais wanted his pupil to 'visit the trees and plants, to sing after meals, to go and see how metals were extracted, how cannon were cast, to learn and consider industry and the invention of trades.' All this is in Milton, and we have not yet carried it out. On one point the man of Touraine outdoes the Englishman; on wet days, Gargantua studied painting and sculpture. In Milton there is not a word about the plastic arts. On the other hand, when he speaks of music, his homely prose becomes music.

The personality of the master, an all-important element in pedagogy, comes to light again in other places:

[1] *Of Education*, Bohn III, 478.
[2] Cf. Lord Vansittart, *The Mist Procession*, 1958. 'Our headmaster taught according to ancient lights. The Bible with Bishop Usher's date for creation—4004 B.C. and what precision!—was still in use, and the giant strides of geology were not mentioned to us. The other foundation of knowledge was, of course, Latin.'
[3] Bohn III, 477.

K

...; in those vernal seasons of the year when the air is calm and pleasant, it were an injury and sullenness against nature, not to go out and see her riches, and partake in her rejoicing with heaven and earth.[1]

Logic, therefore, so much as is useful, is to be referred to this due place with all her well-couched heads and topics. . . . To which poetry would be made subsequent, or indeed rather precedent, as being less subtile and fine, but more simple, sensuous, and passionate.[2]

This would make them soon perceive what despicable creatures our common rhymers and play-writers be; and shew them what religious, what glorious and magnificent use might be made of poetry, both in divine and human things.[3]

But here the main skill and groundwork will be, to temper them such lectures and explanations, upon every opportunity, as may lead and draw them in willing obedience, inflamed with the study of learning and the admiration of virtue; stirred up with high hopes of living to be brave men, and worthy patriots, dear to God, and famous to all ages.[4]

The end of learning is to repair the ruins of our first parents by regaining to know God aright.[5]

When the treatise appeared the Presbyterian pack was barking at the divorcer's heels, but the wife of an Irish peer, 'London's queen', 'the incomparable Lady Ranelagh', entrusted to Milton her son Robert Jones and her nephew, the Earl of Barrimore. The need for a new school could not escape her; she was the sister of Robert Boyle and quite worthy of him through her vigour of mind.

The Commonwealth was to be born and to die without making any attempt to realize Milton's dream. Under Charles II, he reprinted his treatise without any more success. About 1830, when the middle class at last had a share in the power, English education took some steps in the direction pointed out by Milton. Dr. Thomas Arnold initiated at Rugby a reform of the upper class boarding-schools. Since that time, as Milton predicted, many a continental family has sent its son to the English school-master.

---

[1] Bohn III, 477.   [2] Ibid., 473.   [3] Ibid., 474.
[4] Ibid., 468.   [5] Ibid., 464.

'AREOPAGITICA'

SIX months after this letter, in November 1644, Milton addressed to Parliament a 'Speech for the Liberty of Unlicensed Printing': *Areopagitica*. The first in date, exhaustive, sometimes solemn in tone, sometimes sarcastic, always burning with conviction, this plea is one of the proudest title-deeds of the Western world. It owed its birth to an historical conjuncture.

From time immemorial the law had required that new books should be registered by the Stationers' Company. In addition, Laud had instituted a preliminary censorship. The Parliament of 1640 had at first allowed books to be published without restrictions, but it had soon regretted so doing. Milton's remark 'All mouths opened against the bishops' was a generalization. In fact, both the Royalists and the parties on the Left were also causing a good deal of stir. Moreover, in the absence of any control, unscrupulous printers reproduced a book without paying anything to the author or to the rightful publisher. In 1642 Parliament ordained that every publication should at least bear the name of the printer. Milton approved this measure and considered it adequate. It safeguarded all rights without hampering writers of good faith. Unfortunately, too few conformed to it. In June 1643 a law that was both severe and meticulous brought back the preliminary censorship. Twenty censors were appointed. The booksellers united in a corporation had a double interest in having the irregular editions seized, since they thus discouraged fraud and also contrived to dispose of the confiscated copies themselves. Order made rapid progress: between January and June 1643, nine out of ten works published had been illegal; during the following six months, the proportion fell to two out of ten. Therefore the opposition press and the freedom of debate were in danger of perishing.

Milton cannot be accused of acting under the impulse of anger—the censorship had been functioning for seventeen months when his protest appeared. Neither were his motives purely personal. He had been begged to intervene by fellow-scholars, as pressing as the Sicilians of old when they adjured Cicero to act against Verres (B. II, 83). Above all, he was speaking for the very large majority of the English. The dissidents demanded the complete neutrality of the State in the matter of faith and the vanquished prelates now advocated tolerance. For practical purposes, the only opponents of liberty were the Presbyterians, but lately victims of Laud, but now decided, as Milton here points out, to equal his severity.[1] Parliament would have been satisfied with striking at seditious publications, but the Westminster Assembly, almost entirely Presbyterian, wanted much more. Its power indeed was considerable because the Parliamentary army was in need of the support of the Covenanters. It was, in short, because the Blue Bonnets fought well that the London booksellers could search the printers' premises.

Once this is known, Milton's curious relations with the censorship become clear. In 1641 and 1642 the law was dormant, and Milton published his anti-episcopal treatises without submitting them to censorship or registration. His *Doctrine of Divorce* appeared two months after the order of 1643—it was, however, neither authorized, registered nor even signed.

Milton reprinted it in February 1644. He signed it, in conformity with the order of 1642, without having it authorized or registered. In June he produced *Of Education*, a booklet clearly unexceptionable; no censor passed it, but the booksellers registered it. The *Bucer* (July) was a sacred text for Calvinists. Milton, perhaps ironically, had it duly registered and censored.

At this juncture (July) the Scots contributed to the defeat of Charles at Marston Moor. Immediately, the Assembly condemned several pleas for toleration to be burnt, and so they were, on August 11th. Two days later, Palmer preached against toleration and drew attention to illegal

---

[1] They made no secret of it. In 1644 an Oxford theologian, the Anglican Chillingworth, known for his appeal for toleration—*The Religion of Protestants*—died. The Presbyterian Cheynell was entrusted with the funeral. He threw the book into the open grave crying—'Go, then, accursed book! Earth to earth, ashes to ashes! Go and perish with thine author!'

books, such as the *Doctrine of Divorce*. On August 24th, the booksellers went to the House of Commons to complain and, among others who treated their privileges with contempt, denounced Milton. On September 13th, however, Cromwell persuaded Parliament to grant toleration to the Independents.[1] Milton took action. At this date the question was already mooted of creating the New Model which, with the overwhelming influence of Cromwell and the Independents, promised toleration. The proposal to reorganize the army came before the Commons on November 25th—*Areopagitica* had been issued the day before. In it Milton took the Presbyterians to task. He therefore made his plea not to the Assembly, but to the two Houses alone. He ignored, of course, both censors and booksellers. On December 9th the latter went to complain to the Lords, but the Lords declined to intervene; they had been informed, by Milton himself, of the corporation's double game. Again it was outside the legal conventions that *Tetrachordon* and *Colasterion* appeared in March 1645.

The title *Areopagitica* does not signify that Milton is addressing an areopagus. He is deeply conscious of the delicacy and importance of his enterprise—to obtain from a sovereign assembly the abrogation of a law voted by itself, which set the thought of a whole nation at the mercy of a score of public servants. He therefore takes as his model the Greek orator Isocrates, an ordinary member of the public like himself, who also loved his country and liberty, wrote like him instead of speaking, and one day addressed to the Five Hundred of Athens a 'Discourse for the Areopagus', *Logos areopagitikos*. The Council of the Five Hundred, the Boulè, which emanated from the people, had reduced the powers of the Areopagus, the aristocratic body. Isocrates implored the Boulè to rescind this spoliation. In 1644 the Areopagus was the English people, deprived of the right to read and write at their pleasure. The law of 1643 outraged the majesty of the English people. Such

[1] See above, p. 112.

was one of the main ideas of Milton's discourse. It inspired
him with whole pages and he formulated it clearly (B. II,
84)—'liberty of printing must be enthralled again, under a
prelatical commission of twenty; the privilege of the people
nullified.'

Despite Milton's natural impetuosity and his fever of hope
and impatience during the autumn of 1644, his discourse
to Parliament stands apart in his prose works. We certainly
do not find there the crystal-clear brook of Isocrates, but
at least the Miltonian torrent is stemmed by several weirs.

In a grandiose *exordium*, Milton eulogizes Parliament,
cites the text of the law whose abrogation he is demanding,
announces that he is going to plead on four counts, and
finally recommends prudence to his hearers, for *books are
living beings.*

> I deny not, [Lords and Commons of England,] but that it is
> of greatest concernment in the church and commonwealth,
> to have a vigilant eye how books demean themselves, as well
> as men; and thereafter to confine, imprison, and do sharpest
> justice on them as malefactors; for books are not absolutely
> dead things, but do contain a potency of life in them to be as
> active as that soul was whose progeny they are; nay, they do
> preserve as in a vial the purest efficacy and extraction of that
> living intellect that bred them. I know they are as lively, and
> as vigorously productive, as those fabulous dragon's teeth:
> and being sown up and down, may chance to spring up armed
> men. And yet, on the other hand, unless wariness be used,
> as good almost kill a man as kill a good book: who kills a
> man kills a reasonable creature, God's image; but he who
> destroys a good book, kills reason itself, kills the image of
> God, as it were, in the eye. Many a man lives a burden to
> the earth; but a good book is the precious life-blood of a
> master-spirit, embalmed and treasured up on purpose to a life
> beyond life.[1]

*First argument: preventive censorship can only be odious to
Parliament because of its origin.*—History of police measures
against books since Ancient times. Preliminary censorship
was born in Rome after the Council of Trent. The *imprimatur*

----

[1] Bohn II, 55.

flourishes in Catholic countries. Reproduction of several *imprimaturs* and this caricature in support:

> Sometimes five imprimaturs are seen together, dialogue wise, in the piazza of one titlepage, complimenting and ducking each to other with their shaven reverences, whether the author, who stands by in perplexity at the foot of his epistle, shall to the press or to the spunge.[1]

It will be said that despite its origin, preliminary censorship has its good points. But so simple a means has occurred to all governments: wise governments have discarded it.

Secondly: the bad and the good are offered to us together.— No book is wholly bad in itself, the good reader finds his good everywhere.

> . . . the knowledge cannot defile, nor consequently the books, if the will and conscience be not defiled. . . . Whereof what better witness can ye expect I should produce, than one of your own now sitting in Parliament, the chief of learned men reputed in this land, Mr. Selden; whose volume of natural and national laws proves, not only by great authorities brought together, but by exquisite reasons and theorems almost mathematically demonstrative, that all opinions, yea, errors, known, read, and collated, are of main service and assistance toward the speedy attainment of what is truest.[2]
>
> It was from out the rind of one apple tasted, that the knowledge of good and evil, as two twins cleaving together, leaped forth into the world. And perhaps this is the doom that Adam fell into of knowing good and evil; that is to say, of knowing good by evil.[3]
>
> As therefore one state of man now is, what wisdom can there be to choose, what continence to forbear, without the knowledge of evil? . . . I cannot praise a fugitive and cloistered virtue unexercised and unbreathed, that never sallies out and seeks her adversary, but slinks out of the race, where that immortal garland is to be run for, not without dust and heat.[4]
>
> . . .; but then, all human learning and controversy in religious points must remove out of the world, yea, the Bible itself; for

[1] Bohn II, 61.　　　　　[2] Ibid., 65–66.　　　　　[3] Ibid., 67–68.
[4] Ibid., 68. St. Columba wrote to Attalus—'Without an enemy, no struggle; without a struggle, no crown; without liberty, no merit'. *Si tollis hostem, tollis et pugnam. Si tollis pugnam, tollis et coronam . . . Si tollis libertatem, tollis dignitatem.*

that ofttimes relates blasphemy not nicely, it describes the carnal sense of wicked men not unelegantly, it brings in holiest men passionately murmuring against Providence through all the arguments of Epicurus:[1]

If it be true that a wise man, like a good refiner, can gather gold out of the drossiest volume, and that the fool will be a fool with the best book, yea, or without book; there is no reason that we should deprive a wise man of any advantage to his wisdom, while we seek to restrain from a fool that which being restrained will be no hindrance to his folly.[2]

Third point: the censorship can never be perfect.—Embargo on foreign books; expurgation of ancient books; censors who are ignorant, corrupt, overworked or revolted by this fastidious and servile toil. And even if it were perfect, it would remain inadequate. Vice and error spread themselves without the help of books. 'The Christian faith (for that was once a schism!) is not unknown to have spread over all Asia, ere any gospel or epistle was seen in writing' (B. II, 76). Finally, do we see that the countries ruled by the *imprimatur* are particularly virtuous?

If we think to regulate printing, thereby to rectify manners, we must regulate all recreations and pastimes, all that is delightful to man. No music must be heard, no song be set or sung, but what is grave and doric. There must be licensing dancers, that no gesture, motion or deportment be taught our youth, but what by their allowance shall be thought honest; . . . It will ask more than the work of twenty licensers to examine all the lutes, the violins, and the guitars in every house; they must not be suffered to prattle as they do, but must be licensed what they may say. And who shall silence all the airs and madrigals that whisper softness in chambers? The windows also, and the balconies, must be thought on; there are shrewd books, with dangerous frontispieces, set to sale: . . . The villages also must have their visitors to inquire what lectures the bagpipe and the rebec reads, even to the ballatry and the gamut of every municipal fiddler; . . . And what shall be done to inhibit the multitudes that frequent those houses where drunkenness is sold and harboured? Our garments also . . . Who shall regulate all the mixed conversation of our youth, male and female together, as is the fashion of this

[1] Bohn II, 69.   [2] Ibid., 70-1.

country? . . . These things will be and must be; but how they shall be least hurtful, how least enticing, herein consists the grave and governing wisdom of a state.[1]

No, the evil is not in books, it is in us: 'Though ye take from a covetous man all his treasure, he has yet one jewel left, ye cannot bereave him of his covetousness'.[2]

Fourthly: this censorship, incapable of procuring any good, will on the contrary be very certainly harmful.—It will paralyse research, discourage writers, revolt readers, humiliate the whole nation, discredit ministers of religion, a general increase of stupidity will follow. See what has happened in Italy.[3] The Presbyterians forget what they suffered yesterday. The acquisition of truth implies a free and constant effort.

I cannot set so light by all the invention, the art, the wit, the grave and solid judgment which is in England, as that it can be comprehended in any twenty capacities, how good soever;[4]

Had anyone written and divulged erroneous things and scandalous to honest life . . . if after conviction this only censure were adjudged him, that he should never henceforth write, but what were first examined by an appointed officer . . . it could not be apprehended less than a disgraceful punishment. Whence to include the whole nation, and those that never yet thus offended, under such a diffident and suspectful prohibition, may plainly be understood what a disparagement it is.[5]

This may have much reason to discourage the ministers, when such a low conceit is had of all their exhortations and the benefiting of their hearers, as that they are not thought fit to be turned loose to three sheets of paper without a licenser; that all the sermons, all the lectures preached, printed, vended in such numbers, and such volumes, as have now well-nigh made all other books unsaleable, should not be armour enough against one single enchiridion, without the castle of St. Angelo of an imprimatur.[6]

Truth is compared in scripture to a streaming fountain; if her waters flow not in a perpetual progression, they sicken into a muddy pool of conformity and tradition . . . if [a man] believes things only because his pastor says so . . . though his belief be true, yet the very truth he holds becomes his heresy.[7]

[1] Bohn II, 73.   [2] Ibid., 75.   [3] See above, p. 76.   [4] Bohn II, 80-1.
[5] Ibid., 81.   [6] Ibid., 82.   [7] Ibid., 85.

There follow satirical portraits (B. II, 85–8) of two laymen and a parochial minister who rely on others.

It is not sufficient to have left Rome and Anglicanism; we must not 'pitch our tent here', but go ever forward.

> Truth indeed came once into the world with her divine Master, and was a perfect shape most glorious to look on: but when he ascended . . . then straight arose a wicked race of deceivers who . . . took the virgin Truth, hewed her lovely form into a thousand pieces and scattered them to the four winds. From that time ever since, the sad friends of Truth . . . went up and down gathering up limb by limb still as they could find them. We have not yet found them all, Lords and Commons, nor ever shall do, till her Master's second coming. . . . The light which we have gained was given us, not to be ever staring on, but by it to discover onward things. . . . To be still searching what we know not by what we know, still closing up truth to truth as we find it, this is the golden rule . . .[1]

The ample *peroration* develops two cognate themes— *trust in England, trust in liberty*.

> Lords and Commons of England! consider what nation it is whereof ye are, and whereof ye are the governors: a nation . . . of a quick, ingenious and piercing spirit . . . so that even the school of Pythagoras . . . took beginning from the old philosophy of this island. . . . Nor is it for nothing that the grave and frugal Transylvanian sends out yearly from as far as the mountainous borders of Russia, and beyond the Hercynian wilderness, not their youth but their staid men. . . . Yet that which is above all this, the favour and the love of Heaven, we have great argument to think in a peculiar manner propitious and propending towards us. . . . And had it not been the obstinate perverseness of our prelates against the divine and admirable spirit of Wickliffe . . . perhaps neither . . . the name of Luther or of Calvin, had ever been known.[2]

> Now, once again . . . God is decreeing to begin some new and great period in his church, even to the reforming of reformation itself; what does he then but reveal himself to his servants, and as his manner is, first to his Englishmen? . . . Behold now this vast city, a city of refuge, the mansion-house of liberty, . . . surrounded with his protection; the shop of war hath not there

---

[1] Bohn II, 89–90.   [2] Ibid., 90–1.

more anvils and hammers waking, to fashion out the plates and instruments of armed justice in defence of beleaguered truth, than there be pens and heads there, sitting by their studious lamps, musing, searching, revolving new notions and ideas wherewith to present, as with their homage and their fealty, the approaching reformation.[1]

Some people deplore 'the schisms and the sects' (the Presbyterian formula). They are still impregnated with the episcopal tradition. It is they who are the instigators of disorder, since they are opposed to the natural law of humanity—research.

... as if, while the temple of the Lord was building, some cutting, some squaring the marble, others hewing the cedars, there should be a sort of irrational men, who could not consider there must be many schisms and many dissections made in the quarry and the timber ere the house of God can be built. And when every stone is laid artfully together, it cannot be united into a continuity, it can but be contiguous in this world.[2]

This movement of mind in England is as happy a symptom as the movement of the blood in the veins. England is in full vigour:

Methinks I see in my mind a noble and puissant nation rousing herself like a strong man after sleep, and shaking her invincible locks: methinks I see her as an eagle mewing her mighty youth, and kindling her undazzled eyes at the full midday beam; purging and unscaling her long-abused sight at the fountain itself of heavenly radiance.[3]

Should ye set an oligarchy of twenty engrossers over it, to bring a famine upon our minds again? ... Liberty which is the nurse of all great wits: this is that which hath rarified and enlightened our spirits like the influence of heaven: this is that which hath enfranchised, enlarged and lifted up our apprehensions degrees above themselves. ... Ye cannot make us now less capable, less knowing, less eagerly pursuing of the truth, unless ye first make yourselves, that made us so, less the lovers, less the founders of our true liberty. ... Although I dispraise not the defence of just immunities,[4] yet love my peace better, if that were all. Give me the liberty to know, to utter, and to argue freely according to conscience, above all liberties.[5]

[1] Bohn II, 91–92.   [2] Ibid., 92.   [3] Ibid., 94.
[4] An allusion to ship-money.   [5] Bohn II, 94–5.

And though all the winds of doctrine were let loose to play upon the earth, so truth be in the field, we do injuriously by licensing and prohibiting to misdoubt her strength ... who ever knew truth put to the worse, in a free and open encounter? Her confuting is the best and surest suppressing. . . . For who knows not that truth is strong, next to the Almighty; she needs no policies, nor stratagems, nor licensings to make her victorious; those are the shifts and the defences that error uses against her power: give her but room, and do not bind her when she sleeps.[1]

The core of Milton's protest is his conviction, valid for all time, that men must search, for no truth can be regarded as sufficient for ever. If Rome, Canterbury, Geneva—or Moscow—succeeded in imposing a golden rule universally, the divine plan would be overthrown, man would sink to an automaton.

Many there be that complain of divine Providence for suffering Adam to transgress. Foolish tongues! when God gave him reason, he gave him freedom to choose, for reason is but choosing; he had been else a mere artificial Adam, such an Adam as he is in the motions.[2]

Middleton Murry, in his *Problem of Style*, has given *Areopagitica* high praise. He discerns in it 'the soul of the great movement of Puritanism, the secret of Cromwell's army, the spirit which has made toleration possible in the world of to-day'. It must, however, be pointed out that Milton refuses liberty of expression to Catholics: 'I mean not tolerated popery, and open superstition, which as it extirpates all religions and civil supremacies, so itself should be extirpated' (B. II, 97). But then, he is no less rigid towards the Presbyterians: 'It would be no unequal distribution in the first place to suppress the suppressors themselves' (B. II, 99–100). Last, we must remember that Protestant England was then as hostile to Catholics as he was. Jeremy Taylor, so broad-minded, Locke, author of *Letters on Toleration*, thought like Milton that the Catholic

---

[1] Bohn II, 96. Here again we find Pascal: 'Quand on oppose les discours aux discours, ceux qui sont véritables et convaincants confondent et dissipent ceus qui n'ont que la vanité et le monsonge. . . . La vérité subsiste éternellement, et triomphe enfin de ses ennemis, parce qu'elle est éternelle et puissante comme Dieu même.' *Provinciales*, Lettre 12.   [2] Ibid., 74.

had shut himself off from the community of free men. And yet, as we shall see, one friend of Milton's was more charitable.

Naturally, the Ordinance for Printing of 1643 was maintained—the war spoke with a louder voice than a pamphlet. Parliament contented itself with being moderate in the application of it. Under the Commonwealth and the Protectorate, the political press was to be strictly watched, the religious press hardly at all. The constraint became heavier under Charles II. However, a plagiarized version of the *Areopagitica* appeared in 1679, the year of *Habeas Corpus*. Another appeared in 1693 under William III, and the preliminary censorship was abolished the following year—which was to see two booksellers hanged in Paris for a libel.

According to Lord Birkett (*Does Pornography matter?*) 'England had a completely free press only between 1695 and 1727'. In France, *Areopagitica* made its appearance under the following title: *Sur la Liberté de la Presse, imité de l'anglais de Milton par le Comte de Mirabeau*, Londres, 1788. 'Londres' was a fiction that could deceive nobody, but it allowed authority to save its face. The neatly worded booklet was reprinted openly in 1789, 1792, 1814 and 1819. It inspired Marat in 1790, Chateaubriand in 1827, and Victor Hugo in January 1850, at the critical time when 'Badinguet' was quietly preparing his coup d'Etat.

In the course of the nineteenth century, *Areopagatica* was translated in Italy, Russia, Spain, German Switzerland, and three times in Germany. In 1872, Lobb published in Calcutta a transcription into modern English for the benefit of Indians. In 1956 Professor Lutaud published a complete and annotated French version with a vigorous introduction of over a hundred pages.

Areopagitica, let us hope, will find many readers yet. For the moment, frontiers are closed against it over more than half the globe. 'C'est une étrange et longue guerre', said Pascal, 'que celle où la violence essaye d'opprimer la vérité'.

VIII

SILENCE
1645–1649

WE have seen Milton in March, 1645, publishing under the nose of the censors his two tracts with the surprising titles, the powerful *Tetrachordon* and the insulting *Colasterion*. His left hand was to give nothing more to the public until 1649, and what his right hand was able to write in these four years scarcely counts, or escapes notice.

Voltaire was living in England in 1727, the year when Deborah Clarke, Milton's daughter, died. He was told that, according to her, when Milton had abandoned his drama of the Fall, an act and a half of it were already composed. Was Milton working on it at this particular period of his life? We do not know. The only poems dating from this period are three angry sonnets against the Presbyterians (1645), one for Lawes (1646), a fifth 'to the religious memory' of a Mrs. Thomason (1646), a Latin ode (1647) to John Rous, Bodley's Librarian in Oxford, and lastly, written in 1648, the paraphrase of nine psalms and a sonnet to Lord Fairfax, Commander-in-Chief. The sonnet to Lawes was published by the latter in 1648, the sonnet to Fairfax was not printed until 1694. The other poems were not made known to the public until a year before the poet's death. Yet it was in this apparently sterile phase that Milton tried to reveal himself as a poet.

At the beginning of the war the flood of English poetry seemed to have dried up. Little more can be mentioned than Denham's *Cooper's Hill*, a moralizing picture of the outskirts of London, which appeared in 1642. The Puritan satirist, Wither, famous (but imprisoned) under King James, had long been something less than mediocre. Carew had died in 1639, Suckling in 1642. Davenant and Cowley were living as refugees in France. Herrick, writing his *Noble Numbers* and *Hesperides* in his country parsonage, was still unknown.

In 1644, the year of Marston Moor, the breeze freshened. Within the next four years Cleveland, Crashaw, Lovelace and Vaughan were to appear on the horizon. *Hesperides* was to blossom in the fatal year 1649.

In 1644 the publisher Moseley, a man of taste and courage, issued the poems of Edmund Waller, a very rich cousin of Cromwell's. He had been condemned to death in the previous year for conspiring against the Parliament—of which he was a member!—and, after saving his life by betraying his accomplices, had just been exiled. In January 1646, Moseley published Milton, although he was then in 'a world of disesteem'. The ambitious poet who had dreamt of sudden fame, now considered himself fortunate to be able to let people know that he was something better than a pamphleteer. He allowed Moseley to present him as a disciple of Spenser, greater than his master. He allowed his portrait to be published. Better still—the engraver having made him look old, Milton made him add on his plate four lines of Greek inviting the reader to 'laugh at a bad portraitist'. Finally, to show that these few poems were merely an earnest, he had inscribed at the beginning of the collection the prayer of Thyrsis in Virgil's *Seventh Eclogue:*

Baccare frontem cingite, ne vati noceat mala lingua futuro.[1]

Alas! the poems of youth found fewer readers than the *Doctrine of Divorce*. Those who could have appreciated them best had for the most part migrated to France. Through a double irony, it was a Catholic, Pope, who was to discover these masterpieces of Puritan poetry for the greatest profit and encouragement of a Miltonian school which was to repudiate Pope.

We still have to find an explanation for Milton's silence. It coincided with the most violent period of the war. The New Model, victorious at Naseby in 1645, seized the King and the last Royalist stronghold in 1646, drove out the Presbyterian government in 1647, subdued London and

---

[1] With foxglove bind my brow,
Lest evil tongues should hurt the bard to be.

Scotland in 1648. Terrible years for the King, who disguised himself as a servant to seek refuge with the Scottish army, was then sold to the Parliamentarians, and lived henceforward as a prisoner. Terrible years for the country—several sieges lasted months, a number of districts changed hands more than once. In his *Ode to Rous*, Milton exclaimed:

> But now what God, what seed of heavenly Line,
> Pitying the pristine genius of our race
> (If our old faults are all aton'd, and base
> Degen'rate slackness, grown to sloth supine),
> These monstrous Civil Jars will terminate?
> What Power restore our peaceful Arts, of late
> From almost all the bounds of England sent
> With the unhous'd Muses into banishment?
> Who will with shafts from Phoebus' quiver pierce
> This obscene wingèd Brood, of talons fierce
> To rapine? Who this Phinean Plague will strive
> Afar from Thames' Muse-haunted Stream to drive?[1]

The 'obscene wingèd Brood' were the war profiteers. Every victory of one side or the other involved confiscations and sequestrations, the dismissal of public servants, evacuations of towns. Informers and unjust judges grew rich. The informer would contrive to have entrusted to him the sale of the confiscated property, and would feather his nest by means of a faked adjudication. To pillage were added scarcity of food, lack of fuel, plague and taxation. If Parliament paid its costs, it was by putting pressure on the civil population. So much the worse for the Londoners who had property in royalist territory. Milton complained of this double incidence:

> I usually kept myself secluded at home, where my own property, part of which had been withheld during the civil commotions, and part of which had been absorbed in the oppressive contributions which I had to sustain, afforded me a scanty subsistence.[2]

To increase his resources he took new pupils in 1645 and rented a larger house in the Barbican, to which he moved in September.

---

[1] Tr. Skeat, Nonesuch, pp. 815–16.   [2] *Second Defence*, Bohn I, 260.

SIGNATURE OF MILTON, NOV. 19, 1651

In June, 1646, the war dealt him a blow which paralysed him. When his wife was expecting a child due in a month's time, he had the whole Powell family descend upon him, driven from Forest Hill by the fall of Oxford. He would now have to feed his parents-in-law and the seven or eight children who were still under their care. He himself had a dozen pupils, the majority of whom boarded with him, and for the last three years he had been giving his father a home.

On July 29th, 1646, Mary gave birth to their first child, Anne, who was deformed.[1] Six weeks later Powell, crushed by grief—and also by remorse, for he had declared himself a Presbyterian to escape confiscation of his possessions— went to bed never to leave it again. He died (it is thought a Catholic) on January 1st, 1647. In March it was old John Milton, the poet's first admirer, his generous friend, and also a guest who had not given him 'the least trouble imaginable' (Phillips), who departed from this world and left his son to the mercy of the Powell tribe. Milton could not expect any relief from his brother. We have seen that Christopher had been driven from Reading to Exeter in April, 1643. In April, 1646, the Parliamentarians took Exeter. Christopher reached London with his family to take refuge with his wife's mother, not without having sworn to the Covenant and made honourable amends for his severity towards Parliamentarians.

We must also note the beginning of Milton's blindness. We have fairly full information on the subject from the poet himself. In 1654 one of his admirers, the Athenian Philaras, who represented Parma in Paris, wanted to consult the oculist Thévenot on his behalf. Milton described his symptoms to him.[2] He may have been suffering from glaucoma, perhaps complicated by cataract, but more probably from amaurosis, the paralysis of the optical nerve. The trouble had begun about 1644—'about ten years ago', wrote Milton. By 1649 the left eye was useless. From 1645–49 Milton thus went through an apprenticeship in blindness, accustoming himself to arranging things, to

---

[1] See p. 107.   [2] Bohn III, 507-8.

L

classifying, to dictating. This apprenticeship was made particularly painful by violent headaches and attacks of dizziness. Moreover, as Milton was his own doctor, and did not spare himself, he 'suffered in the kidneys and intestine'.

His morale is known to us in part, thanks to a letter he sent on April 21st, 1647, to his young Florentine friend, Carlo Dati.

> But as soon as I came to that passage in which you tell me you had previously sent me three letters which must have been lost, then the simplicity of my joy began to be imbued with grief and agitated with regret. But something more disastrous soon appears. It is often a subject of sorrowful reflection to me, that those with whom I have been either fortuitously or legally associated by contiguity of place, or some tie of little moment, are continually at hand to infest my home, to stun me with their noise and waste me with vexation, while those who are endeared to me by the closest sympathy of manners, of tastes and pursuits, are almost all withheld from my embrace either by death or an insuperable distance of place; and have for the most part been so rapidly hurried from my sight, that my prospects seem continually solitary and my heart perpetually desolate. . . . I appeal to the tomb of Damon,[1] which I shall ever cherish and revere; his death occasioned the most bitter sorrow and regret, which I could find no more easy way to mitigate than by recalling the memory of those times, when, with those persons, and particularly with you, I tasted bliss without alloy. . . .
>
> Though I must confess that I found other reasons for silence in these convulsions which my country has experienced since my return home, which necessarily diverted my attention from the prosecution of my studies to the preservation of my property and my life. For can you imagine that I could have leisure to taste the sweets of literary ease while so many battles were fought, so much blood shed, and while so much ravage prevailed among my fellow-citizens?[2]

Milton was very discreet, for he made no mention of his father's recent death or the state of his eyes, or even of his hard work and responsibilities as a pedagogue.

---

[1] Dati was named in the *Epithaphium Damonis*, see p. 85.
[2] Bohn III, 500–2.

Teaching is, if one may say so, the most engrossing of
the accessory occupations. Spinoza could polish a lens and a
definition, Maupassant could write a novel on government
foolscap, but when a master is conscientious (as Mallarmé
was not), to create is forbidden him. His day ended, it
only remains for him to read, check, and fill up index-
cards, all these works of patience which might be called
the knitting of men of letters. Milton occupied himself
with such things during these silent years. In 1646, he
undertook a history of Great Britain, four books of which
were ready at the beginning of 1649. In the meantime he
was enriching, with a word here, a phrase there, his Latin
thesaurus, analogous to that of Robert Estienne.

Everything leads us to think that his *Index theologicus* of
Horton days took a new direction in these years from
1645–49.
He was obsessed by the religious problem. He had ceased
to hear the deep notes of the *Ode to the Nativity*. He had
written, in connection with his disappointing marriage:
'Almost the strongest Christian will be ready to despair in
virtue and mutiny against Divine Providence. . . . An over-
tossed faith endangers to shipwreck.'[1]
Milton has not revealed the investigations he was led
to pursue. All that we find is this—in 1641, when he was
attacking the Laudians, his religious ideas were more or
less the same as Young's. When he came to write his epic,
they would no longer be those of any group. The change
seems to have taken place during this period of silence.
His solitude was much deeper than he admitted to Dati.
For a long time past, he had broken with the Anglicans,
the Presbyterians had just spurned him, the rabble dis-
honoured his plea for the rights of the soul, the sermons
of the Independents would have made him die of boredom.
In Cromwell's army a prayer lasted two hours, a sermon
three. And of what use were sermons to him?

Hence we may conclude, if men be not all their lifetime under
a teacher to learn logic, natural philosophy, ethics or mathe-

[1] *The Doctrine and Discipline of Divorce*, Bohn III, 194.

matics, which are more difficult, that certainly it is not necessary
to the attainment of Christian knowledge, that men should sit
all their life long at the feet of a pulpited divine; while he, a
lollard indeed over his elbow cushion, in almost the seventh
part of forty or fifty years teaches them scarce half the principles
of religion.[1]

In these apparently passive years, Milton remade his
religion. He was helped in this notably by Servet, the
Mortalists, Vane and Williams.

Servet had maintained opinions such as—the Trinity is
irrational (Milton would say: 'Scripture does not say in
express words that the Father and the Son are one in
essence. . . . Reason protests strongly against the doctrine
in question . . . a notion as absurd as it is removed from all
human comprehension')[2]—there has been no creation *ex
nihilo*—a part of God is subject to laws—God is at the same
time universal matter and the will that rules it—the Word
is the energy that orders the chaos and executes the decrees
of the divine will—all things have existed from all time in
the mind of God; their manifestations alone, including the
birth of Christ, are inscribed in time—man can please God
by his works and contribute to his own salvation (for
Calvin, man's works were 'stinking' before God)—we
are saved by faith, but not by faith received passively (the
baptism of new-born infants is valueless); only active faith
is accepted as living—we are justified not by the works of
the law: fasts, vows, etc., but by the works of faith, which
are works of love—and God wills our salvation, his spirit
is born in us—the Scriptures make no mention of predestination to perdition, but only predestination to belief.

All these ideas can be found in Milton,[3] veiled in *Paradise
Lost*, openly expressed in his *Christian Doctrine*.

The doctrine of mortality was condemned by Calvin
in his *Psychopannychia*. The English Mortalists in 1643
set forth their teaching in *Man's Mortality*. They maintained
that the whole of man dies to come to life again, body and
soul, on the appointed day. A French critic, the late Denis

[1] *The likeliest means to remove Hirelings out of the Church*, Bohn III, 24.
[2] *Christian Doctrine*, ch. V, Bohn IV, 7 et seq.
[3] See Larson, *Milton and Servet*, PMLA of America, 1926.

20

Saurat, has shown that Milton owed much to this sect, and rendered them services. *Man's Mortality* was reprinted in 1644. Saurat maintains that the following edition, published in 1655, was revised by Milton.[1]

The Mortalists indeed borrowed from the Jewish Cabbala the following ideas—God is light, light is divine. As it was mixed with darkness in the beginning, it has 'retracted' to purify itself—hence the 'outer darkness'. Perfect light is inaccessible to men; but between that and absolute darkness there are degrees. One of such degrees is that state of matter that we call 'light'. The sun forms a screen between us and the unbearable splendour.[2] Light which is contracted, for example in passing through a lens, produces fire. In becoming further condensed, it produces the other elements and all beings.

The origin of the universe is therefore the withdrawal of God. But if God is everywhere, if he is the All, the idea of a soul distinct from the body becomes a useless hypothesis. What an absurdity, moreover, to claim that the body must die because it has been 'the instrument of sin'! We might as well say that the judge should send the axe to the scaffold and acquit the assassin. No, the whole of man dies. But his resurrection will seem to him immediate since, all movement ceasing, time is no longer measurable. On this point Milton quotes Aristotle, for he had adopted the foregoing ideas. The majority of the Mortalists, however, were not quite sure of the resurrection. Others extended it to animals and plants. As to Milton, he asserted that 'God is neither willing, nor, properly speaking, able to annihilate anything altogether'.[3]

The Mortalists, we should note, like Servet or Milton, based themselves on the Bible, but there are many ways of interpreting Scripture. For instance, to elucidate the assertion of The Preacher, 'The spirit shall return to God

---

[1] *Milton et le matérialisme chrétien en Angleterre*, Rieder, 1928.
[2] Hugo had read the Cabbala. He wrote: 'Dans la nuit que vous nommez l'azur'—See *Contemplations* (Ce que dit la bouche d'ombre), and *Dieu* (La Lumière); see also Saurat, *La Religion de Victor Hugo*, Hachette, 1929.
[3] *Christian Doctrine*, ch. VIII. The science of that time denied the organic origin of fossils principally for the reason that God could not have allowed any single one of his works to perish.

who gave it', Milton quotes the passage of the *Suppliant Women* in which Theseus declares that 'each part that constitutes man returns to the place whence it has come— the spirit to the ethereal heaven, the body to the earth'.

We see, says Milton, that 'every constituent part returns, at dissolution, to its elementary principle. This is confirmed by Ezechiel, 37, v. 9: "Come from the four winds, O breath; and breathe upon these slain that they may live". It is certain, therefore, that the spirit of man must have previously departed thither whence it is now summoned to return.'[1]

Sir Henry Vane, who was five years younger than Milton, will often appear in this narrative. Guizot calls him 'le plus éminent, le plus sincère, le plus capable et le plus chimérique des républicains civils'.[2] Clarendon, the historian of the Rebellion, recognized in Vane extraordinary talents and an intelligence which penetrated other people's designs with marvellous sagacity. Cardinal de Retz, who received Vane in 1650, considered him to be astonishingly able, 'd'une capacité surprenante'.

To the great annoyance of his father who was one of Charles's Privy Councillors, Vane had given up Oxford rather than subscribe to the Anglican creed. At twenty-three he was governor of Massachusetts but he had to return the following year because he had defended Mrs. Hutchinson, a Quietist, against the Boston clergy. He was elected to the Short Parliament, and Charles gave him a knighthood and appointed him Treasurer of the Navy. He sat on all the important committees. It was he and Cromwell who, in 1641, had proposed the abolition of the episcopate in the Commons. In 1643 he directed the negotiations with Scotland. Under the Commonwealth he was to organize the navy and become Cromwell's most subtle adversary.

Now this man of outstanding intelligence held in his head a mystic metaphysics of his own, which Cromwell himself, his close friend for years, found beyond his comprehension. His followers, the Vanists, closely resembled

---

[1] Bohn IV, 279.
[2] Guizot, *Histoire de la République d'Angleterre*, Livre I, p. 5.

the Seekers, who did not recognize any church, being persuaded that man had not yet received the full revelation, but must seek it unremittingly. Vane and Milton had at least one common friend in Williams. Directly or indirectly, Sir Henry strengthened Milton's anticlericalism. We can recognize the Seekers or the 'Vanists' in the myth of the virgin Truth, the pieces of which have not all been found.

It was in Massachusetts that Vane linked himself with Roger Williams. Son of a London tailor, singled out by the famous jurist Sir Edward Coke, whose speeches he took down in shorthand, and sent by him to Oxford, he entered the Anglican Church, but was soon repelled by Laud's demands. In 1631, he went into voluntary exile in America. There he became a Congregationalist, then a Baptist, then a Seeker, then an individualist, despite the adjurations of the Reverend John Cotton, the idol and tyrant of Boston, who had also fled from Laud's despotism, but only to become an American Laud.

Now Williams did not only reject Rev. Cotton's theology. He told the colonists that the King had assigned Indian lands to them without any right to do so, and that they ought to have bought them from the natives. He was expelled from the colony the year Vane landed there. He then purchased from the Indians a piece of land in the territory now known as Rhode Island, where he founded the town of Providence. Slavery was forbidden there, and all the inhabitants, without any distinction of religious or philosophical opinions, enjoyed the same rights. This first lay city has to-day as large a population as Leicester.

In 1643 Williams returned to London to obtain a charter from Parliament for his city; some jobbers were trying to appropriate it. At first he lodged with Vane. Milton became his friend. Williams read to him a manuscript that he meant to publish in London, for Providence did not yet possess a printing-press. Milton took him to his own publisher. Roger Williams's manifesto, *The Bloudy Tenent* (i.e. *The Bloody Tenet*) *of Persecution for Cause of Conscience*, came out shortly before *Areopagitica*. The Presbyterians immediately had it condemned to be burnt, but it circulated in the army.

In this pamphlet Williams paid homage to the Baptists, who, in 1614, had been the first to declare themselves for the lay character of the State. He related how one of them continued his propaganda after he was put into prison. Receiving as he did a pint of milk each day, he wrote with milk on the paper wrapped round the bottle. A friend from outside made this sympathetic ink legible by warming the paper, and took care of the printing. 'It was with milk', exclaimed Williams, 'with this mild and beneficial beverage, that they were writing for the peace of souls and of states. The reply was written in blood.'

> Jesus did not institute a national church.—A religion which needs arms of flesh and blood to maintain itself cannot be true.—Evil is always evil, but to permit it may be a good.— The spiritual and temporal swords cannot be in the hand of one and the same person.—The civil magistrates [are] bound to preserve the bodies of their subjects, and not to destroy them for conscience sake.—The civil magistrate owes two things to false worshippers: firstly, Permission; secondly, Protection.[1]

Williams was less well-read than Milton, but he was better able to bear with his fellow-creatures and manage them. His tolerance excluded neither atheists, Turks nor Papists. He confessed, however:

> I have little hope till those flames [kindled in the bloody persecutions of Queen Mary] are over, that this Discourse against the doctrine of persecution for cause of conscience should pass current . . . even among the sheep of Christ themselves. Yet *liberavi animam meam*; I have not hid within my breast my soul's belief.

Williams often spoke of 'soul liberty'. It might be said that Milton never spoke of anything else.

The ideas entertained by Milton at the time were therefore very nearly those of the Quakers. George Fox possibly never met Milton, but his ideas were spreading throughout the land. This inspired cobbler was announcing from county to county, with exceptional power, that the Christian ought to entrust himself to the Light Within. He began his campaign in 1646. He was twenty-two.

[1] Masson III, 112–19.

Imprisoned over and over again, he yet made numerous disciples who soon came to be named the Quakers and called themselves simply Children, or Friends, of the Light, strange people who took off their hats to no one, thee'd and thou'd everybody, and forbade themselves adornment in dress and the use of arms. They did not swear, even before a judge, did without sacraments and clergy, and called churches 'steeple-houses'. Met together in the house of one of them, they awaited in silence, 'a silence of Quakers', sometimes with trembling, the impulses of the Spirit. Voltaire spoke of them with respect. It was the sect for which Milton had the least contempt.

Milton, however—was it pride or modesty?—never took part in these collective appeals to the supernatural. Reason is, moreover, a permanent Inward Light.

Again, Milton differed from the Quakers in his veneration for the Bible. To them the Scriptures were but a 'secondary rule, subordinated to the Spirit', who still deigns to speak to men directly. Milton considered that we ought to believe all that is clearly expressed in the Bible. When it says that 'God was angry' or 'repented', we may be certain that other terms would translate the unknowable reality less faithfully. The immediate meaning, however, is not necessarily the only one. Here a personal factor intervenes. If God has permitted the sacred text to be corrupted by copyists, 'it is to teach us by the very circumstance that the Spirit which is given to us is a more certain guide than Scripture; whom therefore it is our duty to follow'.[1]

When, despite our diligence, a certain passage remains closed to us, it is because it is concerned with a truth we do not yet need. To each one his truth,[2] and ours, provisionally, stops there.

To be certain that Milton held, or believed he held, his rule of faith solely from the Bible, it is sufficient to consult his *Tractatus de Doctrina Christiana* at which he worked until his last days and which he set above his poems ('my best and richest possession'). The theologians had repelled him by 'their formal sophisms and grammatical quibbles'.[3] They

[1] *Christian Doctrine*, ch. II.   [2] See p. 132.
[3] Preface to *Christian Doctrine*.

gave themselves up to lengthy demonstrations punctuated with a few verses of Scripture in support. Milton's method was wholly otherwise. He put forward concise affirmations and proved each of them by a succession of Scriptural verses. That was his method at Horton when he grouped under various headings facts and ideas supplied by his reading.

Shortly after the letter to Dati, his father's legacy enabled Milton to dismiss his pupils and, accordingly, to move once more. His new house, in High Holborn, had at least two advantages—it looked on to the gardens of Lincoln's Inn and it was too small to lodge the formidable Powells. Milton installed himself there in September, 1647.

It was there that in April 1648 he turned into verse a few psalms, because Parliament wanted to give a modernized version of them, in common metre (scanned 4, 3, 4, 3, and rhymed abab). He quickly grew weary of the task. 'My mother bore me a speaker of what God made mine own, and not a translator.'[1] He had begun with *Psalm* 80: 'Give ear, O shepherd of Israel . . . come and save us'. He stopped at *Psalm* 88: in which the same lament resounds as in the letter to Dati—'Lover and friend hast thou put far from me, and mine acquaintance into darkness'.

Perhaps he was discouraged by the resumption of the war. Since the two years that Charles had been a prisoner, he had exploited the disagreements of the victors and at the same time was calling to his aid at one time the Irish, at another Mazarin. Moreover, Queen Henrietta and her two sons, who had taken refuge in France, were working in his favour. In this very month of April, 1648, the Welsh rose, soon followed by South-East England, then by the navy. A fleet led by the Prince of Wales blockaded the Thames, and the Scots crossed the Tweed. Fairfax and Cromwell, however, reacted with such force that by the month of August all was virtually over.

[1] *Bucer*, Bohn III, 314.

On August 27th Milton, happy but impatient, addressed
to the Commander-in-Chief of all the forces, the Presbyterian Fairfax, the sonnet mentioned earlier. In it he
extolled Fairfax, stigmatized the 'false North', the Scots
whom Cromwell had just crushed at Preston, and warned
the master:

> O yet a nobler task awaites thy Hand;
>   For what can Warr, but endless warr still breed,
>   Till Truth, and Right from Violence be freed,

This 'nobler task' was to put a stop to the brigandage of
the profiteers:

> . . . In vain doth Valour bleed
> While Avarice, and Rapine share the Land.

In October Milton's wife bore him a second daughter,
Mary, who resembled her mother, and was to sadden the
old age of her father.

IX

AT THE SERVICE OF THE COMMONWEALTH

1649

MILTON had written to Fairfax: 'For what can Warr, but endless warr still breed?' Fairfax might have answered: 'Thy sonnet, friend, must endless pamphlets breed'. Four months later, Milton demonstrated that it was lawful to depose a bad king and to put him to death. Up till that time he had always spoken of the monarchy with respect, and of Charles with hope, but circumstances had dispelled whatever illusions he might have cherished.

The victorious regiments had gone back to their garrisons filled with fury against the 'man of blood' who had forced them to reconquer the country. When they saw Parliament negotiating a fresh compromise with him—probably leading to a fresh war—they resolved upon the King's death.

The Presbyterians held the majority in Parliament by more than 140 votes against 96 to the Independents, and it was in the interests of their party that Charles should not even be deposed, for he had promised the Scots, in December, 1647, that he would impose Presbyterianism on the English, to the exclusion of all other systems, for three years. Three years was not much, but now that the royalist rising was crushed, more could be hoped for.

In any case, it was essential to save the King. If the army and toleration prevailed, the Presbyterians could no longer hope to rule every soul and hold every living. Therefore they now proclaimed that for good Protestants the person of a king was inviolable.

On this point they were in agreement with the instinct of the country and even with the military leaders, from Commander-in-Chief Fairfax downwards. The commander of the cavalry, Cromwell, was attached to the old institutions. Skippon, who commanded the infantry, although a firm Republican, had a repugnance against shedding the blood of a king. Other Republicans, such as Vane or Algernon Sidney, took into account the national spirit of loyalty to the Crown and feared a military dictatorship.

It thus seemed as if the Presbyterians ought to win this duel between themselves and the army, which had now been going on for two years. Yet their success would have plunged the country into the worst religious servitude. Just when the Scots were crossing the border, in May 1648, Parliament had taken advantage of the disorder to vote, amongst other measures scarcely credible, the death penalty for anyone who should deny the Trinity, and terms of imprisonment for the partisans of free will! Thus by a fatal sequence of events, it was necessary either to renounce liberty of conscience or to sacrifice this King who insisted on being absolute.

Milton considered it urgent to set up against the Presbyterians a rational theory of monarchy, the opinions of their own highest authorities, from Zwinglius to John Knox, and finally their own example. The theory derived from an undisputed principle:

> No man, who knows aught, can be so stupid to deny, that all men naturally were born free, being the image and resemblance of God himself, and were, by privilege above all the creatures, born to command, and not to obey.[1]

Now this liberty comes from God, who could take it back again. Man can only delegate it, and under conditions. Nations can and should demand an account from their mandatories. The unfaithful magistrate is to be dismissed from his office. A king who makes war on his own people becomes *ipso facto* a tyrant and deserves death.

> For look how much right the King of Spain hath to govern us at all, so much right hath the King of England to govern us tyrannically. If he, though not bound to us by any league, coming from Spain on person to subdue us, or to destroy us, might lawfully by the people of England either be slain in fight,

[1] *Tenure of Kings and Magistrates*, Bohn II, 8.

or put to death in captivity, what hath a native king to plead,
bound by so many covenants, benefits and honours, to the
welfare of his people; ... Nor is it distance of place that
makes enmity, but enmity that makes distance.[1]

How could the Presbyterians forget that they had already
virtually deposed the King by refusing him obedience in
1637, that they had persecuted and beleaguered him, that
they would have killed him twenty times over if chance or
flight had not saved him from their hands? The reason of
their completely changed attitude was their cupidity.

Milton called this new manifesto *Of the Tenure of Kings and
Magistrates*. This title expressed everything. Among the
Anglo-Normans, *tenure* designated the land of a 'tenant'
(*tenancier*) or the conditions on which he 'held' it (*la tenait*).
The King was not, as the Presbyterians repeated, 'the Lord's
anointed', but one magistrate among others, who held his
power from a contract.

Milton hoped to convince those of the Independents
who hesitated and even the conscientious Presbyterians
like Thomas Young.

As for the party called presbyterians, of whom I believe
very many to be good and faithful Christians, though misled
by some of turbulent spirit, I wish them ... not to compel
unforcible things, in religion especially ...[2]

Whilst, however, he was hastily marshalling arguments
and quotations, the army was taking action. On December
6th, 1648, Colonel Pride, a foundling and former carter,
'purged' the House of Commons by reducing it to the
'ninety Independents'. Vane protested against this violent
measure. He protested even more loudly and retired to
his estate, when this truncated assembly, the Rump Parliament, decided to have the King judged for high treason
against the nation by a High Court specially appointed.
Vane would have liked Charles to appear before a normal
jury, like any private person. By virtue of this impeccably
democratic procedure, the King's life would have been

---

[1] Bohn II, 19.   [2] Ibid., 35.

saved. The affair, however, was hurried through, in spite of the solicitations of foreign powers and powerful opposition in England itself. Out of one hundred and thirty-five judicial commissioners appointed, so many failed to attend the sittings that the death sentence was carried, unanimously, by only sixty-seven votes. The President of the Court was John Bradshaw, a lawyer to whom Milton, according to Aubrey, was related through his mother. We know with what dignity Charles behaved before his judges and on the scaffold.

Chateaubriand liked to imagine that Milton 'perhaps assisted as a spectator at the beheading of his sovereign, and returned home to write some lines of poetry or to arrange for some children a paragraph of his Latin grammar'. It may be that Milton, on that Tuesday, January 30th, 1649, was present before Whitehall, but then, assuredly, as soon as his poor eyes had seen the axe fall, his ears reminded him how precarious was the position of the conquerors. There rose from the crowd, wrote an eyewitness, 'such a groan as I never heard before and desire I may never hear again'. When Milton returned home, he must have thought very little of the various pieces of writing on which he was then engaged, but much more of the anxieties of Vane. Without his having played any part in it, the irrevocable was accomplished. What would happen now? That was not his business. The men of action would decide.

> When I was released from these engagements [his contest with the Treasury and the writing of *Tenure*] and thought that I was about to enjoy an interval of uninterrupted ease, I turned my thought to a continued history of my country, from the earliest times to the present period. I had already finished four books . . .[1]

He had just been living the Danish invasions over again, when his now superfluous manifesto at last came from the printer's, ten days after the King's execution. Almost immediately, he was torn away from his private pursuits for ten years.

[1] *Second Defence*, Bohn I, 260.

On February 6th, the Rump abolished the House of
Lords. On the 7th, it suppressed the monarchy and
appointed a Council of State, charged with executing its
decisions, for one year. Among the forty-one councillors,
we find about fifteen nobles, among them the Earl of
Salisbury; about ten military men, including Fairfax,
Cromwell and Skippon; two judges; Bradshaw the lawyer,
and finally Vane, who had come out of his retreat at the
entreaties of his colleagues. At first the Council felt its
way: it was heterogeneous and feared the military. On
March 10th, Bradshaw was elected president. On the 13th,
six councillors, Vane among them, were entrusted with the
administration of Foreign Affairs, and requested to 'speak
with Mr. Milton, to know whether he will be employed
as Secretary for the Foreign Tongues'.[1] On the 15th Milton
took the oath. On the 17th the Commonwealth introduced
itself to the European Powers in a manifesto in Latin,
French and Dutch. Milton had made his début.

Phillips assures us that 'he was courted . . . and at last
prevailed with (for he never hunted after preferment, nor
affected the tintamar and hurry of public business)'. Here
again Phillips is not wholly accurate. His uncle probably
hesitated, but, as we have just seen, for less than forty-
eight hours. His visitors had certainly not been lacking in
arguments. The situation of the Commonwealth was a most
precarious one. Six out of the twelve Judges of the High
Court had refused to swear loyalty to it. The Prince of
Wales had been proclaimed king by Scotland and Ireland.
Out of the forty-one Councillors, twenty-two regretted the
Lords and the monarchy. Some Republicans demanded
general elections, which would have caused the Civil War
to break out again. The lands confiscated from the Cavaliers
had passed to new men who rarely troubled themselves
with their feudal obligations and made people regret their
former masters. In short, free England stood in need of all
her friends and every talent available. Now among the
Independents, Milton alone handled Latin, the diplomatic

[1] Masson IV, 79.

language of the time, as a master. He alone, moreover, wrote, spoke or read five or six modern tongues. He could not refuse.

He had no idea, nor had the Council, what tasks were going to fall to him. Because the Government team was so restricted, Milton would have not only to attend diplomatic receptions and receive foreigners of distinction at his table, but also to unmask the royalist emissaries, control the Record Office, supervise the official gazette, *Mercurius politicus* (and often collaborate in it), penetrate the secrets of parties and sects. . . . In short, he was going to be the intellectual jack-of-all-trades of the young Commonwealth.

On this painful subject we are exactly informed by the Order-Books of the Council. As an example, here is an order of May 15th, 1650—

> Ordered: 'That a certain person . . . be searched by Mr. Serjeant Dendy, and that his trunks be brought in and thoroughly searched by Mr. Milton, who is to report to-morrow what he finds in them'.[1]

That Milton may have lent himself to certain unpleasant tasks willingly, is not really surprising. We have seen him in 1641 ready to acquit himself of 'the meanest under-service if God enjoins it'. But he gloried indeed in his abasement!

> Hence, while I applaud those who were victorious in the field, I will not complain of the province which was assigned me; but rather congratulate myself upon it, and thank the Author of all good for having placed me in a station, which may be an object of envy to others rather than of regret to myself.[2]

Yet the Commonwealth kept a close watch on the political press and spared neither seditious writers nor their accomplices. Happily for Milton, the preliminary censorship was dormant, and his position allowed him to help more than one offender. It grieved him that those devoted to the service of ideas, were they political opponents, should

---

[1] Masson IV, 226.   [2] *Second Defence*, Bohn I, 219.

M

have to undergo physical punishment. He had several of them released, won over others, scandalized the Council by letting off a Socinian and even, it is thought, in 1650 saved the life of the poet Davenant, although the latter had fought against the Commonwealth not on paper but in action.

We have seen that Milton entered upon his duties on March 15th. The Council allocated to him as salary two hundred and eighty-eight pounds (the Secretary-General received seven hundred and thirty, the Assistant Secretary three hundred and sixty-five). His personal income amounted at that time to about two hundred pounds.

As Holborn was too far from Westminster for his convenience, and Whitehall was not ready to lodge the the Commonwealth officers, he took two rooms in Charing Cross, between a garden and the tavern where the Invisible College met. Edward Phillips had just gone up to Oxford. Thus the two rooms harboured, besides Milton and his wife, Anne who was not yet three, little Mary aged six months, and John Phillips, a boy of seventeen.

On March 26th, the Council demanded a report on *England's New Chains*, the work of the famous Colonel John Lilburne, leader of the Levellers, and a friend of Cromwell. He accused the officers of fraternizing with the propertied classes instead of maintaining the interests of the people, foretold a dictatorship, demanded the abolition of the privileges of the nobles and a reformed system of suffrage. He had already roused the army in 1647 and been thrice imprisoned; the people of London and a third of the army followed him. To proceed against his book, however, was a delicate matter for Milton. Lilburne detested the Presbyterians, he wanted more liberty for men's consciences and for the press; the leader of the Mortalists was his right arm; certain of his formulae were taken from *Areopagitica*. Milton had the report drawn up by a subordinate. Shortly afterwards, Lilburne was in the Tower, and the army, again in a state of mutiny, was taken in hand by Cromwell once more.

On March 28th the Secretary for Foreign Tongues was invited to write for the public a clear account of the complex situation in Ireland. The whole island had risen at the call of Ormond, the governor appointed by the late King. Southern Ireland, Catholic, was claiming the quasi-autonomy that Charles had promised her. As to the Scottish Presbyterians of Ulster, they could but defy the authority of the regicides. To Englishmen of that time, Erin was *terra incognita*. In Milton's eyes it was sufficient that Ireland was either Papist or Presbyterian, and that the papists had massacred (as he thought) over two hundred thousand of his compatriots a few years earlier.[1] He maintained that the Irish, 'by their own foregoing demerits and provocations, had been justly made the vassals of England'.[2] In fact, the Council wanted to prepare public opinion for the punitive expedition begun by Cromwell in 1650 and completed by his son-in-law, Ireton, in 1652. By the time the repression was accomplished, one-third of the population had disappeared. Thousands of young men and girls were sold to the planters of Barbados and a third of the soil reserved for English colonists.

Only ten days after the execution of Charles, a small book, unique of its kind, *Eikôn Basilikè*, 'Portrait of the King', had been published in London in great secrecy. It purported to be the work of the late King, but was mostly from the hand of one of his chaplains, Gauden, who had made use of materials provided by his master. In it Charles described his sufferings in his prisons, justified his policy with the reservation that he ought to have saved Strafford's life; last, not least, Charles displayed deep piety at every page. This moving book was to become the Royalists' Bible. In twelve months, despite the police, forty-six editions of it appeared, and others arrived from Holland, despite the customs officials. It is estimated that fifty thousand copies were disposed of in a year, an extraordinary figure for the times. Many of the Commonwealth Party

[1] *First Defence*, Bohn I, 117 and above p. 111, n. 2.
[2] *Articles of Peace*, Bohn II, 180.

were disturbed over it; a French version went all over Europe; Milton was ordered to provide a counterblast. On October 6th, 1649, he published *Eikonoklastes*.

He had had wind of Dr. Gauden's pious fraud, but preferred to ignore him and strike at the head, refuting the King point by point, with as much violence as scorn. Kings are poor polemists, he wrote in his introduction, and to argue with them has nothing glorious about it, yet 'I shall make no scruple to take up this gauntlet, though a king's, in the behalf of liberty and the commonwealth' (B. I, 308). To certain allegations of Charles or Gauden, Milton opposed a recent history of the Parliament.[1] To the confidences of the 'Martyr-King', he replied by jeers or the worst calumnies. It was not the moment to be impartial. Charles, like all tyrants, was a fool, a hypocrite, a profligate. Milton, drawing on the *Grand Remonstrance*, compared him to Shakespeare's Richard III and recalled that earlier, when public rumour accused Buckingham of the unexpected death of King James, Charles had forbidden Parliament to open an inquiry.

Milton's arguments, derived mainly from parliamentary documents, reassured some readers, but many more were sickened by his harshness. The work, however, was reprinted in 1650, and the next year the Council ordered that it should be put into French.

A month after the publication of *Eikonoklastes*, Milton was occupying an apartment in the palace of Whitehall and furnishing it with hangings which had belonged to the late King, when a powerful indictment originating from Holland was directed at the Commonwealth.

Charles II's advisers had thought it would be excellent tactics to have the pious regicides publicly condemned precisely by a Protestant authority. Calvinists and Lutherans considered themselves compromised. On the death of Charles I, Holland had immediately recognized his son, who was then taking refuge in that country. Holland was also sheltering at the time a Burgundian Huguenot

[1] *History of the Parliament of England*, by Thos. May, secretary to Parliament, 1647.

known throughout Europe, the man whom Gui Patin[1] called 'le savant et incomparable M. de Saumaise, ce grand personnage qui savait tout et entendait tout, le grand héros de la république des lettres'. Selden spoke of him as 'most admirable'. Saumaise (in literature Salmasius), then aged sixty-one, had been reigning over the university of Leyden for the last twenty years. Richelieu and Mazarin had in vain tried to attract him to France; he loved liberty. He had even refused to write Richelieu's life. At the request of Charles II, he readily promised to brand the English 'parricides'.

In a very short space of time he had written five hundred pages of Latin, which he forthwith turned into French. In November 1649—a month, that is, after *Eikonoklastes*, the *Defensio Regia pro Carolo I* issued from the press. The Council forbade it to enter England as early as November 20th, and on January 8th decided that a refutation was imperative. Milton happened to be present.

> They were not long in looking about for an opponent, but immediately appointed me.[2]

After three hundred years we are in a position to realize the importance of the incident. In the persons of their champions (as Trevelyan tells in his *England under the Stuarts*), two very unequal groups confronted each other—on the one hand 'the white races of Europe and America, in whom the hope of mankind lay, were developing a political structure and a fashion of public sentiment akin to those of Czarist Russia'; on the other, 'the English, unaware of their destiny and of their service, tenacious only of their rights, their religion, and their interests, evolved a system of government which differed as completely from the new continental model as it did from the chartered anarchy of the Middle Ages'. The numerical disproportion was so great that Saumaise himself could have no idea of the significance of the contest. 'La République d'Angleterre', says Guizot, 'parut un fait singulier, purement local, dont

---

[1] A physician, whose racy, sarcastic *Correspondence* is still worth reading. 1601–72.
[2] *Second Defence*, Bohn I, 261.

même dans les Etats encore travaillés par des dissensions civiles, on n'avait pas, sur le continent, à redouter beaucoup la contagion.'[1]

But such was Milton's faith in his country and in liberty that he disregarded the material weakness of his cause. We shall soon hear him glorifying the rôle assigned by God to his country and himself in the interests of the whole world. Since he alone, of all the republican host, could measure himself against Saumaise, he refused to take account of the state of his eyes. In this connection he has left a page that is both characteristic and well known.

> Thus, therefore, when I was publicly solicited to write a reply to the Defence of the royal cause, when I had to contend with the pressure of sickness, and with the apprehension of soon losing the sight of my remaining eye, and when my medical attendants clearly announced, that if I did engage in the work, it would be irreparably lost, their premonitions aroused no hesitation and inspired no dismay. I would not have listened to the voice even of Esculapius himself from the shrine of Epidauris, in preference to the suggestions of the heavenly monitor within my breast; my resolution was unshaken, though the alternative was either the loss of my sight, or the desertion of my duty: and I called to mind those two destinies, which the oracle of Delphi announced to the son of Thetis:
>
> > Two fates may lead me to the realms of night;
> > If staying here, around Troy's wall I fight,
> > To my dear home no more must I return;
> > But lasting glory will adorn my urn.
> > But, if I withdraw from the martial strife,
> > Short is my fame, but long will be my life.
> >
> > *Iliad ix.*
>
> I considered that many had purchased a less good by a greater evil, the meed of glory by the loss of life; but that I might procure great good by little suffering; that though I am blind, I might still discharge the most honourable duties, the performance of which, as it is something more durable than glory, ought to be an object of superior admiration and esteem; I resolved, therefore, to make the short interval of sight, which

[1] Op. cit., Vol. I, p. 206.

was left me to enjoy, as beneficial as possible to the public interest.[1]

Thus, during the year 1650, at the same time that he was attending to his manifold tasks (the trunks of 'a certain person' were searched in May), Milton reconstructed the trial of Charles, and scoffed at the great Saumaise. His left eye was useless, his right eye was hurting at the end of an hour, but neither the King nor Saumaise lost anything thereby. The *Defence of the English People* was registered on December 31st, 1650, and appeared at the end of February—260 in-folio pages, replying point by point to the *Royal Defence*.

When Saumaise could read this he was no longer at Leyden. At the beginning of 1650, the English Council had succeeded in having his book banned in Holland itself. Hurt by this disavowal, Saumaise had accepted the invitation of Queen Christina, who had just lost Descartes and wanted to have some other genius to fill the vacancy. Therefore, Milton's broadsides hit their mark in Stockholm. Christina found Milton's reply so trenchant, so well written and so amusing, that she lost all consideration for 'the great hero of the republic of letters' and made no secret of it. Smarting under this new blow, he whom his colleagues called 'the Terrible' went back to Leyden, there to set to work to refute this insolent Englishman.

Saumaise had proved exceptionally erudite and insulting. Milton repaid him with interest. He ranged from Egypt to Assyria, from the Exodus to the siege of La Rochelle, and called to witness not only 'the divine Plato' (B. I, 140), but the Gaulish king Ambiorix (134). As to the rude personal remarks, let us pass by such commonplaces as *rogue*, *slave*, *ass*, at which no polemist worth his salt could take offence; but many other taunts were definite charges and therefore can shed light on the accuser himself. We will try to marshal them as follows.

A 'foreigner' who 'intrudes into English affairs' (Bohn I, 158 etc.) is a 'pragmatical puppy' (159). Your case is far

---

[1] *Second Defence*, Bohn I, 238 sqq.

worse, since you are 'both a Frenchman and a vagabond' (27), 'a French mountebank' (204) who earns his bread 'by selling of smoke' (16). 'You pedagogue' (203), 'though one should turn you topsyturvy, and inside out, you are but a grammarian' (30). And 'but a poor grammarian' (5), 'a two-penny professor' (14), 'a blot and a stain to all learned men' (28). Besides, your facts are wrong, 'you impudent liar . . . I am ashamed of your lies' (92). Then you repeat yourself, 'you are but a raving distracted cuckoo' (139). Time was when you defended Christian liberty, but now, 'more hungry than any dog, you return greedily to what you have vomited so often' (92). Perhaps you obeyed 'that hotspur your wife' (159), for 'you are the wife of a woman, a he-wolf impregnated by a she-wolf' (166); she 'cried to you: "Either write, or let us fight" ' (211). At any rate, 'O mercenary advocate' (7), you were 'bribed with Charles's jacobuses'[1] (116). To conclude (211): you are 'a second Balaam called upon by another Balak; a very talkative ass rid by a woman . . . the image of that Beast in the Revelation'; a second Judas: 'you will hang yourself and burst asunder as he did, and send beforehand your conscience . . . to that place of torment that is prepared for you'.

In fact, Saumaise was really disinterested and his indignation was not feigned. Only a fortnight after the execution, in a letter to a friend, he had vehemently accused the 'parricides'.[2] The hundred jacobuses promised by Charles II would certainly not have been an adequate fee for a defence like his. Moreover, Charles was so poor that Saumaise had to pay the printer himself. Further, Milton reiterated with increasing violence his atrocious accusations against Charles I, but did not prove any of them. Of all his arguments the strongest was that the Protestants, by rejecting the authority of the popes, went further than they did in rejecting that of kings.

We should do Milton a grave injustice, however, if we ignored those moments when he allows us to survey the battle-field from his *templa serena*. Then we understand his

---

[1] A gold coin, minted in King James's reign, worth about 25*s*.
[2] February 17th, 1649.

indignation and almost excuse his violence. Here is one of those passages. Nowhere has the Christian poet stated his philosophy of liberty more clearly. Discussing the famous text *Matthew* XXII, 21: 'Render unto Caesar the things which are Caesar's', Milton declares:

> Our liberty is not Caesar's; it is a blessing we have received from God himself; it is what we are born to; to lay it down at Caesar's feet, which we derive not from him, which we are not beholden to him for, were an unworthy action, and a degrading of our very nature. If one should consider attentively the countenance of a man, and inquire after whose image so noble a creature were framed, would not any one that heard him presently make answer, that he was made after the image of God himself?[1] Being therefore peculiarly God's own, and consequently things that are to be given to him, we are entirely free by nature, and cannot without the greatest sacrilege imaginable be reduced into a condition of slavery to any man.[2]

It goes without saying that the English Royalists were disgusted. One of them on his copy of the *Defence* inscribed the words—*Liber igni, Author furcâ, dignissimi*—the book richly deserves the fire, the author the gallows. This critic is known to us: he was John Egerton, one of the two brothers who had performed in *Comus*.

Europe, generally, however, was of the opinion of Christina. Many a brother-scholar, moreover, was not sorry to see 'the great Salmasius' thrown off his pedestal. 'Our little David', says Phillips, 'had the courage to undertake this great French Goliath, to whom he gave such a hit in the forehead, that he presently staggered, and soon after fell.' The Council gave their secretary a reward of one hundred pounds. The latter could not accept them after having said so much about the jacobuses of 'young Charles'. The allocation was accordingly cancelled and a vote of thanks recorded in the Order-Book instead.

Right from its first year the *Defence* was reprinted several times and translated into Dutch. (Intended as it was for

---

[1] Cf. 'human face divine' (*Paradise Lost* III, 44); also Francois Mauriac, *Bloc-Notes*, September 26th, 1962: '. . . sur le visage humain, fût-ce le plus ingrat, au fond du regard le plus morne, brille une lumière qui ne saurait venir de la matière aveugle et sourde, ni de ce monde animal, dont la loi est de s'entre-dévorer'.
[2] Bohn I, 63.

Europe, it was not to appear in English until 1692.) It had the honour to be burnt by the hangman in Paris and in Toulouse as early as 1652. In the years that followed, cultured foreigners passing through London did not fail to see, some with admiration, others with horror, first of all Cromwell, and then 'the blind man who had refuted Saumaise'. Some of them visited the house in Bread Street and the room in which he was born. Thus the man who, through patriotism, had sacrificed fame in Europe as a poet, became famous there as a prose writer, for having obeyed his patriotism.

To his pride as a polemist was added in 1651 a great but simple joy: a son, whom he called John, was born to him on March 16th.

His darkness was becoming deeper. After July, 1651, he was seldom present at the Council's sessions. In December he had to give up his rooms to a member of Parliament. He took refuge near St. James's Park, in an attractive house in Petty France (or Petite-France, as people often still wrote). The house (to-day 19 York Street) had a garden around it, and communicated with the Park. Three months later Milton was completely blind.

In order to omit nothing, some account should be given of how Madame de Saumaise was avenged.

In 1646 old Richard Powell, the day-dreamer, had left a succession such as we find in the pages of Balzac, of property mortgaged, secretly owned, undervalued, fictitiously made over to friends trustworthy or not so trustworthy. There remained due to Milton three hundred pounds from the 1627 debt, plus the thousand pounds of the dowry. Mrs. Powell had tried in 1649, by petitioning to Parliament, to recover something of the confiscated property. Milton had obtained the usufruct of certain lands until such time as the debt of 1627 should be liquidated. In 1650 he was fined as a 'retainer of property which had belonged to a delinquent'. He argued that he paid over one-third of the revenue, twenty-six pounds, to Mrs. Powell, but the Parliamentary Commission judged that this rent was purely gratuitous. Milton therefore paid the fine, but suspended the rent, promising his mother-in-law in writing that he would resume his payments when she should have obtained the ruling that they would be taken into account. She petitioned in this sense, but was referred to the Courts. Whereupon she replied to the Commissioners that she was too poor to prosecute her son-in-law and that, moreover, 'she was afraid that her daughter might suffer the consequences of it since Mr. Milton was a harsh and choleric man, who had turned away his wife heretofore for a long space upon some other occasion' (Masson IV, 236–46, 336–41).

Mrs. Powell was to survive her son-in-law and finish her days in comfort.

DARKNESS

(For those blind and their kinsfolk)

Blind at forty-three! 'Ere half my days', Milton protested, by virtue of the tradition which estimated the normal span of a human life at a hundred years.[1] He has left several allusions to his state, which differ considerably. Convinced that nothing happens without the will of God or his permission, he was at first scandalized. He lets something of this appear in the cry of Samson:

O loss of sight, of thee I most complain!
Blind among enemies, O worse then chains,
Dungeon, or beggery, or decrepit age!
Light the prime work of God to mee is extinct
And all her various objects of delight
Annull'd, which might in part my grief have eas'd,
Inferiour to the vilest now become
Of man or worm; the vilest here excell me,
They creep, yet see, I dark in light expos'd
To daily fraud, contempt, abuse and wrong,
Within doors, or without, still as a fool,
In power of others, never in my own;
Scarce half I seem to live, dead more then half.
O dark, dark, dark, amid the blaze of noon,
Irrecoverably dark, total Eclipse
Without all hope of day!
O first created Beam, and thou great Word,
Let ther be light, and light was over all;
Why am I thus bereav'd thy prime decree?[2]

Milton did not indeed imagine these grievances. When we read the words 'fraud', 'abuse', we should think of his daughters selling his books to the rag-merchant to buy themselves ribbons. If he speaks of insult, it is because his adversaries printed in Latin, for all Europe to read, that he was expiating the hours he had spent in Italy or his subversive writings. Would Samson have complained as bitterly of being always in the power of others, if this constant bondage had not been unbearable to a man like Milton? Pierre

---

[1] 'For every wrong he has committed a man must pay the penalty in turn, ten times for each, that is to say, once every hundred years, this being reckoned as the span of a man's life'. Plato, *The Republic*, XI, 615.
[2] *Samson Agonistes*, 67–86.

Villey, whose name is familiar to lovers of Montaigne, was blind.
He declared in his Monde des Aveugles:

> La dépendance de l'aveugle, une dépendance de tous les
> instants, lui pèse lourdement. . . . Il se sent enchaîné. . . . Par-
> dessus tout, il est le jouet du préjugé: quoi qu'il sache faire, il
> est aveugle.

Villey stresses the point that blindness would be bearable in
itself; the majority of blind men are gay, very few commit suicide.
Their suffering comes to them chiefly from men. Samson said this,
Milton experienced it.
The revolt may take on another form. Samson laments that we
can only see with our eyes.[1]

> Since light so necessary is to life,
> And almost life itself, if it be true
> That light is in the Soul,
> She all in every part; why was the sight
> To such a tender ball as th'eye confin'd?
> So obvious and so easie to be quencht,
> And not as feeling through all parts diffus'd,
> That she might look at will through every pore?[2]

Against the reactions of the natural man stand out those of the
believer. The latter are known to us from a sonnet written in 1652,
which is an echo of that of 1631—'How soon hath Time . . .'
Both make reference to the same parable, mark the same anxiety
and terminate similarly in submission.

> When I consider how my light is spent,
>   Ere half my days, in this dark world and wide,
>   And that one Talent which is death to hide,
>   Lodg'd with me useless, though my Soul more bent
> To serve therewith my Maker, and present
>   My true account, least he returning chide,
>   Doth God exact day-labour, light deny'd,
>   I fondly ask; But patience to prevent
> That murmur, soon replies, God doth not need
>   Either man's work or his own gifts, who best
>   Bear his milde yoak, they serve him best, his State

---

[1] Adam wonders why God created woman—see above, p. 115.
[2] *Samson Agonistes*, 90–97. Same idea in Diderot. See also Balzac, *La Messe de l'Athée*, and the studies of Jules Romains.

Is Kingly. Thousands at his bidding speed
And post o're Land and Ocean without rest:
They also serve who only stand and waite.

*This admission of an inward struggle was not known until 1673,
long after victory had come. Friends and the public saw only the
victor. A sonnet dictated in 1655 shows him as proud of his blindness as a veteran of his wounds.*

To Mr. Cyriack Skinner *upon his Blindness*

Cyriack, this three years day these eys, though clear
    To outward view, of blemish or of spot;
    Bereft of light, thir seeing have forgot,
    Nor to thir idle orbs doth sight appear
Of Sun or Moon or Starre throughout the year,
    Or man or woman. Yet I argue not
Against heavns hand or will, nor bate a jot
    Of heart or hope; but still bear vp and steer
Right onward. What supports me, dost thou ask?
    The conscience, Friend, to have lost them overply'd
    In Liberties defence, my noble task,
Of which all Europe talk from side to side.
    This thought might lead me through the worlds vain mask
    Content though blind, had I no better guide.

The 'defence' mentioned here was the reply to Saumaise. In the
Second Defence, *published before this sonnet was composed,
Milton had asserted that blindness could be a mark of the divine
favour. In ancient times certain blind men were venerated for their
wisdom to the point that their misfortune was attributed to the
jealousy of the gods. Did not Apollonius write of Tiresias in the*
Argonautica:

To men he dar'd the will divine disclose,
Nor fear'd what Jove might in his wrath impose.
The gods assigned him age, without decay,
But snatched the blessing of his sight away.[1]

*But, argued Milton, our God is Truth: those who spread the
truth are dear to him, their blindness can be a mark of his love.
Moreover, how many blind men were 'as distinguished for wisdom
in the cabinet as for valour in the field'. And, after all, what are
my crimes?*

---

[1] *Second Defence*, Bohn I, 236.

And with respect to myself, though I have accurately examined my conduct, and scrutinized my soul, I call thee, O God, the searcher of hearts, to witness, that I am not conscious, either in the more early or in the later periods of my life, of having committed any enormity, which might deservedly have marked me out as a fit object for such a calamitous visitation. . . . I again invoke the Almighty to witness, that I never, at any time, wrote anything which I did not think agreeable to truth, to justice, to piety.[1]

It is voluntarily, said Milton, that I have become blind, and if I had to choose, I should prefer my lack of physical sight to the deprivation of moral vision of my adversaries.

[My blindness] keeps from my view only the coloured surfaces of things, while it leaves me at liberty to contemplate the beauty and stability of virtue and of truth. . . . There is, as the apostle has remarked, a way to strength through weakness.[2] Let me then be the most feeble creature alive, as long as that feebleness serves to invigorate the energies of my rational and immortal spirit; as long as in that obscurity, in which I am enveloped, the light of the divine presence more clearly shines, then, in proportion as I am weak, I shall be invincibly strong; and in proportion as I am blind, I shall more clearly see. O that I may thus be perfected by feebleness and irradiated by obscurity! And, indeed, in my blindness, I enjoy in no inconsiderable degree the favour of the Deity, who regards me with more tenderness and compassion in proportion as I am able to behold nothing but himself. . . . For the divine law not only shields me from injury, but almost renders me too sacred to attack; not indeed so much from the privation of my sight, as from the overshadowing of those heavenly wings which seem to have occasioned this obscurity; and which, when occasioned, he is wont to illuminate with an interior light, more precious and more pure.[3]

Finally, in Paradise Lost *the sublime opening of Book III,* 'Hail holy Light . . .,' *brought the poet to speak of his state in definitive terms—I am blind, but poetry remains to me; blind, but I still possess the inward light.*

[1] *Second Defence*, Bohn I, 237.
[2] A thought dear to Milton, inscribed by him in the albums of friends.
[3] *Second Defence*, Bohn I, 239.

I sung of *Chaos* and *Eternal Night*,
Taught by the heav'nly Muse to venture down
The dark descent, and up to reascend,
Though hard and rare: thee I revisit safe
And feel thy sovran vital Lamp; but thou
Revisit'st not these eyes, that rowle in vain
To find thy piercing ray, and find no dawn;
So thick a drop serene[1] hath quencht their Orbs,
Or dim suffusion veild.[2] Yet not the more
Cease I to wander where the Muses haunt
Cleer Spring, or shadie Grove, or Sunnie Hill,
Smit with the love of sacred song; but chief
Thee Sion and the flowrie Brooks beneath
That wash thy hallowd feet, and warbling flow,
Nightly I visit: nor somtimes forget
Those other two equald with me in Fate,
So were I equald with them in renown,
Blind *Thamyris* and blind *Mæonides*,[3]
And *Tiresias* and *Phineus* Prophets old:
Then feed on thoughts, that voluntarie move
Harmonious numbers; as the wakeful Bird
Sings darkling, and in shadiest Covert hid
Tunes her nocturnal Note. Thus with the Year
Seasons return, but not to mee returns
Day, or the sweet approach of Ev'n or Morn,
Or sight of vernal bloom, or Summers Rose,
Or flocks, or herds, or human face divine;
But cloud in stead, and ever-during dark
Surrounds me, from the chearful waies of men
Cut off, and for the Book of knowledg fair
Presented with a Universal blanc
Of Natures works to mee expung'd and ras'd,
And wisdome at one entrance quite shut out.
So much the rather thou Celestial Light
Shine inward, and the mind through all her powers
Irradiate, there plant eyes, all must from thence
Purge and disperse, that I may see and tell
Of things invisible to mortal sight.[4]

[1] Glaucoma.   [2] Cataract.   [3] Homer.
[4] *Paradise Lost* III, 18-55.

X

THE COMMONWEALTH'S GREATNESS
AND FALL

1649–1653

MILTON had been blind for several weeks when, on May 2nd, 1652, his wife gave him a third daughter. This child was to resemble her father and to become his favourite assistant. He enrolled her forthwith among the poets and the regicides by calling her Deborah. How could he do otherwise than apply to the victories of the Commonwealth the song of triumph of the Prophetess: 'The kings came and fought . . . the stars in their courses fought against Sisera'? Assuredly this birth of his daughter seemed to Milton a good omen.[1]

The young mother, however, died three days after her confinement, and a month later little John, the only son, died too 'through the ill usage or bad constitution, of an ill-chosen nurse' (Phillips).

How the blind man's life was organized, responsible as he was for three children, the eldest not yet six, it did not occur to Phillips to note. We know, however, that the Council and a few friends came forward with offers of help. Milton declared proudly:

> Nor do the persons of principal distinction in the commonwealth suffer me to be bereaved of comfort, when they see me bereaved of sight, amid the exertions which I made, the zeal which I shewed, and the dangers which I run for the liberty which I love.[2]

Without reducing his salary, they lightened his service. He was no longer seen receiving ambassadors or searching suspects. As early as January 1652, he had ceased to edit the *Mercurius politicus*. From March onwards he was seconded, or if necessary replaced, by an elderly German

---

[1] He had alluded to the prophetess in the *First Defence*, Bohn I, 26.
[2] *Second Defence*, Bohn I, 240.

polyglot and poet, Weckherlin, then by the famous Secretary-General to the Council, Thurloe, who in turn had recourse to a young Latinist of the name of Meadows. Milton was fully worthy of this consideration. He dictated as many official letters in 1652 as during the whole of the three previous years.

Among the friendships with which he was blest, first to be mentioned is that of Lady Ranelagh, the Royalist who had entrusted her son to him in 1644. Nothing does them greater honour than their mutual sympathy. Men of talent thronged the receptions of the most cultured Englishwoman of the times. To meet the man who was then the most cultured of Englishmen, she had only to cross St. James's Park. She watched over Milton and his children until the day when, in 1656, she had to accompany her husband to Ireland. That year, in May, Milton was to write to her son, then an undergraduate at Oxford:

> Farewell, my well-beloved Richard, and allow me to exhort and incite you to virtue and piety, like another Timothy, by the example of that most exemplary woman, your mother....[1]

Again, in September 1656:

> Now your most excellent mother, on her way to Ireland— whose departure ought to be a matter of no ordinary regret to both of us (for to me also she has stood in the place of all kith and kin: *nam et mihi omnium necessitudinum loco fuit*), carries you this letter herself.[2]

This 'all kith and kin' doubtless means that the Agars and the Christophers were prevented from helping him. Edward Phillips, who left Oxford in 1651, was working for the booksellers and giving private lessons. His brother John was an additional responsibility for Milton and worried him by his flightiness. None the less he did something for his uncle in this year 1652. Proud of his intelligence and of his Latin, he took upon himself to refute one of the scurrilous pamphlets which from time to time were thrown like mud at the regicide. In a fatherly way, the veteran helped his young avenger. On Christmas Eve

[1] Masson V, 268, or Bohn III, 514.
[2] Masson V, 277-8, or Bohn III, 511.

an octavo volume—*Joannis Philippi Angli Responsio* ...
crowned this collaboration.

Two other of his former pupils brought some gaiety
into the Milton home. Henry Lawrence, not an outstanding
figure, was the son of the Parliamentarian who was to
preside over Cromwell's successive councils. Cyriack
Skinner, then aged twenty-five, was the son of a Lincolnshire squire and the grandson on his mother's side of Sir
Edward Coke. His revenues allowed him to study sciences
and politics and to watch over his former master. In 1654
he came to live near him, to be at his disposal at any moment.
A sonnet that Milton addressed to him has just been quoted
and we shall have occasion to refer to another.

Why did Milton never honour with a line brave Roger
Williams, who had fought at his side in 1644 and who sailed
back from America for the second and last time at the very
beginning of this sad year 1652? He came to plead for
new guarantees for Providence, whose freedom was
threatened by the neighbouring colonies. Moreover, he
wanted to publish his reply to fresh attacks from the tyrant
of Boston. This reply came out as early as April, but
Williams spent two years besieging government offices
before he could cross the seas again, in possession of his
charter. He thus had ample time to consort with his friend.
For instance, they worked together, Williams perfecting
Milton's Dutch (New York was still Nieuwe-Amsterdam)
and Milton, Williams' Greek and Hebrew. Had the need
arisen, Williams could have taught him something about
intrepidity.

It will be recalled that Williams had been secretary to
Sir Edward Coke. One of this lawyer's daughters, Mrs.
Sadleir, was an Anglican and a Royalist. Doubtless through
gratitude to his former patron, Williams resolved to snatch
this poor benighted woman from her ignorance. He first
of all sent her some meditations he had published and she
thanked him for them politely. He then offered her his
Bloody Tenet of 1644. She returned it to him forthwith,
begging him that he would 'trouble her no more in this
kind'. Whereupon in a third missive, Williams recast

the King's trial for her, and recommended her to read
Eikonoklastes in the conviction that Milton's eloquence
would leave the good lady without a reply. But she did
reply, and did not mince her words:

> It seems you have a face a brass so that you cannot blush. . . .
> For Melton's book that you desire I should read, if I be not
> mistaken that is he that has wrote a book of the Lawfulness of
> Divorce; and, if report says true, he had at that time two or
> three wives living. This perhaps were good doctrine in New
> England, but it is most abominable in Old England. For his
> book that he wrote against the late King that you would have
> me read, you should have taken notice of God's judgment
> upon him, who struck him with blindness; and, as I have
> heard, he was fain to have the help of one Andrew Marvell,
> or else he could not have finished that most accursed libel.
> God has begun his punishment upon him here; his punishment
> will be hereafter in Hell.[1]

Andrew Marvell was, of all men living, the most capable
of understanding Milton. The worth of Skinner and
Williams lay chiefly in their moral qualities. Marvell was
a poet, a scholar, a Puritan without prudery and a broad-
minded republican. Born in 1621, a graduate of Cambridge
in 1639, during four years in Europe he had learnt Dutch,
French, Italian and Spanish. Fairfax gave him to his only
daughter as her tutor. In his childhood he had been linked
with the Skinner family, and it was as a friend that he
was welcomed in Petite-France. In February 1653, since
Weckherlin was given up by his doctors, Milton asked
Bradshaw, the President of the Council, to reserve the post
for Marvell:

> . . . Mr. Marvell: a man who, both by report and the converse
> I have had with him [I can recommend as] of singular desert
> for the State to make use of; who also offers himself if there be
> any employment for him. . . . This, my Lord, I write sincerely,
> without any other end than to perform my duty to the public in
> helping them to an able servant,—laying aside those jealousies
> and that emulation which mine own condition might suggest
> to me by bringing in such a coadjutor.[2]

We must now revert to the remarks of Mrs. Sadleir.

[1] Masson IV, 530.   [2] Ibid., 479.

In the first place, because, in her naive way, she reflected her orthodox but indifferently informed entourage. This in turn was representative of the average Englishman. Her letter confirms that the poet Milton was unknown to the mass of English readers and that, moreover, unlike the scholars of England or of Europe, this mass knew scarcely anything of Milton's learned dissertations on the government of the church or the city, whereas his opinions on marriage, written in English, had spread over the whole country and scandalized all right-thinking people. The divorcer was a depraved man, a reprobate, probably a polygamist, in any case a man never to be read. It was this ostracism by all his fellow-countrymen, by this nation whom he esteemed so highly, and not the bites of a few enraged attackers, that caused Milton to say sorrowfully: 'For God, it seems, intended to prove me, whether I durst alone take up a rightful cause against a world of disesteem, and found I durst' (*Bucer*, Bohn III, 281).

Secondly, the very uncertainties of honest Mrs. Sadleir provide us with one certainty well worth having. Writing from the provinces in 1652 or 1653, she asked if the abettor of regicide and the 'divorcer' were the same man. Although Milton had then been Latin secretary for three or four years, she had not heard of the fact. And yet she did know of his quite recent blindness. She was quite sure that God had struck him for having written against the King and that he had needed 'the help of one Marvell'. How could she be ignorant of almost everything concerning 'Melton' and give him as collaborator the man most capable of helping him?—Skinner was her nephew. Some scrap of news emanating from London had enlightened her as to what her nephew's friend was about. Now Milton had needed no help to finish *Eikonoklastes*; it was the reply to Saumaise which had cost him his sight. We are entitled, therefore, to associate Marvell with the success of the *Defence of the English People* and we can understand better Milton's letter to Bradshaw.

Milton in turn surprises us by having neglected poetry so much in these years 1652–53. It seems most probable that the sonnet 'When I consider how my light is spent' dates from the early months of 1652. In May came a sonnet for Cromwell, in July another for Vane. In August an anonymous factum arrived from the Hague, *Regii Sanguinis Clamor ad Coelum*, 'the royal blood cries to heaven', so trenchant and so well informed that the Council called upon Milton to answer it. He was still a sick man and wanted first of all to finish with Saumaise, whose smashing retort could not be long in coming. So he spent several months inquiring who had written *Regii Sanguinis*, correcting his nephew's Latin, and revising Durie's French version of *Eikonoklastes*,[1] which arrived in France about January 1653. In August, 1653, his strength being recovered because he had given up his now purposeless barbarous medical treatment, he played, like a beginner, with putting into rhyme eight psalms in eight days in eight different metres, and translated one of Horace's odes[2]—the maestro was practising his scales. In September came great news— Saumaise was dead and without having printed anything more. His reply was ready for publication, but who knew when it would appear? The field was clear. Helped, it would seem, by Marvell, Milton began his refutation of *Regii Sanguinis — Pro Populo Anglicano Defensio Secunda*.

To sum up, the poet's contribution at this time consisted of three sonnets and a few exercises in prosody. Yet Milton had considerable leisure and his virtuosity was not diminished. Is it possible to think that his apprenticeship in darkness, his bereavements, his household cares perhaps, paralysed his creativeness? The three sonnets will provide the answer.

In the first, 'When I consider . . .', he deplored his unused talent. He held, therefore, as null and void all his letters in Ciceronian Latin to the rulers of the Continent. But he concluded that, since he was blind, he was dispensed from producing his real work, a great poem. Patience said to him: 'God has willed it so, resign thyself'. The proposition which was implied, namely that blindness was

[1] *Eikonoklastès*, par le Sr. Jean Milton, traduite et corrigée par l'autheur. Dugard, London, 1652 (old style).
[2] I, 5, *Ad Pyrrham*: 'What slender youth, Pyrrha . . .'

incompatible with poetic creation, was left untouched. Yet, before proving that a blind man could be inspired by the poetic Muse, Milton had affirmed this possibility again and again. In the final analysis we are here dealing with three Miltons—the poet, grieved at remaining silent; the politician, delighted with playing a rôle; last, the Puritan, who approved both.

The poet's regret was justified, since to hide one's talent is worthy of death. But to serve liberty is also a duty. The dignified excuse of blindness was a kind of alibi supplied by the Puritan. What is called in France *un cas de force majeure* is known in England as an Act of God. The man who wrote with his left hand could thus continue without remorse and his next two sonnets are political gestures. Milton did not care to admit the fact to himself, but he was fascinated by the drama which was unfolding so close to him. He watched its every act and scene. This was basically what he meant by 'only stand and wait'.

The spectacle was all the more absorbing for being far from clear. A fairly good sign of this confusion was that Milton addressed in rapid succession the head of the army and the spirit of Parliament, as if he refused to choose between them. Yet, from one sonnet to the other, differences appear, revealing as to the author's position. To make this point clear, let us recall the happenings and doings that Milton observed with most eagerness at this time.

In three years, the Commonwealth had united the people of the British Isles, a task in which eight hundred years of monarchy had failed; it had the best soldiers in Europe; the American territories had been won over, willingly or by force; the navy, thanks to Vane, was excellent; the Navigation Act ensured the future of commerce. After a long lapse, England was making her appearance again in Europe. In turn Spain, Florence, Genoa, Venice, the Swiss cantons, the Hansa towns, sought the regicides' friendship. In September 1650, just after Dunbar, Henry Vane had gone to Cardinal de Retz with offers of alliance. In February 1652, Mazarin was already talking of surrendering Dunkirk. Ten months later, Louis XIV would recognize the English Commonwealth. This resurgence elated Milton: he saw in it the hand of God, and the dream of Grotius surpassed by the predestined race.

Unfortunately, the masters of the house were not agreed among themselves. Parliament represented the propertied middle classes, the army came from the people. The members of Parliament, who had almost all been sitting for more than ten years, formed cliques. No longer having either king, lords, or prelates to guide or restrain them, their power was absolute and extended to all domains. About a hundred men made the appointments to all the vacant posts, handed out all privileges, administered all the wealth of the State and intervened in affairs as paltry as the Powell inheritance. On one occasion, they argued for three weeks over some legal jargon. The inevitable had occurred. If the leaders remained honest, in the secondary—and yet active—ranks, greed, a cynical selfishness, easy morals, tarnished the memory of the Pyms and the Eliots.[1]

The forty thousand invincibles of the New Model Army found it burdensome to obey a handful of 'lawyers and babblers', that Rump which, after all, owed its existence to Colonel Pride. The army clamoured for social and political reforms, a new Chamber which would be honest and up to normal strength. The Rump adjourned elections and reforms, suspended army pay, reduced the strength of the regiments.

No incident of this civil cold war could escape Milton; even the schemes and scoops of the sharks were known to him, for one of his assiduous visitors was Needham, the versatile journalist of doubtful loyalty, formerly a detractor of the Court, then of Parliament, imprisoned on the strength of a report by Milton, brought back to the straight path by Milton, finally entrusted, thanks to Milton, with editing the official weekly, *Mercurius politicus*. Milton, however, counted on the disinterested group of which Vane was the

---

[1] The French 'Convention Nationale' (1792–95) accomplished a remarkable amount of excellent legislation, but was followed by the corrupt 'Directoire' to which Bonaparte put an end in 1799.

leader. As to the verbiage, it was better than the silence which follows the death of liberty.

Cromwell was difficult to assess. At Westminster he could comment on a psalm for an hour at a time. Yet he loathed speechifiers. He would say to his soldiers, in the same breath and without smiling: 'Trust in God and keep your powder dry'. He was right to want to 'settle the land', but why did he hint in a select meeting that 'some mixture of monarchy might be useful'? From that day the prudent Whitlocke kept an eye on him. Vane had always watched him. As for Milton, despite the impure contacts of politics, he could still repeat what he had declared to Diodati in former days: 'When any one ... dares to feel and speak and be that which the highest wisdom throughout all ages has taught to be best, to that man I attach myself forthwith by a kind of real necessity, wherever I find him'.[1] For the Cavaliers Cromwell was 'the Brewer'; Needham had formerly nicknamed him Noll Maggotface, Nose Almighty, Copper-face, the Town-Bull of Ely; the Levellers called him a despot and the Scots a blasphemer. But Milton paid homage to his genius. Marvell was justified in writing:

> 'Tis madness to resist or blame
> The force of angry Heaven's flame;[2]

Cromwell, moreover, was something more than the lightning that strikes and kills. Milton and Marvell could but praise his piety, his application to work, his civic and domestic virtues.

On one point, however, he disappointed Milton and Vane. This was in regard to the 'soul liberty' dear to Williams. Personally, Cromwell claimed to be merely a Seeker, and he respected a man's conscience. To the fanatical Parliamentarians he declared: 'I would rather that Mahometanism were permitted among us than that one of God's children should be persecuted'[3] ... But he grieved to see the parishes without accredited pastors, given over to the rivalries of the sects, and drifting into paganism. He wanted to give them a pious and tolerant

---

[1] See above, p. 58.   [2] Masson IV, 478.   [3] Ibid., 394.

clergy, recruited from all denominations and, in addition—
there Milton was no longer with him—paid by the State.

Milton was persuaded that State-support makes hirelings
and that a national clergy always tended to appeal to the
temporal sword. He learnt with anguish that certain
Presbyterians and so-called Independents were obstinately
manoeuvring with a view to being hall-marked and hand-
fed by the State. Until something better could be had,
they had persuaded Parliament to vote on June 7th, 1650,
an 'Order for the preparation of a General Bill for the
Advancement of the Gospel in all parts of this Commonwealth'. Acute problems had immediately arisen. How
was this home mission to be financed? The tithe-system
was a relic of popery, but could anything better be devised?
What theological compromise could satisfy Presbyterians
and Independents alike? Would this mission be adequate?
Was it not essential to have a resident Puritan in each
rectory? Would the squires relinquish their centuries-old
right of presentation?

The months went by in debate after debate. The name
of the Act was altered several times. The partisans of the
separation of Church and State, Vane at their head, vied
with each other in energy. On April 29th, 1652, however,
a committee on which Cromwell sat was charged to
examine 'how a godly and able ministry might be settled'
without having recourse to tithes, and at the same time
it was decreed that 'provisionally' the tithes would be
maintained. A few days later Milton sent to Lord-General
Cromwell a petition in fourteen lines entitled *On the pro-
posalls of certaine ministers at the Committee for the Propagation
of the Gospell*.

The construction repeats that of the sonnet to Fairfax—
praise of the soldier, reminder of the difficulties which
await him, finally the petition:

> *Cromwell*, our cheif of men, who through a cloud
>   Not of warr onely, but detractions rude,
>   Guided by faith and matchless Fortitude
>   To peace and truth thy glorious way hast plough'd,

> And on the neck of crowned Fortune proud
>> Hast reard Gods Trophies, and his work pursu'd,
>> While *Darwen* stream with blood of Scotts imbru'd,
>> And *Dunbarr feild* resounds thy praises loud,
> And *Worsters* laureat wreath; yet much remaines
>> To conquer still; peace hath her victories
>> No less renownd then warr, new foes arise
> Threatning to bind our soules with secular chaines:
>> Helpe us to save free Conscience from the paw
>> Of hireling wolves whose Gospell is their maw.

Milton found himself in agreement with two-thirds of the country. Neither the Episcopalians, nor the mass of the Independents wanted a subsidized Puritanism. The maintenance of the tithe had only won twenty-seven votes out of forty-four. The matter rested there—until the following year.

The sonnet to Vane was inspired by the declaration of war on Holland. In its early days the Commonwealth had proposed to its neighbour the fusion of the two States into one—which would have ruled the seas. Holland ruled them already, and rejected the plan. Hence the Navigation Act (August–October 1651), by which goods coming to England were to be carried in English ships, or in ships belonging to the country from which the goods came. The 'waggoners of all seas' often displayed their dissatisfaction and there was a possibility of a war breaking out. Vane wanted it to break out for three reasons—'Tout régime nouveau sent le besoin de s'agrandir pour s'affermir' (Guizot); English commerce was impatient; finally Vane counted on the exploits of his navy to take down Cromwell's army a peg or two.

On May 17th, 1652, Vane was elected President of the Council. On the 19th, Tromp put in an appearance off Dover. Blake happened to be there, and without anyone knowing the reason even yet, Dutch and British exchanged shots for four hours. London was furious. The Dutch strove in vain to smooth over the incident, and sent an ambassador who arrived in London on June 11th. Vane resigned on the 14th and the machine functioned without him. On July 7th, Parliament passed a 'Declaration of the

Causes of the War against the Dutch', and ordered the same to be translated into Dutch, French and Latin. The Latin translation was Milton's task. He acquitted himself of it gladly. This monstrous war between Protestant republics might indirectly ensure liberty of conscience for the English. In a lively sonnet, he congratulated Vane on having prepared it, and here and there blamed Cromwell implicitly.

> *Vane,* young in yeares, but in sage counsell old,
>   Then whome a better Senatour nere held
>   The helme of *Rome,* when gownes not armes repelld
>   The feirce *Epeirot* and the *African* bold,
> Whether to settle peace, or to unfold
>   The drift of hollow states, hard to be spelld,
>   Then to advise how warr may best, upheld,
>   Move by her two maine nerves, Iron and Gold
> In all her equipage; besides to know
>   Both spirituall powre and civill, what each meanes
>   What severs each thou'hast learnt, which few have don.
> The bounds of either sword to thee wee ow.
>   Therfore on thy firme hand religion leanes,
>   In peace, and reck'ns thee her eldest son.

Milton was filled with passionate hope. Although it was only a month since the deaths of his wife and son, he jested. He punned on Holland and hollow, he complained smilingly ('names hard to be spelled') of having had to consult atlases or his friend Roger Williams. The general tone was optimistic. The success of the navy was certain, there would be no State-hired church. . . .

Holland, however, knew how to fight. She was still far from capitulating when Milton had lost on all counts. In four ballots, between February 25th and April 1st, 1653, Parliament instituted a national clergy, maintained the tithe, and charged the magistrates to prosecute those who proved refractory. In vain did Williams and others besiege influential Parliamentarians, such as Lawrence, or entreat Cromwell himself. Williams went so far as to write and distribute a tract entitled *The Hireling Ministry none of Jesus Christ's,* and another, *Ill News from New England,* in which he recounted the troubles of the American Baptists and other sectarians. Nothing had any effect. Cromwell was determined to 'settle the land'.

Immediately afterwards, the army triumphed over the Rump. About the middle of February, 1653, a success on the part of Admiral Blake made such a sensation in London that the Rump dared to brave the armed forces. It had promised to dissolve itself in November. Instead of leaving with a good grace, the members of Parliament discreetly agreed on a surprise vote to keep their seats and to invalidate those elected whom they considered none too reliable. Learning of this at the last minute, Cromwell came to take his seat on April 20th, ballot day, accompanied right to the door by musketeers, and at the very moment of the ballot, had the fifty members present expelled. Vane protested to no purpose. A few hours later Cromwell dismissed the Council. London did not stir. 'There was not so much as the barking of a dog', said Cromwell.

For new wine, new wineskins. The Puritan ideal wanted servitors beyond reproach. Cromwell charged a small interim Council to assemble a 'Constituent Convention', in which the three nations of the British Isles would be represented. Appointed by their churches, one hundred and forty 'saints' came to take their seats at Westminster where Cromwell gave them an enthusiastic welcome on July 4th, 1653. Unfortunately, these constituents interfered with the making of laws and the majority were visionary and un-practical. London called them Barebone's Parliament, after one of them, a Baptist leather merchant with a sad coun-tenance. They ended in displeasing Cromwell himself, by claiming to separate Church from State. On Novem-ber 11th they retired once more into their obscurity.

Cromwell's Council of Officers then drew up a constitu-tion, the *Instrument of Government*, which foreshadowed the United States of to-day by giving important powers to the head of the State, who was to be known as Protector (the title of King was rejected by Cromwell). Elected for life, he would convene the legislative assembly nominated for three years, and see that it did not infringe the constitution. He could dissolve it after five months, but he himself would be assisted and controlled by an irremovable Council of State. At his death, this Council would appoint his successor.

The generals counted on Puritan and Republican elections. Meanwhile Cromwell was proclaimed Protector on December 16th, 1653. The elections to the Assembly could not be terminated before September 1654. Until that time Cromwell would be all powerful.

It was in this period of expectancy, on May 30th, 1654, that Milton published the *Second Defence of the English People*. It will readily be supposed that he had a good deal to say.

XI

THE SOLEMN APPEAL TO CROMWELL

1654

THE title of the new work: *Second Defence of the People of England in response to an infamous anonymous libel entitled 'Cry of the King's Blood to Heaven against the English parricides'* announced nothing more than the refutation demanded by the Council in 1652. In fact, one half of these 173 pages turned on the situation of the country in 1654.

The refutation, the negative portion, would to-day be only dead wood if Milton had not been forced by the ferocious attacks of the anonymous writer to give his antecedents and even his description. A man likened to Virgil's Polyphemus: 'A monster hideous, ugly, huge, bereft of sight',[1] with the immediate aggravation: 'No, not "huge", for nothing is more puny, pale, and shrivelled than he',[2] is called upon to make the necessary correction. No one has written on Milton without having recourse in lesser or greater degree to what he here reveals of his life and person. The remainder of the refutation, however, consisted of ponderous and cruel invectives, and worse— they were derisory, for they were sometimes aimed at the dead Saumaise, sometimes at some mere underling, while they left the elusive author untouched. Milton was the victim of a hoax imposed by the vigilance of Thurloe's police. To relate the whole business would be tiresome, but certain details throw light on the poet. There is no better index to a man than the character of his enemies.

The *Regii Sanguinis Clamor* had been printed at the Hague by a publisher called Ulac, under the attentive and exclusive supervision of a well-known minister named More. The Dutch were naturally convinced that More had written the book. In fact, he had only written the preface, and even so had contrived to have it signed by Ulac. In following

[1] *Monstrum horrendum, informe, ingens, cui lumen ademptum.* Aen. III, 658.
[2] Masson IV, 454.

this false trail, however, Milton made some sensational discoveries. Alexandre More (in literature Morus), born at Castres in the south of France in 1616 of a Scottish father and a French mother, learned, highly eloquent, dearer to his female parishioners than to his colleagues, professor of Greek in Geneva at the age of twenty, was teaching theology in Middleburg. Now he owed this post to Saumaise. He frequently went to Leyden to see the Saumaises. A young English girl, Bontia, who was in the service of Madame de Saumaise, was said to have been 'moralized' by him to the point that her condition was visible. An epigram was spreading through the town:

> *Galli e concubitu te gravidam, Bontia, Mori,*
> *Quis bene moratam morigeramque neget?*[1]

In his *Mercurius* of September 23rd–30th, 1652, Needham published this murderous couplet and gave Morus as the author of the book. Morus prosecuted Bontia and the Saumaises for defamation, managed to whitewash himself ('the Moor badly whitewashed', sneered the Dutch) and went off to teach sacred history in Amsterdam. Milton had the archives of Geneva consulted. In 1649 the City fathers had removed Morus discreetly, but firmly, for adultery. Milton blessed heaven (so he wrote) for having granted him an enemy so vulnerable. Therefore he refused to listen to Hartlib when the latter, who had it from Ulac, warned him that he was on the wrong track.

Much later, in April 1654, when Morus learned with terror that a book was being printed in London in which Milton was tearing him to pieces, he revealed the name of the author, but under the seal of secrecy, to the Ambassador of the Low Countries in London, begging him to inform Milton. Milton was informed, but what was the word of a Morus worth? 'Well, that was all one; he having writ it, it should go to the world; one of them was as bad as the other' (Aubrey).

---

[1] With child by Morus, Bontia? Who'll deny
That we descry
Your morals more, your breeding more, thereby?
Masson IV, 463.

John Milton was born the 9th of December
1608 die Veneris half an howr after 6 in the
morning
Christofer Milton was born on Friday about
a month before Christmass at 5 in the morning
1615
Edward Phillips was 15 year old August 1645
John Phillips is a year younger about October.

My daughter Anne was born July the 29th
on the fast at eebning about half an houre
after six 1646.
My daughter Mary was born on Wedensday
Octob. 25th on the fast day in the morning about
6 a clock 1648.
My son John was born on Sunday March the
16th about half an hower past nine at night 1650
My daughter Deborah was Born the 2 of May
Being Sunday somwhat before 3 of the clock in the
morning. 1652.
this my wife hir mother dyed about 3 days after. And my
son about 6 weeks after his mother.
Katherin my daughter, by Katherin my second wife, was
borne ye 19th of October, between 5 and 6 in ye morning,
and dyed ye 17th of March following, 6 weeks after hir
mother, who dyed ye 3rd of Feb. 1657

FLYLEAF OF JOHN MILTON'S BIBLE

The other was a respected Londoner, the Anglican clergyman Pierre Du Moulin, a zealous Royalist, former tutor to the Ranelaghs, a friend of Boyle and Hartlib, son of a well-known Calvinist theologian, Pierre Du Moulin, mentioned with respect in *Animadversions*, and brother of an Oxford professor who had put into Latin part of the *Eikonoklastes*. He had succeeded in getting his manuscript to Saumaise with a request to publish it without betraying him. Saumaise, who was very ill at the time, had asked Morus to satisfy Du Moulin's wish.

To the misdirected indictment of Milton, Morus was to reply skilfully in a *Fides publica* and a *Supplementum* to which Milton opposed a *Personal Defence*. This passage-at-arms is of no interest to us. It should merely be noted that More never revealed to the public the name of the culprit. It was Du Moulin himself who, under the Restoration, proclaimed his exploit:

> It had the effect, moreover, of making enemies for Morus in Holland; for at that time the English Tyrants were very much feared in foreign parts. Meanwhile I looked on in silence, and not without a soft chuckle, at seeing my bantling laid at another man's door, and the blind and furious Milton fighting and slashing the air, like the hoodwinked horse-combatants in the old circus, not knowing by whom he was struck and whom he struck in return.[1]

In 1652 Du Moulin wrote in the *Regii Sanguinis*: 'Verily an egg is not liker an egg than Cromwell is like Mahomet'. In 1656, he would present his 'Humble Petition' to the Protector to be admitted into his clergy. It was granted.

It is now time to return to the *Second Defence* and look at its constructive pages. Like the sonnets of 1652, they are impregnated with enthusiasm and anxiety.

The exordium is triumphant. Milton thanks God for what his nation and he himself have accomplished and for his restored health which allows him to go into action once more. Then he congratulates himself on addressing so extensive an audience. His book was in the press when

---

[1] Masson V, 220.

O

pacts were signed on April 5th with Holland and her allies—
Denmark, Protestant Switzerland, the German princes—and
on the 28th with Sweden. Milton had known what was
afoot and he exults:

> It has excited such general and such ardent expectation, that I
> imagine myself not in the forum or on the rostra, surrounded
> only by the people of Athens or of Rome, but about to address
> in this, as I did in my former Defence, the whole collective
> body of people, cities, states and councils of the wise and
> eminent, through the wide expanse of anxious and listening
> Europe. . . . Surrounded by congregated multitudes, I now
> imagine that, from the columns of Hercules to the Indian
> Ocean, I behold the nations of the earth recovering that liberty
> which they so long had lost; and that the people of this island
> are transporting to other countries a plant of more beneficial
> qualities, and more noble growth, than that which Triptolemus
> is reported to have carried from region to region; that they are
> disseminating the blessings of civilization and freedom among
> cities, kingdoms and nations.[1]

A little further on the enthusiast plunges fully into the
events of the moment. Christina was still hesitating at the
time when he wrote, but she had taken up her stand against
Saumaise and had just told Whitlocke, who had come to
see her as Cromwell's deputy, how much she admired
Milton. Accordingly he thought he could influence her.
All he had to do was to allow the expression of his gratitude
to expand into flattery.[2]

> You, O queen will for ever be the object of my homage,
> my veneration, and my love (249).—Henceforth, the queen of
> the South [of Sheba] will not be alone renowned in history; for
> there is a queen of the North . . . to whose court others [other
> kings] may from all parts repair (250).—Her reign has proved
> that she is fit to govern, not only Sweden, but the world (251).

Events in England must not make her distrustful. One
can punish a tyrant and still honour kings.

> I have not written a word against kings, but only against
> tyrants, the spots and the pests of royalty (249).

Since Du Moulin had blackened Bradshaw, Milton had
to defend him, but there were more ways than one of so

---

[1] Bohn I, 219–20.   [2] Ibid., 248–51.

doing. Bradshaw was wholeheartedly Republican. When Cromwell dismissed the Council, Bradshaw, who was President, said to him: 'Sir, we have heard what you did at the House in the morning, and before many hours all England will hear it. But, sir, you are mistaken to think that the Parliament is dissolved, for no power on earth can dissolve them but themselves; therefore take you notice of that.'[1] After the *coup d'Etat*, Bradshaw had retired into the country. Milton, instead of touching lightly on the matter, devoted two whole pages to the praises of the intransigent. In particular he praised his modesty ('He does not cease to extol the merits of others and to belittle his own') and pointed out another of his virtues in ominous terms:

> But the great character which he then sustained, he with perfect consistency still sustains, so that you would suppose that not only then, but in every future period of his life, he was sitting in judgement upon the King.[2]

Further on it was to Fairfax that Milton's admiration went out. Yet this Royalist Presbyterian had resigned in 1650 rather than repress Scotland, and he held the Commonwealth in horror. But the stealthy slanderer took him to task, so Milton praised his courage and his victories. Then he went further: he also praised Cromwell's former leader for his taste in literature, his modesty, and . . . his love of liberty.

> Nor was it only the enemy whom you subdued, but you have triumphed over that flame of ambition and that lust of glory which are wont to make the best and the greatest of men their slaves. . . . But whether it were your health, which I principally believe, or any other motive which caused you to retire, of this I am convinced, that nothing could have induced you to relinquish the service of your country, if you had not known that in your successor liberty would meet with a protector, and England with a stay to its safety, and a pillar to its glory.[3]

This tendentious praise was inserted among the twenty pages devoted to Cromwell. Cromwell came of illustrious

[1] Ludlow, *Memoirs* (Ed. C. H. Firth, Oxford, 1894) I, 357.
[2] Bohn I, 268.
[3] Bohn I, 287. Milton's judgment of Fairfax is of great value: he had his information from Marvell.

lineage which distinguished itself in civil functions under the monarchy, and still more in working to re-establish and implant in England the true religion.[1] At first nothing marked him out but 'the strictness of his religious habits and the innocence of his life'. When war came he 'almost surpassed' the greatest of captains. Nothing was more natural:

> He had either extinguished, or by habit had learned to subdue, the whole host of vain hopes, fears, and passions, which infest the soul. . . . The whole surface of the British empire has been the scene of his exploits, and the theatre of his triumphs.[2] . . . in about the space of one year you entirely subdued, and added to the English dominion, that kingdom which all our monarchs, during a period of eight hundred years, had in vain struggled to subject.[3]

He did well to send away the selfish Parliamentarians and the incapable Convention. He merited the supreme power.

> . . . nothing in the world is more pleasing to God, more agreeable to reason, more politically just, or more generally useful, than that the supreme power should be vested in the best and the wisest of men. Such, O Cromwell, all acknowledge you to be.[4]

Cromwell, however, was logical in refusing the crown, for the title of king was unworthy of the transcendent majesty of his rôle, and a man who overthrows an idol does not permit himself to adore it. There followed a pressing appeal, solemn in tone and stamped with the words 'revere' and 'liberty'.

> Do you then, sir, continue your course with the same unrivalled magnanimity; it sits well upon you; to you our country owes its liberties; nor can you sustain a character at once more momentous and more august than that of the author, the guardian, the preserver of our liberties; . . . Often reflect what a dear pledge the beloved land of your nativity has entrusted to your care; and that liberty which she once expected only from the chosen flower of her talents and her virtues, she now expects from you only, and by you only hopes to obtain.

---

[1] A reference to the evil genius of Henry VIII, Thomas Cromwell, known as 'the Hammer of the monks'.

[2] Bohn I, 286.   [3] Ibid., 287.   [4] Ibid., 288.

Revere the fond expectations which we cherish, the solicitudes of your anxious country; revere the looks and the wounds of your brave companions in arms, who, under your banners, have so strenuously fought for liberty; revere the shades of those who perished in the contest; revere also the opinions and the hopes which foreign states entertain concerning us, who promise to themselves so many advantages from that liberty which we have so bravely acquired . . . and lastly, revere yourself; and, after having endured so many sufferings and encountered so many perils for the sake of liberty, do not suffer it, now it is obtained, either to be violated by yourself, or in any one instance impaired by others. You cannot be truly free unless we are free too; for such is the nature of things, that he who entrenches on the liberty of others, is the first to lose his own and become a slave.[1]

The glory of Cromwell is here involved—a matter of interest to the whole of humanity. His future reputation is concerned—history will search into his life and will overlook nothing.

And now the victorious soldier must approach the tasks of peace 'compared with which the labour of war is mere pastime'.

And this you can, in my opinion, in no other way so rapidly effect, as by associating in your councils the companions of your dangers and your toils; men of exemplary modesty, integrity, and courage; . . . and who are more zealously interested in the preservation of liberty, in proportion as they have encountered more perils in its defence.[2]

Here a very delicate operation is initiated—to bring the master to allow himself to be kept up to the mark by staunch Republicans.

The Council foreseen by the Instrument of Government had been in existence for four months; Milton does not mention it. It is necessary to look closely to realize that he has replaced some of the members by men after his own heart. There were sixteen Councillors, eight of them soldiers. Six were relatives of Cromwell, either soldiers or civilians. Milton retained eight of these men and proposed to add to them four more. In the Council that he had in

---

[1] Bohn I, 289–90.   [2] Ibid., 290–1.

mind, the followers of Cromwell would still have been six, but the soldiers would have been seven against five civilians. Yet Milton had not a very high opinion of the military; as he has just reminded us, it is easier to kill than to govern. The army, however, was Republican; it must have the last word.

Milton then designated in the first place General Charles Fleetwood, Cromwell's son-in-law. ('I shall commemorate the names of some of those who have most conspicuously signalized themselves in these times: and first thine, O Fleetwood! whom I have known from a boy...') Now in the existing Council Fleetwood came after the civilians Lawrence and Lisle. (Fleetwood was, in fact, to oppose absolutely in May 1657 the suggestion of Cromwell's accepting the crown.) Milton also retained Lambert and recalled his exploits. (This second choice was a less happy one, but at least Lambert was jealous of his chief.)

It is amusing to see how cautiously the impetuous Milton chose and put forward his four new men. He passed over in silence those who were notorious anti-Cromwellians—Bradshaw, Marten, Ludlow and Vane himself. He proposed Whitlocke, highly appreciated by Cromwell for his clear mind and legal knowledge. Whitlocke had shown Cromwell in 1652 that by making himself king he would destroy himself. Milton named Colonel Whalley, Cromwell's cousin, who had seconded Pride and voted for the King's death. He suggested Colonel Algernon Sidney, younger brother of Councillor Lisle, the latter being tacitly eliminated. Sidney, when the musketeers tore him from his bench, swore to curse the tyrant Cromwell every day of his life. But there had been no open clash between him and Cromwell, and Sidney was a man of great parts and high principles.[1] Skilfully, Milton slipped him into a group, remembering incidentally that Sidney the poet had died fighting against Spain, with this effect:

Whitlocke, Pickering, Strickland, Sydenham, Sydney (a name indissolubly attached to the interests of liberty),

[1] His political writings were to inspire the founders of the United States and the French revolutionaries. Robespierre quoted him as an example. After an eventful career, he was beheaded in 1682.

Montacute, Lawrence, both of highly cultivated minds and polished taste; besides many more citizens of singular merit.[1]

The fourth new man would have been Colonel Robert Overton, a former lawyer who had saved the situation at Marston Moor, then governed a region in Scotland with as much talent as humanity. Milton exclaimed:

> ... and yours, O Overton, who have been most endeared to me now for so many years by the similitudes of our studies, the suavity of your manners, and the more than fraternal sympathy of our hearts. . . .[2]

Then he called attention to the successes of the soldier and the administrator. Never did he express more affection for anyone than he did for this Overton. They were of the same age and perhaps had been linked together at the time when Milton frequented the lawyers in Gray's Inn. It is easy to place Overton politically. He had highly approved of the *coup d'Etat*, but he and other officers stationed in Scotland had grumbled when the Protectorate was proclaimed, so much so that Lieutenant-General Monk, their commander, had sent Overton to govern Hull. Interrogated at that time by Cromwell, Overton declared that 'if he perceived his Lordship did only design the setting up of himself, and not the good of these nations, then he could not continue to serve him'. Cromwell's answer was: 'Thou wert a knave if thou wouldst'.[3] Overton was, then, like Milton, for the *status quo*.

Having thus composed his government, Milton traced out for it a programme inspired by the single desire for liberty—to laicise the State completely; to legislate very little and even to abrogate superfluous or harmful laws, such as those which condemned innocent pleasures, or forbade the use of a thing to prevent its abuse ('the intention of the laws is to repress the manifestations of vice, but the best school of virtue is liberty'); to endow schools and universities more generously, but reserving the rewards of merit for those deserving them; totally to abolish the censorship of the press. It was essential that the Protector should 'not dread to hear any truth or any falsehood'.

[1] Bohn I, 293.   [2] Ibid., 292.   [3] Masson IV, 608.

Then you will always be dear to those who think not merely that their own sect or faction, but that all citizens of all descriptions, should enjoy equal rights and equal laws.[1]

The peroration followed. It was addressed to the English, disappointed by Parliament, ruined by the army, demoralized by ten years of war. The aristocratic Republican developed in five pages the maxim of his *Comus*: 'love virtue, she alone is free'. And he concluded by asserting that he at least had done his whole duty:

Unless you will subjugate the propensity to avarice, to ambition, and sensuality, and expel all luxury from yourselves and from your families, you will find that you have cherished a more stubborn and intractable despot at home, than you ever encountered in the field. . . .[2]

But from such an abyss of corruption into which you so readily fall, no one, not even Cromwell himself, nor a whole nation of Brutuses, if they were alive, could deliver you if they would, or would deliver you if they could.[3]

I have delivered my testimony, I would almost say, have erected a monument, that will not readily be destroyed, to the reality of those singular and mighty achievements which were above all praise. As the epic poet, who adheres at all to the rules of that species of composition, does not profess to describe the whole life of the hero whom he celebrates, but only some particular action of his life, as the resentment of Achilles at Troy, the return of Ulysses, or the coming of Aeneas into Italy; so it will be sufficient, either for my justification or apology, that I have heroically celebrated at least one exploit of my countrymen; I pass by the rest, for who could recite the achievements of a whole people? If after such a display of courage and of vigour, you basely relinquish the path of virtue, if you do anything unworthy of yourselves, posterity will sit in judgment on your conduct. They will see that the foundations were well laid; that the beginning (nay, it was more than a beginning) was glorious; but with deep emotions of concern will they regret, that those were wanting who might have completed the structure. They will lament that perseverance was not conjoined with such exertions and such virtues. They will see that there was a rich harvest of glory, and an opportunity afforded for the greatest achievements, but that men only were wanting for the execution; while they were not

[1] Bohn I, 294.   [2] Ibid., 295.   [3] Ibid., 297.

wanting who could rightly counsel, exhort, inspire, and bind
an unfading wreath of praise round the brows of the illustrious
actors in so glorious a scene.[1]

It does not appear that the *Second Defence* changed the
course of events. The polemist's sallies amused the one
camp and irritated the other, without modifying the balance
between the two forces. As to the project of a reshuffle, it
had against it, besides Cromwell himself, eight powerful
men, the Councillors whom it dislodged. The eloquent
peroration could not bring the English, even if they had
understood Latin, to forsake their besetting sins. There
remained the appeal to the Protector.

Chateaubriand thought it admirable that Milton's boldness did not win him any blame. 'Au temps de la toute-
puissance de Napoléon, qui aurait osé lui dire qu'il n'avait
obtenu l'empire que pour protéger la liberté?' This aggra-
vating circumstance moreover must be added—to get
printed at the expense of the State advice which it did not
ask for. It must be believed that the Cromwell régime
was not, as a French critic recently claimed, 'one of the most
brutal dictatorships known to history'. The martyrdom
of Ireland will always weigh on Cromwell's memory,
but he made no war on ideas. He said: 'A man's ideas can
harm only himself'.

In the very year 1654, the Quaker, George Fox, came to
speak to him on behalf of his persecuted brethren. He has
related how he was received, having called when the
Protector was dressing.

> When I came in, I was moved to say: 'Peace be in this house';
> and I bid him to keep in the fear of God, that he might receive
> wisdom from Him. . . . I spake much to him of Truth, and
> much discourse I had with him about religion; wherein he
> carried himself very moderately. But he said we quarrelled
> with priests, whom he called ministers. I told him I did not
> quarrel with them, but they quarrelled with me and my friends.
> . . . . Then I shewed him that the prophets, Christ, and the
> apostles declared freely, and against them that did not declare
> freely, such as preached for filthy lucre, and divined for money,
> and preached for hire . . . like the dumb dogs that can never

[1] Bohn I, 299–300.

have enough. . . . As I spake, he several times said it was very good and it was truth. . . .

Many more words I had with him, but people coming in, I drew a little back; and as I was turning, he caught me by the hand, and with tears in his eyes said, 'Come again to my house, for if thou and I were but an hour of a day together, we should be nearer one to the other'; adding that he wished me no more ill than he did his own soul. I told him if he did he wronged his own soul; and I bid him hearken to God's voice, that he might stand in His counsel. . . . If he did not hear God's voice, his heart would be hardened. He said it was true. Then I went out.[1]

This would show that the hypothesis of an interview of the soldier with his *idéologue*[2] on the subject of the *Second Defence* is very plausible. If it did actually happen, the more mystical of the two could have no difficulty in proving to his mentor that he was preaching to the converted but that a man of action is 'the slave of the most merciless tyrant: the nature of things'.

May it perhaps be said that there was a good deal of pride in Milton's intervention? That was what Morus told him. Milton had protested that 'the great Saumaise' was not worthy to be called great, being only a grammarian. Morus retorted in *Fides publica*:

All which has so elated you that you would be reckoned next after the very first man in England, and sometimes put yourself higher than the supreme Cromwell himself; whom you name familiarly, without giving him any title of rank, whom you lecture under the guise of praising him, to whom you dictate laws, assign boundaries to his rights, prescribe duties, suggest counsels, and even hold out threats if he shall not behave accordingly. You grant him arms and rule; you claim genius and the gown for yourself. '*He only is to be called great*', you say, '*who has either done great things*'—Cromwell, to wit!—'*or teaches great things*'—Milton on divorce, to wit!—'*or writes of them worthily*'—the same twice-great Milton, I suppose, in his Defence of the English People![4]

---

[1] *Journal of George Fox*, ch. VI.
[2] Term applied by Napoleon to some of his own critics.
[3] A saying of Napoleon about himself.
[4] Masson V, 160.

The years passed, Morus's irony evaporated, the homage remains. Milton was in fact 'next in England after Cromwell', or even his equal or perhaps his better. He had the right, the duty, to put him on his guard.

Milton had sent his book to an admirer and friend named Oldenburg, Aulic Counsellor to the city of Bremen, a friend of Spinoza and son-in-law of John Durie. Oldenburg congratulated him on his great talent, but at the same time expressed the desire that he would soon employ it on 'some work more useful and more noble'. Milton answered him in July 1654:

> To prepare myself, as you suggest, for other labours,—whether nobler or more useful I know not, for what can be nobler or more useful in human affairs than the vindication of Liberty?—truly, if my health shall permit, and this blindness of mine, a sorer affliction than old age, and lastly the 'cries' of such brawlers as there have been about me, I shall be induced to *that* easily enough. An idle ease has never had charms for me, and this unexpected contest with the Adversaries of Liberty took me off against my will when I was intent on far different and altogether pleasanter pursuits: not that in anyway I repent of what I have done, since it was necessary; for I am far from thinking that I have spent my toil, as you seem to hint, on matters of inferior consequence. But of this another time. . . .[1]

What could these 'far different and altogether pleasanter pursuits' be? The planning of *Paradise Lost* surely extended over several years, but so did the composition of *Doctrina Christiana*.

[1] Masson IV, 626–7, or Bohn III, 506.

XII

CROMWELL'S PROTECTORATE

1653-1658

CROMWELL, when Milton dared to offer him his advice, had no more than four years left in which to juggle with the impossible.

He did not dismiss his presumptuous secretary, nor did that secretary tender his resignation. In addition to the reasons we already know, Milton was held back by a weighty scruple. All that survived of the Commonwealth was henceforward at the mercy of a dagger-thrust. How could one abandon a man so necessary and so threatened by danger? It was impossible even to seem to approve these blind Republicans, who, to avenge liberty, would have brought back first of all chaos and then the King.

Overton, so dear to Milton, was one such Republican. In September 1652, Cromwell had given him back his command in Scotland. Immediately he and his comrades had resolved to depose Monk and to march on London to crush the tyrant there. The Levellers were in the affair and were counting on the Royalists, who were already in intelligence with Spain.

No less dangerous was the folly of Harrison, formerly Cromwell's right-hand man. He was now directing the Men of the Fifth Monarchy, a numerous and turbulent sect, who justified their hare-brained programme by the Bible. There had been four universal monarchies (we should say four empires)—Assyria, Persia, Macedonia and Rome. The Reformation had sounded the knell of the Roman hegemony; therefore the return of Christ was imminent. He would reign on earth for a thousand years before judging the living and the dead, and the mission of preparing this Fifth Monarchy had devolved on the Kingdom of the Saints, the Puritan Commonwealth. In itself this pious imperialism had little about it to alarm Milton or

Cromwell. If Milton had known Pascal's phrase—'Cromwell was going to ravage all Christendom',[1] he would have replaced 'ravage' by 'liberate'. In 1654, Cromwell wrote to the Dutch: 'Who will say what God, at the hour chosen by him, thanks to our two republics, will perhaps accomplish for the deliverance of the oppressed peoples?' Milton had predicted that an England rid of prelates would rally the Protestants of the Continent, and now his prophecy was coming true. But Harrison's fanatics had had no part in this success. On the contrary, if allowed a free hand they would have wrecked all. They declared in their tracts that all governments usurped the prerogative of Jesus Christ and that, in order to follow Moses, England must be governed by a sanhedrin. Already they had contributed to the fall of the Barebones Parliament, in which they had been powerful.

Was Vane himself reasonable? He wanted a government chosen by the notables, and would have resigned himself to a parliamentary monarchy. Why, then, was he bad friends with Cromwell? Who was his candidate?

An example will show how Cromwell was at the same time both so weak and so strong that a friend of liberty had no right to desert him. In November 1657, he married his daughter Frances to the grandson of the Earl of Warwick, and a week later his daughter Mary to Viscount Falconbridge. The second marriage was blessed first by a minister of the 'Cromwellian' church, then by a former chaplain of Charles I, Dr. Hewit. In the course of a sumptuous reception, two songs by the Puritan Marvell were followed by an Epithalamium by the Royalist Davenant. Cromwell was radiant. He danced again and again. He who wanted to be only 'the parish constable', at last saw his villagers fraternizing.

Now Hewit, who used his drawing-room as a chapel, counted among his faithful Cromwell's favourite daughter, Lady Claypole, and the new bride, Mary. It was Mary—and not Falconbridge—who had wanted the second ceremony. Cromwell had yielded on so serious a point through fatherly

---

[1] *Pensées*, 176: 'Cromwell allait ravager toute la chrétienté, sans un petit grain de sable, qui se mit dans son uretère'.

weakness and the desire of appeasement. Shortly after the marriage, however, Thurloe discovered that Hewit and a certain Slingsby, Falconbridge's uncle, were directing a vast plot, in which people like Fairfax and *Lord* Lambert (Lambert, the Republican ennobled by Cromwell!) were involved. Harrison and his followers were of the number. Their plan was to raise London and certain counties at the very moment when Charles II should land from Belgium with 8,000 Spaniards. Mary's spiritual director and her husband's uncle were executed on June 8th, 1658.

Here, however, is the other side of the Protectorate. A week after the execution, the keys of Dunkirk were handed to Cromwell's nephew, Lockhart, by Louis XIV in person. After exactly one hundred years, the loss of Calais was repaired; the regicide avenged the kings.

The new régime, however, was a burden for a Milton. He resigned himself to this makeshift, as did sensible men such as Whitlocke, Thurloe, Lawrence, or Monk. His acceptance of it, however, did not go beyond his official task. In 1655 he even had that lessened and an annuity of one hundred and fifty pounds was guaranteed to him if he should retire altogether. He did not attend the Lord Protector's receptions or his weekly concerts. Like his father before him he preferred to have music at home, with a few friends. To a young diplomat, Heimbach, who in 1657 solicited his support, he replied (B. III, 518): 'I have little familiarity with those who have favours to bestow, since I have more pleasure in keeping myself at home. . . .'

During these few years the Protector's first concern was to protect himself; he wore armour, no longer opened his letters himself, changed his bedroom frequently, and Milton lived not unhappily indeed, but secluded. According to Phillips, 'he was frequently visited by people of quality . . . and all learned foreigners of note'. He welcomed them with his usual courtesy. A visitor of that particular time, the German pastor Arnold, wrote to a friend: 'The strenuous defender of the new republic, Milton, enters readily into talk'. Milton, however, complained of disturbance by too many passing callers. Some wrote to him, but his replies, apparently, did not give them his confidence.[1]

Between him and clergymen of any persuasion, the aversion was mutual, and he would not have taken one step to approach a university man. He read, certainly, but probably never met the Cambridge neo-Platonist, Henry More, 'the Chrysostom of Christ's College', though the don's learning and breadth of mind were very worthy of him. In June 1656, he wrote to Oldenburg, then staying in Oxford (B. III, 510): 'I see not what advantage you can have in that retirement, except in an access to a multitude of books', and he severely criticized both masters and methods. In the 'Invisible College'[2] he reckoned a few friends besides Hartlib and Durie, but these scientific investigators were scarcely interested in literature (or in Hebrew, like Lady Ranelagh), and Milton would rather have re-read the *Timaeus* than discussed an experiment in chemistry.

Concern for facts, for clarity, for logic, now also invaded the realm of letters. Fifteen years of controversy had generalized the critical sense; a Puritan Commonwealth could only deny the 'fine frenzy' of the Elizabethans, the gallantries of the 'amorists' and of the Cavaliers, or the riddles of the 'metaphysicals', and by this time France was rapidly supplanting Italy as the teacher of Europe. Under the Protectorate the youthful Newton studied Descartes' *Géométrie analytique*. The authors who counted then were, besides Bacon, two other prose writers, Hobbes and Harrington.

Hobbes had been Francis Bacon's favourite secretary. A refugee in France since 1640, he had corresponded with Descartes and taught mathematics to the future Charles II in Paris. His doctrines having alarmed the French clergy, he recrossed the Straits in 1651 to publish that masterpiece of materialistic dialectic, *Leviathan*. There he showed, as rigidly as another Euclid, that the visible universe and the moral world, including the life of societies, can be reduced

---

[1] It must be said that when Milton's widow retired to Nantwich, she took his papers with her, and few of them have come down to us.
[2] See page 119, n.

to mere motion. Every society, at the outset, is a deadly conflict of selfish interests. To make sure of a lasting peace for itself it must surrender its strength to a man or to an assembly and empower them to will in its place. Henceforward this man or assembly, as the case may be, must remain absolute. Divine right is pure fiction. It is mutual consent which creates the 'mortal god' like Job's Leviathan 'created fearless'. Two other works of 'Hobbes the atheist' came out in 1655 and 1656. Milton would acknowledge him to be a man of great parts, and a learned man, but he did not like him at all. Their interests and tenets 'did run counter to each other' (Aubrey).

The Puritan Harrington, formerly one of the household of Charles I, anticipated the French physiocrats[1] by bringing agriculture into the foreground. His *Commonwealth of Oceana* (1656) brought against Hobbes the objection that Leviathan could do nothing without an army, and that an army was 'an animal with a large appetite' which required extensive pasture-lands. It was essential to found a stable society by fixing a limit to fortunes in land (Harrington gave figures) and by making the ownership of landed property accessible to all. This agrarian republic would be ruled by two permanent chambers, annually renewable by a third, that is a senate of 300 important landowners of mature years who would prepare legislative measures for submission to a popular assembly three times more numerous. All votes would be secret. This programme rallied the Levellers. It also attracted rich landowners like Cyriac Skinner. Milton was too much the son of a scrivener to give his approval to tampering with title-deeds by the State, but he retained the idea of a permanent legislature, periodically rejuvenated. The group of the Harringtonians owed the surname of 'Rota Club' to this important suggestion of rotation.

Thus Milton, the man of politics, was enriched by a political writer. As to Milton the poet, he could expect

[1] A school of economists emanating from Quesnay in 1770. They coined the maxim 'Laissez faire, laissez passer'. Their doctrine inspired Turgot and the Convention.

BUST OF JOHN MILTON AT THE AGE OF 46 CIRCA

nothing from the poets of that time, whom he called, as we have seen, 'despicable creatures'.[1]

The last two Cavalier poets were ending their days in the provinces, Cleveland as a tutor, Lovelace behind bars. In Wales a doctor who was something of a mystic, Vaughan, author of *Silex Scintillans*, was living in obscurity. The sensitive Herrick, driven from his parish, was vegetating in London, no less unknown.

Waller had spent eight years in France after his condemnation in 1643. There he associated with Saint-Evremond[2] and La Fontaine. Recalled by his cousin, Cromwell, he introduced Corneille to the English, although he himself was hardly worthy of Corneille's heroes. He left only occasional poems, polished, pretty, somewhat cold. He turned skilfully enough the rhymed couplet which was to serve Pope's antithesis so well. Milton was not unknown to him. He had heard tell of a blind translator who had formerly been a schoolmaster. . . . Pope exhorted his readers to praise

> the easy vigour of a line
> Where Denham's strength and Waller's sweetness join.[3]

Denham's reputation was long-lasting; it rested on *Cooper's Hill* which had appeared in 1642. In the reprint of 1653 he added four lines about the Thames to define the poetry he desired to write:

> O, could I flow like thee, and make thy stream
> My great example, as it is my theme!
> Though deep, yet clear; though gentle, yet not dull;
> Strong without rage; without o'erflowing full.

The Restoration was to see the wise Sir John Denham Surveyor of Works to His Majesty and member of the Royal Society.

---

[1] Above, p. 124.

[2] Charles de Saint-Denis, sieur de Saint-Evremond (1613–1703), soldier (brigadier in 1653), man about town, man of letters, shunned all passions, even that of glory, but had a deep appreciation of love, friendship, good books and good food. Only twice in his life did he give anything to the printers. He judged the Ancients or Racine on their merits. His prose was worthy of Voltaire. He found verse too little compatible with common sense.

[3] *An Essay on Criticism*, 360–1.

P

Milton once named Cowley in the same breath with Shakespeare and Spenser. (After all, Goethe and Saint-Beuve admired Béranger.) Pope, however, was presently to ask: 'Who now reads Cowley?' At first he won admiration by his precociousness. Learned, pious, witty, he had become the most accomplished of the metaphysical poets. He lacked sensitivity, however, the sciences attracted him; a friend of Hobbes and an admirer of Bacon, he was to be one of the founders of the Royal Society. He abandoned poetic conceits and buried in oblivion the metaphysical school. As cipher-secretary to Queen Henrietta and to her chief officer, Lord Jermyn, he had lived for a long time in France, but Cromwell's successes had dissuaded him—as he himself wrote—from 'weaving laurels for the conquered'. Returning in 1656, he immediately published his complete poems, plus an epic, the *Davideis*, as mortal in both senses as its contemporary *La Pucelle*.

It is possible that Davenant sometimes called at Petite-France. He and Lawes collaborated, and we have seen that he probably owed his life to Milton. He was, however, above all a man of the theatre and a man of the Court who sought for immediate success. On coming out of prison he had published *Gondibert*, an epic romance in one thousand five hundred quatrains. In 1656 he produced *The First Day's Entertainment at Rutland House*, a rather dull opera in the Italian fashion, immediately followed by *The Siege of Rhodes*, a noisy and vapid opera drama which set up a fashion.

There we have clear indications of a situation without parallel. Even if the poets of the time had been better equipped with talent and character, even if they had not all been Royalists and anti-Puritans, their conception of poetry would have separated them profoundly from Milton. Paradoxically, as one or another disciplined himself, they moved even further away from him, so disciplined as he was himself. This was because the poetry of the Protectorate was moving towards the negative purity of melody, whereas Milton wanted both order and superabundance, the unity of the symphony. Moreover he completely ignored France.

He held to the Bible, the Italian Renaissance, and the sub-
limity of Greece. He denied that a tragedy was more worthy
of Euripides for being written in rhymed couplets. Any
man, especially if he be a creator, has his share of solitude,
but the case of Milton was exceptional. The author of
Hernani boasted of having made Boileau grind his teeth
and of having changed the orderly 'wig' of the classical
age into the wild 'mane' of the Romanticists.[1] How he
exaggerated his audacity! His famous declaration: 'Sur
le Racine mort le Campistron pullule'[2] proves clearly
enough that Romanticism had the field open before it.
Hugo swam like an athlete, but with the current. Nothing
could shake Milton's principles, but could poetry such as he
understood it, 'simple, sensuous and passionate', find an
audience? When they appeared *Gondibert* and the *Davideis*
had been very well received. Milton was anxious about the
future of his work.

> Mee of these
> Nor skilld nor studious, higher Argument
> Remaines, sufficient of it self to raise
> That name, unless an age too late, or cold
> Climat, or Years damp my intended wing
> Deprest; . . .[3]

> : still govern thou my Song,
> *Urania*, and fit audience find, though few.[4]

It is now time to review the principal acts and deeds of
Cromwell in these years between 1654 and 1658, and also
the modest activity of the Latin secretary and his retired life.
It has been said[5] that in 1654 a Protestant league was
taking shape. All the merit of it reverted to Cromwell.
It was in spite of his lieutenants that he made an ally of
Holland instead of crushing her. In June he demanded of
Portugal, guilty of favouring the Royalist fleet in 1649,
an indemnity and free access to her colonies. In August,
despite Lambert and other Hispanophiles, he opted for
France against Spain. Solicited for long months past by

---

[1] *Les Contemplations*, I, vii.
[2] Ibid., Jean Galbert de Campistron (1656–1723), an unworthy imitator of Racine,
popular in his day.   [3] *Paradise Lost* IX, 41–46.
[4] *Paradise Lost* VII, 30–31.   [5] Above, p. 188.

both one and the other, he ended by preferring the country of the Edict of Nantes to that of the Inquisition (and then . . . Spain had very fine colonies!). He therefore equipped two naval squadrons. That of Penn would attack Hispaniola;[1] the other, under Blake, would keep an eye on Spain. While the ships were getting ready or at sea, Cromwell repressed a Royalist movement in Scotland (August), opened his first Parliament (September), buried his mother in Westminster (November) and put down Overton's mutiny (December).

This first Parliament of Cromwell's included no professed Royalists and no Catholics. Commonwealth supporters and Presbyterians held the majority. They immediately contested the new régime. Cromwell demanded a signed oath of fidelity. One hundred members, Bradshaw among them, refused it and were excluded. The three hundred left demanded, however, that the Protector should be responsible to them, the army reduced, and 'heresies and blasphemies repressed'. Cromwell seized the opportunity; and in the name of threatened liberty of conscience, he dismissed these fresh 'prattlers' on January 22nd, 1655.

During this year, 1654, the blind secretary dictated seven official letters, worked until May at his *Second Defence* and from October onwards meditated on his reply to the *Fides Publica* of Morus.

For twenty months (February 1655–September 1657), Cromwell again held all power. A serious Republican plot and several Royalist risings induced him to try what he called 'a little poor invention'—that of dividing England into eleven regions and having them administered by so many Major-generals. Unfortunately, those men ruthlessly enforced the Puritan taboos, and dragged a tenth of their revenue out of refractories proved or presumed. Cromwell organized Scotland as a conquered country and appointed his son Henry as governor of Ireland. Moreover, he defined the status of his clergy. Despite the existing laws, his own clergy and public opinion, he mitigated the lot of Catholics and Quakers. Despite his clergy again, and the City, he

---

[1] Later called St. Domingo, then Hayti.

readmitted the Jews to England, whence they had been excluded since the thirteenth century.

During this period, for the first time in history, an English fleet was active in the Mediterranean. Blake demanded indemnities from Tuscany and from the Pope, both guilty in 1650 of the same fault as Portugal. He also obtained liberty of worship for the English in Florence. Then he forced the Barbary States to release their English captives, and showed himself in Malta, Venice, Toulon, Marseilles, and in several Spanish ports. At this date Admiral Penn, driven off from Hispaniola, seized Jamaica (April 14th, 1655).

On April 17th a drama blazed out in the Piedmontese valleys about Pignerol,[1] inhabited to this day by the evangelical Vaudois or Waldenses. The Marquis di Pianezza, an officer of the Duke of Savoy, let loose on these misbelievers his troop of Piedmontese, reinforced by a detachment of French and Irish. The massacre lasted eight days, attended with such cruelties that a French officer protested in writing. About two thousand peasants were slaughtered and their villages burned.

The beliefs and organization of the Waldenses perhaps went back to the early Church; Milton believed that they did.[2] Reinerius, an Inquisitor in the thireenth century, wrote to the Pope: 'They have existed from time immemorial'.[3] It was at their expense, in large part, that the Olivétan Bible had been printed at Neuchâtel in 1535. The whole of Protestantism revered them.

Cromwell and his people, forgetting the atrocities in Ireland, were shocked. London published illustrated tracts, there was a national fast, a national subscription, and the Protector invited his Protestant allies, and also France,

---

[1] Now Pinerolo, in Italy, the key of Piedmont; 24,000 inhabitants. Annexed to France several times. It was French at the time, but not the Valleys.

[2] '. . . those churches in Piedmont have held the same doctrine and government since the time that Constantine . . . poisoned . . . the whole Church . . . Others affirm they have continued there since the Apostles' (Eikonoklastes, Bohn I, 437). In Hirelings, Milton quotes them again as an example; see next chapter, p. 221.

[3] Innocent III, in the thirteenth century, had decreed a crusade against them. Innocent VIII another, in 1488. More than 20,000 had been massacred in 1544. Many had migrated to Germany and to Calabria. They have only had legal status in Italy since 1848.

which was tolerant and favourably placed, to common
intervention. Mazarin was polite, but temporized. The day
Blake threatened Nice,[1] Mazarin ousted Cromwell's envoys
at Turin (John Durie among them) and acted alone. In
August the Duke signed a 'Patent of Grace and Pardon'. So
the Waldenses continued to be regarded as guilty; they
were only pardoned on severe conditions.

This half-success did not palliate the abuses of the major-
generals, and in England there was an under-current of
anger. In August 'scandalous' publications were forbidden,
then the newspapers disappeared, except for two weeklies,
the *Mercurius* and the *Intelligencer* edited by Needham under
the eyes of Thurloe. In October, Cromwell having signed
a treaty of peace and commerce with France, declared war
on Spain.

To Milton's credit balance for the year 1655 should be
assigned a sonnet to Skinner on his blindness,[2] ten letters
to Europe (May–July) on the occasion of the 'Waldensian
Easter', the sonnet *Avenge O Lord*, the most eloquent in
English literature, and also 'text of an inexhaustible lesson
in art' (E. Legouis), the *Personal Defence* (August), and a
Manifesto against the Spaniards (October) which justified the
taking of Jamaica after the event. In the meantime,
relieved by Thurloe and rid of Morus, Milton was
progressing with his history of England, his thesaurus,
and his theological treatise. The year ended with two
elegant sonnets inviting Skinner and Lawrence to a 'neat
repast . . . light and choice, of Attick tast, with Wine',
followed by Italian music. Perhaps Milton wanted to
celebrate his birthday. These invitations worthy of Horace
are far removed from the elegy of 1630, in which he assured
Diodati that Homers 'drink from the brook' (*rivi potor
Homerus*).[3]

We find his sense of well-being all the more remarkable,
as his nephews had just passed over to the enemy. They
loved and respected their uncle, but their generation was
not Puritan. John had even begun to give trouble. To
keep him away from temptation, Milton had found him a

[1] The county of Nice was at the time a possession of the Duke of Savoy.
[2] Above, p. 168.   [3] Above, p. 31.

job in Scotland. He came back from it almost immediately
to resume the life of the tavern and to publish, in August
1655, *A Satyr against Hypocrites*, twenty-two pages of burlesque verse, often coarse though not devoid of colour,
in which he jeered at the Puritans, relating, for instance, how
their weekly fast-day, Wednesday, ended in a gorge. It is
possible that the blind poet knew nothing of this insolence,
which, moreover, was not signed. In April of the following year, however, when 'the August Council of State'
presided over by the elder Lawrence, having examined a
licentious miscellany entitled *Sportive Wit or the Muses'
Merriment*, summoned the compiler, imposed a fine and
condemned the book to be burnt, was it possible to hide
from Milton the fact that the culprit was his adopted son?
John was to have a long and undistinguished career,
selling his pen to whoever offered most and finishing as a
wine-bibber. Edward, less gifted, but a respectable member
of the middle-class, had already published a few popular
works and volumes of criticism. Of his own two nephews,
brought up by him entirely, Milton had only succeeded in
making a bohemian and a 'grammarian'.

It will be remembered that in 1656 Lady Ranelagh had
followed her husband to Ireland. Perhaps on the advice of
this true friend Milton remarried. Katherine Woodcock,
the orphan daughter of a Royalist officer, was twenty years
younger than Milton. She was gentle and pious and this
time he was loved. Since the Barebones Parliament, civil
marriage was obligatory. Milton judged it sufficient. The
couple were united in the Guildhall on November 12th,
1656.

That year the blind secretary dictated about thirty State
letters, but it was in England that the most important
scenes were played. The Venetian Ambassador Giovanni
Sagrado, who had come from Paris to London, wrote to
his government: 'Here are no smart cavaliers as in France,
but cavalry and infantry; instead of music and ballet,
trumpets and drums; no patches on the ladies' faces, but
muskets on the men's shoulders. . . .'[1] So many troops

---

[1] The ambassador punned upon *mosca* (patch) and *moschetto* (musket).

assure Cromwell's power, but they ruin the country and
exhaust it. The machine is strong but I do not deem it
lasting, for it is violent'.[1] These lines were written on
October 6th, 1656, three weeks after the second Parliament
of the Protectorate had at last begun to function.

Cromwell was not unaware of the precarious nature of
his power. Both his interest and his conscience urged him
to obtain the sanction of his people. On March 4th, 1656, he
proclaimed 'a day of solemn humiliation and prayer to be
upon Friday 28th':

> That we in all these Nations have more than ordinary cause
> to humble Ourselves and to lay Our mouthes in the dust in
> Fasting and Prayer before the Lord at this time will undoubtedly
> be agreed by all.

The Council deliberated secretly on the matter of new
elections in May and June, and the writs went out on July
10th.

Vane, in retirement in Lincolnshire in his country-house
of Belleau, had scented the danger and issued a pamphlet.
In actual fact many Englishmen had come to wish that the
protectorate might be changed into a monarchy. Some were
content to bow to a leader who was invariably successful;
others had to admit that he was just and merciful; others
said to themselves that once the throne was re-established,
Charles II would ascend it; others finally assured themselves that Cromwell crowned would be less dangerous,
because 'the royal prerogative was as exactly bounded as
an acre of land'. Petitions coming in from the provinces
called upon Cromwell to take the throne.

When the electors were convened, in July 1656, they
read Vane's pamphlet eagerly. He exhorted the English
to recover their liberties. At a pinch the executive could be
reduced to a single man, but assisted by irremovable councillors, and controlled by a freely elected assembly. A second
pamphlet, plainly anti-Cromwell, appeared anonymously in
August. The Republicans seethed but were mastered. Vane,
accused of having written the second pamphlet, was rele-
gated to the Isle of Wight.

[1] Guizot, op. cit., II, 239.

Shortly afterwards, on September 17th, 1656, Cromwell's second Parliament opened.

A hundred opponents were excluded at the outset. The rest showed themselves as 'boldly servile' (Guizot). Cromwell very soon secured the vote for the abolition of the military prefectures, partly in order to resume control of subordinates who had become over-powerful. In December he released Vane and defended against Parliament a Quaker preacher, Nayler, who had allowed some ranting women to offer him honour as if he were the special representative of Jesus Christ. It must be said that Nayler had too much success not to excite the jealousy of the regular ministers. It was he who converted the son of Admiral Penn, the future founder of Pennsylvania. A majority condemned him to barbarous penalties and to life imprisonment. Cromwell denounced this encroachment of the legislative upon the judiciary power; Parliament took no notice. It was a crying scandal and Cromwell's attitude opportunely tightened the links between him and his soldiers. His powerlessness to help Nayler made the Protector regret he was not a king.

In October 1656, in sight of Cadiz, English frigates captured some galleons from Peru. Cromwell made considerable capital out of their success and Waller wrote:

> His conquering head has no more room for bays,
> Then let it be, as the glad nation prays:
> Let the rich ore forthwith be melted down,
> And the state fix'd by making him a crown;
> With ermin clad and purple, let him hold
> A royal sceptre, made of Spanish gold.[1]

Waller was not the man to talk in the air, and he was a member of Parliament. Four months later, in February 1657, the Commons offered Cromwell the crown. He hesitated, well knowing that neither his talents nor a rite could make him the lawful heir of Edward the Confessor. In April a delegation of which Waller formed part tried a more pressing overture. Cromwell dared not brave the army and finally refused the crown on May 8th.

[1] Waller, *Poems*, London, 1810, p. 63.

So a kind of parliamentary monarchy without a king was agreed upon. The Protector appointed for life would designate his successor. He would create an irremovable Upper Chamber, the counterpart of the Lords, and the Parliament thus constituted would alone be qualified to legislate. On June 26th, Cromwell swore fidelity to this constitution between the hands of the Speaker of the Commons, and the assembly broke up for vacation.

During the first months of 1657, Cromwell ceaselessly intervened in Europe. The Czar had broken with the regicides as far back as 1649, but Cromwell had renewed commercial relations through Archangel in 1654. In March 1657, he sent an envoy extraordinary to Moscow.

In the same month he signed a military alliance with France for one year. Learning that the six thousand infantry he sent to that country were assigned to operations inland he threatened Turenne that he would recall them. In September they were to take Mardyck, a village near Dunkirk.

The previous month, to restore peace among his Northern allies, he had sent Meadows to Denmark and Downing to Holland. In the meantime, on two occasions, he had arranged for monetary help to be sent to the Waldenses.

Milton's share in this activity amounted to about twenty State letters, including one to the Czar Alexis. Two events gave him personal pleasure—in September Marvell was given to him as assistant in place of Meadows, and in October a little daugher, Katherine, was born to him.

As soon as Parliament re-assembled on January 20th, 1658, discord broke out between the Commons and the Upper Chamber, which they called 'the other House'. Cromwell had appointed to it seven peers of the realm and more than fifty members of Parliament of whom he was sure. Two peers only, however, deigned to sit. As to the members of Parliament ennobled for the occasion, the majority, like Colonel Pride, now Sir Thomas, came from the people. Moreover, the promotions to the Upper Chamber had weakened Cromwell in the Commons. They refused to hold discussions 'with carters and cobblers'. As early as

February 4th, Cromwell, furious and bitterly disappointed, had to dismiss his Parliament.

On the 10th Milton lost his young wife, and six weeks later the child followed the mother. To the memory of his wife Milton dedicated a sonnet which is not the work of a misogynist. The mention of the 'veiled face' will be noted—Milton had never seen Katherine.

> Methought I saw my late espoused Saint
>   Brought to me like *Alcestis* from the grave,
>   Whom *Joves* great Son to her glad Husband gave,
> Rescu'd from death by force though pale and faint.
> Mine as whom washt from spot of child-bed taint,
>   Purification in the old Law did save,
>   And such, as yet once more I trust to have
> Full sight of her in Heaven without restraint,
> Came vested all in white, pure as her mind:
>   Her face was vail'd, yet to my fancied sight,
>   Love, sweetness, goodness, in her person shin'd
> So clear, as in no face with more delight.
>   But O as to embrace me she enclin'd
>   I wak'd, she fled, and day brought back my night.

In March 1658, Cromwell renewed his treaty with Louis XIV for one year, then sent him fresh troops and placed the whole expeditionary force under the orders of his nephew and ambassador Lockhart. Dunkirk was besieged.

The illness and death of his wife had interrupted the secretary's activities for three months. On March 30th he wrote to the King of Sweden. In May he published a manuscript attributed to Sir Walter Raleigh, entitled *The Cabinet Council*, and now printed for the first time. It was an account of the methods of work practised by princes. It was of little interest in itself, but its publication at this date associated Cromwell with Elizabeth and Lockhart with Raleigh. Raleigh also had fought Spain at the side of the French.

Again in May, when Cromwell learnt that the Waldenses were in danger, Milton wrote two letters in his name, one to recommend them to Louis XIV, the other to charge Lockhart to suggest to Louis a means of saving them—to acquire their Valleys in exchange for some Catholic territory. Of the many letters dictated by Milton, that of May 26th, 1658, to the young King Louis XIV is not the least interesting. Here are a few lines:

> Most Serene and Potent King, and most August Friend and Confederate: . . . All things seem to threaten the utter extermination of those deplorable wretches, whom the former massacre spared. Which I most earnestly beseech and conjure ye, Most Christian King. by that RIGHT HAND which signed the league and friendship between us, by that same goodly ornament of your title MOST CHRISTIAN, by no means to suffer, nor to permit such liberty of rage and fury uncontrolled. . . . But as for you, great prince, suffer not, while you reign, your titles, nor the confines of your kingdom, to be contaminated with this same Heaven-offending scandal. . . . Remember, that they submitted themselves to your grandfather Henry, most friendly to the protestants, when the victorious Lesdiguieres pursued the retreating Savoyard over the Alps. There is also an instrument of that submission registered among the public acts of your kingdom, wherein it is excepted and provided among other things that, from that time forward, the Piedmontois should not be delivered over into the power of any ruler, but upon the same condition upon which your invincible grandfather received them into his protection. This protection of your grandfather these suppliants now implore from you as grandchild.[1]

In June 1658 Cromwell's 'tolerant' clergy succeeded in obtaining from him, as Milton had feared, the imposition of a more exacting creed. On the other hand the Immortal Six Thousand triumphed on the Dunes and took Dunkirk.

Cromwell was counting (rather cynically) on proposing to France a partition of the Low Countries. He was hoping moreover to establish himself on the Baltic by seconding the ambitions of Sweden, then engaged in a struggle with Poland and Austria. Finally, he was thinking of providing a counterpart to the Roman Congregation of Propaganda by instituting a 'Council of the Protestant religion' sitting in Chelsea. Would his Third Parliament, for which he had been preparing since March, have granted him the necessary credits? He was worn out and fell ill. The death of his

[1] Bohn II, 311–12 or Masson V, 387–9.

dearly loved daughter, Lady Claypole, broke his heart. He died three weeks after her, on September 3rd, his 'fortunate day', the day of Dunbar and of Worcester. The dictator in spite of himself, the solitary of Whitehall, was not yet sixty.

This death in full activity deeply troubled the solitary of Petty France, as we know from *Samson Agonistes*. One consequence was that he had become, as used to be said not so long ago in the land of the Japanese Samurai, a *rōnin*, a warrior without a lord.

He felt the blow all the more deeply as the previous month Edward himself, the respectable Edward, had humiliated and almost disavowed him by publishing a sort of fashionable manual of seduction. It was called *Mysteries of Love and Eloquence, or the Arts of Wooing and Complementing, as they are managed in the Spring Garden, Hide Park, the New Exchange, and other Eminent Places*, dedicated 'to the Youthful Gentry'. Godwin wrote in 1815, in his *Lives of Edward and John Phillips:* 'The book is put together with conspicuous ingenuity and profligacy, and is entitled to no insignificant rank among the multifarious productions which were at the time issued from the press to debauch the manners of the nation and bring back the king'.

Cromwell had been lying in the vaults of Westminster for a month when a new edition of the reply to Saumaise came out. It contained two additional pages, of which the conclusion was as follows:

> I have for some time understood that not only all the best of my own countrymen, but all the best also of foreign men, sanction and approve this persuasion of mine by no silent vote over the whole world. Which highest fruit of my labours proposed for myself in this life I both gratefully enjoy and at the same time make it my chief thought how I may best be able to assure not only my own country, for which I have already done my utmost, but also the men of all nations whatever, and especially all of the Christian name, that the accomplishment of yet greater things, if I have the power—and I *shall* have the power if God be gracious—is meanwhile for their sakes my desire and meditation.[1]

[1] Masson V, 573–4.

What is the exact meaning of this grandiloquent sentence?
Masson supposes that it was an indication of the coming
Paradise Lost. Aubrey reported, in fact, that, according to
Phillips, Milton began his epic 'about two years before the
King came in'.

Professor Tillyard,[1] however, thinks that Milton refers
here to the theological treatise already mentioned several
times.[2] The *Defensio* was exactly suited to the announcement
of this *Doctrina Christiana*, since both were in Latin. It
would be less easy to explain that Milton should have
promised in Latin, *i.e.* to the whole of Europe, an epic
accessible to the English alone.

But we can easily reconcile the two interpretations if
we try to imagine Milton at this critical hour of his life.
Seeing Cromwell gather together Protestant Europe, the
Latin secretary eagerly hoped to propose to that Europe
the system of theology he had composed over the years
for his personal satisfaction. He still had to put the final
touches to it. It would be natural for him to take advantage
of the new edition of the first *Defence* to announce vaguely,
but solemnly, this ambitious project. But new edition and
post-scriptum were still in the press when the Protector's
death suddenly overcast the future of England and of
Europe. Milton may then have interrupted the revision of
his *Doctrina Christiana* to devote himself entirely to his epic.

Such, we think, is the true meaning of the information
supplied by Phillips to Aubrey: 'he began about two years
before the King came in'. For we have seen (p. 99) that
the apostrophe of Satan to the sun was written as far back
as 1642, and that Milton did not abandon the drama for
which this passage was intended until he had composed an act
and a half (p. 136). Who knows what other fragments of this
drama, and also what purple passages, what descriptions,
episodes, images suitable for an epic, had been waiting
a longer or a shorter period for the day when the poet
should have completed his plan? From 1658 onwards, the
composition was to continue without interruption.

Several scholars have sought to date the books and even

[1] *Milton,* 1956, p. 207.   [2] Pp. 45, 141, etc. See Index.

particular passages of *Paradise Lost*. Their conclusions are not always convincing, the alchemy of poets has secrets even for themselves. A work of art is a living thing, and as such reaches beyond our understanding. What we can and should do is to recall, for those who are interested in the mystery of artistic creation, the stages through which Milton passed.

As a boy he was attracted by du Bartas and by Spencer: *Genesis* and Chivalry; how man has risen from clay and of what nobility he is capable. In Cambridge his dreams were of Hesiod and of Tasso: under other names the rivers that mirrored him were still the same. In Italy, Tasso predominated. Milton returned home longing to sing the first exploits of his race and drafted a few epic lines. But 'these new pipes apart did slip, snapping their band'.[1] He then turned aside to tragedy and examined possible subjects. Since legend and history seemed to him less propitious than the Bible, he returned to *Genesis* and began a drama of the Fall. One act and a half were in existence when the Long Parliament went into action. Religious and political disturbance, a foolish marriage, a bloody revolution, an official post, everything turned Milton aside from his task as a poet. As far back as 1641, however, seeing the Episcopal tyranny crumbling, he had imagined to himself that the liberation of England would supply him with the theme of an epic. Twice he let this be understood.[2]

Thirteen years went by. He was blind and was perhaps frightened by the vastness of an epic of the Fall. In any case, observing the European success of his reply to Saumaise, and intoxicated with political passion, he believed, or wished to believe, that his plea for the Commonwealth

---

[1] *The Lament for Damon*, Nonesuch, p. 812.
[2] In *Of Reformation in England*, in May 1641 (Bohn II, 418): 'But let them all take counsel together, and let it come to nought; let them decree, and do thou cancel it; let them gather themselves, and be scattered . . . for thou art with us. Then amidst the hymns and hallelujahs of saints some one may perhaps be heard offering at high strains in new and lofty measure to sing and celebrate thy divine mercies and marvellous judgments in this land throughout all ages. . . .'—A month later, in *Animadversions* (Bohn III, 72): 'O perfect and accomplish thy glorious acts . . . but thou art God, thy nature is perfection. . . . When thou hast settled peace in the Church and righteous judgment in the Kingdom . . . he that now for haste snatches up a plain ungarnished present as a thank offering to thee . . . may then perhaps take up a harp, and sing thee an elaborate song to generations.'

had as much value as an epic. Common sense protests, but this was indeed the theory he formulated in 1654.[1] If the Republicans had won their cause, perhaps Milton would have left matters so. But already, in 1654, the Commonwealth was tottering. Milton realized it, for he warned the Protector and exhorted the English to Republican virtues. Despite *Eikonoklastes* the Royal Image still shone bright, Milton's nephews sided with Saumaise, his people wanted a king, whether he were called Oliver or Charles. England's liberating mission was a mirage; there was no elect people. 'All have sinned', says the Apostle, 'and come short of the glory of God'. The incredible successes of Cromwell had been able to uphold the poet in his illusions; this premature death brought him back to reality. Like a man who finds his way in the glow of his burning house, Milton understood that he must return to the supreme theme of the Fall and treat it in all its fullness, that is, under the form of an epic.

---

[1] See above, p. 194: 'As the epic poet . . .'

XIII

RICHARD—THEN MONK

1658–1660

THE Commonwealth had signed its own death-warrant by thrusting aside social reforms. The Protectorate, a make-shift solution, a defeat in disguise, had only been held together by Cromwell's genius. Richard might make a good king, but a Protectorate was beyond him, and his merit was to recognize the fact. The generals expected to govern in his name. When they saw him prudently relying on the civil administration, they threw him over. They them-selves, however, were not equal to the task. One among them, Monk, brought back the monarchy in spite of them. We may sum up thus the twenty months which elapsed between Cromwell's death and the Restoration.

At the outset there was complete calm. Since Richard was neither soldier, Puritan nor innovator, and some people even believed him to be a Royalist, both friends and adver-saries of his father awaited events. To wait is to hope. Milton resumed the struggle for liberty of conscience.

In June 1658, Cromwell had promised that the teaching of his Church would be clearly defined. On September 27th, three weeks, that is, after his death, a hundred Independent ministers opened a minor council of war against 'heresies and blasphemies'. The tune had a familiar ring about it. If the Independents themselves chimed in with the Presby-terians, soul liberty had everything to fear. Fortunately, the state of finance necessitated the prompt convening of a parliament. On January 27th, 1659, Westminster opened its doors to Cromwell's sixty senators and nearly six hundred commoners.

Among the latter figured Bradshaw and Vane once more and, for the first time, Marvell. Richard, however, had appealed to electors whom his father had thrust aside, so that liberty of conscience had even less supporters in the new representation than in the previous one.

A fortnight after their installation, the members of
Parliament had brought to their notice a pamphlet of about
a hundred pages entitled *Treatise of Civil Power in Ecclesiastical Causes, showing that it is not lawful for any power on earth
to compel in matters of Religion.* In the opening lines Milton
declared:

> Two things there be, which have ever been found working
> much mischief to the Church of God and the advancement of
> truth: force on one side restraining, and hire on the other side
> corrupting, the teachers thereof.[1]

Milton dealt with the first point only, reserving the second
for his next treatise. He established, Bible in hand, the
four following propositions. Our only common rule is
Scripture, such as the Holy Spirit interprets it to each one.—
The State is incapable of appreciating different beliefs, and
even if it could, it has not the right to do so.—Christianity
is spiritual in its essence, its first principle is liberty.—
Finally, force can neither instruct nor inspire repentance;
it alienates the mind, hardens the heart, encourages formal-
ism and hypocrisy. The rôle of the magistrate is not to
control the churches, but to assure their liberty.

The style was perfectly simple, for Milton was no longer
dealing with the cultured parliamentarians of 1640. He
wanted to be understood even by Sir Thomas Pride.

> Pomp and ostentation of reading is admired among the
> vulgar; but doubtless in matters of religion, he is learnedest
> who is plainest. The brevity I use, not exceeding a small
> manual, will not therefore, I suppose, be thought the less
> considerable, unless with them, perhaps, who think that great
> books only can determine great matters. I rather choose the
> common rule, not to make much ado, where less may serve;
> which in controversies, and those especially of religion, would
> make them less tedious, and by consequence read oftener by
> many more, and with more benefit.[2]

Such simplicity, however, did not mean dryness of style:

> How many persecutions, then imprisonments, banishments,
> penalties, and stripes; how much bloodshed have the forcers of

[1] Bohn II, 522.   [2] Ibid., 548.

conscience to answer for, and protestants rather than papists!
For the papist, judging by his principles, punishes them who
believe not as the Church believes, though against Scripture;
but the protestant, teaching every one to believe the Scripture,
though against the Church, counts heretical, and persecutes
against his own principles, them who in any particular so
believe as he in general teaches them; them who most honour
and believe divine Scripture, but not against it any human
interpretation though universal.[1]

The Parliament was Presbyterian to a very large extent.
It took care not to touch the ecclesiastical organization.
Its primary object was to reduce the power of the army.
The generals put Richard under the necessity of choosing
between them and Parliament. He dismissed Parliament,
reluctantly, on April 22nd, 1659, and then stood aside. His
abdication a month later was to pass unnoticed.

On May 7th the army recalled the Rump Parliament
which Cromwell had driven out in 1653. A new Council
was appointed including Vane and Bradshaw. This time
the members of Parliament were almost all fervent
supporters of the Commonwealth. Milton was delighted
and offered them in the month of August his second treatise,
*Considerations touching the likeliest means to remove Hirelings
out of the Church*—one hundred and fifty pages, as arrogant
as they were explicit. No more tithes, no more fees—which
he called 'vails'. Let the pastors live from the offerings of
the faithful or from some secular trade or profession, as it
is the rule among 'the Waldenses, our first reformers' (B. III,
32). It was useless to maintain the universities at great expense: the clergymen they formed would be replaced with
advantage by itinerant preachers who would leave behind
them lay monitors and libraries. A 'competent' library would
not cost them more than £60.

> But [they say,] papists and other adversaries cannot be con-
> futed without fathers and councils, immense volumes, and of
> vast charges. I will shew them therefore a shorter and a better
> way of confutation: Tit. i, 9, 'Holding fast the faithful word,

[1] Bohn II, 532.

as he hath been taught, that he may be able by sound doctrine, both to exhort and to convince gainsayers': who are confuted, as soon as heard, bringing that which is either not in Scripture, or against it. To pursue them further through the obscure and entangled wood of antiquity, fathers and councils fighting one against another, is needless, endless, not requisite in a minister, and refused by the first reformers of our religion.[1]

Luckless Milton! When his second treatise saw the light, it was already more than a month since the Rump had voted for the maintenance of the national church and of the tithe. The great problem of the parliamentarians still was how to reduce the army to obedience. Among other measures, Cromwell's European policy was abandoned, all the generals were stepped down to the rank of colonel, and the officers of both land and sea forces must in future hold their warrant from the Speaker of the Commons.

In August 1659, Lambert had suppressed a Royalist rising in the provinces. In September he demanded semi-Cromwellian powers. On October 12th the Rump relieved him of his command. The next day his regiments encircled Westminster before it was daylight and prevented the members from entering. This eclipse of the Rump was to last two months. The Council remained in office (a statement of payments attests that at the end of October Milton and Marvell were still Latin secretaries), but the administrative machine no longer had any impetus. Milton in a curious *Letter to a Friend* dated October 20th[2] compared the fragile Commonwealth to a child subject to ruptures. A political personage, perhaps Vane, had consulted Milton. He replied:

> Upon the sad and serious discourse which we fell into last night, concerning these dangerous ruptures of the Commonwealth, scarce yet in her infancy, which cannot be without some inward flaw in her bowels, I began to consider more intensely thereon than hitherto I have been wont, resigning myself to the wisdom and care of those who had the government.[3]

[1] Bohn III, 37–38.
[2] It was not to be published until 1698, but it was circulated.
[3] *On the Ruptures of the Commonwealth*, Bohn II, 102.

Milton was indignant that the army should have dared to gag the Parliament. Such insubordinations would never have been seen in France, in Venice, or in Holland.

> Being now in anarchy, without a counselling and governing power; and the army, I suppose, finding themselves insufficient to discharge at once both military and civil affairs, the first thing to be found out with all speed, without which no commonwealth can subsist, must be a senate, or general council of state, in whom must be the power, first to preserve the public peace; next, the commerce with foreign nations; and lastly, to raise monies for the management of these affairs.[1]

This Council would have to swear to respect liberty of conscience and to oppose government by one man alone.

> That which I conceive only able to cement, and unite for the army, either to the parliament recalled, or this chosen council, must be a mutual league and oath, private or public, not to desert one another till death: . . . If such a union as this be not accepted on the army's part, be confident there is a single person underneath.[2]

> With this you may do what you please, put out, put in, communicate or suppress: you offend not me, who only have obeyed your opinion, that in doing what I have done, I might happen to offer something which might be of some use in this great time of need.[3]

This letter was perhaps useful. Six days later, on October 26th, 1659, despite a solemn warning from Bradshaw, the Council of the Rump surrendered its powers to a Committee of Safety appointed by the Council of the Officers. The twenty-three members swore loyalty to 'the Good Old Cause'. Seven, Lambert among them, were of the military; Vane and nine others came from the suppressed Council. Vane seems to have seen through the game of Monk, the commander of the forces in Scotland, and to have relied on the officers of London to save the Commonwealth.

As early as October 20th, Monk had written to Speaker Lenthall of the Rump: 'I am resolved, by the grace and

---

[1] Bohn II, 104.   [2] Ibid., 105   [3] Ibid., 106.

assistance of God, as a true Englishman, to stand and assert the liberty and authority of Parliament'. This sounded well, but what did he mean by Parliament? Then he took certain steps. In particular he dismissed those of his officers whom he knew to be supporters of the Commonwealth. On November 3rd the Committee of Safety entered into negotiations with Monk, and instructed Lambert, who had been promoted Major-General of the forces in England and Scotland, to prevent his marching into England. On this same November 3rd, Monk invited the Committee to restore the Rump, or, if the Rump would not be restored, then to elect 'a full and free Parliament'. ('The Good Old Cause' and 'a full and free Parliament' were the slogans of the time.)

On December 13th, Monk was at the frontier, whence he continued his dilatory negotiations, while Lambert's troops deserted. On December 26th, the Committee gave place to the Rump, which appointed a new Council. Matters were thus back again at the deadlock of May. Since the visit of the unknown friend, Milton had been searching for a rapid and definitive solution.

Without firing a shot, Monk's troops, regularly paid, well in hand, and acclaimed as they advanced, marched through England in the snow. On January 28th, 1660, they were at the gates of London, then in complete anarchy and clamouring for 'a full and free Parliament'. For those in Westminster three solutions were possible, as in 1653: to proceed to free general elections (which would probably sweep them from power), to recall the Royalist members excluded in 1648 (which would put them in a minority), or to proceed to partial, controlled elections, they themselves keeping their seats and invalidating the election of those not sufficiently Republican. This was the combination which had earned them their dismissal by Cromwell in 1653, but they opted for it again. Whereupon London set up barricades everywhere and refused to pay the taxes.

Monk knocked down the barricades on February 8th and 9th, then enjoined the Rump on the 11th to recall within a week the members excluded in 1648. The Londoners lit bonfires at which they roasted rumps of every kind.

On February 21st Monk gathered together about a hundred of Pride's victims, handed them his written instructions and had them escorted to Westminster. The 1640 Parliament was reconstituted.

For all Milton's haste—demonstrated by the printing errors in his pamphlet—it was only about this fatal February 21st, 1660, that he was able to launch a project of solution which he had destined for the Rump, *The Ready and Easy Way to Establish a Free Commonwealth*, a small quarto of eighteen pages. At the same time, in a private letter of three pages, he sent Monk a summary of it: *The Present Means and Brief Delineation of a Free Commonwealth, Easy to be put in Practice and without Delay.*

Inevitably the Parliament now re-established was royalist, but its first care, since Monk insisted upon it, was to swear loyalty to the Commonwealth. It then sent Lambert to the Tower and, in conformity with a royal decision, handed over to Monk the command of all the forces by land and sea. For the last five months Harrington's club, the Rota, had been demanding a single assembly renewable by rotation. Needham was a member of it, Cyriack Skinner often presided over the meetings in which all social classes thronged together. On seeing the rebirth of the Commons of 1640, the Rota dissolved itself. The extent of the House's dislike of Milton's ideas is proved by a single fact. It had only twenty-five days before it to acquit itself of its only mission: to convene a Parliament-Convention. It dared to take advantage of this brief delay to have the Covenant posted up in every parish in England.

As to Monk, from Land's End to the Hebrides, there was no man more determined not even to glance at the lucubrations of one such as Milton. He classed all the Independents, Baptists, Quakers and others, under the name of fanatics. Milton could not have expected much of him, for on February 6th, addressing the Rump, Monk disappointed it and made it uneasy by his ambiguity. Monk, however, gave himself out as a supporter of the Commonwealth. During his march on London he had horse-whipped an officer for having insinuated that he, Monk, would bring back the King. On the evening of February 21st, he had written to the regiments of the three nations that the government was still to be that of a Commonwealth. To the secluded members of 1648 he affirmed that 'in God's presence, he had nothing before his eyes but the glory of God and the settlement of these nations upon Common-wealth foundations'. Last, not least, he was all-powerful. The friends of liberty would have to keep silence or implore Monk's good will.

The Ready and Easy Way was chiefly a parallel between monarchies and republics, accompanied by predictions and objurgations, and by a plan which owed a good deal to Harrington. Not a word about the ecclesiastical situation. Milton addressed himself solely to saving the Common-wealth.

... to betray a just and noble cause ... not only argues a strange, degenerate contagion suddenly spread among us, fitted and prepared for new slavery, but will render us a scorn and derision to all our neighbours.

And what will they at best say of us, and of the whole English name, but scoffingly, as of that foolish builder men-tioned by our Saviour, who began to build a tower, and was not able to finish it? Where is this goodly tower of a Com-monwealth, which the English boasted they would build to overshadow kings, and be another Rome in the West? ...[1]

... making vain and viler than dirt the blood of so many thousand faithful and valiant Englishmen, who left us in this liberty, bought with their lives; ...[2]

There will be a queen of no less charge; in most likelihood outlandish and a papist; besides a queen-mother such already; together with both their courts and numerous train: then a royal issue, and ere long severally their sumptuous courts; to the multiplying of a servile crew, not of servants only, but of nobility and gentry, bred up then to the hopes not of public but of court-offices, to be stewards, chamberlains, ushers, grooms even of the close-stool ... who (the king) for any-thing wherein the public really needs him, will have little else

[1] Bohn II, 114.   [2] Ibid., 115.

to do, but to bestow the eating and drinking of excessive dainties, to set a pompous lace upon the superficial actings of state, to pageant himself up and down in progress among the perpetual bowings and cringings of an abject people on either side deifying and adoring him for nothing done that can deserve it. For what can he more than another man? who, even in the expression of a late court-poet, sits only like a great cipher set to no purpose before a long row of other significant figures. Nay, it is well and happy for the people, if their king be but a cipher, being ofttimes a mischief, a pest, a scourge of the nation, and, which is worse, not to be removed, not to be controlled, much less accused or brought to punishment, without the danger of a common ruin, without the shaking and almost subversion of the whole land: whereas in a free commonwealth any governor or chief counsellor offending may be removed and punished, without the least commotion.[1]

And what madness is it for them who might manage nobly their own affairs themselves, sluggishly and weakly to devolve all on a single person; and more like boys under age than men, to commit all to his patronage and disposal, who neither can perform what he undertakes, and yet for undertaking it, though royally paid, will not be their servant but their lord![2]

Now is the opportunity, now the very season, wherein we may obtain a free Commonwealth and establish it for ever in the land, without difficulty or much delay.[3]

Is it such an unspeakable joy to serve, such felicity to wear a yoke? to clink our shackles, locked on by pretended law of subjection, more intolerable and hopeless to be ever shaken off, than those which are knocked on by illegal injury and violence?[4]

To save the Commonwealth it was necessary to set up 'forthwith' a permanent legislative body, the Grand or General Council of the Nation. This Council could not be elected by the people, who were too ignorant not to fall into 'unbridled democracy'. The chief gentlemen of the counties, called up and instructed by Monk, would divide England into as many constituencies as there were important towns, and would install in every chief town an assembly which would occupy itself with local affairs, including justice and education. At first some of the 'ablest

[1] Bohn II, 116–18.   [2] Ibid., 118.   [3] Ibid., 121.   [4] Ibid., 129.

knights and burgesses' would be chosen by those assemblies
to sit in London 'or in some more convenient place' and
constitute the Grand National Council, entrusted with
national affairs, commerce, war and peace, finance, and
Foreign Affairs. Later, this Council would fill up its vacancies by summoning to itself regional councillors. In this way
every councillor making his début in London would
already have experience of affairs. To discourage ambitions
and prevent jealousies, it might prove necessary to recon-
stitute the Council by one third, either annually or at longer
intervals, although it would be better to confine oneself
to filling the vacancies as they occurred. The periodical
replacement of a third of the Council Milton called 'partial
rotation'.[1] Whether it was resorted to or not, continuity
would be ensured. Continuity was of paramount importance. 'The ship of the Commonwealth is always under
sail' (B. II, 122). Such a permanent senate would be more
stable than any dynasty.

Therefore, Milton's republic would have been an oligarchy
like Venice and a federation like the United Provinces.[2]
Milton foresaw, moreover, that the electorate would grow
larger as education progressed. He had heard the mob
roaring at the barricades. His appeal to the members of
Parliament insisted on the necessity of educating the people.

Since it was necessary to address oneself to Monk, it
was to him that on March 21st a Republican group sent
out a desperate appeal: 'We fear a knife is at the very throat
not only of our and your liberties, but of our persons also'.
The pamphlet, not signed, was entitled *Plain English*.[3] On
March 23rd Needham published a final pamphlet, also
anonymous, *News from Brussels*.[4] A characteristic incident
then occurred.

[1] 'The known expedient may be used, of a partial rotation' (B. II, 108); 'this they call "partial rotation" ' (Ibid., 122).
[2] Indeed, Milton boasted that his federation would be the stronger of the two: ' . . . we shall also far exceed the United Provinces, by having not as they (to the retarding and distracting ofttimes of their counsels on urgentest occasions), many sovereignties united in one commonwealth, but many commonwealths under one united and intrusted sovereignty'. Bohn II, 136.
[3] Masson V, 664.   [4] Ibid., V, 671–2.

Monk absolutely forbade any public reference to the Restoration, but London lived through it in anticipation and London's joy voiced itself loudly. On March 25th a former chaplain to Charles I named Griffith dared to preach on the text from *Prov.* xxiv, 21-2: 'My son, fear thou the Lord and the king; and meddle not with them that are given to change, for their calamity shall rise suddenly; and who knoweth the ruin of them both?' After this, completely losing his head, Griffith published his sermon, dedicating it to General Monk. Monk was forced to send him to Newgate. Milton replied to Griffith by *Brief Notes* and, paradoxically, was not molested. There he said, however:

> I affirmed in the Preface of a late discourse, entitled 'The Ready Way to Establish a Free Commonwealth, and the dangers of readmitting Kingship in this Nation', that the humour of returning to our old bondage was instilled of late by some deceivers; and to make good, that what I then affirmed was not without just ground, one of those deceivers I present here to the people: and if I prove him not such, refuse not to be so accounted in his stead.[1]

Now a few days before the appearance of *Brief Notes*, on March 28th, the police had arrested Chapman, the printer of *Plain English*, who had also printed *Ready and Easy Way*. Would Milton be keeping Chapman company? He was beginning to be spoken of. Prynne, who had passed from prison to the House, had taken up his pen again to abuse Milton. On March 17th, an anonymous libel, *Character of the Rump*, attacked Milton, Harrington and Needham. On the 30th an amusing pamphlet, *Censure of the Rota*, not signed, imagined the club discussing Milton's project. All his work as a controversial writer was reviewed. Nothing was more just, since he had been the sole champion of the regicides. Why had he not the decency to let it be forgotten?

At this date the Commonwealth had no defenders left. Bradshaw had died in November, Sidney was on a mission in Denmark and Lambert under lock and key. Haselrig, known for his boldness, did not move from his home and

---

[1] *Brief Notes on Dr. Griffith's Sermon*, Bohn II, 354.

groaned: 'We are undone. We are undone.' Ludlow walked
up and down before the House to show that he had not
fled like so many others, and had not either, like so many
others, changed camps; but he was silent. Barebones,
whose windows the crowd had broken, had promised to
keep quiet. Vane had gone back to his country-house of
Belleau. Blind Milton alone held the field.

He was attacked on April 1st in a reply to *Plain English*.
Treason arraigned claimed to recognize in *Plain English* the
style of *Eikonoklastes*:

> . . . not content barely to applaud the murder of the King, the
> execrable author vomits upon his ashes. . . . Betwixt him
> [Milton] and his brother Rabshakeh [Needham?] I think a
> man may venture to divide the glory of it. . . . Say, Milton,
> Needham, either or both of you, or whosoever else, say where
> this worthy person [Monk] ever mixed with you. . . .[1]

In this month of April, 1660, London was consumed with
impatience, Monk kept an eye on the progress of his comedy,
tracts poured out, and the electors nominated the Parliament-
Convention which would open on the 25th. Milton, alone
in the breach, revised his *Ready and Easy Way*, which had
been written and printed too hastily. He pruned, corrected,
amplified. He even attached to his new version one of his
pregnant epigraphs:

> . . . *Et nos*
> *Consilium dedimus Syllae: demus Populo nunc.*
> We have advised
> Sulla himself: advise we now the People.[2]

The first part is from Juvenal, *demus Populo nunc* is Milton's.
Sylla is Monk who had not deigned to answer him; the
people was England in the process of voting. Milton had
very little hope, but at least he had liberated his soul. He
experienced a bitter pleasure:

> If their absolute determination be to enthral us, before so
> long a Lent of servitude, they may permit us a little shroving-
> time first, wherein to speak freely, and take our leaves of liberty.[3]

[1] Masson V, 665.   [2] Ibid., 678.
[3] *Ready and Easy Way*, Bohn II, 109.

The name of the printer is unknown. Nor do we know on which day in April the book came out. Its publication must be placed among the following events: on April 9th Needham was relieved of his functions as official publicist and Lambert escaped from the Tower to recruit an army in the provinces. (Needham was to abscond to Holland, Lambert would find no troops and be imprisoned again on April 24th). The next day, 25th, the Parliament-Convention assembled. Five hundred Commons and half a score of Lords. The same day Roger L'Estrange, a royalist pamphleteer, published without a signature *No Blinde Guides: in answer to a seditious Pamphlet of J. Milton's entituled 'Brief Notes on a late Sermon etc.'* It is a long apostrophe of which it will be sufficient to quote the beginning:

> Mr. Milton,
>
> Although in your life and doctrine you have resolved one great question, by evidencing that devils may indue human shapes and proving yourself even to you own wife an incubus, you have yet started another; and that is whether you are not of that regiment which carried the herd of swine headlong into the sea, and moved the people to beseech Jesus to depart out of their coasts.[1]

Shortly afterwards came a new and curious attack, cautiously signed G.S. In this connection the circumspection of Charles's champions should be noted. Monk remained masked until the last moment, L'Estrange did not sign; the shadow of Cromwell still had power to frighten. The pamphlet of this G.S. is particularly enlightening. *The Dignity of Kingship Asserted* . . . recapitulated Milton's scandalous past, but at the same time kept within reasonable limits.

> I am not ignorant of the ability of Mr. Milton . . . Concerning his answer [to Salmasius] thus much must be confessed, that nothing could be therein desired which either a shrewd wit could prompt or a fluent elegant style express.[2]

The body of the work, however, dated back several weeks. The dedication, on the contrary, a lengthy epistle

[1] Masson V, 690.　　　　　[2] Ibid., 692.

to His Majesty, written at the moment when the Restoration was at last certain, denounced Milton to the vengeance of the King in impassioned terms:

> ... this Murder, I say, and these Villainies, were defended, nay extolled and commended, by one Mr. John Milton, in answer to the most learned Salmasius ... he did so bespatter the white robes of your Royal Father's spotless life (human infirmities excepted) with the dirty filth of his satirical pen that to the vulgar, and those who read his book with prejudice, he represented him a most debauched, vicious man (I tremble, Royal Sir, to write it), an irreligious hater and persecutor of Religion and religious men, an ambitious enslaver of the nation, a bloody tyrant, and an implacable enemy to all his good subjects; and thereupon calls that ... Murder ... Restoring of the nation to its Liberty.[1]

The second edition of *The Ready and Easy Way* awakened no response. England was delirious and events were moving too fast. It is even probable that the work was seized at the printer's or remained in the printer's warehouse. We only know the text of it from a Dutch reprint in 1698.

When the Convention entered upon the scene, Cromwell's troopers demanded their dismissal *en masse*. After a series of decisions arrived at months earlier between the King and Monk, the assembly declared on May 1st that 'according to the ancient and fundamental laws of this kingdom, the Government is, and ought to be, by King, Lords and Commons'.

All that was left to Milton was to put himself and his children in safety. An unknown friend found him a safe retreat. An act of transfer dated May 7th, on which the blind man's signature is in the hand of a secretary, but authenticated by the family seal of the double-headed eagle, tells us that the loyal Skinner handed him, against a Treasury bond, four hundred pounds, the wherewithal to live for two years.

On the morrow Charles was proclaimed king.

Three weeks later, on May 29th, 1660, London at last welcomed her King, a handsome cavalier of thirty, thin

[1] Masson V, 693.

and sunburnt, a fine figure of a man, with gracious gestures, and with a shrewd intelligent look. The bells answered the salvoes of artillery, along the flower-strewn streets the crowd shouted for joy. Charles laughed and with characteristic irony said to a person in his suite that it was his own fault that he had not come back sooner; for he found nobody who did not tell him that he longed for his return. At the time Milton was in hiding, perhaps with his daughters, in Bartholomew Close, an obscure backwater of the City.

At the announcement of the King's return, several persons died of joy. Milton, despite his sorrow as a patriot and a lover of Soul-liberty, had the solid satisfaction of having fought right to the end, and alone. These unique hours were to have their echoes in his major poems. He had shown something of their intensity already in that second edition of *The Ready and Easy Way*, which most probably never reached the public; it ended as follows (B. II, 138):

However, with all hazard I have ventured what I thought my duty to speak in season, and to forewarn my country in time. . . .

What I have spoken is the language of that which is not called amiss 'The good old Cause': if it seem strange to any, it will not seem more strange, I hope, than convincing to backsliders. Thus much I should perhaps have said, though I was sure I should have spoken only to trees and stones; and had none to cry to, but with the prophet, 'O earth, earth, earth!' to tell the very soil itself, what her perverse inhabitants are deaf to. Nay, though what I have spoke should happen (which thou suffer not, who didst create mankind free! nor thou next, who didst redeem us from being servants of men!) to be the last words of our expiring liberty. But I trust I shall have spoken persuasion to abundance of sensible and ingenuous men; to some, perhaps, whom God may raise from these stones to become children of reviving liberty; . . . to exhort this torrent also of the people, not to be so impetuous but to keep their due channel, and at length recovering and uniting their better resolutions, now that they see already how open and unbounded the insolence and rage is of our common enemies, to stay these ruinous proceedings, justly and timely fearing to what a precipice of destruction the deluge of this epidemic madness would hurry us, through the general defection of a misguided and abused multitude.

Here Milton was comparing himself to the prophet Micah. Seven hundred years before Christ, this impassioned seer reproached Israel for her infidelities, foretold the ruin of Jerusalem, and announced a Saviour. He knew, however, that his people would refuse to listen to him. 'If a man . . . do lie, saying, I will prophesy unto thee of wine and of strong drink; he shall even be the prophet of this people.' Therefore he addressed himself to the whole world and to God: 'Hear, all ye people: hearken, O earth, and all that therein is: and let the Lord God be witness against you, the Lord from his holy temple'.

XIV

THE LANDSLIDE
1660–1662

ON May 1st, 1660, the Convention heard the Declaration of Breda read, in which Charles promised his loving subjects a general pardon, 'excepting only such persons as shall hereafter be excepted by Parliament,—these only to be excepted'. Could Milton be otherwise than 'excepted'? The *Character of the Rump* mentioned earlier already put him in the list for the future hangman:

> John Milton is their goose-quill champion [the Rump's];... an old heretic both in religion and manners, that by his will would shake off his governors as he doth his wives, four in a fortnight.... He is so much an enemy to usual practices that I believe, when he is condemned to travel to Tyburn in a cart, he will petition for the favour to be the first man that ever was driven thither in a wheel-barrow. And now, John, *you* must stand close and draw your elbows, that Needham, the Common-wealth didapper, may have room to stand beside you....[1]

The furious Prynne, the man without ears, with the nose cleft, with his cheek scorched, wanted a hecatomb. The majority of his colleagues, however, were anxious to save some relative or a friend. There were reciprocal concessions and more than one generous gesture.

The Commons agreed in the first place that only those men who had been directly responsible for the crime of 1649—judges, clerks of the court, executioners—would be excepted. Twelve were designated as worthy of death— in the first place the valiant, simple Harrison, the visionary of the Fifth Monarchy, and lastly the Independent pastor Hugh Peters, who had returned from America to throw himself into the fight. Eloquent, devout, indefatigable, Cromwell had made him chaplain to the army and to the Council. He had preached vehemently against the King.

[1] Masson V, 659.

On mere hearsay, the Convention thought he had been one of the masked men on the scaffold.

On June 9th the Commons went further. They resolved to demand imprisonment for a time or for life for twenty Republican leaders, discreetly designated as 'political delinquents'. This time Milton was in danger.

Marvell brought the influence of sympathizers into play. There was no lack of them. Influential Parliamentarians such as Morrice and Clarges, relatives of Monk, Annesley, the Privy Councillor, and Lord Broghill, brother of Lady Ranelagh, were favourable to Milton. Pope had it on good authority that Davenant saved the man who had saved him in 1650, a very plausible contention, for all depended on Chancellor Hyde, the future Clarendon, and he and Davenant had been close friends in their youth. However this may be, a first list of 'delinquents' was drawn up on the 16th—it included thirteen names, among them those of Vane, Thurloe, Haselrig and Lambert. It omitted Milton, but the sword hanging over his head might fall on the morrow. Was it Marvell who managed to have the blow deflected straight away? At the close of the session the Convention voted that three works should be burnt by the executioner and their authors forthwith taken into custody by the Sergeant-at-Arms. The works were a pamphlet of the Independent pastor John Goodwin, a learned defender of toleration, together with *Eikonoklastes* and the first *Defence*.

Since June 16th fell on a Saturday, Milton in his hiding-place had twenty-four hours to think over his situation, as Marvel had for further action. On the Monday the members completed the list of the twenty 'delinquents' worthy of prison; Goodwin was included in it but not Milton.

In July it was the turn of the Lords to discuss the sanctions. They demanded capital punishment for all those who had voted for the King's death and, in addition, for Vane, Haselrig and Lambert, although none of these three had voted for it.

In August the Commons examined the list drawn up by

the Lords, then deliberated about it with them. Since agreement could not be arrived at in the cases of Vane and Lambert, Hyde had this compromise adopted—to demand from the judges condemnation to death and from the King that the sentence be commuted to life imprisonment. On August 27th the public executioner burnt the books of Milton and Goodwin. On the 29th Charles signed the Law of Amnesty, which gave the list of those excepted. Milton was not of the number; his books had paid his debt and he was free.

Unfortunately the Sergeant-at-Arms of Parliament, Norfolke, understood nothing but his formal orders . . . and what the payment for board and lodging of his prisoners brought him in. He arrested his man, who doubtless went out from Bartholomew Close too soon. The Convention rose after September 13th and did not sit again until November 6th. Not until December 15th could Marvell obtain his friend's liberation. One characteristic and often quoted trait must be mentioned. Parliament had ordered that Milton should be 'forthwith released, paying his fees'. Now Norfolke had demanded the exorbitant sum of one hundred and fifty pounds. Milton lodged a complaint and obtained justice.

To set up once more the fine house in Petty France would have been ruinous and out of place. The Royal Parliamentary City of Westminster now belonged to the new race. It was in his birth-place, the City of London, that the defeated man went to take refuge permanently.

He first of all found a modest, provisional retreat in Holborn, near the Red Lion Inn. He discovered that his captivity was continuing under another form. The booksellers had just received at long last the shattering reply announced by Saumaise in 1653. But no one paid attention to it, and if Milton had ventured to refute it, no one would have published his book. Released from custody he found himself lost in the world of the deaf, reduced to following in silence events which verified his prophecies and often went further—impudent retractions, loyalty punished, foul deeds honoured, scandals of one sort or another, pious reprisals. In principle it would be sufficient to mention these commonplaces of history, but generalizations do not bring home how much the Miltonian epic merited its melancholy title.

Charles II inaugurated his reign in a very delicately balanced situation. Brought up by a Catholic mother, detesting the moral exigencies and the political claims of the Presbyterians, he had nevertheless contracted serious engagements towards them. In 1650, when a refugee in Scotland, he had been forced to swear to the Covenant, like his grandfather hearing mass to gain Paris. Thus in 1659, writing from Breda, he had promised Parliament to respect the Presbyterian system. From the month of May 1660, however, seeing London at his feet, he declared himself personally as Anglican. Immediately, a number of Anglican clergymen found their livings restored and sometimes acquired a good deal more. Pierre Du Moulin, but recently a humble petitioner of the tyrant, obtained a prebend at Canterbury, a Welsh rectory and the office of King's chaplain, while his brother, Louis, the professor who had translated Milton, was driven from Oxford and was making shift to live in London. The insignificant Pory, Milton's former fellow-pupil at St. Paul's and at Cambridge, was distantly related to the new Archbishop of Canterbury—he was made Archdeacon of Middlesex, rector of St. Botolph's and a prebendary of Willesden. He was to end his days as a canon of St. Paul's. Honest Edmund Calamy, the E.C. of the cypher 'Smectymnuus', trusted the King and agreed to be one of his Presbyterian chaplains.

In October 1660, Charles promised an official Anglicanism, mitigated by Presbyterianism. In November he re-established the episcopal framework, while assuring that non-Anglican forms of worship were still authorized. Poor Ireland, Catholic and Presbyterian, received four Anglican archbishops and eighteen bishops, Scotland detached itself, hundreds of Independents were imprisoned—like the Baptist Bunyan, who was to spend twelve

years of his life as a prisoner. As to Calamy, the kindly—
and cynical—King offered him the bishopric of Coventry,
but Calamy refused to forswear himself.

All this was only a prelude.

Three events of different kinds occurred in October 1660
—the disbanding of the army, the execution of ten regicides
and the affair of Hyde.

The dispersal of the invincibles was justified. One
consequence of it, at once unexpected and capital, was that
it contributed to the rehabilitation of Puritanism. The
Commonwealth and the Protectorate had been compromised
by the ambition of a few generals, the greed of some
politicians, and the eccentricities of too many fools and
hypocrites, but now, in every corner of the country, tens
of thousands of farmers, gardeners, domestics, sailors,
artisans, won admiration for their piety, their professional
conscientiousness and their self-control.

The regicides detained by the Convention appeared before
a Court of Justice which applied to them this clause of a
statute of Edward III: 'Quant homme fait compasser ou
imaginer la mort de nostre Seignur le Roy'.[1] Milton
must have congratulated himself that the Convention
had not thought of this old law. Hugh Peters satisfied the
Court that he was not one of the masked men on the
scaffold, but was sentenced to death for his inflammatory
sermons. Between October 11th and 19th, fifteen of the
accused were condemned to capital punishment, but
reprieved, and ten more were executed. Despite the
barbarism of the rites of the scaffold—suppressed by
Cromwell but now re-established—the King witnessed the
spectacle on four occasions. Did he see Hugh Peters die?

The unhappy man had been afraid of weakening. When
the executioner had disembowelled under his eyes a certain
Cook, consulting barrister in 1649, he turned to Peters
and asked him, while ostentatiously rubbing his hands in
their gauntlets of blood: 'How do you like this work, Mr.

[1] To fall foul of a French law would have justified Milton's dislike for the French.
In this connection we may note that French remained the legal language of the
English until 1731, except under Cromwell. See *Of Education*, Bohn III, 468.

Peters?' Cromwell's friend, however, died as a brave man, under the jeers of the crowd.[1]

Milton had written that a Court would prove debauched, servile and ruinous. He had not foreseen that noblemen would serve Charles on their knees.

Nor could he have imagined the Hyde scandal. While they were disembowelling the regicides, the Chancellor learnt that his daughter Anne was pregnant by the King's brother, the Duke of York. Honourable to the point of severity, Hyde cursed his daughter, spoke of executing or imprisoning her, and when it was represented to him that there was perhaps a secret marriage, replied that 'he would rather know that she was the Duke's wench than his wife'. Whereupon an officer of the Duke of York claimed the girl and offered reparation.[2] This time it was the Duke James who stormed. Finally, thanks to the King, everything was cleared up and arranged—the Duke married officially and the officer was ennobled. This, too, was but a prelude. Chateaubriand called the reign 'vingt-cinq ans de débauche sous des fourches patibulaires ... une orgie funèbre'.[3]

Milton was still lodging near the Red Lion Inn when the Convention, desirous of ending gloriously, ordained that the death of the holy King should be commemorated on January 30th, 1661, by a fast, sermons, prayers, and the posthumous punishment of Cromwell, Ireton and Bradshaw, whose remains were reposing at Westminster. On Monday, 28th, the coffins of the tyrant and his son-in-law were dragged on a hurdle along the Strand to the acclamations of the populace, then deposited provisionally—in Holborn, in the courtyard of the Red Lion Inn. On the morrow, there was the same procedure with the remains of Bradshaw. Thus, during a night, a day and another night, the blind man heard under his windows the trampling and uproar of the crowd. On the 30th, the regicides were hanged at Tyburn in their coffins, then, when evening came, buried at the foot of the gallows.[4] The heads, however,

---

[1] Masson VI, 97.   [2] Ibid., 106–8.
[3] Not exempt from rhetoric, but see Taine, Book III, ch. I, i–viii.
[4] Close to the present site of Marble Arch.

were to blacken in the wind and rain on the gables of Westminster Hall. '. . . the best and wisest of men. Such, O Cromwell, all acknowledge you to be.'

In April, 1661, Charles distributed titles and was crowned. From now onwards Hyde was Earl of Clarendon and Annesley Earl of Anglesey.

On May 8th began what was known as the 'Cavalier' Parliament, which showed itself at first 'more Royalist than the King and more Anglican than the bishops'. The month had not run out when the Covenant, which had been posted up in all the churches for a year past, was publicly burnt. In July Parliament declared that the Law of Amnesty was too indulgent. The King had to point out that he could not go back on his word. Vengeance was taken on the dead. In September, twenty-five corpses, including that of Cromwell's mother, were thrown into the common ditch by order of the Dean of Westminster. In December, the Corporation Act stipulated that no one would be allowed to hold a municipal office 'unless he took the oath of loyalty and had, during the year preceding the nomination, communicated in accordance with the Anglican rite'. The day after Christmas, a certain Baptist minister named James was drawn and quartered for a sermon which had 'disquieted His Majesty'.

It was in this year 1661 that Milton, in addition to disgust and horror, experienced fear. Some young Cavaliers, disappointed by Charles II's moderation, undertook to avenge his father themselves. Algernon Sidney, for instance, who had remained unpunished because he was in Denmark at the time of the King's return, had encounters with assassins, well-born men, or well paid, in Rome in 1661 and 1662, in Switzerland in 1663, in Augsburg in 1664, in Holland in 1665. One of the late King's judges, John Lisle, was killed in Lausanne, at the instigation, it was believed, of the Queen Mother. Those self-appointed avengers and their emissaries easily found people to aid and abet them, and their cause seemed to them to justify all means. Richardson recounts that at this period the blind poet 'was in a perpetual terror of being assassinated . . .

[and] so dejected that he would lie awake whole nights, and kept himself as private as he could'.

At the beginning of 1662, Milton had a surprise. On January 12th and 30th, the King and the Court heard the most eloquent pastor in Paris, namely, our old acquaintance Alexander Morus, preach in French. Having the secret of attracting congregations and of provoking scandal, he had had to leave Amsterdam in 1657, only to be immediately called to Paris. At this time, since Paris likewise had become too hot for him, he was endeavouring to obtain the office of minister to the French Reformed Church in London. Hence these two trial sermons. Milton's indignation may be imagined. But the sermons did not have the good fortune to please. After putting up a valiant fight, Morus went back to France in June, and the assembly of Charenton[1] was in a ferment as before.

Milton had foretold to his countrymen the coming of an 'outlandish' and Catholic queen. In May 1662, in fact, the King married the Portuguese princess Catherine of Braganza, who despite her affection for him, was to do harm to his cause by surrounding herself with Catholics and not giving him a child.

In this same month of May, Parliament took new measures against the dissidents. The Quaker Act forbade Quakers to meet. The famous Act of Uniformity ('uniformity', the dream of Laud!) declared that no one was to exercise any ecclesiastical function unless he had been ordained or accepted by a bishop, or to teach, even in a private capacity, unless he were an Anglican. The persons concerned had until August 24th to regularize their position. Finally, the press was submitted to an efficiently organized censorship. Poetry, for instance, depended for the future, as did science and theology, on the Archbishop of Canterbury, and the Bishop of London.

In August 1660, Charles II had spared the lives of Vane and Lambert. They were awaiting deportation in their dungeons when the Cavalier Parliament, in July 1661, decreed new proceedings against them. Whether or not

---

[1] A village five miles distant from the Louvre, where Parisian Protestants were allowed a place of worship.

they were responsible for the death of the Martyr King, from the date of that death they had become guilty of lèse-majesté *in respect of his successor*! The unfortunate men were thus tried again in June 1662, while the King and his young bride were spending their honeymoon at Hampton Court. Lambert offered complete submission, Vane defended himself with an eloquence and audacity that cost him his life. Both were condemned to death; then, according to precedent, recommended to the King's mercy. Lambert was deported to a small island in Plymouth harbour, then to Guernsey, where he was to end his days in 1694. As for Vane, Charles wrote to Clarendon: 'He is too dangerous a man to let live, if we can honestly put him out of the way'. On the intercession of his relatives, Vane was spared the ignominy of Tyburn, and honourably beheaded on Tower Hill. He succeeded, although the executioner took his notes away from him and despite the trumpets and drums, in broadcasting to the hostile crowd a supreme eulogy to liberty. He was fifty. Was it not the end of Sir Henry Vane that inspired these lines of Milton:

> Nothing is here for tears, nothing to wail
> Or knock the brest, no weakness, no contempt,
> Dispraise, or blame, nothing but well and fair,
> And what may quiet us in a death so noble.[1]

On the date stipulated by the Act of Uniformity, August 24th, 1662, two thousand Nonconformist pastors, one-fifth of the English clergy, had to leave their parishes, and thousands of masters to abandon their public or private teaching. This was what the English people called the Presbyterian St. Bartholomew. The majority of the victims were doomed to indigence. One of them was Calamy, who through a scruple had refused a bishopric.

In October Charles ceded Dunkirk and Mardyck to Louis XIV in exchange for four hundred thousand English pounds. What they were used for was never known. London suspected Clarendon of having drawn his commission on the deal, and christened his new home 'Dunkirk House'.

---

[1] *Samson Agonistes*, 1721–24.

Since the month of August 1662, Charles had been secretly negotiating with Rome. In December, he promulgated an Edict of Toleration which was cleverly planned—it relieved the dissidents, who were numerous, considerably, and the few Catholics very little. Even so Parliament, in agreement with the majority of the nation, considered that Charles had done too much for the papists. The Edict was to be annulled the following year.

Writers praised the new order, followed its lead, or were silent. Cromwell, living or dead, had been praised in verse by his cousin Waller and by the youthful Dryden. Both offered incense to the new master. Needham, who had returned on the occasion of the amnesty, was immediately attacked in the press. He cleared his name by reprinting his Royalist epigrams of former times and then he threw down his pen and turned physician. John Phillips re-issued in 1661 his anti-Puritan verses of 1655. In November 1662 appeared the first part of an epic in doggerel, Butler's *Hudibras*, caricaturing the Presbyterians and the Independents. Fashioned upon *Don Quixote*, often witty, generally as scurrilous as Scarron,[1] it delighted the Court. The King learnt some of its tirades by heart. Its prolixity, however, its lengthy discussions of Puritan casuistry, and above all its unrelieved malignity, discouraged some readers. Pepys bought a copy of it for half a crown, and sold it the same evening for eighteen pence. He noted in his Diary: 'It is so silly an abuse of the Presbyter knight going to the wars that I am ashamed of it'. But he noted it in cypher for himself alone. Marvell did not raise his voice. Government Intelligence was well organized, and how was one to stem 'the deluge of this epidemic madness'?

[1] A master of burlesque (1610–60). His *Virgile travesti* was imitated many times, notably by John Phillips (see below, p. 337).

'UP...INTO THE HEAVEN OF HEAVENS'

Paradise Lost VII, 12–13

XV

'ALL PASSION SPENT'

1662–1667

MILTON was now established, probably since 1661, in Jewin Street, between Bread Street and Aldersgate. He could no longer afford to send to France or Holland for a collection of Byzantine historians or atlases in several volumes. Of the sums lent to the Commonwealth, he would never see one penny again. He had acquired Church property; the Church had taken it back from him. A broker had despoiled him of two thousand pounds. He was left with one thousand five hundred pounds variously invested, and his house in Bread Street, that is about two hundred pounds in revenue instead of three times that amount.

It would have been cruel to remind him of his political career. His heroes were dead, his people had betrayed his expectations, he had lost twenty years of his life and those the best. After his victory over Saumaise, he had thought that Europe was hanging on his words. What Englishmen of standing thought of him at this time, we learn from the comte de Comminges, Louis XIV's ambassador in London. In 1661, rendering account to his master of the state of learning in England, he wrote: 'Le nommé Miltonius s'est rendu plus infâme par ses dangereux écrits que les bourreaux et les assassins du feu roi'.

One consequence of his relative poverty was that he had to do without a paid secretary. As a rule, friends put their children at his disposal, and sometimes adults were glad to profit by his learning, but these various instances of goodwill did not always follow each other at the right moment. From hints by Phillips and Aubrey a legend grew up which painters and poets have exploited—the poet's three daughters, interchangeable like the Graces, taking down his dictation and reading to him in half a dozen languages of which they knew nothing. It may be interesting to sift the evidence for this.

In 1658, when *Paradise Lost* was already on the way, Anne was twelve, Mary ten, and Deborah six. Anne was lame and deformed ('decrepit', says Phillips), and a defect in her speech made her unintelligible; she did read English a little, but could not write her name. We have receipts from her signed with a cross. There remained the two younger girls. They read to their father, says Phillips, 'the Hebrew, the Greek' [four more languages] 'and I think the Syriac.'—Why this 'I think'?—Phillips was writing in 1694. Twenty years earlier, Aubrey noted: 'Deborah was his amanuensis; he taught her Latin, and to read Greek'. Besides, she read French and Italian. This indeed would seem very likely. Mary, moreover, is known to us only by her traits of rebellion, whereas Deborah had her father's features and his memory, loved him, and must have rendered him service without great effort and very willingly. Many years after his death, in 1721, the engraver Virtue showed to Deborah several portraits and asked her 'whether she had ever seen such a face'. Rejecting the rest, she exclaimed 'in a transport' at the sight of a portrait in pastel:[1] ' 'Tis my father, 'tis my dear father! I see him, 'tis him!'; 'and then', says Richardson, 'she put her hands to several parts of her face. " 'Tis the very man! here, here!"' She wept as she said this and spoke of Milton with reverence and fondness. On another occasion, a Professor Ward, of Gresham College, made her recite long passages not only of Ovid, but of Homer and Euripides. It must be added, however, that she did not understand a word of what she recited. It sometimes happened that a friend or a visitor would remark on the ignorance of the girls, but a frequent joke of Milton was that 'one tongue was enough for a woman'. Was he to admit that he had given a governess to his daughters, but that they were as impervious as their mother to the things of the mind? The case of the eldest is all too clear. Mary signed 'millton' and bartered the

---

[1] This pastel had been executed by Faithorne, most likely for the Earl of Anglesey. See pp. 301 and 354, and plate facing p. 314.

poet's books. Deborah, who signed 'Deboroh', might surely have shown a little more intellectual curiosity.

Yet, even when the legend has been shattered, a core of truth remains. Milton could not forgive his daughters for being of the race of the Powells. In giving them a governess, he doubtless considered that he had done all his duty towards them and more also.

One of those who read to the poet, Thomas Ellwood, occupies a modest but honourable place in the history of his work. Incidentally, his case shows how difficult it was for Milton always to have an assistant to his hand.

The Penningtons, rich Quakers who had taken refuge in the country, had recommended to Dr. Paget, a friend of Milton's, this young man of twenty-three who, after a period spent in idleness and field-sports, had been converted by Nayler and wished to follow a course of education over again. Milton liked Quakers. Young Ellwood, fervent, upright, a poet on occasion, pleased him. Ellwood has related in his memoirs[1] that every afternoon, 'except on the first day of the week' (the word *Sunday* must be left to the heathen), he would seek out Milton in the dining-room at Jewin Street, to read Latin to him. From their first meeting Milton taught him to pronounce it in the Roman manner, the only way to feel the beauty of the language and of making oneself understood in every country. When the pupil hesitated over the meaning, the master, 'having a curious ear', noticed the change of tone; 'he would stop me, examine me, and open the most difficult passages to me'.

This exchange of kind offices was interrupted when Ellwood, for reasons of health, had to stay for a time with the Penningtons. It was interrupted again in October 1662. For having infringed the Quaker Act by praying with his brethren, Ellwood was sent to Newgate for three months.

[The common side of Newgate he describes as] a type of hell upon earth; . . . there lay, in a little by-place, like a closet, near

[1] *Ellwood's Life*, ed. 1714.

the room where we were lodged, the quartered bodies of
three men. . . . At length . . . the bloody quarters were removed
from the closet, the friends of the dead men having obtained
leave to bury them; but the heads were kept, to be set up in
some parts of the city. I saw the heads, when they were
brought up to be boiled. The hangman fetched them in a dirty
dust-basket . . . and, setting them among the felons, he and they
made sport of them. They took them by the hair, flouting,
jeering, and laughing at them; and then, giving them some ill
name, boxed them on the ears and cheeks. Which done, the
hangman put them into his kettle, and parboiled them with
bay-salt and cummin-seed: *that* to keep them from putrefaction,
and *this* to keep off the fowls from seizing on them.[1]

His prison sentence accomplished, Ellwood came to bid
Milton good-bye; the Penningtons had engaged him as tutor
to their children.

A month later, on February 24th, 1663, in the church of
St. Mary, Aldermanbury, Milton married a relation of
Paget, Elizabeth Minshull.

Signature affixed by Milton to his request for a marriage licence, February 11th, 1663.[2]

She was twenty-four, healthy, sensible, 'a gentle person',
says Aubrey who knew her, 'of a peaceful and agreeable
humour'. Her handwriting denotes a certain education.
Milton liked the tones of her voice, while regretting that
she had not a very true ear.

One of her first cares was to bring her step-daughters to

---

[1] Masson VI, 471.   [2] Ibid., 475.

heel. They were in league with the servant to deceive their father as to the price of food. One day the maid-servant said to Mary: 'Great news! your father is marrying again!' Mary replied that 'that was no news, to hear of his wedding, but, if she could hear of his death, *that* was something'.[1]

Shortly after the marriage, the family went to establish itself elsewhere in the parish of St. Giles, in a poor suburb where a dozen new cottages, packed close together on the side of a rough road for carts, looked out over an artillery practising ground. The road, Artillery Walk, led to Bunhill Fields, formerly an ossuary (Bonehill). Beyond stretched the open country. The house had a garden; it included a first storey, but only four of the rooms had fireplaces.

Such was the retreat in which Milton was to finish *Paradise Lost*. He had never been weaker—or stronger. Far from Westminster and Hampton Court, the little man clad in rough grey cloth in winter, in light black cloth in summer, smoking his pipe at his door as he let the sun warm his lifeless eyes and his gouty hands, at last enjoyed the peaceful hermitage of *Il Penseroso*, where he won for himself a place among the kings of poetry.

It was a monastic existence. He got up, normally, at four o'clock in summer, at five in winter, for he loved, as Valéry would love 'l'heure entre la lampe et le soleil, pure et profonde'. His man came to read the Bible to him in the original. He breakfasted, then went up to his room again, to contemplate. At seven o'clock, the man returned. Until noon the voices alternated, the one reading, the other dictating. At noon there was a light meal. Although he could appreciate a dish 'of Attic taste', he was 'extraordinarily' abstemious (Richardson). He took very little wine, no alcohol. As to tea and coffee, they were still almost unknown to the people of England.

He walked up and down his garden for three or four hours at a time. If it rained, he would swing himself to and fro in a seat suspended from the ceiling, pulling on a

[1] Masson VI, 476.

S

rope. Then came music, the organ, the bass-viol, songs sung alone or among friends. About four o'clock he went up to his books again. From six until eight he received his visitors or had poetry read to him 'to store his fancy against morning'. Then he took 'a few olives or some other light thing', smoked a pipe, drank a glass of water and went to bed at nine o'clock.

It was during the night that inspiration came to him. Even so, according to Phillips, 'his vein never happily flowed but from the autumnal equinoctial to the vernal', that is from the end of September to the end of March. He awaited the awakening of the household in order to dictate ten to thirty lines. Sometimes, in his impatience he would call them up, and complain that he 'wanted to be milked'. Usually, when he dictated, 'he sat leaning obliquely in an easy chair, with his leg flung over the elbow of it' (Richardson). The lines which the night had given him, he polished during the day, sometimes suppressing half of them. Like Flaubert he might have said: 'Le génie, c'est Dieu qui le donne, mais le talent nous regarde'.

His nephew, Edward, was tutor in the household of a rich Royalist, John Evelyn, botanist and numismatist, known to-day for his diary. Edward visited his uncle from time to time to take his sheets covered with erasures and insertion marks, and carry them away to make fair copies.

His visitors included at least two of the victims of the new régime: Louis Du Moulin and Edmund Calamy. The Earl of Anglesey, the Annesley who had supported Marvell, greatly appreciated the poet's conversation and admired his character. Lady Ranelagh, who had become a widow in 1659, had returned from Ireland to keep house for her brother the chemist. To have no doubt that she, too, appreciated Milton's conversation, it is sufficient to note with what lucidity, writing to her brother in 1659, she judged the superficial Waller.[1] John Durie was wandering about the Continent. Lawes and Hartlib both died in 1662. John Phillips did not approach the house, neither did

[1] Masson VI, 456–7.

Needham the trimmer. But Marvell, although his Parliamentary duties took much of his time and he was kept away from London in 1663–65 by a mission to Russia, did his best to keep in touch with the household. As to Cyriack Skinner, who did not move from London and had plenty of leisure on his hands, he was to attend his old master to the very end with the devotion of a son. Paget, one of the best medical practitioners in London, had served the Commonwealth as physician to the Tower and therefore had known Milton a long time. Now, his skill was indispensable to a man afflicted with gout to the extent that his fingers were deformed and that, as he said to a visitor, 'was he free from the pain this gave him, his blindness would be tolerable'. (Yet he sang during the attacks.)

The censor of the political press was now that L'Estrange who had trampled on Milton four years earlier. In October 1663, he seized from a small printer named Twyn, the proofs of an anonymous pamphlet according to which the people had the right to judge and execute tyrants. This was a plagiarism of the *Tenure of Kings*. In February 1664, Twyn suffered the punishment of traitors.

In May, a Conventicles Act forbade non-conformists to meet if they numbered more than five in addition to members of a family. Moreover, despite Clarendon, purely from commercial jealousy, Parliament declared war on Holland in February 1665. At this date, in London and elsewhere, a few deaths heralded the Great Plague which was to sweep away seventy thousand Londoners, one-fifth of the population.

Despite L'Estrange, gout, plague, and war, the poet went on with his dialogues between Adam and the archangels. The work was finished in June 1665. By that time about twenty plague-stricken were dying each day. Those Londoners who could do so went into the country.

When Ellwood came up to London, he did not fail to come and pay his respects to his master. At his request he found him a refuge. It was a brick and timber cottage situated at Chalfont St. Giles, near the Penningtons' village.

The poet's other dwellings have disappeared, but to-day this is a national museum and receives ten thousand visitors a year. There Milton discovered memories of Horton. At ten minutes' distance stood the Norman manor where he had seen at play Cromwell's future son-in-law, Charles Fleetwood, and the owner of Chalfont, his brother George, the regicide. A few miles further a noble audience had applauded *Arcades*.

On their arrival at Chalfont in August, the Miltons were surprised that Ellwood did not come to do them the honours of the place. The little Quaker was again under lock and key. Despite the Conventicles Act, he had followed the funeral procession of a co-religionist, and that in broad daylight. The police had made a rush at the procession, the coffin had fallen on to the road. Only in September was Ellwood able to present himself at Chalfont and read to his master some lines written in prison.

> After some discourses had passed between us, he called for a manuscript of his; which, being brought, he delivered to me, bidding me take it home with me and read it at my leisure, and, when I had so done, return it to him, with my judgment thereon. When I came home . . . I found it was that excellent poem which he entitled *Paradise Lost*. After I had . . . read it through, I made him another visit, and returned him his book, with due acknowledgment of the favour. . . . He asked me how I liked it, and what I thought of it; which I modestly, but freely, told him: and after some further discourse about it, I pleasantly said to him, 'Thou hast said much here of Paradise Lost, but what hast Thou to say of Paradise Found?' He made no answer, but sat some time in a muse; then brake off that discourse, and fell on another subject.[1]

In October 1665, when the plague was carrying off five hundred Londoners a day, Parliament, having taken refuge at Oxford, completed what is improperly called 'The Clarendon Code'. Since the Anglican clergymen had left London, their non-conformist predecessors had dared to take their places. The Five Mile Act cut short this scandal. It forbade non-conformist ministers to reside or to exercise

---

[1] *Ellwood's Life*, pp. 246-7. Masson VI, 496.

their ministry within five miles of any town or of their former parish.

From December onwards the plague subsided rapidly. In February or March 1666, the Court returned to Westminster and Milton to his suburb. The quarter was still dangerous. It was in Bunhill Fields that the largest of those pits had been dug into which so many unfortunate wretches sometimes threw themselves of their own accord.[1]

Publishing the epic without authorization was not to be thought of. For having omitted this formality in reprinting certain sermons of Hugh Peters, those responsible had been punished with life imprisonment. The author of *Areopagitica* experienced the humiliation of submitting 'la fleur de ses ans', to quote Mistral,[2] to the chaplain of the Archbishop of Canterbury, a certain Tomkyns, aged twenty-eight, author of a treatise on *The Inconveniences of Toleration*. It was Tomkyns or nothing—Hobson's choice.

We know from experience that when war scatters a population, some refugees are written off as dead. This was what happened to the refugee of Chalfont. A man from whom he had not heard for nine years having learnt that he was safe and sound, wrote to say how delighted he was, and as he had deeply meditated on the merits of one he had thought dead, he was lyrical in his praise.

> I, who admired in you not so much your individual virtues as the marriage-union of diverse virtues . . . by the union of a grave dignity (exhibited in a face worthy of the wearer) with the calmest politeness, of kindness with prudence, of piety with policy, of policy with immense erudition, and, I will add, of a generous and far from timid spirit . . . with a genuine love of peace . . .[3]

Thus wrote Heimbach, Counsellor of State to the Elector of Brandenburg, whom Milton in happier days had asked to procure him some books. His letter was dated June 8th,

---

[1] The territory was afterwards enclosed by a wall and became the burial ground of the non-conformists. To-day three of the Cromwells, George Fox, Bunyan, Defoe and the poet William Blake, lie there.
[2] Frédéric Mistral (1830–1914), poet of Provence, in his dedication of *Mireio* (*Mireille*) to Lamartine—'es la flour de mis an'.
[3] Masson VI, 501.

1666. Milton replied on August 15th, not without irony and sadness:

> That after so long an interval I should have come into your mind is very agreeable; although, from your exuberant expression of the matter, you seem to afford some ground for suspecting that you have rather forgotten me, professing as you do such an admiration of the marriage-union in me of so many different virtues. Truly, I should dread a too numerous progeny from so many forms of the marriage-union as you enumerate, were it not an established truth that virtues are nourished most and flourish most in straitened and hard circumstances; albeit I may say that one of the virtues on your list has not very handsomely requited me the hospitable reception she had. For what you call *policy*, but I would rather have you call *loyalty to one's country*,—this particular lass, after inveigling me with her fair name, has almost expatriated me, so to speak. The chorus of the rest, however, makes a very fine harmony. One's country is wherever it is well with one (*Patria est, ubicunque est bene*).— And now I will conclude, after first begging you, if you find anything incorrectly written or without punctuation here, to impute it to the boy who has taken it down from my dictation, and who is so utterly ignorant of Latin, that I was forced, while dictating, not without misery, to spell out the letters of the words one by one.[1]

Two weeks after this reply, on September 2nd, broke out the Great Fire, which in three days consumed two-thirds of the City, including St. Paul's, built by the Normans, and larger than that of to-day. The fire subsided at five hundred paces from Artillery Walk, but it destroyed the Bread Street house. Dryden judged it opportune to celebrate in three hundred quatrains this *Annus Mirabilis* which had seen the English sink some Dutch ships and the King go all over the still smoking City. With Bread Street Milton lost a third of his property.

The political situation, however, gave ground for some slight hope. 'Unaccountable terrors of popery, ever since the accession of the house of Stuart, had prevailed throughout the nation.'[2] Enlightened people were free from this

---

[1] Masson VI, 502, and Bohn III, 521. Query: What were the three martyr daughters doing that day? Also, cf. this '*Patria est . . .*' and below p. 285.
[2] Hume, *History of England*, ch. LXV, 8.

psychosis, but day by day the King and his brother made England more uneasy. The former, tolerant, and therefore under suspicion, was in fact working surreptitiously for the Catholics, and the latter supported them with open countenance. The Court was cluttered with Frenchmen, the Queen had foreign chaplains, England was fighting against Holland at the side of France. The double disaster of 1665–66 could not but have great and mysterious causes. After the Plague, London had accused the Catholics of having spread the contagion, for vengeance and the profits to be gained from the pillage. After the Fire, people came down to details—eighty or eighty-six agents of the Jesuits and of France had thrown seven hundred fire-balls and pilfered goods from the fire to the amount of fourteen thousand pounds! The Jesuits had also raised another fire on St. Margaret's Hill, another at Southwark! They were determined to burn all the chief cities in England! The country was shaken out of its complacency by a tornado similar to the 'Grande Peur' which swept over France in 1789. Parliament was forced to institute an inquiry. Naturally, it gave no result, but in 1667, on the Monument which still commemorates the Great Fire, the two Houses had an inscription set which incriminated the Catholics.[1] Moreover, they obtained from Charles the proclamation of the banishment of priests and Jesuits. The King took good care not to have his order carried out, but the wind had veered. Moderate men drew closer to Geneva, the dissidents had a respite. In London, first of all, and then in the counties, non-conformist preachers drew large congregations.

At the beginning of 1667 Tomkyns at last granted the *imprimatur*. Nothing had shocked him, it would appear, other than a certain allusion to revolutions:

> . . . his form had yet not lost
> All her Original brightness; nor appeard
> Less then Arch-Angel ruind, and th'excess
> Of Glory obscur'd: As when the Sun new ris'n

---

[1] Removed under James II, replaced under William III, it was suppressed in 1831.

Looks through the Horizontal misty Air
Shorn of his Beams; or from behind the Moon
In dim Eclips disastrous twilight sheds
On half the Nations, and with fear of change
Perplexes Monarchs.[1]

It now remained to find a publisher. Everyone's budget was in a state of confusion and the great printing houses clustered round St. Paul's had vanished with it. The suburb of Aldersgate, however, spared by the fire, possessed a bookseller, Samuel Simmons, whose father or uncle had published *Tenure of Kings* and other works of Milton; he accepted the manuscript. Not without fears, indeed: he was new in the business; the author was known as a seditious pamphleteer, unknown as a poet; epics, even classical epics, no longer sold. And to crown everything this strange old man had dispensed with rhyme. Simmons offered a contract which is one of the curiosities of literary history. The manuscript would be his property; he would pay the author five pounds immediately, five after the first edition was sold out, five more after the sale of the second, and five after the third; he could print fifteen hundred copies each time, but an edition would be considered out of print when thirteen hundred copies had been sold. Thus Milton would get twenty pounds at most, and he could not get ten unless the work was bought by at least thirteen hundred persons. . . .

He would have paid to be published. On April 27th, 1667, by the side of his name traced by a third party, he put on the contract the imprint of a finger and that of the spread-eagle.

In the months that followed, the English fleet having been laid up for want of funds, Ruyter sailed up the Medway as far as Chatham, burnt or captured sixteen ships, and blockaded London for several weeks. Evelyn wrote: 'The King's Counsellors would merit . . . I well know what'. The people cursed the royal mistresses, and visited their sins on Clarendon by wrecking the gardens of 'Dunkirk House'. 'Everyone to-day', noted Pepys, 'reflects upon Oliver, what brave things he did, and made all the neighbour Princes fear him.'

[1] Book I, 591-9.

Public opinion accused Clarendon, the King was weary of his tutelage, the Lords condemned him, the King exiled him.

The first copies of *Paradise Lost* made their appearance at the end of the month of August. They were small quartos of 342 pages, carefully printed, tastefully bound, and were sold at three shillings. The poem was divided into ten cantos and was presented without a preface.

XVI

PARADISE LOST

1667

In no other of his works has Milton so largely revealed himself, deliberately or not, as in what we might call his *Comédie humaine*—and more than 'humaine'. As we have seen, he does not hesitate to speak at length on his blindness. We shall also see that he boasts of his civic courage. The language was new. As to the design, it rests on a few lines of *Genesis* in which Satan is not even named. Before we examine this creation of ten thousand lines, let us try to summarize it.

'*The diagram of the universal infinitude.*'—Masson VI, 543.

Books I and II.—In the depths of Chaos, on a lake of fire, millions of mighty beings have been floating inert for nine days. They are the rebel angels, cast down from the Empyrean. Lucifer exhorts them to revenge. There was a rumour up in Heaven of the creation to take place shortly, of a world and of a race that would be very dear to the Tyrant. Would there be nothing to attempt in this direction? Then comes the construction of Pandemonium, where the fallen deliberate. Beelzebub gets the leader's suggestion adopted. Now, he says, 'whom shall we send in search of this new world?' *Hell is silent*. Satan assumes this mission and insists on accomplishing it alone. The gate of Hell opens on to Chaos. The gate is guarded by two children of Satan—Death and Sin. They let him pass through The King of Chaos shows him an opaque bubble suspended from the Empyrean. It is our cosmos; Satan flies there.

III.—Hymn to the light, for the scene is in Heaven. God foretells to his Son that man will succumb. He is ready to pardon him since he will be less guilty than his tempter, but since he will try to be equal with God, he will have to die. . . . Unless someone dies in his place. 'Dwels in all Heaven charitie so deare?' *Heaven is silent*. The Son offers his life. Song of the angels.

Satan reaches our cosmos, finds the opening to it, and plunges towards the sun. Disguised as a young cherub, he flatters the guardian of the star, who completes his information. He lands on Mount Nephates, whence issues one of the rivers of Paradise, and from the summit of Nephates he curses the sun.

IV.—In Paradise, under the form of a cormorant, Satan admires and pities the human couple. The man warns his companion that if they taste of a certain fruit, they will die. This is information of the utmost value! When night comes Satan turns himself into a toad, crouches against Eve's ear as she is asleep, and suggests to her thoughts of pride. But the cherubim on guard discover him and God drives him out. Before man be tempted, it is only right that he should know all that is involved.

V—VII.—Therefore Raphael comes down to reveal to Adam the rebellion of one-third of the angels, their defeat, the creation of the world, the threat hanging over Eden.

VIII.—Adam questions him about the stars, then, to detain him, relates his memories, in particular his first vision of Eve. Raphael warns him against passion. When evening falls the angel departs. Adam blesses his guest.

IX.—Seven nights later Satan, who has now returned to Eden, insinuates himself into the sleeping serpent. When Eve awakes she, despite Adam, decides to 'tend Plant, Herb, and Flower' alone, because now she finds Adam's tutelage burdensome. She is virtually lost. The serpent approaches her. How can he speak, and that so well? It is because he has eaten a certain fruit. Eve recognizes the forbidden tree, but her curiosity prevails. Adam comes along. Through 'vehemence of love' he chooses sin and death. The culprits experience voluptuousness, then shame.

X.—The Son comes to tell them that they will have to suffer and die, but promises them that the posterity of the woman will crush the serpent's head. Satan speeds to Pandemonium to recount his exploit. He is answered by hisses. All, himself included, have become reptiles. The globe has deviated from its axis, the seasons change, Death takes his first step in the universe, the stars turn pale. Adam bitterly deplores his fall and the lot reserved to his race. Eve suggests that they should refrain from begetting children, or should kill themselves. But he reminds her of the promise of an avenger. No, they must strive to obtain grace by repentance.

XI and XII.—God accepts their repentance, but maintains their exclusion from Eden. The Archangel Michael intimates this to them, then comforts Adam. Leaving Eve to rest, the archangel and the man climb a height whence they can see one half of the globe and a succession of centuries. Under the eyes of Adam, Cain kills Abel. Adam exclaims: 'But have I now seen death? Is this the way I must return to native dust?'—Then appears 'a place like a Lazar-house, wherein are laid all maladies'. The next visions are dances, a besieged city, a battle, the Flood. There follows the history of Israel and of Christendom. Adam understands and adores. On his return he goes on in advance of the angel to speak alone with Eve; but she has already been informed by a dream, she will leave Eden comforted. Before the cherubim cast the flame over the garden, Michael leads the banished couple away with him and then disappears. Our humanity has begun.

The drama thus extends over several days, and thanks to time-honoured devices, we are informed as to its origins and its farthest consequences. The 'flashback' of Raphael (V—VII) is Aeneas recounting the Trojan war. Virgil had predicted the fortune of Rome, Michael predicts the lot of humanity.

This difference of scope enables us to measure Milton's boldness. It was this above all that struck his contemporaries. In 1674, the second edition was presented to the public by Barrow, the King's physician, and by Marvell. As if the two men had consulted each other, the Latin lines of the physician, and the English lines of the member for Hull, pointed out in the first place that the poem was encyclopaedic. 'Thou who readest *Paradise Lost*', said Barrow, 'this grand poem of the great Milton (*grandia Magni carmina Miltoni*), what readest thou, if not all things (*cuncta*)?'

> When I beheld [wrote Marvell] the Poet blind, yet bold,
> In slender Book his vast Design unfold . . .
> Heav'n, Hell, Earth, Chaos, All; the Argument
> Held me a while misdoubting his Intent . . .
> Pardon me, Mighty Poet. . . .[1]

Milton, too, as we have seen, was uneasy.[2] But what reassured him somewhat was the very span of his work. He had seen his generation turn away from the battle epic, imitated from Homer or from Tasso, and dear to the previous generation. His account, such as he intended it, concerned men of all times and of all countries. Age had weakened him, but Urania had guided him. At least a few readers would be found to understand him ('fit audience find, though few'); they would pass over his weaknesses in consideration of his boldness, they would applaud:

> . . . my adventrous Song,
> That with no middle flight intends to soar
> Above th' *Aonian* Mount; while it persues
> Things unattempted yet in Prose or Rime.[3]

---

[1] Masson VI, 715.   [2] See above, p. 205.   [3] *Paradise Lost*, I, 12–16.

Milton in fact saw his friend Haak, a naturalized German, one of the founders of the Royal Society, put half his epic into German verse, so that it should be admired in his native country. In 1688 the London bookseller Dring was to present Milton to the rest of Europe by having Book I translated into Latin verse. Two years later, Tonson was to produce the entire poem in a luxury edition, in folio and illustrated.

Since that time *Paradise Lost* has appeared in Hebrew, in Persian and in Japanese. Messiaen's recent version is the twenty-fourth published in French. France has done much for the reputation of Milton, and in our own days, in the country of Voltaire and in the century of the atom, the fabulous narrative can still charm—as witness this homage from a French Academician, Jean Guehenno:

> [Pendant les vacances] au fond de quelque campagne, loin de la petite foire littéraire . . . il arrive qu'on retourne aux vieux et vrais livres, aux livres des livres. Il n'en est pas beaucoup. Il n'en est pas dix peut-être. . . . Je veux parler de ces livres qui nous paraissent contenir, résumer et commander tous les autres, qui, à toutes les pages, nous parlent de nous-mêmes et nous atteignent au plus profond, qui nous semblent égaux au monde, à notre condition, à notre destinée, de ces livres enfin, qui sont, chacun d'eux, en quelque sorte, ce livre unique, adéquat à la Création, dont rêvait Mallarmé. Les chrétiens, tout de suite, nommeront l'Évangile . . . Pour moi, le livre des livres, durant ces vacances, ç'aura été le *Paradis perdu* . . . Quel maître livre! Je ne sais s'il est un de ces livres que nous cherchons, mais c'est sûrement le roman des romans.[1]

In short, if we compare the Miltonian epic with works that seem to be analogous, the *Adamus Exul* of Grotius, the two *Semaines* of du Bartas, or the *Lucifer* of Vondel, we find that it belongs to a different family, that of the world's masterpieces.

Yet it disappoints on so many heads that its success poses a problem. It is true that an evocation of our origin always commands our interest, but here all the characters are supernatural or fictitious, and Milton's inventions are not always happy. For instance, Hell should not have as gaolers

[1] *Le Figaro*, September 30th, 1953.

the very children of the principal prisoner. Why do the faithful angels wage a battle which only the Son can win? Has the Son created the angels (III, 383)? Or on the other hand was he 'begot' after them (V, 603)? It is necessary to turn to his *Doctrina Christiana* to know that Milton used 'beget' in the metaphorical sense of 'to exalt'. The subject bristled with difficulties and Milton has added to them.

Is it the abstract content which attracts the reader? Mallarmé one day startled Degas by declaring that one cannot make a poem with ideas. Milton judged otherwise and his readers regret it. Adam, Eve, God, the angels, the serpent, all indulge freely in ratiocination. When God the Father inflicts on his heavenly and deferential audience a dissertation upon free will (III, 96–134) we turn the page. Again certain assertions, on the loves of the angels for instance (VIII, 615), or on their digestion (V, 404), although accepted at that time by grave scholars cannot but surprise the average reader.

Naturally, despite the best efforts of the Devil's advocate, there would still remain five or six thousand admirable and characteristic lines, far more than many justly famous poets have left. It is, however, true that the material here gathered together by Milton is very unequal in value and that he owes his renown to its presentation.

It should be made clear at once that 'presentation' here does not mean the art of selecting and handling syllables. On this, in the 1930's, several English-speaking critics were mistaken. They claimed that in Milton the excellence of the form hid the poverty of the substance. We have, however, two good reasons for not agreeing with them.

In the first place the great majority of the poet's admirers have known him only in translation. Then, for a long period, the English themselves found him cacophonic, and obscure too. Addison, who established his reputation, yet avowed 'Our language sunk under him'. About the same time, the learned Bentley wondered how such a great poet could have written so badly. Surely the blind man had been the victim of his secretaries! Whereupon Bentley, no less bold than learned, produced in 1732 a *Paradise Lost* conformable to good taste and good sense. Some of his emendations were justified, but in general his platitudes helped the English people to augur better of the original. It baffled them to such an extent, however, that Bentley's help failing them, they looked to a Frenchman. The episode is unique in the history of European literature. Voltaire having revealed *Paradise Lost* to the French in 1727, Dupré de Saint-Maur produced the first French version in 1729. It was neither accurate nor complete, but it read so easily that the English wanted to have the benefit of its clarity in their own language, and this re-translation was printed not once but ten times! Twenty years later Bishop Joseph Butler was still reproaching Milton for his 'Babylonish dialect'. Dr. Johnson confirmed his verdict.

The decisive merit of the epic of the Fall, therefore, is its style in the sense in which artists understand the term—that is, the general character of the productions of an epoch, a country, or a man. In Elizabethan plays we sometimes read the direction, *Flourish*. Tune or performer mattered little, the sound of the trumpets was sufficient to announce the entrance of a prince. Similarly, the oboe indicated a festal occasion, the flute signified mourning. So, too, in *Paradise Lost*, a particular tone warns us, despite the strangeness of an episode, the heaviness of a disquisition or the unexpectedness of the syntax, that we are in the presence of greatness. From generation to generation and without distinction of frontiers, Milton has been called 'sublime'.

That is a word which we avoid, and to define it would be difficult. We can, however, feel the difference between the 'Qui te l'a dit?' of Hermione[1] and the 'Qu'il mourût!' of the old Horace.[2] The one does credit to a psychologist and the other to human nature capable of surpassing itself.

[1] Racine, *Andromaque*, V, iii. Orestes loves Hermione, who loves Pyrrhus, who disdains her love. She orders Orestes to kill him. Much against his will, he obeys. She is desperate, and lays the blame on Orestes; he is 'a monster'; how could he kill such a man? 'Who told you to?'

[2] Corneille, *Horace*, III, vi. His three sons are fighting against three champions of Alba. He is told that two are fallen, and the survivor is running away. He curses the coward. A woman pleads: 'What could he do against three?'—'He could have died'.

Shakespeare disturbs us, Milton uplifts us. We cannot read his epic without approving Voltaire's phrase, 'C'est un ouvrage qui ne semble pas fait pour l'homme'.

Our impression of transcendence is partly due to the fact that the stage is without limits and the characters of giant stature. There is something puerile in the gigantic, but it is no less justified here than it is in Homer. Milton has recourse to it with pleasure and success. There was an affinity between the volcanic element of his nature, the dawn of the world and the eternal youth of God. He embraced whole entities and handled masses with the ease of a Jehovah.

His reading of the Bible in Hebrew each day enabled him to rival the Psalmist without effort. When Raphael relates the creation of the world to the first man, he tells him that the Son, his work once finished, went back to heaven escorted by angels who sang his praise. 'They sang . . .', said Raphael. Here Milton took over a verse of *Psalm* 24 and made the archangel say:

Op'n, ye everlasting Gates, they sung,
Op'n, ye Heav'ns, your living dores; let in
The great Creator from his work returnd
Magnificent, his Six Days work, a World;
Op'n, and henceforth oft; for God will deigne
To visit oft the dwellings of just Men
Delighted, and with frequent intercourse
Thither will send his winged Messengers
On errands of supernal Grace. So sung
The glorious Train ascending: He through Heav'n,
That op'nd wide her blazing Portals, led
To Gods Eternal house direct the way,
A broad and ample rode, whose dust is Gold
And pavement Starrs, as Starrs to thee appeer,
Seen in the Galaxie, that Milkie way
Which nightly as a circling Zone thou seest
Pouderd with Starrs.[1]

Another element of majesty is the constant presence of Him who has evoked from nothingness theatre, actors and poet. God surveys the unfolding of the drama he has

---

[1] VII, 565–81.

T

foreseen. Or rather, he follows the trial from which he will emerge absolved. Humanity complains of him, Milton defends him. He claims to 'justifie the wayes of God to men' (I, 26). Sometimes the advocate calls upon the accused to speak. Yet the accused is the Sovereign Judge who declares 'What I will is Fate' (VII, 173).

The writer has resources which the painter and the sculptor may well envy. Rodin had to leave his *Porte de l'Enfer* unfinished. Milton has decribed its 'thrice threefold gates' with their folds of brass, iron and rock (II, 645), and gives us their measure:

> ... the Gates wide op'n stood,
> That with extended wings a Bannerd Host
> Under spred Ensigns marching might pass through
> With Horse and Chariots rankt in loose array;[1]

If the gates of heaven, 'on gold'n Hinges moving', open harmoniously (VII, 207), but:

> On a sudden op'n flie
> With impetuous recoile and jarring sound
> Th' infernal dores, and on thir hinges grate
> Harsh Thunder, that the lowest bottom shook
> Of *Erebus*.[2]

In Dante, who was capable of imposing upon himself the discipline of the *terza rima*, hell is the work of an architect, a subterranean Coliseum. That of Milton defies not only the architect but the painter:

> At once as farr as Angels kenn he views
> The dismal Situation waste and wilde:
> A Dungeon horrible, on all sides round
> As one great Furnace flam'd, yet from those flames
> No light, but rather darkness visible
> Serv'd onely to discover sights of woe,
> Regions of sorrow, doleful shades, where peace
> And rest can never dwell, hope never comes
> That comes to all;[3]

Rivers wind through it, it includes 'a frozen continent',

> ... many a Frozen, many a Fierie Alpe,
> Rocks, Caves, Lakes, Fens, Bogs, Dens, and shades of death.[4]

[1] II, 884-7.   [2] Ibid., 879-83.   [3] I, 59-67.   [4] II, 620-1.

The Chaos, of which this immensity is only an enclave, far from defeating Milton's imagination, stimulates it. He is happy to unleash his energy amid this violent confusion. He gives it life and peoples it. Satan is welcomed there by King Chaos and his Queen Primitive Night, surrounded by sinister courtiers, among them Chance.[1] Death and Sin (II, 649–870). Here is Death at the moment when the news of the Fall reaches the denizens of the abyss:

> So saying, with delight he snuffd the smell
> Of mortal change on Earth. As when a flock
> Of ravenous Fowl, though many a League remote,
> Against the day of Battel, to a Field,
> Where Armies lie encampt, come flying, lur'd
> With sent of living Carcasses design'd
> For death, the following day, in bloodie fight.
> So sented the grim Feature, and upturnd
> His nostril wide into the murkie Air,
> Sagacious of his Quarrey from so farr.[2]

And here is the Son, accompanied by angels, in the presence of the Chaos:

> On heav'nly ground they stood, and from the shore
> They viewd the vast immeasurable Abyss
> Outrageous as a Sea, dark, wasteful, wilde,
> Up from the bottom turnd by furious windes
> And surging waves, as Mountains to assault
> Heav'ns highth, and with the Center mix the Pole.
> Silence, ye toubl'd waves, and thou Deep, peace,
> Said then th' Omnific Word, your discord end:
> Nor staid, but on the Wings of Cherubim
> Uplifted, in Paternal Glorie rode
> Farr into *Chaos*, and the World unborn;
> For *Chaos* heard his voice: him all his Traine
> Followd in bright procession to behold
> Creation, and the wonders of his might.
> Then staid the fervid Wheeles, and in his hand
> He took the gold'n Compasses, prepar'd
> In Gods Eternal store, to circumscribe
> This Universe, and all created things:
> One foot he centerd, and the other turnd

[1] II, 890–967. Cf. 'Necessitie and Chance / Approach not Mee', VII, 172—the will of the Creator rules the cosmos entirely.
[2] X, 272–81.

Round through the vast profunditie obscure,
And said, Thus farr extend, thus farr thy bounds,
This be thy just Circumference, O World.
Thus God the Heav'n created, thus the Earth,
Matter unformed and void:[1]

Victor Hugo is the only poet west of Suez who has
disposed of space and time with this prodigality, or depicted
with the same eagerness 'l'Olympe monstrueux des époques
obscures'. Between the two titans many points of similarity
could be found. For instance, Hugo, too, struggled twenty
years for the republican ideal. But their respective conceptions of Satan, of evil, of liberty, differ profoundly. Hugo,
in a curious passage in his *William Shakespeare*, pities Milton
for having been a Puritan.[2] He himself indeed suffered no
inhibitions and boldly sang of the flesh of woman, 'argile
idéale', 'fange auguste' and concluded:

   ... on ne peut, à l'heure où les sens sont en feu,
   Etreindre la beauté sans croire embrasser Dieu.[3]

Whereas Milton was contented with 'imparadis't in one
another's arms'.[4]

Hugo never wrote in praise of discipline. He considered
that man was definitely in debt to the Tempter. The angel
Liberty was born 'from a feather which had dropped from
the archangel's wing'. God, who worked this metamorphosis, would one day say to the Great Rebel:

   Viens! l'ange Liberté, c'est ta fille et la mienne,
   Cette paternité sublime nous unit ...
   Satan est mort: renais, ô Lucifer céleste.[5]

There is nothing like this in Milton, he hated Satan.
Puritanism was a passion. For Milton 'the Adversary of
God and Man' was condemned without possible remission.
He endowed him, however, with a personality so strong

[1] VII, 210-33.
[2] *William Shakespeare* (Hetzel, p. 74). Having named twenty great minds from
Hesiod to Voltaire, Hugo declares that they have 'ni exagération, ni ténèbres, ni
obscurité, ni monstruosité'. And he asks: 'Que leur manque-t-il donc?' — 'Cela'·
Cela, c'est l'inconnu. *Cela*, c'est l'infini. Si Corneille avait *cela*, il serait l'égal
d'Eschyle. Si Milton avait *cela*, il serait l'égal d'Homère. (...) Avoir, par tristesse
puritaine, exclu de son oeuvre la vaste nature, le grand Pan, c'est là le malheur de
Milton'.
[3] *Légende des Siècles*, I. Le sacre de la femme, 146-51.
[4] P.L. IV, 506. See also IX, 1008-11.
[5] *La Fin de Satan*, iv, 'Satan pardonné', *in fine*.

that it has been used against him. He must have been a man of great pride, it has often been said, to paint the first proud being so well. It is very true that God and Heaven here are put in less relief than Satan and Hell, but evil is dramatic of its very nature—it causes fear, it attacks, it destroys. Good can only defend itself, or may even be defenceless. We pity Desdemona, we admire Iago. We say 'a perfect crime'. In consequence, the Prince of Darkness has inspired numberless writers. Does Milton prevail over them all because he was inordinately proud? We might as well say that the creator of Iago must have been a double-dealer.

'*Ecco Dite*', cries Virgil to Dante, pointing out to him a gigantic man-eater with three faces. But this ogre was barely up to champing three sinners at the same time, he never could have recruited one. As to Goethe's Mephistopheles, he can be but an underling, unless Satan is fallen very low indeed. He behaves like a salacious jester out of a mystery play.[1]

Milton shows us Lucifer in person, on the morrow of his fall. The meteorite is still shining brightly. The vanquished leader still has his troops in hand and has lost nothing of his wonderful gifts. He knows how to re-establish the morale of an army, to raise an assembly, or to lull the suspicions of an innocent woman. He still has some heart. When he is rallying his legions, their fidelity to the leader who has brought them to ruin, fills him with emotion to the extent of preventing him from speaking.

> Thrice he assayd, and thrice in spite of scorn,
> Tears such as Angels weep, burst forth: at last
> Words interwove with sighs found out their way.
> 'O Myriads of immortal Spirits, O Powers
> Matchless, but with th' Almighty . . .'[2]

At the sight of the sun, recalling his lost splendour, he deplores his pride and his ingratitude. At the moment of

[1] Mephistopheles presents himself with a modest vagueness: 'Ich bin ein Teil des Teils der anfangs alles war': i.e. a part of the darkness which was everything before God's withdrawal. For Goethe too knew the Cabbala. Heine's devil is completely tamed—'ein lieber, charmanter Mann', etc. To find another Miltonian Satan, one would have to go to Baudelaire.
[2] I, 619–23.

attacking the couple, he pities them. There is no more sensuality or baseness in him than there is in his followers. The latter still had the heavenly hymns in their ears. They sang 'to many a harp their own heroic deeds and hapless fate' with so much art that 'the harmony . . . suspended Hell' (II, 554). Neither they themselves nor their captain have yet injured the earth, and we regret on their account their refusal to serve. Their only crime is our own: pride. *Superbia radix omnium vitiorum*, declares a Bible of the Middle Ages. At first their pride is only at the stage of the 'root', and we witness their downfall with pity. Whereas Adam and Eve are progressing towards 'a paradise within them, happier far', the first-born of the Sons of the Morning ends as the dragon of the bottomless pit.

A few quotations will give us a clearer picture of Milton's Lucifer. Still chained on the burning lake, he comforts his lieutenant Beëlzebub and defies 'him with his Thunder'.

> What though the field be lost?
> All is not lost; th' unconquerable Will,
> And study of revenge, immortal hate,
> And courage never to submit or yeild:
> And what is else not to be overcome?
> That Glory never shall his wrauth or might
> Extort from mee. To bow and sue for grace
> With suppliant knee, and deifie his power
> Who from the terrour of this Arm so late
> Doubted his Empire; that were low indeed,
> That were an ignominy and shame beneath
> This downfall;[1]

To this moral strength corresponds physical force:

> . . . or that Sea-beast
> *Leviathan*, which God of all his works
> Created hugest that swim th' Ocean stream:
> Him haply slumbring on the *Norway* foam
> The Pilot of some small night-founderd Skiff,
> Deeming some Iland, oft, as Sea-men tell,
> With fixed Anchor in his skaly rinde
> Moors by his side under the Lee, while Night
> Invests the Sea, and wished Morn delayes:

[1] I, 105–16.

So stretcht out huge in length the Arch-fiend lay
Chaind on the burning Lake.[1]

The Almighty, however, permits and even wills that Satan should free himself. He must be free to damn himself completely, and must work to cause the love of God for man to burst forth.

Forthwith upright he rears from off the Pool
His mighty Stature; on each hand the flames
Driv'n backward slope thir pointing spires, and rowld
In billows, leave i' th' midst a horrid Vale.
Then with expanded wings he stears his flight
Aloft, incumbent on the dusky Air
That felt unusual weight . . .[2]

This vertical flight enables him to discover his empire:

Is this the Region, this the Soil, the Clime,
Said then the lost Arch-Angel, this the seat
That we must change for Heav'n, this mournful gloom
For that celestial light? Be it so, since hee
Who now is Sovran can dispose and bid
What shall be right: fardest from him is best
Whom reason hath equald, force hath made supream
Above his equals. Farewel happy Fields
Where Joy for ever dwells: Hail horrours, hail
Infernal World, and thou profoundest Hell
Receive thy new Possessor: One who brings
A mind not to be chang'd by Place or Time.
The mind is its own place, and in it self
Can make a Heav'n of Hell, a Hell of Heav'n.
What matter where, if I be still the same,
And what I should be, all but less then hee
Whom Thunder hath made greater? Here at least
We shall be free; th' Almighty hath not built
Here for his envy, will not drive us hence:
Here we may reign secure, and in my choice
To reign is worth ambition though in Hell:
Better to reign in Hell, then serve in Heav'n. . . .[3]

It is much further on, at the end of the following book, that Satan sets off to reconnoitre. Before doing so, he changes his wings:

[1] I, 200–10.   [2] Ibid., 221–7.   [3] Ibid., 242–63.

> Mean while the Adversary of God and Man,
> *Satan* with thoughts inflam'd of highest design,
> Puts on swift wings,[1] and toward the Gates of Hell
> Explores his solitary flight; som times
> He scours the right hand coast, som times the left,
> Now shaves with level wing the Deep, then soares
> Up to the fiery Concave touring high.
> As when farr off at Sea a Fleet descri'd
> Hangs in the Clouds, by *Æquinoctial* Winds
> Close sailing from *Bengala*, or the Iles
> Of *Ternate* and *Tidore*, whence Merchants bring
> Thir spicie Drugs: they on the Trading Flood
> Through the wide *Ethiopian* to the Cape
> Ply stemming nightly toward the Pole. So seemd
> Farr off the flying Fiend:[2]

Tennyson asked: 'Was ever a simile so vast as this?'

Bentley, the Greek scholar, erased this passage, as being too remote from the simplicity of classical antiquity. He did not see that Milton was himself a classic, a great force controlled.

When Milton praised 'sweetest Shakespear, fancies childe, warbling his native Wood-notes wilde' his homage was perhaps not unmixed with envy. He himself took a great deal of trouble. The classical Dr. Johnson admired the profusion of emendations on the manuscript of *Comus*, and we have seen Milton polishing in the day-time what he had received in the night from his heavenly muse. All his verse follows the rule laid down by Cézanne: 'The artist does not record his emotions as the bird warbles its notes— he composes'. If Milton discarded rhyme, it was not for greater facility.[3] The verse of *Paradise Lost* is of so complex a structure that good poets like Cowper and others who tried their hand at it gave up in despair. Robert Bridges, poet laureate and a master of metre, studied it for several years without discovering all its resources.

The 'Babylonish dialect' evinces a set purpose no less exacting. Milton's verse had always been remarkable for

---

[1] 'puts on swift wings'. One hardly dares write it, but is not this, after the helicopter, the jet-plane?
[2] II, 628–43.   [3] See above, pp. 36, 47–8, and below, p. 303.

its terseness. Here, the fugue is defined in sixteen words.[1]
It was in order to be exact and brief that the poet, when
English would not meet his need, borrowed from Italian,
French, Greek or Hebrew, a word sometimes, often a
construction.

Similarly, if many Miltonian images are unexpected or
seem protracted, examination will generally reveal that they
mean more than meets the ear. For instance, the one that
Bentley suppressed suggests far more than the aerial voyage
of a giant being. It calls up a *night* flight, the crossing of
oceans, sailing vessels gliding by in *silence*. We cannot help
but catch a glimpse of the image of the Prince of this world
flying over his kingdom while mankind is asleep.[2]

And is it not also the sea, night and silence that we find
in the adventure of the Norwegian sailor? Assuredly,
Leviathan does not come into the account solely by reason
of his size. The scene is grandiose and sad, the sailor is
alone, lost, infinitely weak. His imprudence makes us
anxious for him. And all the more so if we have read *Job*,
Isaiah or the *Psalms*, or even *Moby Dick*. Leviathan sleeping
on the foam, inoffensive in appearance, portrays a being
whose prodigious force and ferocity we all forget.

It is again the poet's desire to say a great deal in a few
words that explains that well-known feature of Milton's
style, the abundance of proper names. The common noun
is linked to a concept, it implies a bold use of only part of
reality; it is the sign and instrument of our struggle against
the universe; thought begins with it. But, like our mind,
it is always surpassed by the real. Any proper name, on the
other hand, designates a complete entity, including its
unknown or unknowable elements. How insipid and in-
consistent does the common noun appear in comparison

[1] Book XI, 561-3:
                    ... his volant touch
     Instinct through all proportions low and high
     Fled and persu'd transverse the resonant fugue.
According to Speath (*Milton's knowledge of music*, Weimar, 1913), this definition would
be the oldest known.
    [2] See Book IX, 48-86: Satan, wishing to discover the animal who would interpret
him best, flies over the earth seven nights running.
          By Night he fled, and at Midnight returned
          From compassing the Earth, cautious of day.

with the other, bursting with realities, firmly set in time
and space. The one gives us 'horse' and man's noblest
conquest remains a shadow. But the other, by enunciating
Pegasus, Bucephalus or Rossinante, releases three clusters
of living images.[1] All the poets have made use to a greater
or lesser degree of the evocative power of the proper noun.
Here, the serpent's splendour is suggested by nine proper
nouns in six lines (IX, 505–10), the wonders of the garden
by twenty proper nouns in seventeen lines (IV, 269–85),
the great epic poems by fifteen proper nouns in eleven lines
(I, 577–87).

Unfortunately, many of the names which probably or
possibly stirred the English imagination during Milton's
lifetime have little or no effect on readers to-day, especially
outside England. For instance, the Bible has never been
familiar to the French and their present acquaintance with
Greek mythology just permits them to follow Offenbach's
Orpheus in the Underworld. In the second place, the emotional
contents of a geographical name partly depends on its
historical connotations. To the first readers of *Paradise
Lost*, Book XI, lines 385–411, such names as 'Ecbatan',
'Ophir', 'Ercoco', probably gave the same impression of
immeasurable distance in space and time as they do to
ourselves. But in the same passage Milton mentions Agra,
Mexico, Algiers and several more cities or countries, and
what their names meant for him we cannot even guess.

The passing of the centuries also explains why certain
episodes are no longer for us anything but ineffective fictions,
whereas on the original readers they exercised the pressure
of reality. For instance, the contemporaries of Milton
must have been moved by the passage in which the rebel
angels invent artillery (VI, 469–628). We say of such and
such a recent weapon that it is 'infernal'. For them this was
no mere manner of speaking. They believed in devils, they
burnt witches. Moreover these angelic gunners were not
the invention of Milton. Tasso and Ronsard had treated
the same theme.

[1] See my article: 'Du Nom propre en littérature', *Mercure de France*, 1936.

To sum up, Milton is to be ranged among those rare artists who have learnt how to submit their exceptionally powerful impulses to a no less demanding discipline. The story of Mazeppa, the guilty lover chained on a wild horse that bolts with him into a far country where he is made king, delighted the Romanticists. Byron, Hugo, several French painters treated this theme, in which they read the fate of genius. But Romanticism of one sort or another has existed at all times, and we have seen (p. 46) what Milton thought of the Mazeppas of his day. His own horse, although immensely powerful, always obeyed the hand and the heel of the strong-willed and expert rider, Milton.

Self-discipline had been pressed upon Milton as a duty and made more easy for him, both by his Puritan training and by his study of the great models. A third influence, even more effective perhaps, was his natural sensibility, which deprecated excess. Some critics have denied him this gift, but Chateaubriand puts them out of court: 'Il n'a jamais existé un génie plus sérieux et en même temps plus tendre que celui de cet homme'. True, Milton could imagine nightmare landscapes, boundless and cruel, but his heart belonged to the modest and gentle English countryside. He had always had his garden, and risen with the dawn to listen to 'the charm of earliest birds'.[1]

Again, twenty years of fierce controversy had left the best of himself unscathed. He 'contemplated' every morning. He believed as firmly at sixty as at twenty that all our acts gave a 'perfect, all-judging' witness. His private life has been combed through a hundred times by enraged adversaries; they have failed to establish that he ever committed anything base. If we admit that the frescoes of Fra Angelico derive part of their spell from the faith and life of the Dominican of Fiesole, let us believe also that to the life and faith of Milton we owe a number of passages universally known for their other-worldly serenity and their plenitude of innocent bliss. 'Ses paysages', said Taine,

---

[1] *Paradise Lost* IV, 642; also IV, 264–6; V, 7–8; VIII, 515; *Paradise Regained* IV, 434–8; and *Reformation* (Bohn II, 417); ' . . . expecting . . . to reinvolve us in that pitchy cloud of infernal darkness, where we shall . . . never more hear the bird of morning sing'.

'sont une école de vertu'. Voltaire had declared: 'Dans tous les autres poèmes, l'amour est regardé comme une faiblesse: dans le seul *Paradis perdu*, il est une vertu. . . . Comme il n'y a point d'autre exemple d'un pareil amour, il n'y en a point d'une pareille poésie.' Maurice Baring, diplomat and novelist, while staying in Czarist Russia, questioned a village schoolmaster who used to lend books to the peasants. According to him, his moujiks could not tolerate Gogol, but appreciated Dostoyevsky and *Monte-Cristo*. And every year they asked him for *Paradise Lost*. 'When I ask them why they like *Paradise Lost* they point to their heart and say: "It is near the heart; it speaks; you read and a sweetness comes to you".'[1]

> With thee conversing I forget all time,
> All seasons and their change, all please alike.
> Sweet is the breath of morn, her rising sweet,
> With charm of earliest Birds; pleasant the Sun
> When first on this delightful Land he spreads
> His orient Beams, on herb, tree, fruit, and flour,
> Glistring with dew; fragrant the fertil earth
> After soft showers; and sweet the coming on
> Of grateful Eevning milde, then silent Night
> With this her solemn Bird and this fair Moon,
> And these the Gemms of Heav'n, her starrie train:
> But neither breath of Morn when she ascends
> With charm of earliest Birds, nor rising Sun
> On this delightful land, nor herb fruit, floure,
> Glistring with dew, nor fragrance after showers,
> Nor grateful Eevning milde, nor silent Night
> With this her solemn Bird, nor walk by Moon,
> Or glittering Starr-light without thee is sweet.[2]

It is Eve who speaks thus, naïve as Miranda, but it might well be Adam. We are in 'the green paradise' of Baudelaire.[3]

Among the personalities which go to make up Milton's character, we must include a certain sermoniser trained doubtless by Young. His interventions are rare, but

[1] *A Year in Russia*, London, 1907, p. 149.   [2] IV, 639–56.
[3] 'Mais le vert paradis des amours enfantines . . . Est-il déjà plus loin que l'Inde et que la Chine?'=*Les Fleurs du Mal*, LXIV.

through his fault the epic flight can crash on a pedantic digression as in the following passage:

> No sooner hee with them of Man and Beast
> Select for life shall in the Ark be lodg'd,
> And sheltered round, but all the Cataracts
> Of Heav'n set op'n on the Earth shall powre
> Raine day and night, all fountains of the Deep
> Broke up, shall heave the Ocean to usurp
> Beyond all bounds, till inundation rise
> Above the highest Hills: then shall this Mount
> Of Paradise by might of Waves be moovd
> Out of his place, pusht by the horned floud,
> With all his verdure spoild, and Trees adrift
> Down the great River to the op'ning Gulf,
> And there take root an Iland salt and bare,
> The haunt of Seales and Orcs, and Sea-mews clang:
> To teach thee that God attributes to place
> No sanctitie, if none be thither brought
> By Men who there frequent, or therein dwell.[1]

This 'or therein dwell' reminds us that 'God visits the dwellings of just Men',[2] that Milton attended no place of worship and that his little house frequented by Urania was in his eyes as good as a church. Granted; but he should not have transported us so brusquely from the Persian Gulf to Artillery Walk.

Much more regrettable than a few false notes of this kind is the inconsistency of the poet's religious ideas. It long escaped most of the readers, for Milton was discreet and skilful; but it was strongly suspected on the publication of *Doctrina Christiana* in 1825. The sales of *Paradise Lost* in Holland fell at once. In 1836, Chateaubriand stated: 'Milton wavered among a thousand systems. . . . All the philosophical theories known to the poet have found a place, either greater or lesser, in his beliefs. . . . He is a fatalist. . . . Again he is a pantheist or a follower of Spinoza, but his pantheism is of a curious nature. . . . Nevertheless, in the midst of this confusion of principles, the poet remains Biblical and Christian.' We have seen in fact that this

[1] XI, 822–38. [2] See above, p. 267.

Puritan was a Platonist, an Arian and a Mortalist,[1] and owed something to the Cabbala.

It is highly probable that the innate or acquired tendencies which contended for the poet's soul would account in large measure for the indefiniteness of his religious views. The fact remains that we find a discord at the very centre of his epic. He respectfully reels off the orthodox sequence— a mysterious prohibition, a single act of disobedience, death for all the human race. But he does so in spite of his reason and his sensibility. He loves the guilty pair and makes us love them. Are they so very guilty? Whatever the archangel may say, Adam has yielded to love that is most noble. Eve has only been slightly susceptible to flattery, a little inquisitive, a little greedy. Milton has tender compassion for this 'Fairest unsupported flower'.[2] When she has to leave Eden the garden-lover shares her grief.

> Must I thus leave thee Paradise? thus leave
> Thee Native Soile, these happie Walks and Shades,
> Fit haunt of Gods?[3] where I had hope to spend,
> Quiet though sad, the respit of that day
> That must be mortal to us both. O flours,
> That never will in other Climat grow,
> My early visitation, and my last
> At Eev'n, which I bred up with tender hand
> From the first op'ning bud, and gave ye Names.[4]

Pure compassion is not the only impulse that makes Milton hesitate. He is a Westerner and a humanist. In spite of his subtle speeches and impressive descriptions, we still have the feeling that he is not quite sure that Adam and Eve would have been happy for long in their perfect garden. Happiness lies in action, in difficulty overcome. Aeschylus, a Westerner too, was on the side of Prometheus. The late Dr. Tillyard rightly said that 'Milton, stranded in his own Paradise, would very soon have eaten the apple on his own responsibility and immediately justified the act in a polemical pamphlet'.[5]

---

[1] See Chap. VIII, pp. 142-4.
[2] IX, 432. Compare in Ralph Hodgson's *Eva*—'Poor motherless Eve'.
[3] Worthy of the angels—see *Paradise Lost* III, 391.
[4] XI, 269-77.
[5] *Milton*, London, 1956, p. 282.

Bearing in mind that the scholarly poet has enriched his
epic with reminiscences from over two thousand authors,
can we believe that he blamed unreservedly the inquisitive-
ness of our first parents? Is it not his secret protest that
Satan formulates for him:

> . . . Knowledge forbidd'n?
> Suspicious, reasonless. Why should thir Lord
> Envie them that? can it be sin to know,
> Can it be death? and do they onely stand
> By Ignorance, is that thir happie state,
> The proof of thir obedience and thir faith?
> O fair foundation laid whereon to build
> Thir ruin![1]

It is true that for Milton, who follows St. Augustine, our
parents were guilty not of curiosity but of disobedience.
A fresh difficulty, however, then crops up, of which Milton
was fully aware. Since God foreknows everything, and he is
all goodness, ought he to have embarked[2] our race on a ship
which he knew would be wrecked? Adam, that is to say
Milton, does not speak of an embarkation. He recalls the
office in Bread Street, and speaks of a contract. He is none
the less incisive.

> . . . O fleeting joyes
> Of Paradise, deare bought with lasting woes!
> Did I request thee, Maker, from my Clay
> To mould me Man, did I sollicit thee
> From darkness to promote me, or here place
> In this delicious Garden? as my Will
> Concurrd not to my being, it were but right
> And equal to reduce me to my dust,
> Desirous to resigne, and render back
> All I receav'd, unable to performe
> Thy terms too hard, by which I was to hold
> The good I sought not. To the loss of that,
> Sufficient penaltie, why hast thou added
> The sense of endless woes? inexplicable
> Thy Justice seems;[3]

Adam himself at once finds the answer—a son has not

---

[1] IV, 515-22.
[2] Pascal, *Pensées*, 233—'Il faut parier; cela n'est pas volontaire, vous êtes embar-
qué'.   [3] X, 741-55.

the right to question his father's decisions. Before the mystery of his destiny, every man must imitate the patriarch Job: 'Then Job answered the Lord and said, "Behold, I am vile; what shall I answer thee? I will lay mine hand upon my mouth".' But what then was the value of Milton's project? Was not his attempt to 'justifie the wayes of God' the very fault committed by Job's friends.

Thus it may happen that a particular passage perfectly written and constructed, and dealing with a question of capital importance, cannot completely satisfy us. We know or have the presentiment that Milton, with equal eloquence and on the same point, may elsewhere defend or does defend a different theory. On the other hand, we read over again with unqualified pleasure the many pages which are simply human, in which the poet forsakes dogma for a while and gives free rein to his sensibility, passages such as the famous *andante* which ends the poem:

> [Eve speaks] . . . but now lead on;
> In mee is no delay; with thee to goe,
> Is to stay here; without thee here to stay,
> Is to go hence unwilling; thou to mee
> Art all things under Heav'n, all places thou,
> Who for my wilful crime art banisht hence.
> This furder consolation yet secure
> I carry hence: though all by mee is lost,
> Such favour I unworthie am voutsaft,
> By mee the Promisd Seed shall all restore.
> So spake our Mother *Eve*, and *Adam* heard
> Well pleas'd, but answerd not; for now too nigh
> Th' Arch-Angel stood, and from the other Hill
> To thir fixt Station, all in bright array
> The Cherubim descended; on the ground
> Gliding meteorous, as Ev'ning Mist
> Ris'n from a River ore the marish glides,
> And gathers ground fast at the Labourers heel
> Homeward returning. High in Front advanc't,
> The brandisht Sword of God before them blaz'd
> Fierce as a Comet; which with torrid heat,
> And vapour as the *Libyan* Air adust,
> Began to parch that temperat Clime; whereat

In either hand the hastning Angel caught
Our lingring Parents, and to th' Eastern Gate
Led them direct, and down the Cliff as fast
To the subjected Plaine; then disappeerd.
They looking back, all th' Eastern side beheld
Of Paradise, so late thir happie seat,
Wav'd over by that flaming Brand, the Gate
With dreadful Faces throngd and fierie Armes:
Som natural tears they dropd, but wip'd them soon;
The World was all before them, where to choose
Thir place of rest, and Providence thir guide:
They hand in hand with wandring steps and slow,
Through *Eden* took their solitarie way.[1]

Bentley castigated this page with unflinching hand. For instance he struck out 'wandering', since the exiles were guided by Providence, and suppressed 'solitary' since there were two of them.[2] Logic is logic. Yet Milton's art here reaches a depth of calculation which is scarcely credible; here are two examples.

The final speech of the drama is entrusted to the principal culprit, but then the final word of this last speech is 'restore'. In the second place, a comparison such as Milton loves, *suggests* to us that the banished pair, while awaiting the promised Redeemer, will not be without consolation. This 'labourer homeward returning' in the evening mist is much more than an obvious—and uncalled for—reminiscence of the reed-beds of Cambridge; he is a presage, unperceived of the couple, but presented to us in confidence. Henceforward, the lot of Adam and Eve will be toil, but they will return at nightfall to the comforts of their fireside.

We should like to be sure that this calm conclusion was written during the Restoration, but we have nothing to date it. Several passages, on the contrary, and even more certain silences, lead us to think that the soul of the defeated republican had undergone a change as momentous as that of the seasons after the Fall. For instance, it is from the

---

[1] XII, 614–49.
[2] His emendation ran:
    They hand in hand with social steps thcir way
    Through Eden took, with Heav'nly Comfort cheer'd.

Restoration that we must date this courageous lament at
the beginning of Book VII:

> Standing on Earth, nor rapt above the Pole,
> More safe I Sing with mortal voice, unchang'd
> To hoarce or mute, though fall'n on evil dayes,
> On evil dayes though fall'n, and evil tongues;
> In darkness, and with dangers compast round,
> And solitude; yet not alone, while thou
> Visitst my slumbers Nightly, or when Morn
> Purples the East . . .[1]

It was also after his struggle in 1660 that the poet
imagined or worked out the important episode of the seraph
Abdiel. Of all Lucifer's subordinates, only Abdiel had
refused to revolt against God. Milton twice praises him.
He remained, says Raphael, 'unmov'd, unshak'n, unseduc't,
unterrifi'd (V. 899). And God welcomes him in these terms:

> Servant of God, well done, well hast thou fought
> The better fight, who single hast maintained
> Against revolted multitudes the Cause
> Of Truth, in word mightier then they in Armes;
> And for the testimonie of Truth hast born
> Universal reproach, far worse to beare
> Then violence: for this was all thy care
> To stand approv'd in sight of God, though Worlds
> Judg'd thee perverse:[2]

Obviously, this refers to Milton the republican remaining
alone in the breach in the fatal spring of 1660.

One very strong feeling in Abdiel is scorn. In coming
out of the ranks to go and put himself to the service of God,
he passed:

> Long way through hostil scorn, which he susteind
> Superior, nor of violence feard aught;
> And with retorted scorn his back he turnd
> Of those proud Towrs to swift destruction doomd.[3]

And perfect scorn is mute. Raphael, recounting the battle,
names a few combatants on both sides, himself among
them, but adds:

> I might relate of thousands, and thir names
> Eternize here on Earth; but those elect
> Angels contented with their fame in Heav'n

[1] VII, 23–30.   [2] VI, 29–37.   [3] V, 904–7.

Seek not the praise of men: the other sort
In might though wondrous and in Acts of Warr,
Nor of Renown less eager, yet by doome
Canceld from Heav'n and sacred memorie,
Nameless in dark oblivion let them dwell.
For strength from Truth divided and from Just,
Illaudable, naught merits but dispraise
And ignominie, yet to glorie aspires
Vain glorious, and through infamie seeks fame:
Therefore Eternal silence be thir doome.[1]

There is the explanation—what other would be possible?
—of two amazing omissions—England and the Reformation
ignored. The vastness of his scheme, the boldness of his
comparisons, enabled the poet to touch on every sphere.
In connection with Satan's buckler, he manages to bring in
Florence and Galileo (I, 284–91). True, he does complain
here, and that twice (I, 497–502 and VII, 32–8), of the
young Cavaliers who disturbed his nights by their drunken
songs, but not a word from him evokes, even indirectly, a
single one of the men or events of which the polemist
had been so proud, because they attested to the world
God's predilection for 'his Englishmen'.[2] England had for-
sworn herself in 1660, she was 'illaudable'.

Similarly, Milton ignores Protestantism. At the beginning
he jeers at the theologians. In this quite new Hell which
prefigures our earth,[3] while Satan is flying towards Paradise,
the fallen angels indulge in our own pastimes—music,
sport, travel and . . . theology:

Others apart sat on a Hill retir'd,
In thoughts more elevate, and reasond high
Of Providence, Foreknowledge, Will, and Fate,
Fixt Fate, free Will, Foreknowledge absolute,
And found no end, in wandring mazes lost.
Of good and evil much they argu'd then,
Of happiness and final misery,
Passion and Apathie, and glory and shame,
Vain wisdom all, and false Philosophie:[4]

But neither in this passage nor elsewhere does Milton

---

[1] VI, 373–85.   [2] *Areopagitica*, see above, p. 132.
[3] 'Car l'Enfer est partout où l'Eternel n'est pas.' Du Bartas, *Première Semaine
Premier Jour*, l. 570.   [4] II, 557–65.

discriminate between Rome and Geneva. If he makes fun of certain customs of the Catholics (III, 476–97), he is silent about their articles of faith. In the summarized history of Christianity which comes in the last book, there is not a word on the rent in the sixteenth century. After the Apostles come the wolves, wolves whom they had predicted, and the continuous corruption of the whole of Christendom. The time when Milton had advocated the Presbyterian system is past and gone. Like their Anglican predecessors, the Presbyterians have betrayed the religion of the spirit. As to the self-styled Independents, the majority have hired themselves out to the civil power. Milton now ignores the light barriers between the denominations. What matters to him is the gulf between the free and tolerant believers and those who, on the contrary,

> Spiritual Lawes by carnal power shall force
> On every conscience . . .
> [and] force the Spirit of Grace it self, and binde
> His consort Libertie . . .[1]

If Milton despises theological systems, he has not much esteem for the sciences either. When Adam questions Raphael on the movements of the stars, the archangel's reply is reticent and vague. He 'does not blame' Adam:

> To ask or search I blame thee not, for Heav'n
> Is as the Book of God before thee set,
> Wherein to read his wondrous Works, and learne
> His Seasons, Hours, or Days, or Months, or Yeares:[2]

The Copernican system, still very much discussed, is only suggested ('What if the Sun be centre to the world'). But Raphael advises Adam to seek knowledge that is less vain. The great Architect has hidden his secrets from angel and from man. Perhaps he has left 'his Fabric of the Heavens' to the disputes of men 'to move His laughter at thir quaint Opinions wide' (VIII, 78).

> Sollicit not thy thoughts with matters hid,
> Leave them to God above, him serve and feare;[3]
> . . . be lowlie wise;[4]

---

[1] XII, 521–2, 525–6.   [2] VIII, 66–9.   [3] Ibid. 167–8.
[4] Ibid., 173. Cf. 'humile sapiemus' in the letter of 1637 to Diodati, p. 58.

Pascal also declared, perhaps in the same year:

> Je trouve bon qu'on n'approfondisse pas l'opinion de Copernic: mais ceci . . . ! Il importe à toute la vie de savoir si l'âme est mortelle ou immortelle.[1]

This comparison suggests others. Pascal had written on the paper which never left him:

> Oubli du monde et de tout, hormis Dieu . . . Père juste, le monde ne t'a pas connu, mais je t'ai connu . . . Joie, joie, joie, pleurs de joie . . . Jésus-Christ, Jésus-Christ . . . Renonciation totale et douce.

Milton proclaims his faith in Adam's very last words:

> Henceforth I learne, that to obey is best,
> And love with feare the onely God, to walk
> As in his presence, ever to observe
> His providence, and on him sole depend,
> Merciful over all his works, with good
> Still overcoming evil, and by small
> Accomplishing great things, by things deemd weak
> Subverting worldly strong, and worldly wise
> By simply meek; that suffering for Truths sake
> Is fortitude to highest victorie,
> And to the faithful Death the Gate of Life;
> Taught this by his example whom I now
> Acknowledge my Redeemer ever blest.[2]

The difference of tone is here so marked that we suspect there must exist deeper ones.

The author of the *Pensées* declares (233) that the justice of God towards the reprobate is less 'enormous' and should shock us less than his mercy towards the elect. But for Milton it was not this 'tipping the beam' in favour of the elect that justified the ways of God to men. He returns to the matter a score of times—God is unimpeachable because man is free, endowed with reason, entirely responsible. For Pascal reason is 'impotent' and must be silent.[3]

---

[1] *Pensées*, 218.   [2] XII, 561–73.
[3] *Pensées*, 434: 'Humiliez-vous, raison impuissante; taisez-vous, nature imbécile . . .' Not so Milton; see *Samson Agonistes*, 322: 'Down Reason then, at least vain reasonings down'.

C'est la grâce, et non la raison, qui fait suivre [notre religion] ... D'un homme plein de faiblesse, de misères, de concupiscence, d'orgueil et d'ambition, [mon Rédempteur] a fait un homme exempt de tous ces maux par la force de sa grâce, à laquelle toute la gloire en est due, n'ayant pour moi que la misère et l'erreur.[1]

Owing everything to grace, Pascal is filled with gratitude and love. Milton, of course, does not fail to remind us that love is necessary. It is a Gospel truth. Is it for him a truth he has personally experienced? To Adam's profession of faith quoted above, Michael replies sententiously:

> onely add
> Deeds to thy knowledge answerable, add Faith,
> Add Vertue, Patience, Temperance, add Love,
> By name to come calld Charitie, the soul
> Of all the rest; then wilt thou not be loath
> To leave this Paradise, but shall possess
> A paradise within thee, happier farr.[2]

There was a programme—one dares not say a prescription—that Marcus Aurelius would not have disavowed. Pascal exclaimed: 'I hold out my arms to my Deliverer'.

The Puritan and the Jansenist both condemn the world. Pascal says in his *Prayer to God for a good use of sickness*:

> O Dieu qui ne laissez subsister le monde et toutes les choses du monde que pour exercer vos élus ou pour punir les pécheurs ... Je sens que je ne puis aimer le monde sans vous déplaire, sans me nuire et sans me déshonorer.[3]

Milton's Archangel Michael is scarcely less severe:

> ...so shall the World goe on,
> To good malignant, to bad men benigne,
> Under her own waight groaning, till the day
> Appeer of respiration to the just,
> And vengeance to the wicked, at return
> Of him so lately promisd to thy aid,
> The Womans seed, obscurely then foretold,
> Now amplier known thy Saviour and thy Lord. ...[4]

But whereas Pascal 'forgets everything except God',

[1] *Pensées*, 564 and 550.
[2] *Paradise Lost* XII, 581-7. This happier Paradise than Eden will, however, demand a vigilant struggle. Our recent suspicion (p. 280) was justified.
[3] *Pensées et Opuscules*, ed. La Bonne Compagnie, Paris, 1947, pp. 76 and 79.
[4] XII, 537-44.

Milton will not renounce either poetry or politics—a decisive proof that he judges the snares and ambitions of the world, its tears, its triumphs, more worthy of a man than passive innocence. He served with equal fidelity the only two spiritual fatherlands that Europe still consciously remembers, Palestine and Greece. Hence, sometimes, inconsistencies such as those we have noted on the subject of Eden.

But when his two fatherlands were in harmony on a particular point, with what force and obstinacy could Milton demonstrate, blame or warn. There is a well known axiom, easily ignored as a rule—'Liberty presupposes discipline'. The Greeks were aware of it. 'Cosmos' signifies order and consequently hierarchy. But the world is solid,[1] no one in it can move freely except in his 'active Sphear assignd' (V, 477). Whoever wishes to go beyond it will be broken by the cosmos. To want to go beyond it was what the Greeks called *hubris*, excess, the outrage which the gods did not forgive.[2] Milton found this idea again in the Bible. *Hubris*, which destroyed the Titans, also destroyed Lucifer.

It was the cult of order which prompted the polemist. The prelates and the King, by presuming to rule by right divine, were going beyond their 'active Sphears assignd'. To break or eliminate them was a duty not only patriotic, but cosmic. On the *hybris* of the bishops the indignation of Milton could express itself with supreme irony:

And that the prelates have no sure foundation in the gospel, their own guiltiness doth manifest; they would not else run questing up as high as Adam to fetch their original, as it is said one of them lately did in public. To which assertion, had I heard it, because I see they are so insatiable of antiquity, I should have gladly assented, and confessed them even more ancient: for Lucifer, before Adam, was the first prelate angel; and both he, as is commonly thought, and our forefather Adam, as we all know, for aspiring above their orders, were miserably degraded.[3]

[1] Balzac: 'Notre globe est plein, tout s'y tient'. *Z. Marcas.*
[2] A hybrid is an outrage against nature.
[3] *Church Government*, Bohn II, 450.

As to tyrants and absolute kings, it was no less clear to Milton that they infringed the laws of the cosmos:

> Though I am of opinion, Salmasius, and always was, that the law of God does exactly agree with the law of nature . . . [I will now] demonstrate that nothing is more suitable to the law of nature, than that punishment be inflicted upon tyrants[1] . . .; the right of the people must be acknowledged, according to the law of nature, to be superior to that of princes; and therefore, by the same right, that before kingship was known, men united their strength and counsels for their mutual safety and defence; by the same right, that for the preservation of all men's liberty, peace, and safety, they appointed one or more to govern the rest; by the same right they may depose those very persons . . . if they find them unfit for government; since nature does not regard the good of one, or of a few, but of all in general.[2]

On the other hand, Milton warned the English people, with the same vigour and sometimes in the same pamphlet in which he belaboured absolute monarchy, that their commonwealth would necessarily perish if they refused to discipline themselves.

If it is permissible to say all too briefly that the keynote of the *Essais* is 'What do I know?' and of the *Pensées* 'We must wager', it could be said that Milton's whole work was already summarized in the closing lines of *Comus*: 'Love vertue, she alone is free'.

This maxim might serve as a motto to *Paradise Lost*. The origin of the drama is a challenge—man believing that he can liberate himself by disobedience. The universe is altered by it up to the very stars. And it all begins, the cosmos being a continuum, with the gesture of Eve:

> So saying, her rash hand in evil hour
> Forth reaching to the Fruit, she pluckd, she eat:
> Earth felt the wound, and Nature from her seat
> Sighing through all her Works gave signs of woe,
> That all was lost.[3]

Eve, in her ignorance, then wonders if she should not keep for herself the secret of the marvellous properties of

---

[1] *First Defence*, B. I, 108-9.   [2] Ibid., 111.   [3] IX, 780-4.

the forbidden fruit. Surely she would thus be able to go beyond her 'Sphear assignd'. Very logically, she forges for herself a principle which is the exact opposite of the law of the cosmos:

> ... so to add what wants
> In Femal Sex, the more to draw his Love,
> And render me more equal, and perhaps,
> A thing not undesireable, somtime
> Superior; for inferior who is free?[1]

This outline has necessarily omitted many important aspects of the vast poem. But perhaps it may have thrown a little more light on the man who is the subject of this book. Of his double allegiance we were already aware; now we can discern better its consequences. They have been exactly weighed up by Professor Kenneth Muir in his *John Milton*:

> The rift between humanism and puritanism, between poetry and theology, between human sympathy and religious belief may set up stresses and strains in the structure of the poem: but it is impossible to wish that Milton had been more of a Puritan, because in that case he would have been more didactic and less poetical, and the characters of Satan, Adam, and Eve would have been treated with less imaginative sympathy; and if he had been less of a Puritan he would not have been drawn to this particular subject. It may be that the greatness of the poem depends in a very real way on the tension between the two sides of Milton's mind and temperament.

[1] IX, 821–5.

XVII

IN PARTIBUS INFIDELIUM
1667–1671

CHARLES II, despite his intelligence, soon disappointed his subjects. He was determined 'never to set on his travels again', and yet he did not take kindly to his 'Sphear assignd'. He did not think he was a king, he said to the Earl of Essex, so long as a company of fellows were looking into his actions and examining his Ministers as well as his accounts. Yet it was indeed necessary that Parliament should regulate its credits to a man whose mistresses vied with one another in rapacity. How could he be granted a permanent army when his dream was to be as absolute as his cousin the King of France? And then, when he gave relief to the Quakers, the nation suspected some ulterior motive and already saw itself beneath the yoke of the Vatican.

He resorted to a desperate means—to leaning on Louis XIV, the man in the whole world who made the English most uneasy. He had sold him Dunkirk and two years later had offered to let the French annex Flanders if Louis would send him ten thousand infantry with cavalry in proportion. The offer was disregarded, and since Louis was preparing to invade Holland, Charles, in 1668, made common cause with Holland and Sweden. Louis suspended operations; he must have realized that the help of England was a valuable asset. In 1670 Louis and Charles came to a secret understanding against Holland, *and against the English conscience*, by the Treaty of Dover. Charles was to supply fifty ships; a substantial pension would be paid to him each quarter for the duration of the war, and at the time of the share-out his part would be the mouths of the Scheldt. Secondly, he would declare himself a Catholic as soon as he deemed it possible; a large indemnity would facilitate this conversion, and if England stirred, Louis would send six thousand men.

The higher Anglican clergy, supported by Parliament,

persecuted the non-conformists even more fiercely than Laud had harried the Puritans. The Act against Conventicles was applied in Scotland, despite the protests of the King, by a drunken general who had recourse to dragooning. In 1666 the Scots revived the Covenant and embarked upon a guerilla warfare which was to last for twenty years.

Henceforth non-conformity was ineradicable. Included now in the same measures of repression, Presbyterians and Independents buried their disagreements. They aroused all the more sympathy as their setbacks had rid them of time-servers. Fox, despite his imprisonments, had never enrolled so many adepts. William Penn seconded him to the despair of his father the Admiral. The cynicism of the Court reconciled the middle classes to the Puritan austerities. Last and not least, among those who had yielded to force, many kept their principles and their hopes intact.

The Good Old Cause then was not dead, and Milton knew this. But the republican galaxy was no more, and the regrets of the humble folk could not renew the deeds of the heroes. No one could so much as imagine that America would avenge Cromwell. America did not count. When in 1667 the Dutch ceded New Amsterdam in exchange for a few Indian factories, the English thought themselves to be losing heavily.

Modern England was now coming into being. Among the social and intellectual élite many minds were intrepid, but their ambition was to see clearly, not to reform. The time of apocalyptic utopias and wild controversies was past, Descartes shed his light over Europe, the Middle Ages were forgotten. England respected the Renaissance, but she was looking forward, not backward. She often took her inspiration now from France, no longer from Italy. Charles sent for Le Nôtre, gardens in the French style were multiplied, St. James's Park was designed by André Mollet. Saint-Evremond[1] was the literary arbitrator. He was to have the honour of interment at Westminster.

[1] A difference with Louis XIV, perhaps of a private nature, had forced him to exchange Paris for London in 1661. Love of learning drew him to Holland in 1665, Dutch austerity sent him back to England in 1670, and he chose to stay in England when Louis offered him his pardon.—See W. M. Daniels, *Saint-Evremond en Angleterre,* 1907.

Oxford still played at comparing the Latin of Duns Scotus with that of Cicero, but Cambridge welcomed the new spirit. There people could hear the mathematician Barrow and the theologian Whichcote discussing divinity according to the inductive method. There Newton succeeded Barrow in 1669. Cartesianism was in particular favour there at Christ's College. In the Royal Society, officially founded in 1662, Bacon's word was law. In 1670 the Society was still a club and its hundred and fifty subscribers included the chemist Boyle, the philosopher Locke, the mathematician Wren, who rebuilt London, Waller, Dryden, a certain Reverend Wilkins, Cromwell's brother-in-law, who thought the moon to be inhabited and contemplated making a journey there, men inquisitive of novelties like Buckingham and Pepys, finally three friends of Milton—Haak, Oldenburg and Aubrey. Hobbes, then aged over eighty, was the oracle of the Court. The King and Buckingham practised dissection and were proud of their laboratories.

These researchers felt the need of a clear and stable prose. The Royal Society required communications worded as simply as possible, and thought of nominating a special committee which would have reformed the language. But the English genius attaches more importance to the substance than to the form, and there was a general reluctance to 'pinning down the language'. For thirty years, therefore, Dryden was to demand in vain an Academy of Letters. The fashioning of modern English devolved on him alone, and a heavy task he found it. 'I am often put to a stand, in considering whether what I write to be the idiom of the tongue or false grammar. . . . I have no other way to clear my doubts but by translating my English into Latin, and thereby trying what sense the words will bear in a more stable language'.

In this first part of the reign two prose works are worthy of note. In his *Essay on Dramatic Poetry* (1667) Dryden pleaded for observation, logic and good taste. Bunyan, in *Grace Abounding* (1666), a moving account of his own life, was a forerunner of Defoe, the first novelist. It is but a step from confessions to the novel.

The poetry was rhymed prose, the favourite literary genres the satire and the epistle. Roscommon translated Horace's *Ars Poetica*, Butler continued his *Hudibras*, Denham and Marvell made fun of Waller for having fawned on the powers that were; Marvell railed at these, sometimes in coarse language, but his epigrams circulated only in manuscript or on loose sheets, and were not signed. Rochester composed an epistle *Upon Nothing*, a title which would have fitted the majority of the poems of the time. Dryden, somewhat poor in imagination, but prolific, virile, supple, brilliant, stood head and shoulders above these rhymesters. The King made him Poet Laureate in 1670.

An aristocratic literature must necessarily be small in quantity. The writers of the time were either nobles or under patronage, and their public was as frivolous as it was restricted. The printers' output was but a quarter of that under the Protectorate, about eighty titles a year, including reprints and periodicals.[1]

What pleased Charles, his brother the Duke of York and their following of elegant idlers, was the theatre, propitious for meetings and intrigue. Here again Court and nation were in opposition. London had only two theatres; they did not pay, because the middle classes frowned upon them, yet the staging included machinery, a numerous cast and rich costumes. Whereas the French actresses formerly introduced by Queen Henrietta had been hissed, pelted and forced to leave the country, now certain plays were acted solely by women.

The tragedies of Ben Jonson or of Beaumont and Fletcher were still applauded, but Shakespeare was no longer possible. Pepys found *Othello* 'a mean thing'. After seeing a performance of *A Midsummer Night's Dream*, he put down in his Diary: 'It is the most insipid and ridiculous play that I ever saw in my life'. So Shakespeare was cut down, bolstered up, trimmed, put into rhyme. *Macbeth*, that descent to bottomless perdition, was enlivened by ballets.

[1] Britain to-day produces 20,000 new books each year.

From the *Tempest* Davenant and Dryden derived a sym-
metrically constructed opera; Miranda, the girl who had
never seen a man, was matched with an *inamorato* who had
never seen a woman.

A revival of Davenant's *Siege of Rhodes* in 1662 gave rise
to the 'heroic drama'. The heroism it displayed differed
widely from the supreme virtue exemplified in Corneille's
tragedies, the courage to sacrifice love, power, or life,
at the call of duty. The master of the genre, Dryden,
merely endowed his characters with an inhuman grandeur;
in general his rivals were content with ranting tirades.
Dryden triumphed in 1670 with the *Conquest of Granada*.
Buckingham ridiculed the play, the genre and the author
in a parody, *The Rehearsal*, acted in Dryden's own theatre.
The pseudo-heroic drama was no better than a cover; it
only lasted about ten years or so. What the Court wanted
was gaiety.

The comedies of Ben Jonson were revived, Dryden
transposed Molière, Wilson exposed Puritan hypocrisy (*The
Cheats*, 1662), others painted vices, not without wit, but
with a crudeness which has remained a byword. Etherege
led the way in 1668; he was followed in 1671 by Wycherley,
'le plus brutal des écrivains qui aient sali le théâtre' (Taine).
The 'Restoration Comedy' was launched.

Between the world and himself Milton had always inter-
posed a small circle of intimates. Now the people whom he
could hear moving to and fro behind the screen were no
longer familiar bores or adversaries, but strangers: a new
England surrounded him. The English commonly divide
the history of their literature into 'Ages' presided over
by Chaucer, Shakespeare, Milton, Dryden, and others;
Milton's age beginning in 1625, Dryden's lasting from 1660
to 1700. In fact, when Milton at last took wing, his supposed 'age' was past.

While his epic was gathering its first readers, to what
other works did he devote his time, dictating prose in the
fine season and poetry in the winter months? All we know
is that in 1669 he published a shabby little Latin grammar
of sixty-five pages, which was original on two points—

it was in English, and by twenty devices it saved the pupil's time. 'It hath been long a general complaint', said the preface, 'not without cause, in the bringing up of youth, and still is, that the tenth of a man's life, ordinarily extended, is taken up in learning, and that very scarcely, the Latin Tongue.'[1] This small practical manual was in the spirit of the new England. Masson is of opinion that Milton may have published it at his own expense.

When we think of Waller's comment to the effect that the 'blind schoolmaster' had published a weighty poem on the Fall of man and if length were a merit, it would have that—we have to admit that the fact of having instructed the young did not recommend Milton to the admiration of his contemporaries, and we may wonder why he became a pedagogue again when he no longer had any pupils. The explanation is simple—school books bring in a good return. In his letter to Heimbach of August 1666 Milton wrote: 'I should dread a too numerous progeny from so many forms of the marriage-union as you enumerate, were it not an established truth that virtues are nourished most and flourish most in straitened and hard circumstances'.[2] What he meant was: 'I am already responsible for the support of three grown-up girls and the Restoration has ruined me'. After this letter, the Great Fire made him poorer still.

About 1670 he sent his girls to learn gold and silver embroidery, a luxury trade to which the apprenticeship was onerous. At this period he lodged for some time with an old friend, Millington, antiquarian bookseller and a specialist in auction sales. Why this change of residence? It was quite unnecessary if Milton had only wanted to buy or sell a few volumes.

Phillips does not mention the stay with Millington and does not refer to a sale. For nothing in the world would he have let it be thought that his uncle had experienced money difficulties. Four years later, in 1698, Toland did mention a transaction, but he proved no less careful than Phillips to save the poet's reputation: 'Towards the latter end of

---

[1] Masson VI, 640. [2] See above, p. 256.

his life, he contracted his library, both because the heirs he left could not make a right use of it, and that he thought he might sell it more to their advantage than they could be able to do themselves'. Millington, a mere auctioneer, is not mentioned. We are at liberty to imagine some tactful arrangement, such as that of Diderot with Catherine.[1] Indeed, Toland goes a little further (and just a little too far) by adding: 'His enemies reported that poverty constrained him to part with his books'. In 1734, Richardson mentioned the bookseller, but said nothing of any sale. Masson (VI, 651) prudently confines himself to a truism: 'This stay can have been but for some purpose of a temporary nature'. Pattison (p. 149) follows Richardson, but is bold enough to suggest that Milton, on his third marriage, moved for some time from Jewin Street 'to the house of Millington, the bookseller'.

If we admit that Milton was short of money, everything becomes clear. He possessed rare books, and wanted to sell them to the best possible advantage. Millington suggested to him a well-known device—they would avail themselves of an auction sale and 'pass' the atlases on such a day with other atlases, the precious Euripides the next day with the classics, etc. Milton would himself be present and could withdraw a volume from the sale if the bids for it were too low. To spare him from coming to and fro, Millington would lodge him for as long as was necessary. This attention should not surprise us; Millington was sometimes to be seen leading his friend round the streets of the City.

Was Milton, however, in need of funds? Richardson has supplied the proof. He had remarked on the flyleaf of a copy of *Eikonoklastes* this epigram written by some person unknown:

> That thou escaped'st that vengeance which o'ertook,
> Milton, thy regicides and thy own book,
> Was clemency in Charles beyond compare;
> And yet thy doom doth prove more grievous far.

---

[1] She bought his books but left him in possession of them, with a salary as her librarian.

OLIVER CROMWELL   *Samuel Cooper*

Facing page 298

Old, sickly, poor, stark blind, thou writ'st for bread:
So for to live thoud'st call Salmasius from the dead.[1]

The anonymous Royalist was certainly not thinking of
Paradise Lost, which had practically no monetary value, yet
the Milton he describes can only be the Milton of the
Restoration. The allusion 'writ'st for bread' must refer
not perhaps to the obscure Latin grammar, but to the work
which followed, that *History of Britain* begun in 1641. It
came out in 1670—three hundred pages of text set between
a handsome portrait and a very full index. The publisher,
Allestree, was a zealous Royalist. It was he who in 1660
had issued Saumaise's posthumous reply.

In 1648 Milton was hoping to bring his story of Britain
down to his own times; circumstances had obliged him
to stop at the Conquest. Such as it was, the book was an
innovation.[2] Although this pioneer work has long ago
been surpassed, the historian Sir Charles Firth has spoken
of it with esteem:

> Milton's *History of Britain* is worthy studying. It elucidates
> both his political writings and his poems; like all that he wrote,
> it bears the impress of his character, and is, therefore, of some
> biographical value; finally, the book itself is a work of learning
> and originality, worthy to be remembered in any account of
> historical writing in England.[3]

We need not be surprised that the songster of Eden
should have taken the trouble to sort out the Saxon Hep-
tarchy. 'He did not reckon his talent', says the Anonymous
Biographer, 'but as entrusted with him, and therefore
dedicated all his labors to the glory of God and some public
good. . . . He scarcely left any part of learning unimproved
by him.' Milton considered that what destroyed nations
was presumption (*hubris*), the basis of which was ignorance.
The historian who recounts to his compatriots exactly
what their successes and their setbacks have been, before
all things avoiding flattery, will spare them from engaging
in enterprises beyond their strength. Milton keenly reproached the obscure old chroniclers for their inventions.

---

[1] Masson VI, 717, or Bohn I, XXXIX. [2] See above, Ch. V.
[3] *Essays historical and literary*, Oxford, 1938, p. 61.

X

Rather than imitate them he would 'choose to represent
the truth naked, though as lean as a plain journal'.
This laudable resolution did not prevent him from
remaining consciously a poet and a partisan. He, too,
recounted the fabulous origins of the Britons and the legend
of King Lear. These old tales so fascinated him that his
style shows their influence. And he explains:

> Ofttimes relations heretofore accounted fabulous have been
> after found to contain in them many footsteps and reliques of
> something true. . . . I have therefore determined to bestow
> the telling over even of these reputed tales, be it for nothing else
> but in favour of our English poets and rhetoricians, who by
> their art will know how to use them judiciously.[1]

These concessions to poetry may be excused, but writing
of the Saxon convents, Milton blames the vows of religion;
speaking of the first bishops, he rails at those of his own time;
ecclesiastical history is deliberately omitted. Since woman
was created to obey, Queen Boadicea who roused her
people and fought the Romans becomes with Milton 'a
distracted woman with as mad a crew at her heels'. Nevertheless, certain sharp quips aimed at the Presbyterians were
suppressed by Milton himself, because that body was being
persecuted. Other passages, hostile to the Anglican clergy,
were banned by the censorship, according to Phillips, who
added that the Earl of Anglesey kept them until his death.
A long digression censured in 1670 saw the light eleven
years later, under the title of *Character of the Long Parliament
and of the Westminster Assembly*. Milton had taken occasion
of the chaotic condition of Britain at the departure of the
Romans to describe England on the morrow of the Civil
War.

The Earl of Anglesey's gesture of reverence in preserving
anti-clerical diatribes suggests an hypothesis. Was it not
the earl who, seeing the poet short of money, persuaded
him to publish his work unfinished, pruned the manuscript,
and had it printed at his own expense by Allestree? Masson
found no trace of the work in the Stationers' Registers.
It is unbelievable that so tendentious a history signed by

---

[1] Masson VI, 643–4.

such an opprobrious name should have been not only accepted, but luxuriously presented by a Royalist bookseller, unless we admit the intervention and generosity of some influential personage. The portrait, designed and engraved by Faithorne, is the best there is of Milton. Faithorne had made portraits of Queen Henrietta, Cromwell, the physician Harvey, Fairfax, Hobbes—a crowd of nobles and notabilities. Who engaged him if not Anglesey?

While the *History* was being printed, Westminster was hotly debating a strange case. A certain Lord Roos, rightly or wrongly alleging infidelity on the part of his wife, wished to be authorized by Parliament to marry another, whether after divorce or without it. Buckingham was behind the affair and the whole country was in a state of excitement over it, because the Queen was sterile. Divorce or bigamy made legitimate would permit the King to have an heir who would eliminate the increasingly unpopular Duke of York. In April 1670, Roos was authorized to proceed with the divorce. The King, however, preferred to change nothing in his life. Now, according to Anthony Wood and the Anonymous Biographer, when the Lord Roos Divorce Bill was brought into the Lords by Buckingham, an eminent peer and a chief officer of State consulted Milton, 'as the prime person that was knowing in that affair'. It happened therefore that Bucer's translator played very much the same rôle as Bucer himself.

What had become of *Paradise Lost*? On April 26th, 1669, Milton had given Simmons a receipt for the second payment of five pounds. It means that in those artless days which knew nothing yet of literary juries and prizes, of copies autographed over the counter to the purchasers, or of searching broadcast interviews, in a city of about three hundred thousand souls, and in the space of eighteen months, there had been sold at least thirteen hundred copies of an epic as intimidating in its matter as in its form.

The reactions of the first readers are unknown to us. They must have belonged in great part to those Puritan circles which now kept their own counsel. Richardson

relates that in 1669 one of Charles II's household, Lord
Buckhurst (afterwards Earl of Dorset), as he was going
the round of the booksellers, happened to come upon
Paradise Lost. There had been poets in his family and he
himself wrote passable verses. He turned over the pages,
was surprised, took the volume away, read it and passed it
to his friend Dryden, who sent it back with this note: 'This
man cuts us all out, and the ancients too'.

This eulogy, which is regularly quoted, was an exaggera-
tion. The noble lord admired, the poet chimed in. Dryden
was to admit in his old age: 'When I first read *Paradise Lost*,
I knew not half the extent of its excellency'. Moreover,
he must have already read the poem, it was he who should
have brought it to Dorset's notice. In 1667, in his *Essay on
Dramatic Poetry*, Dryden had formally condemned blank
verse, even in the theatre. In 1668, Milton in his turn
had publicly condemned rhyme. He did not name Dryden,
but the incident leaves little doubt that Dryden was a
very early reader of *Paradise Lost*.

Simmons, in fact, only had two or three hundred copies
bound and put on sale at a time, modifying the title-page
slightly, notably by rectifying the date. Two of these
'bindings' had appeared in 1667, signed 'John Milton'.
Another, dated 1668, now only bore the initials J.M. The
following one, however, still of 1668, again gave the name
in full, and in addition a eulogy of blank verse and the
argument of the poem. Simmons had evidently found
that the sale was dragging. After supposing that the name
of the pamphleteer was frightening off readers, he had
blamed the absence of rhymes and the insufficiency of the
title. He himself boasted, in a heading of four lines, of
having obtained from the author these fourteen useful
pages: '*Courteous Reader*, there was no Argument at first
intended to the Book, but for the satisfaction of many
that have desired it, I have procur'd it, and withall a reason
of that which stumbled many others, why the Poem
Rimes not'.

Now in 1668 the use of blank verse was the subject of
keen discussion. In particular, there had been an exchange

of printed arguments between Dryden and his brother-in-law Sir Robert Howard, a dramatist of talent. At a time when London was bringing out eighty titles a year, Dryden had certainly read Milton's preliminary note, *The Verse*, which bore hard upon him and was favourable to Howard:

> ... Rime being no necessary Adjunct or true Ornament of Poem or good Verse, in longer Works especially, but the Invention of a barbarous Age, to set off wretched matter, and lame Meeter; grac't indeed since by the use of some famous modern Poets, carried away by Custom, but much to thir own vexation, hindrance and constraint to express many things otherwise and for the most part worse than else they would have exprest them. Not without cause, therefore some both *Italian* and *Spanish* Poets of prime note have rejected Rime both in longer and shorter Works . . . as a thing of it self, to all judicious ears, trivial and of no true musical delight. . . . This neglect then of Rime so little is to be taken for a defect, though it may seem so perhaps to vulgar Readers, that it rather is to be esteemd an example set, the first in *English*, of ancient liberty recoverd to Heroic Poem from the troublesom and modern bondage of Rimeing.

It is understandable that Dryden, implicitly classed among the 'vulgar Readers' should have made no attempt to bring forward the man who was cutting out all other poets, both present and past.

The new presentation perhaps speeded up sales, but Simmons must have hoped for more. The contract did not oblige him to reprint, and when the first edition was sold out, he left it at that. Five years were to pass before he discovered that his strange poet could please more than fifteen hundred people.

It may be guessed that Milton scarcely appreciated this refusal to reprint. Simmons', moreover, was a mind of very small calibre. His four lines bordered on insolence and hurt the tongue. Milton had to correct their syntax for the ensuing binding. It was not Simmons who printed *Paradise Regained* and *Samson Agonistes*, but Starkey, the publisher of the Latin grammar. Authorized by the censorship in July 1670, the two poems appeared under the same cover at the beginning of the following year.

XVIII

PARADISE REGAINED

1671

IT will be recalled that at Chalfont, in September 1665, Ellwood had asked with a smile: 'Thou hast said much here of Paradise Lost, but what hast thou to say of Paradise Found?', and that Milton made no answer, but sat some time in a muse, then fell into another subject. Let us return to Ellwood's autobiography:

> And, when afterwards I went to wait on him there (which I seldom failed of doing, whenever my occasions drew me to London), he showed me his second poem, called *Paradise Regained*, and in a pleasant tone said to me, 'This is owing to you; for you put it into my head by the question you put to me at Chalfont; which before I had not thought of'.[1]

We have no reason to call in question the incident. Honest Ellwood was incapable of inventing it. Molière, before putting his comedies on the stage, took care to read them to his cook. We regret, however, the vagueness of the date 'afterwards'. Let us try to define it.

Milton went back to Artillery Walk after the Plague was over, and 'the city had become safely habitable again' (Ellwood), that is in February–March 1666. The Great Fire broke out on September 2nd. If Ellwood had seen the manuscript *after* the Fire, or very soon before it, would he have fixed the date of his visit without any reference to that catastrophe? The chronology is this, then—at Chalfont, about September 1665, Milton took up Ellwood's challenge. His library had remained in London, the long evenings had begun, poetry absorbed him entirely. In about two hundred days (September 1665—February–March 1666), he dictated two thousand lines, and soon after his return to London, he proudly showed them to the little Quaker. But they did not pass the censor until July 1670. Does the Great Fire

[1] *Ellwood's Life*, ed. 1714, p. 247, or Masson VI, 654.

of September 1666 suffice to account for this long delay? Another explanation will appear presently. Meanwhile, let us examine the poem.

Ellwood had naïvely thought of the heavenly paradise opened to men by the sacrifice of Calvary. Milton knew this quite well and took it into account. But, putting on one side the Passion, the Descent into Hell, and the Resurrection, he deliberately chose the Temptation in the wilderness. This crossroads was the point of departure for the whole enterprise. Since the avenues that Satan proposed were rejected, one way alone remained open, that which led to the cross. A well-known chapter of the *Brothers Karamazov* turns on this interpretation of the Gospel text. Clearly Milton's gloss was the same as Dostoyevsky's, for the long expostulation of the Grand Inquisitor can already be found in embryo in this question of Satan:

> Since neither wealth, nor honour, arms nor arts,
> Kingdom nor Empire pleases thee, nor aught
> By mee propos'd in life contemplative,
> Or active, tended on by glory, or fame,
> What dost thou in this World?[1]

Milton had strong personal reasons for choosing this theme. Neither sentimental nor a mystic, dearly loving, on the contrary, a close debate, he would have to imagine a contest between good and evil. He had formerly announced[2] that he would perhaps write 'a brief epic on the model of the *Book of Job*'—with regard to brevity, no other event of equal importance could be told in fewer words than the Temptation in the wilderness. Moreover, as it was the only encounter of Christ with Satan in person, no other page of the Gospel authorized Milton to bring before the public the fallen angel as Prince of this world, proud of his power yet fully conscious of his doom, and bent on the destruction of his prisoners. Milton had 'said much' about him in *Paradise Lost*, but he had left unsaid far more. On this capital point, *Paradise Regained* was a continuation. It was one also on less important matters. For instance,

[1] *Paradise Regained* IV, 368–72.
[2] In *Church Government*, in 1641. See above, p. 97.

the world's view presented by Michael to Adam did not extend beyond the time of the Flood, but some of the stones rejected by the builder of the major epic might and did become part of the brief one.[1] Indeed, they take up no less than one-third of the poem.[2]

Above all, Ellwood's question had awakened in the defeated Republican echoes which the honest youth could not suspect. Paradise reconquered, recovered, regained, was it not this 'paradise within thee, happier farr' promised to the first man on the morrow of his first fault? Had not Milton, too, after faults and struggles, regained peace with God and himself? Was he not as happy at Chalfont as he had formerly been at Horton? Jesus, in rejecting the tempter, had obtained that communion with his Father which is heaven upon earth. Such was the theme unknowingly suggested by Ellwood and announced here:

> I who ere while the happy Garden sung,
> By one man's disobedience lost, now sing
> Recoverd Paradise to all mankind,
> By one mans firm obedience fully tri'd
> Through all temptation, and the Tempter foild
> In all his wiles, defeated and repulst,
> And *Eden* rais'd in the wast Wilderness.[3]

The apostrophe quoted earlier: 'Since nothing pleases thee . . .' implies that the poet has not hesitated to amplify and embellish. In exact terms he has developed the second temptation—'the kingdoms of the world and their glory'. The first—to change stones into bread—runs into forty lines; the last—for Christ to throw himself down from the top of the temple—into eighty. Between that short prelude and that short conclusion the assaults are renewed during a day and a night. In connection with the world and its glory, we see following one another the various means with which the world will try to seduce or reduce us, including fear.

---

[1] After all, we have it from Milton himself, the vision in *Paradise Lost* was but an audacious transposition of the vision in the wilderness. (See *P.L.* XI, 376–384.)
[2] 'For Milton, geography had its romance.' (Bowra, *From Virgil to Milton*, 1962, p. 238.) And so had history. They are inseparable.
[3] *Paradise Regained* I, 1–7.

Before the first temptation, Jesus was already hungry. During the night that followed it, he dreamt that God was feeding him miraculously. On the morrow it is Satan who offers him a feast. From aridity and desolation we are transferred to a scene teeming with life and a gathering as splendid as Poussin ever painted. The table is spread under wide-stretching shade, there is meat, game, fish prepared in a score of ways, a buffet laden with rare wines and 'tall stripling youths rich clad to serve them'.

> ... distant more
> Under the Trees now trippd, now solemn stood
> Nymphs of *Diana's* train, and *Naiades*
> With fruits and flowers from *Amalthea's* horn,
> And Ladies of th'*Hesperides*, that seemd
> Fairer then feignd of old, or fabl'd since
> Of Fairy Damsels met in Forest wide
> By Knights of *Logres*, or of *Lyones*,
> *Lancelot* or *Pelleas*, or *Pellenore*,
> And all the while Harmonious Airs were heard
> Of chiming strings, or charming pipes, and winds
> Of gentlest gale *Arabian* odors fannd
> From their soft wings, and *Flora's* earliest smells.[1]

Such a banquet might have done for Heliogabalus; Jesus rejects it out of hand.[2]

Satan then offers riches—Will 'the dizzy multitudes' follow thee

> Longer than thou canst feed them on thy cost?
> Money brings Honour, Friends, Conquest, and Realms;
> What rais'd *Antipater* the *Edomite*,
> And his Son *Herod* plac'd on *Judahs* Throne
> (Thy throne) but gold that got him puissant friends?
> Therefore, if at great things they wouldst arrive,
> Get Riches first, get Wealth, and Treasure heap,
> Not difficult, if thou heark'n to me,
> Riches are mine, Fortune is in my hand;
> They whom I favour thrive in wealth amain,
> While Virtue, Valour, Wisdom sit in want.[3]

[1] II, 353–65.　　　　[2] See Charles Lamb, *Essays*, 'Grace before Meat'.
[3] II, 421–31.

For lack of these three, replies Jesus, wealth is impotent.

> Yet he who reigns within himself, and rules
> Passions, Desires, and Fears, is more a King;
> Which every wise and vertuous man attains:
> And who attains not, ill aspires to rule
> Cities of men, or head-strong Multitudes,
> Subject himself to Anarchy within,
> Or lawless passions in him which he serves.[1]

—Then, wish for glory, give to the universe the joy of admiring thee. Do not wait, 'Great Julius ... wept that he had lived so long inglorious'.

—What does the people's praise matter to me? 'To be dispraised of them were no small praise'. It is God who gives true glory. Moreover, war is base and cruel.

—Ah! How little thou resemblest thy Father! He created all things for his glory.

—He created all things to manifest his goodness.

—Let us leave glory. Thy people are the slaves of the Romans; fulfil the prophecies and reign; it is thy duty.

—Everything will come in its own time. Who knows if my Father does not want me to suffer first? And what is my kingdom to thee—since it will be thy destruction?

—I know that I am lost.

> I would be at the worst; worst is my Port,
> My harbour and my ultimate repose,
> The end I would attain, my final good.[2]

Thou dost not know what thou art refusing. Every year thou spendest a few days in Jerusalem, but 'the world thou hast not seen, much less her glory'. Come and see!

From the top of a mountain Jesus views the Orient, Nineveh, Babylon, Persepolis.

> *Ecbatana* her structure vast there shews,
> And *Hecatompylos* her hunderd gates,
> There *Susa* by *Choaspes*, amber stream,
> The drink of none but Kings ...[3]

The armies of the Parthians and their satellites march past in the plain, archers and cuirassiers, 'chariots and elephants endorsed with towers'.

---

[1] II, 466–72.　　　[2] III, 209–11.　　　[3] Ibid., 286–9.

—I will procure their alliance for thee, and thou shalt reign 'from Egypt to Euphrates and beyond'.

—Thou has just proved to me that arms are fragile. And what is the good of reigning over idolaters?

> Or as a swarm of flies in vintage time,
> About the wine-press where sweet moust is powrd,
> Beat off, returns as oft with humming sound;
> Or surging waves against a solid rock,
> Though all to shivers dasht, the assault renew,
> Vain battry, and in froth or bubbles end;
> So Satan, whom repulse upon repulse
> Met ever; . . .[1]

He brings our Saviour to the western side of the mountain:

> The City which thou seest no other deem
> Than great and glorious Rome, Queen of the Earth.[2]

The City and the World. Tiberius.

—Old Tiberius is a monster; with my help, thou mayst replace him for the good of his people.

—I have not been sent for Tiberius, nor for his debased people.

> What wise and valiant man would seek to free
> These thus degenerat, by themselves enslav'd,
> Or could of inward slaves make outward free?
> Know therefore when my season comes to sit
> On *Davids* Throne, it shall be like a tree
> Spreading and over-shadowing all the Earth,
> Or as a stone that shall to pieces dash
> All Monarchies besides throughout the World,
> And of my Kingdom there shall be no end: . . .[3]

—Thou disdainest my gifts because I offer them unconditionally; yet they are precious, and I do put one condition upon them; it is that 'thou wilt fall down and worship me as thy superior Lord'.

—It is written—Thou shalt worship God alone. Thou offerest me what is mine.

—Do not be offended and let us leave the transitory

---

[1] IV, 15–22.   [2] Ibid., 44–5.   [3] Ibid., 143–51.

kingdoms of this world. What thou lovest is contemplation
and profound dispute. Be famous then by wisdom. How
canst thou hope to persuade men if thou dost not equal
in them learning?

> Look once more ere we leave this specular Mount
> Westward, much nearer by Southwest, behold
> Where on the *Aegean* shore a City stands
> Built nobly, pure the air, and light the soil,
> *Athens* the eye of Greece . . .[1]

—I know all I need to know;

> . . . : he who receives
> Light from above, from the fountain of light,
> No other doctrin needs, though granted true; . . .[2]

I know the nothingness of philosophies, the sterility of
books when the reader's judgment is weak. Nothing sur-
passes our psalms, which delighted Babylon. It is from us
that Greece holds her poetry and her music, of which she
makes use to sing the vices of her gods and her people.
Our prophets have spoken better of the government of
cities than all the oratory of Greece and Rome.

—Then, *what dost thou in this world?*

Satan 'takes' and brings back to the wilderness the Son of
God. There Jesus spends another night. But his sleep is
disturbed by 'ugly dreams', then a storm breaks out in
which troops of demons vie with the elements. Jesus, however, like Abdiel, like Milton in 1660, remains steadfast.

> O patient Son of God, yet onely stoodst
> Unshak'n; nor yet staid the terror there,
> Infernal Ghosts, and Hellish Furies, round
> Environd thee, some howld, some yelld, some shriekd,
> Some bent at thee thir fiery darts, while thou
> Sat'st unappalld in calm and sinless peace.
> Thus passd the night so foul, till morning fair
> Came forth with Pilgrim steps in amice gray;
> Who with her radiant finger stilld the roar
> Of thunder, chas'd the clouds, and laid the winds,
> And grisly Spectres, which the Fiend had rais'd
> To tempt the Son of God with terrors dire.[3]

[1] IV, 236-40.   [2] Ibid., 288-90.   [3] Ibid., 420-31.

Satan reappears and is sarcastic. 'I am unharmed', replies Jesus, and 'I shall reign past thy preventing'.

—We shall then try another method. Thou art called the Son of God, but the Son of God I am too—I will put thee to the test.

He carries Jesus away, and puts him down on the summit of the Temple of Jerusalem.

> There stand, if thou wilt stand; to stand upright
> Will ask thee skill; . . .
> . . . if not to stand,
> Cast thyself down; safely if Son of God: . . .
> To whom thus Jesus: also it is writt'n,
> Tempt not the Lord thy God; he said and stood.
> But Satan smitt'n with amazement fell;[1]

Angels carry Jesus away into a pleasant valley, offer him celestial food, celebrate his victory and put him on his way again.

> . . . hee unobserv'd
> Home to his Mothers house privat returnd.[2]

As can be seen, the second Paradise is very simply conceived. God and heaven appear only in a few lines at the beginning; Satan no longer dwells in hell but in the air; instead of surveying the early history of humanity, we travel through the empire of Tiberius. Milton keeps to his basic theme—the man-God rejecting the seductions of the world. It has been said that *Paradise Regained* was a work of weariness.[3] 'Of relaxation' seems nearer the mark. There is no proof that Milton was a tired man when he found shelter at Chalfont. But surely he must have been at a loss how to use his time pleasantly and to good purpose so far from his books and his friends. The suggestion of Ellwood had been providential. While the fields were dank and roads were mire, how could a poet better help waste the sullen season than by composing a dozen lines a day, dictating them to his wife, and pondering over the next passage by the log-fire of a cottage? His past, remembered in tranquillity,

---

[1] IV, 551–62.   [2] Ibid., *in fine*.
[3] Chateaubriand: 'une oeuvre de lassitude, quoique calme et belle'.

presented itself to him in its true colours.[1] He felt proud
of his studious childhood, and of his courage in 1660,
but he was sorry that, like Solomon, he had yielded to the
seductions of woman, and that he had sought, with
Cromwell, to save an unworthy nation. As for his learning,
how vain it appeared to him now! And all these memories
and reflections he wove, sometimes with scant disguise,
into the story of the Evangelists. A little logic sufficed
him to introduce some incident or other which at first seems
strange. For instance, when the evil spirits hold council
for the second time (II, 115–235), Belial shouts brutally,
'Set women in his eye', and praises (admirably) the power of
women, recalling the sins of Solomon, but his leader checks
him at once—An Alexander, a Scipio, 'have with a smile
made small account of beauty and her lures!' Solomon
lived at ease, but 'he whom we attempt is wiser far than
Solomon'. To make Satan pronounce the eulogy of chastity
was paradoxical only in appearance. Belial's suggestion
had to be made and had to be refuted.

In short, the poem was in existence without having cost
the poet much effort when, half sincerely, half teasingly,
he thanked Ellwood for having given him the idea.

What happened in the four years that followed? It is
inconceivable that Milton should have put his poem away
in a drawer and forgotten it. It is possible that he revised
the plot. It is certain that he perfected its form, for it
presupposes an exceptional effort on his part. Severe as
the wilderness, rigorous as the rules of fencing, it banishes
the eloquence, so dear to the former polemist.

At the opening a young carpenter uncertain of his destiny
meets an old peasant who seems to be looking for one of his
sheep or some dead wood. In the course of the dialogue,
the former becomes more clearly conscious of his vocation,
and the second betrays ever more the fact that, while knowing much, he understands nothing. But at no moment is

---

[1] O what a multitude of thoughts at once
Awak'nd in me swarm, while I consider
What from within I feel my self, and hear
What from without comes oft'n to my ears,
Ill sorting with my present state compar'd.
                    Paradise Regained I, 196–200

eloquence appropriate to their intercourse. If the final book contains half a dozen images, they are the only ones in the whole poem. The soberness of the Gospels was demanded. Milton has muted his lyricism as far as he can.

His situation was more or less that in which Flaubert struggled for five years when, having renounced what he called the mythological and theological 'flamboiements' of his first *Tentation de saint Antoine*, he exerted himself to the utmost to choose and place each word of *Madame Bovary*. He then wrote to Louise Colet in 1852:

> Je suis dans un tout autre monde ... De même que le sujet est différent, j'écris dans un tout autre procédé ... Je veux qu'il n'y ait pas dans mon livre *un seul* mouvement, *une seule* réflexion de l'auteur. — Toute la valeur de mon livre, s'il en a une, sera d'avoir su marcher droit sur un cheveu, suspendu entre le double abîme du lyrisme et du vulgaire (20-21 mars).

And here is Professor John Bailey's comment on *Paradise Regained*:

> ... a style stripped of almost all ornament especially in the speeches of our Lord: the poet deliberately walking always on the very edge of the gulf of prose and yet always as one perfectly assured that into that gulf his feet can never fall.[1]

Flaubert had written on January 16th, 1852:

> Ce qui me semble beau, ce que je voudrais faire, c'est un livre sur rien, un livre sans attache extérieure, qui se tiendrait de lui-même par la force interne de son style ... La forme, en devenant habile, s'atténue; elle quitte toute liturgie, toute règle, toute mesure, elle abandonne l'épique pour le roman, le vers pour la prose; elle ne connaît plus d'orthodoxie, et est libre comme chaque volonté qui la produit. Cet affranchissement de la matérialité (*liberation from the material*) se retrouve en tout et les gouvernements l'ont suivi, depuis les despotismes orientaux jusqu'aux socialismes futurs.

The sequence conceived by the recluse of Croisset had been experienced by the refugee of Chalfont. It was in wishing to follow the 'liberation from the material' that he had denounced the episcopate, pleaded for divorce and against tyrants, cautioned Cromwell, and finally freed the heroic poem from the 'modern bondage of rhyming'. In

[1] *Milton*, Oxford, 1947, p. 208.

his new poem he dared even more. There dialogue takes the place of action, and 'the speakers are no more than the abstract principles of good and evil, two voices' (Pattison);[1] the absolute spirituality of the hero detaches him from all human activities, his deeds are 'above Heroic' (P.R. I, 15). As to the form adopted, it 'forsakes' indeed 'all liturgy'. Let us listen to Bailey once more:

> Milton has left nothing more Miltonic. He did greater things but nothing in which he stands so entirely alone. There is no poem in English, perhaps none in any language of the world, which exhibits to the same degree the inherent power of style itself, in its naked essence, unassisted by any of its visible accessories. . . . Its grave Dorian music, scarcely heard by the sensual ear, is played by the mind to the spirit and by the spirit to the mind. Ever present as its art is, it is an art infinitely removed from that to which all the world at once responds and surrenders. It is not at first seen to be art at all. The verse which in truth dances so cunningly appears to the uninitiated to stumble and halt. The music, which the common ear is so slow to catch, makes us think of those Platonic mysteries of abstract number seen only in their perfection by some godlike mathematician who lives rapt above sense and matter in the contemplation of the Idea of Good.[2]

It goes without saying that despite its apparent simplicity, such poetry loses infinitely in translation. It was even too little perceptible to the common run of the first readers. Who among the poets of France would come closest to it? Racine, perhaps, who is at once so simple and so elusive. But even so his characters live and hate, weep, shed blood. Milton only gives us a 'rhetorical disputation' (Pattison) and the issue is not even in doubt for an instant. It follows that readers, be they English or foreign, have always liked *Paradise Regained* far less than its predecessor. Milton was indignant at this.[3] Yet experts themselves have praised the form more than the matter in his second poem. 'The most perfect *execution*[4] of anything written by Milton', said Wordsworth. Coleridge emphasized and explained: '*In its kind*[4] it is the most perfect poem extant, though its kind be

---

[1] *Milton*, p. 192.   [2] Op. cit., pp. 209-10.
[3] 'He could not hear with patience any such thing when related to him' (Phillips).
[4] The italics are mine.

JOHN MILTON AT THE AGE OF 62 CIRCA

inferior in interest—being in its essence, didactic—to that
other sort in which emotion is conveyed more effectively'.[1]

The subject-matter is not only too abstract; it is sometimes perplexing. For instance, what must we make of
the famous diatribe against the Ancients (IV, 286–364)?
Jesus, of course, did not rely upon human wisdom; and
when Satan flaunts Greek philosophy before him, he is
bound to disparage it. Yet, at bottom, Milton does not deny
his secular masters—witness the brief parenthesis:

> Unless where moral vertue is exprest
> By light of Nature not in all quite lost.[2]

Jesus—Milton cites as models of disinterestedness four
Romans (II, 446) and likens Socrates to Job (III, 95). Was
not the motto of St. Paul's School *Fide et bonis literis*?[3]

Let us approach a deeper question. How did Milton
conceive the personality of Jesus? A semi-Socinian according to Blondel, Milton was nothing of the sort in the eyes of
Saurat. On the other hand, almost everyone labels him
Arian, yet C. S. Lewis declares *Paradise Lost* Augustinian,
apart from a few elements 'only discoverable by search'
(*A Preface to Paradise Lost*, p. 81). Tillyard rightly says that
'it is an error to tidy up Milton's belief' (op. cit., p. 234).
What can we infer from *Paradise Regained*? Here, towards
the beginning, God announces to Gabriel:

> . . . this man born and now up-grown,
> To shew him worthy of his birth divine
> And high prediction, henceforth I expose
> To Satan; . . .[4]
> He now shall know I can produce a man
> Of femal Seed, far abler to resist
> All his sollicitations, and at length
> All his vast force, and drive him back to Hell . . .[5]
> . . . But first I mean

---

[1] *Lectures and Notes on Shakespeare and other English Poets.*
[2] IV, 351–2.
[3] Calvin declared: 'Nous ne contemnerons pas la vérité partout ou elle apparaistra,
sinon que nous veuillons faire injure à l'Esprit de Dieu'. Aristotle, Cicero and Pythagoras have their statues at Chartres. Yet Milton would have agreed with his
opponent Bishop Hall, who wrote in *The Christian Stoic*: 'True right and peace of
mind are to be won not at Athens but at Jerusalem'.
[4] I, 140–3.   [5] Ibid., 150–3.

Y

> To exercise him in the Wilderness, . . .[1]
> That all the Angels and Ætherial Powers,
> They now, and men hereafter may discern,
> From what consummat vertue I have chose
> This perfet Man, by merit calld my Son,
> To earn Salvation for the Sons of men.[2]

This conception of Jesus differs widely from the creed of St. Athanasius, accepted by three-quarters of Christendom: 'As the reasonable soul and the flesh is one man, so God and man is one Christ'. This 'perfect man' who will obtain the salvation of humanity, is he at least such as he said himself, 'meek and lowly in heart'? The Prologue in Heaven that we have just quoted makes us doubt this. It breathes out warfare and boasting. Jehovah passes over in silence the painful expectation of the earth and the power of love. Jesus is sent forth

> To conquer Sin and Death the two grand foes,
> By Humiliation and strong Sufferance:
> His weakness shall orecome Satanic strength,
> And all the World, and mass of sinful flesh.[3]

He will drive Satan back to Hell,

> Winning by Conquest what the first man lost
> By fallacy surpriz'd.[4]

God has given himself a champion; it is a superman who appears here. Does he love anything at all in the world? It would not seem so. He detests tyrants and despises their slaves. He speaks of our passions and our errors with almost as much disdain as he shows to the father of lies. He obeys his Father and resists evil perfectly; nothing more.

But we notice that he does not exactly resist—he thrusts aside, he rejects, he denies, and that at once. Clearly, it is essential that he should be the victor, but he could sometimes be uncertain of himself or weigh both sides. He could, in short, be tempted in the ordinary sense of the word. But what is most markedly absent in this epic of the Temptation is a temptation worthy of the name.[5]

---

[1] I, 155–6.   [2] Ibid., 163–7.
[3] Ibid., 159–62.   [4] Ibid., 154–5.
[5] Cf. Hebrews iv. 15: He was in all points tempted like as we are.

It will be said that in *Matthew* and *Luke*, our Saviour's replies are immediate and crushing, but then the Evangelists are extremely concise, whereas Milton paraphrases. He paraphrases so freely that he succeeds in evoking his 'serious' childhood or his courage in 1660 and in speaking out against men of war, degraded peoples, and unworthy kings. Yet not a word from him even foreshadows the night of anguish in the Garden of Olives. If his hero is only a man, why is he not human? If he is God incarnate, he is not clothed with our flesh.

Seeley declared that this Jesus was a Marcus Aurelius. According to Bailey, the speeches of Jesus here display 'the self-conscious righteousness of the Pharisee'. Blondel gives a verdict[1] not very far removed from that of Seeley. He finds here an incongruity that we could foresee as we read the end of the major epic. Here, God announces that the Temptation in the wilderness will be only a preliminary trial, the rudiments of the 'great warfare'. The final angelic chorus takes up the same theme. And yet the 'great duel' is recounted as if it had an absolute value in itself. In connection with the 'interior paradise' and with the counsels of the archangel Michael, we spoke of 'programme' and of 'prescription'.[2] Here the programme is carried out, the prescription works.

La victoire du Christ [says Blondel, pp. 72-5] revêt dans *Paradise Regained* avant tout une valeur exemplaire; il a montré la voie et il n'apparaît pas comme le seul chemin qui mène au salut ... La critique a souvent reproché à Milton le titre même de son poème. Louis Racine[3] considérait que le Paradis n'est pas regagné lorsque le Christ a résisté dans le désert ... L'effort de la volonté semble assurer désormais, sans même que l'ombre de la Croix doive se profiler sur le poème, la victoire sur le mal, et les oeuvres de l'homme seront donc bonnes, avant que 'le péché du monde' ait été expié ... Le salut de l'homme,

---

[1] *Le Paradis Reconquis*, Etude critique, Traduction et Notes, Aubier, Paris, 1955.
[2] Above, p. 288.
[3] Louis Racine (1692-1763), son of the dramatist, was a convinced Jansenist. Dupré's translation of *Paradise Lost* delighted him. He learned English and thought still more highly of Milton. He found his theology 'beaucoup plus sage et plus éclairée que celle de Dante'. In 1755 he gave a complete and conscientious translation of *Paradise Lost* which ran into its fifth edition under Napoleon, in 1808.

indépendant du salut cosmique du monde, se réduit ici à une 'imitation de Jésus-Christ'.

Thus we have confirmation that reason, will, virtue, are the master-words of Milton's religion. It has no place for weakness, pardon, redemption, for the injustice of love. When Milton read the parable of the Prodigal Son, his sympathy must surely have gone out to the elder brother.

We had the duty to explore these arduous tracks. Those who are interested less in the man than in his work will read—and re-read—the speech of Belial, Satan's banquet, the pictures of the Orient, of Rome and the Empire, and above all the panegyric of Athens. They will find that Jesus speaks more simply than Satan or than the author, and will admire the fact that Satan, by turns plaintive, sly, insolent, fawning, indignant, or despairing to the point of the sublime, should always argue beside the point. They will note on each page confidences and maxims, but never find a word that is useless or weak. Yet, to render full justice to this fresh masterpiece, one would have to ignore its predecessor. Dr. Johnson has expressed it after his own manner: 'Had this poem been written not by Milton, but by some imitator, it would have claimed and received universal praise'.

XIX

SAMSON AGONISTES

1671

SAURAT calls it 'A pure jewel'. For Tillyard it is with *Lycidas* his most spontaneous poem, of value for its prophetic message only less than for its weight of emotion. The chorus of critics agree—'He has written nothing more impassioned'.

The title has become familiar, but it calls for comment. *Agonistes* is Greek unalloyed, and Milton did not decide to use it as it stood without good reason. An *agonistes* was a competitor in one of those public games by which the Greeks at stated times solemnly honoured Zeus, Phoebos or Poseidon. It can no more be translated by a single word than can *matador*. No English term could indicate that Samson in this particular poem is giving a public exhibition of his strength in honour of his God.

Moreover *agonistes* was a legitimate title to give to a drama of Greek type (in passing we may remark that therein lay a fresh challenge to the disparagement of the Ancients). Twenty years before Racine's *Esther*, we find here a chorus inserted in a tragedy, and one which does not confine itself to mere comment, as in Racine or Euripides. In conformity with Aristotle's *Poetics*, it takes part in the action. To justify this innovation Milton, in his preface, puts forward the example of his beloved Italy. There were choruses in Tasso's *Aminta*, and echoes of them can be perceived here. In 1638 the Italians had created *Il Sansone, dialogo per musica* by a certain Pietro dell'Isola. Italy of the Renaissance, however, chiefly imitated the Romans. Milton goes straight to the Greeks, exploiting Aeschylus, Sophocles and Euripides, both as to form and matter; no one, he claimed, had yet equalled them. Goethe was to declare: 'There is no modern play which has been written so much in the taste of

Antiquity[1] as that one'. Responsive to this informing spirit of Greece, three English writers have translated *Samson* into Greek verse, Glasse in 1788, Graswell in 1832, Lyttelton in 1867.

The work presents itself as an uninterrupted series of about eighteen hundred lines. Yet the usual elements of Greek tragedy—*prologos, parodos, stasima, peripeteia,* can be discerned in it, distributed over five principal divisions.

I.—Lines 1–325

Before the prison in Gaza at break of day the blind man is sitting under the trees; he is wearing fetters but he has a right to repose, for Gaza is to-day celebrating the victory of Dagon over Jehovah. Samson deplores his downfall.

> . . . Promise was that I
> Should *Israel* from *Philistian* yoke deliver;
> Ask for this great Deliverer now, and find him
> Eyeless in *Gaza* at the Mill with slaves,
> Himself in bonds under *Philistian* yoke;
>
>   38–42

He recognizes his fault, however:

> Whom have I to complain of but my self?
> Who this high gift of strength committed to me,
> In what part lodg'd, how easily bereft me,
> Under the Seal of silence could not keep,
> But weakly to a woman must reveal it,
> Orecome with importunity and tears.
> O impotence of mind, in body strong!
>
>   46–52

Former friends and neighbours arrive who will form the Chorus. They admire and pity him. He again accuses himself:

> Who like a foolish Pilot have shipwrackt
> My Vessel trusted to me from above,
> Gloriously riggd; and for a word, a tear,
> Fool, have divulg'd the secret gift of God
> To a deceitful Woman: tell me Friends,
> Am I not sung and proverbd for a Fool
> In every street, do they not say, how well
> Are come upon him his deserts?
>
>   198–205

---

[1] Cf. Chateaubriand (*Essai*): 'La tragédie de Samson respire la force et la simplicité antique'.

... of what now I suffer
Shee was not the prime cause, but I my self,
Who vanquisht with a peal of words (O weakness!)
Gave up my fort of silence to a Woman.
233-6

The Chorus concludes: 'Just are the ways of God ...'

II.—Lines 326-709
Enter Samson's old father, Manoah. Energetic, full of common sense and rich, he has come to ransom his son. He tells him this and speaks to him of the joys that the paternal home can still give him. Better still, come the day when God shall decide to humiliate Dagon, Samson will be able to re-enter the struggle. Doubtless God will restore his sight, since he has restored his strength.

To each of his father's suggestions, Samson opposes his despair and his will to expiate. He confesses his pride and his weaknesses at some length. He has betrayed his mission, has been a scandal to Israel. He is suffering too much to want to live. He prefers to earn his convict's bread until the day when death shall cut short his torture, rather than to live comfortably in his father's house.

Now blind, disheart'nd, sham'd, dishonourd, quelld,
To what can I be useful, wherein serve
My Nation, and the work from Heav'n impos'd,
But to sit idle on the houshold hearth,
A burdenous drone; to visitants a gaze,
Or pitied object, these redundant locks
Robustious to no purpose clustring down,
Vain monument of strength; ...
563-70

All otherwise to mee my thoughts portend,
That these dark orbs no more shall treat with light,
Nor th' other light of life continue long,
But yeild to double darkness nigh at hand:
So much I feel my genial spirits droop,
My hopes all flat, nature within me seems
In all her functions weary of herself;
My race of glory run, and race of shame,
And I shall shortly be with them that rest.
590-8

Manoah, however, is not discouraged, he goes out in search of the enemy leaders. The prisoner complains of being abandoned by God. The Chorus sympathizes and asks in general terms: 'God of our fathers, what is man?'

III.—Lines 710–1060

Dalilah 'comes sailing', 'an Amber sent of odorous perfume her harbinger', reminding us of Baudelaire's 'beau navire' and 'vampire' ('un beau vaisseau qui prend le large. . . . Forte comme un troupeau de démons'). It cannot be material interest that brings her back to this eyeless slave. Her motive is that expressed by Daudet's Sapho—'la vanité de la femme, la fierté bien naturelle de reconquérir après la rupture'.

> . . . But conjugal affection
> Prevailing over fear, and timerous doubt
> Hath led me on desirous to behold
> Once more thy face, and know of thy estate,
> If aught in my ability may serve
> To light'n what thou suffer'st, and appease
> Thy mind with what amends is in my power,
> Though late, yet in some part to recompense
> My rash but more unfortunat misdeed.
> *Sam.* Out, out *Hyaena*; these are thy wonted arts,
> And arts of every woman false like thee. . . .
>
> 739–48

She brings every argument into play, pleads her patriotism, her religion, 'the jealousy of Love', offers to intercede with the Philistines, promises her care as nurse and delights, that even a blind man can appreciate. She reproaches her victim with not having had will enough for two—saying that Samson's weakness should pardon hers. Samson refuses her proferred hand:

> At distance I forgive thee, go with that;
>
> 954

She finally gives up, but throws off the mask before withdrawing. The Chorus (1004–1060) sings of the strange power of beauty and of the deceitfulness of women.

IV.—Lines 1061–1300

A braggart, the giant Harapha, comes to see the famous Samson with his own eyes. He greatly regrets not having been able to measure himself against him in former days. From retort to retort Samson finally comes to challenge the swaggerer to death and the latter goes away muttering threats. 'He will denounce thee', says the Chorus. 'He would never admit his cowardice', says Samson, 'and then, death matters little to me'. The Chorus develops two themes:

> Oh how comely it is and how reviving
> To the Spirits of just men long opprest!
> When God into the hands of thir deliverer
> Puts invincible might
> To quell the mighty of the Earth, th' oppressour . . .
>
> 1268–72

> But patience is more oft the exercise
> Of Saints, the trial of thir fortitude,
> Making them each his own Deliverer,
> And Victor over all
> That tyrannie or fortune can inflict;
> Either of these is in thy lot,
> *Samson*, with might endu'd
> Above the Sons of men; but sight bereav'd
> May chance to number thee with those
> Whom Patience finally must crown.
>
> 1287–96

V.—Lines 1301–1758

An officer comes to order Samson to give a demonstration of his strength before the Philistines, but Samson refuses to participate in any homage to Dagon, and the officer goes away to report to the authorities. The Chorus urges Samson to prudence and reminds him that after all he does consent to work for the enemy. Samson takes the paralogism to pieces and remains unshakeable. But a mysterious impulse makes him change his mind. When the officer returns he follows him unhesitatingly.

Manoah appears again, full of joy—he is authorized to pay the ransom. From the city rises an immense clamour—

Samson has just made his entry down there in the theatre.
Manoah confides his hopes to the Chorus. A terrifying
sound of crashing and cries ensues. A Hebrew who has
witnessed the scene arrives:

> . . . he his guide requested
> (For so from such as nearer stood we heard)
> As over-tir'd to let him lean a while
> With both his arms on those two massie Pillars . . .
> . . . which when *Samson*
> Felt in his arms, with head a while enclin'd,
> And eyes fast fixt he stood, as one who pray'd,
> Or some great matter in his mind revolv'd.
> At last with head erect thus cry'd aloud,
> Hitherto, Lords, what your commands impos'd
> I have performed, as reason was, obeying,
> Not without wonder or delight beheld.
> Now of my own accord such other tryal
> I mean to shew you of my strength, yet greater;
>
> 1630–44

The Chorus sings this 'dearly-bought revenge' and the
immortality of virtue. But it soars too high. As always,
Milton wants to finish *andante dolce*. So Manoah brings us
back to realities.

> Come, come, no time for lamentation now,
> Nor much more cause, *Samson* hath quit himself
> Like *Samson*, and heroicly hath finisht
> A life Heroic, on his Enemies
> Fully reveng'd . . .
> Nothing is here for tears, nothing to wail
> Or knock the brest, no weakness, no contempt,
> Dispraise, or blame, nothing but well and fair,
> And what may quiet us in a death so noble.
> Let us go find the body where it lies . . .
> . . . I with what speed the while
> (*Gaza* is not in plight to say us nay)
> Will send for all my kindred, all my friends
> To fetch him hence and solemnly attend
> With silent obsequie and funeral train
> Home to his Fathers house: there will I build him
> A Monument, and plant it round with shade
> Of Laurel ever green, and branching Palm,

With all his Trophies hung, and Acts inrould
In copious Legend, or sweet Lyric Song.
Thither shall all the valiant youth resort,
And from his memory inflame thir brests
To matchless valour, and adventures high:
The Virgins also shall on feastful days
Visit his Tomb with flowers, onely bewailing
His lot unfortunate in nuptial choice,
From whence captivity and loss of eyes.

1709–44

Then the Chorus concludes by singing, it seems, in a subdued tone, fourteen lines rhymed like a sonnet, but slightly unequal, a veiled sonnet, the last farewell to Italy; the sentiment it expresses, Christian though it sounds, terminates five tragedies of Euripides:

All is best, though we oft doubt,
What th'unsearchable dispose
Of highest wisdom brings about,
And ever best found in the close.
Oft he seems to hide his face,
But unexpectedly returns
And to his faithful Champion hath in place
Bore witness gloriously; whence *Gaza* mourns
And all that band them to resist
His uncontroulable intent;
His servants hee with new acquist
Of true experience from this great event
With peace and consolation hath dismist,
And calm of mind all passion spent.

1745–58

The essential element of the plot is therefore a succession of visits without visible links between them. We understand Dr. Johnson's complaint that the drama 'has a beginning and an end which Aristotle himself could not have disapproved', but that it must 'be allowed to have no middle, since nothing passes between the first act and the last that either hastens or delays the death of Samson'.

It should first of all be noted that if there be a fault, it is one which Molière, too, committed. The Lysidas of the

Critique complains that in the *École des Femmes* no action takes place and the whole consists of the narratives. Faguet has remarked that the whole of Molière's *Don Juan* is nothing but a 'dramatic portrait' and that the *Misanthrope* is 'the triumph of the play without a subject'. If the guaranty of Molière is insufficient, is the *Prometheus* of Aeschylus anything more than a 'dramatic portrait'?

Here, however, we can find something much better than a lesson in anatomy: Samson is alive, he changes from act to act. In the beginning he cries out for death; within an hour or so he marches to his finest victory. His visitors have unwittingly applied to him the method, old as the world itself, which we should call homeopathy and to which Milton lays claim in his preface.

We have just seen that the English Court of that time indulged in extravagances and ribaldry which displeased the Town. Thirty years earlier, when the situation was substantially the same, Milton had put before the two parties his mask-morality play, *Comus*. Would they now accept another synthesis, a Biblical figure in a Greek setting? His preface is addressed to the rigorists.[1] He finds with them that the English theatre has fallen into obloquy, but reminds them that the Apostle Paul quoted Euripides:

> Tragedy, as it was antiently compos'd, hath been ever held the gravest, moralest, and most profitable of all other Poems: therefore said by *Aristotle* to be of power by raising pity and fear, or terror, to purge the mind of those and such like passions, that is to temper and reduce them to just measure with a kind of delight, stirr'd up by reading or seeing those passions well imitated. Nor is Nature wanting in her own effects to make good his assertion: for so in Physic things of melancholic hue and quality are us'd against melancholy, sowr against sowr, salt to remove salt humours.[2]

---

[1] Compare Racine, writing for the intention of Messieurs de Port-Royal, in his preface to *Phèdre* in 1677: 'Il serait à souhaiter que nos ouvrages fussent aussi solides et aussi pleins d'utiles instructions que ceux de ces poètes [les tragiques grecs]. Ce serait peut-être un moyen de réconcilier la tragédie avec quantité de personnes, célèbres par leur piété et leur doctrine, qui l'ont condamnée dans ces derniers temps.'

[2] Preface to *Samson Agonistes*.

A Puritan owed it to himself to attach a particular importance to *catharsis*—purification. Milton quotes Aristotle in English in his preface, in Greek and in Latin on the title-page, and his drama finishes on the words— 'all passion spent'. Now he wanted the remedy applied to the spectators to work the cure of his hero as well. If Samson's visitors do not even know each other, they go to the same goal by the same means—friends or enemies, they try to turn Samson aside from his vocation and in so doing they bring him back to it. There lies the supreme irony of this play in which ironies are not wanting.

Samson is so downcast that when his childhood's friends come to express their admiration and their sympathy, he acknowledges his faults to them—not, however, without incriminating the leaders of Israel.

Manoah finds that God is too severe for his son, but Samson takes all the blame upon himself and makes a complete confession to his old father. He refuses to live in seclusion with his father; that would be to abandon things utterly, a betrayal of himself. He judges himself incapable and unworthy of resuming the combat, but he wants to expiate—which implies some form of action.

The violence of his answers to Dalilah proves that Samson still fears her and that his full confession to Manoah has given him complete light on his weakness. The more she insists, the more he detaches himself.

It is a free man, therefore, whom Harapha comes to flout. Instead of bowing his head, the blind man becomes brutal. When Harapha accuses him of having used magic, Samson suggests a duel between Harapha, the champion of Dagon, and Samson, the champion of the God of Israel. He has found his physical courage again, and his faith in divine support.

This time it is the Chorus which is tempting Samson. It insinuates that since he is blind, he will have to resign himself to patience. He then asserts that a blind man can set force at defiance.

Thrice, however, he refuses to surrender to the call of the Philistines—'I cannot' (1321), 'I will not' (1332), 'I will not' (1342). His moral strength has returned. 'Think of what awaits thee', the officer says to him. 'Regard thyself.' 'My self? my conscience and internal peace' (1334).

At this point the Chorus tempts him again: 'Consider, Samson, thou runnest a grave risk, and then with this strength, thou servest the Philistines'. Samson 'considers' indeed and justifies his refusal logically.

Thus, body, soul, and reason, here he is the complete hero once more. God then sends him a sign—impulses which presage for him 'something extraordinary' (1383). His metamorphosis is now complete, he will die happy.

Such is the background which Dr. Johnson declared was non-existent, and which Milton added to the Bible. What can be more dramatic than the hard-won triumph of a human soul? Is the play too lyrical or too closely woven? It has been performed but on rare occasions. Milton expressly said that he did not divide it into acts and scenes because it was 'in no way intended for the theatre'. Handel transposed it into an oratorio.

Let us realize once more the tenacity of the solitary navigator. Eight years after *Comus* he was wondering if he would give his country an elaborated epic, a short epic, or some sacred tragedy. Thirty years later here they are, all three completed, and they treat of the same theme, which is that of *Comus*—temptation. The solutions, however, differ— the heroine of *Comus* is aided by Heaven; Adam, left to himself, succumbs; Jesus remains untouched; Samson rises after his fall. Moreover, the last two poems are in complete contrast on an important point.

Whereas the hero of *Paradise Regained* restricts himself to passive resistance, to Samson, who is by nature a man of action, impetuous, irascible, inaction means death. Jesus allows himself to be carried away, as if inert, to the summit of a mountain or of the Temple. The facts of the Gospels demanded that it should be so. Milton invented the fall of Satan, but Jesus does not bring about this issue either by a gesture or by an order.

Very logically, the temptations rejected by the 'patient Son of God' are all, except for the storm by night, calls to action. On the contrary, Manoah, Dalilah, Harapha, the Chorus, advise passiveness for the man of action. But to be rejected by God is one thing, to abdicate is another. Samson will act.

For us who are trying to understand Milton, it is not unimportant that *Samson Agonistes* should be placed second in the 1671 volume of his writings. By this device the indomitable finished his work on a hopeful note. At Chalfont, when he was composing his second *Paradise*, he was still in despair about his country, but when he returned to London he had been present at an explosion of 'No Popery', followed by severe measures against the Catholics. Moreover, the Covenanters' rising of 1666 had been punished in 1668 by mass hangings which had caused much talk. It was shortly after this scandal that Milton expunged from his *History of Great Britain* those passages wounding to Presbyterians. *Samson Agonistes* was still on the stocks. Now historians are agreed that although no one then desired to see again either a Civil War or a Commonwealth, yet the background scaffolding against which the 'Glorious Revolution' was to be played was going up piece by piece. Milton had written in 1644: 'Methinks I see in my mind a noble and puissant nation rousing herself like a strong man after sleep, and shaking her invincible locks'.[1] In 1671, he could hear Puritan England awakening once more.

Yet the sombre pages predominate here, and often surprise us by the vehemence of the author of *Paradise Regained*. Some have concluded from this that *Samson Agonistes* was composed well before the Restoration. External proof, however, is lacking, and several important passages were clearly dictated by events or sentiments of recent dates. We cannot doubt, however, that several pages recall, were it only by their inspiration, the poet's immediate reactions after Mary's flight or the loss of his eyes. As we read them, we think more of him than of his hero. He must have been aware of their double import,

---

[1] *Areopagitica*, Bohn II, 94.

and they contain two humiliating admissions. One of his reasons for publishing them doubtless was their beauty. Another was his need, conscious or not, of himself benefiting from the dramatic catharsis.

In Samson's laments and confessions, the recurring themes are—divine election, exceptional gifts, incredible victories, pride, weakness born of pride, divine disavowal, the triumph of the wicked. It is the whole history of the Commonwealth and of Milton. When Samson declares to his father (532):

> Then swoll'n with pride, into the snare I fell,

can we help thinking of the reviler of Hall hoodwinked by the Powells? This 'vessel gloriously riggd' (200), is it not the poet's talent? The 'scandal brought to Israel' (453) takes us back to the sect of the Divorcers or Miltonists. The evident analogies are so numerous that there is a danger of pushing the parallel too far.

Had two happy marriages reconciled Milton with womankind? Here he pays homage to her who keeps the home, but for form's sake and in four lines (1046–9). In a corner of his memory the fury and amazement of 1642 still survived. Hence the diatribe of the Chorus after Dalilah's exit. Whether Milton wrote this about 1642 or dictated it twenty-five years later, matters little. He was ridding himself of an old suffering by dissecting before the public the enigma of woman. As this attempt at analysis exceeded the resources of the Jewish Hercules, it was the Chorus who was entrusted with it:

> It is not vertue, wisdom, valour, wit,
> Strength, comliness of shape, or amplest merit
> That womans love can win or long inherit;
> But what it is, hard is to say,
> Harder to hit,
> (Which way soever men referr it)
> Much like thy riddle, *Samson*, in one day
> Or seven, though one should musing sit . . .
>   1010–17

Is it for that such outward ornament
Was lavisht on thir Sex, that inward gifts
Were left for hast unfinisht, judgment scant,
Capacity not rais'd to apprehend
Or value what is best
In choice, but oftest to affect the wrong?
Or was too much of self-love mixt,
Of constancy no root infixt,
That either they love nothing or not long?
What e're it be, to wisest men and best
Seeming at first all heav'nly under virgin veil,
Soft, modest, meek, demure,
Once joind, the contrary she proves, a thorn
Intestin. . . .

1025-38

Therefore Gods universal Law
Gave to the man despotic power
Over his femal in due awe,
Nor from that right to part an hour,
Smile she or lowre . . .

1053-7

An incredible indictment coming from a good-humoured old husband.[1] In *Paradise Lost*, Adam said simply: 'Or whom he wishes most shall seldom gain through her perversness . . .' (*P.L.* X, 901-2). It was a swift declaration, slipped in among others. Here Milton stresses heavily the moral and mental imperfection of a physically irresistible being, forgetting the essential of the Samson–Dalilah affair, namely that the physique of the male may deceive also. Clearly he was liquidating the old affair John–Mary (and Mary, decidedly, must have been very pretty).

Milton had spoken of his blindness in verse and prose with perfect serenity. He had been silent about the racking hours at last revealed in the wild clamour of Samson (see above, pp. 166, 167).

The poem also makes known to us what a scandal the fall of the Commonwealth and the miserable end of its founders had been to him. In the beginning (237–92),

[1] See below, p. 344.

z

Samson and the Chorus engage in dialogue on the ingratitude and corruptness of the people who 'love Bondage more
then Liberty, Bondage with ease then strenuous liberty'
(270–1). Moreover, they ask themselves how God can
send his elect to defeat, or

> Have prompted this Heroic *Nazarite* . . .
> To seek in marriage that fallacious Bride,
> Unclean, unchaste.
>
> 318–21

Despite a reluctant submission ('Down reason then, at
least vain reasonings down'), the question comes up again,
burning and precise, after Manoah's departure. Under the
cloak of general terms, we recognize Cromwell, his
Immortals, Vane, and even the former Latin secretary,
now poor and, against all justice, afflicted with deforming
rheumatism. Milton succeeds, however, in giving us a page
which seems to be taken from the *Book of Job:*

> God of our Fathers, what is man!
> That thou towards him with hand so various,
> Or might I say contrarious,
> Temperst thy providence through his short course,
> Not evenly, as thou rul'st
> Th' Angelic orders and inferiour creatures mute,
> Irrational and brute.
> Nor do I name of men the common rout,
> That wandring loose about
> Grow up and perish, as the summer flie,
> Heads without name no more rememberd,
> But such as thou hast solemnly elected,
> With gifts and graces eminently adornd,
> To some great work, thy glory,
> And peoples safety, which in part they effect:
> Yet toward these thus dignifi'd, thou oft
> Amidst thir highth of noon,
> Changest thy countenance, and thy hand with no regard
> Of highest favours past
> From thee on them, or them to thee of service.
>   Nor onely dost degrade them, or remit
> To life obscur'd, which were a fair dismission,
> But throw'st them lower then thou didst exalt them high,

Unseemly falls in human eie,
Too grievous for the trespass or omission,
Oft leav'st them to the hostil sword
Of Heathen and prophane, thir carkasses
To dogs and fowls a prey, or else captiv'd:
Or to th' unjust tribunals, under change of times,
And condemnation of th' ingrateful multitude.
If these they scape, perhaps in poverty
With sickness and disease thou bow'st them down,
Painful diseases and deformd,
In crude old age;
Though not disordinate, yet causless suffring
The punishment of dissolute days, in fine,
Just or unjust, alike seem miserable,
For oft alike, both come to evil end.

667–704

Other pages, too, despite hopeful passages, evoke the national failure. Yet the subject is the recovery of a defeated man. Is not Milton himself avenging that prose of his that had been consigned to the public hangman? The King takes his pleasures, the Church persecutes, but a hand is writing upon the wall.

While thir hearts were jocond and sublime,
Drunk with Idolatry, drunk with Wine,
And fat regorg'd of Bulls and Goats,
Chaunting thir Idol . . .

1669–72

But hee though blind of sight,
Despis'd and thought extinguisht quite,
With inward eyes illuminated
His fierie vertue rouz'd
From under ashes into sudden flame . . .

1687–91

Virtue, the virile qualities—energy, will, courage: salvation would come from these.

. . . vertue which breaks through all opposition,
And all temptation can remove . . .

1050–1

It is this that Milton opposes to weakness, the cause of all our faults, here denounced on every page. And virtue is imperishable.

> So vertue giv'n for lost,
> Deprest, and overthrown, as seemed,
> Like that self-begott'n bird
> In the *Arabian* woods embost,
> That no second knows nor third,
> And lay ere while a Holocaust,
> From out her ashie womb now teemd
> Revives, reflourishes, then vigorous most
> When most unactive deemd,
> And though her body die, her fame survives,
> A secular bird ages of lives.
>
> 1697–1707

XX

'WHILE IT IS DAY, FOR THE NIGHT
COMETH...'

1671–1674

CHARLES'S secret pact with his over-powerful cousin held
unsurmountable difficulties in store for him. The English
people would never return to Rome; at most it might be
possible to give Catholics some small measure of relief.
And how was England to be brought to attack her Protestant allies? In any case, the first thing to do was to restore
the navy—but where were the funds to come from? On
this point some trickery was possible, since the treaty was
known only to the King and his two Catholic Councillors,
Clifford and Arlington.[1]

In 1670 the King set his Keeper of the Seals to work.
The latter, in perfect good faith since he was in complete
ignorance, duped the Commons by giving them facts that
were correct: i.e. since the French navy had recently tripled
its strength, the King could not assist Holland and Sweden
unless he refitted the navy. The Commons, never suspect-
ing that the ally to be assisted was now Louis XIV,
immediately voted large supplies and fresh taxes. Unfortunately for Charles, these taxes hit the big traders, who
saw to it that the bill was thrown out by the Lords. The
King dismissed both Houses in 1671.

Four months earlier he had obtained from Versailles
a treaty he could show, as it said nothing either of pension
or religion. After this, Buckingham, a Protestant, went
to 'negotiate' it and came back very proud of an agreement
which had been arranged without his knowledge well
before his departure.

As a new ruse to force the hand of Parliament, Charles

[1] Their initials and those of their colleagues made up the key-word of unhappy
memory—CABAL.

tried to manoeuvre the Dutch into declaring war by creating an incident at sea. They thought, however, that there had been a misunderstanding and offered apologies. That same year 1671 the Duke of York lost his Duchess and had the untimely candour to declare himself a Catholic.

On January 2nd, 1672, Charles suspended payments from the Exchequer overnight without warning. This violent measure caused an upheaval in commerce and brought families to ruin—but the King gained little enough from it.

He then launched an attack on the Dutch Smyrna fleet, consisting of seventy sail valued at £1,500,000. The attack failed, but the die was cast. On March 15th Charles promulgated a Declaration of Indulgence in favour of non-Anglicans, and on the 17th a declaration of war on the Low Countries.

This proved a double failure. Presbyterians and Independents, instead of rallying to the King against Parliament which was throwing them into prison, rejected a benefit which they were neither willing to share with the Papists nor hold at the good pleasure of the prince. As to the Anglo-French fleet, it was quickly rendered harmless by Ruyter, whereas the French regiments were taking town after town in the Low Countries, Louis demanding proportionate commercial advantages and liberty of worship for Catholics.

Since the decline of Spain, for the people of England it was France who personified absolutism and its consequences. English travellers were astonished at the wretched condition of the French peasants. One saying ran—'Popery and wooden shoes'. When, after the murder of the de Witt brothers (August 1672), William of Orange was recognized as Stadtholder, the English strongly upheld this young champion of Protestantism, ready to 'die in the last ditch'. In February 1673, Charles, always short of money, had to abrogate his Declaration of Indulgence and sign the Test Act—no one for the future should serve the State who had not taken Communion publicly according to the Anglican rite and denied Transubstantiation in writing. Numerous Catholic officials handed in their resignations.

The Duke of York himself lost his lucrative office as Lord High Admiral, but he married Mary of Modena, richly dowered by Louis XIV. Popular alarm knew no bounds. The Duke was to succeed his brother. If he had a son (as happened), the crown would pass after him, not to his daughters, brought up as Protestants, but to another Catholic. Parliament in 1674 demanded a separate peace with Holland and went further than the Test Act—Catholics had to leave London and priests were given six weeks in which to quit the realm. This double defeat cost Charles very dear. 'From this moment all trust in him was at an end' (Green).

During these years of intrigue, of controversy, of war— not to mention the scandals—Milton went on dictating, printing, reprinting.

In 1672 Dryden put on the stage *The Assignation*, and *Marriage-à-la Mode, or Love in a Nunnery*, John Phillips brought out *Maronides, or Virgil travestied*, and the solitary of Artillery Walk published two editions of a *Logic after the Dialectics of Ramus*,[1] enriched with exercises and a biographical notice.

In his treatise Milton made use of a commentary published in 1616 by Downham, Praelector of Logic in Cambridge, and followed a biography written by a German who was a contemporary of Ramus. The exercises and examples brought the book up to 235 pages. As the publisher also worked for the Royal Society, we may assume an agreement between the Society and Milton to mark in this way the centenary of the death of Ramus, who had perished in the St. Bartholomew Massacre. The initiative perhaps came from Milton. It is certain that he admired Ramus and was only too glad to make him better known.

Pierre La Ramée (1515–72), one of the early glories of the Collège de France,[2] has been forgotten. He aroused in

---

[1] *Artis Logicae Plenior Institutio ad Petri Rami Methodum Concinnata....*
[2] Founded by Francis I about 1530, to enable the leaders of the New Learning to teach independently of the University of Paris. Still extant. Entrance to all lectures free for all, confers no diplomas, staff self-recruited.

his day as much enthusiasm and as much fury as Darwin caused in the last century. We need not here examine his general conception of the world. Still largely medieval, it was to be abandoned in England for the philosophy of Locke. His logic, on one important point, anticipated Descartes.

Descartes was to thrust aside the medieval disputation in the name of experience; Ramus simplified it. He blamed the scholastics for 'having preferred to living discussion such as poets, orators and philosophers practise, a mass of rules without any connection with it which embarrass rather than enlighten the mind'.[1] The self-styled disciples of Aristotle had invented nineteen types of syllogism! For the triangle of the syllogism Ramus substituted the horns of the dilemma. To decide whether 'Peter is mortal' it is useless to reason from *barbara* or *baralipton* on premises which are themselves doubtful. It is sufficient to posit the alternative— 'mortal or immortal'? The common sense of the first comer replies without error and immediately. It is the method of 'all or nothing' as applied to-day in cybernetics.

According to Ramus, the universe was rational. It followed from this that our reason, the inward light given to each one, can distinguish the true from the false. The logician's part is the 'dichotomy', the dissection of problems in successions of alternatives. Before Descartes proclaimed his faith in common sense, Ramus had written—'*homo animal logicum*', that is, man is capable of choice, and the whole of logic is nothing but choice.

The dialectic of Ramus won over many minds in Europe, particularly in Protestant countries; Descartes found it established in Holland. It had been taught in Cambridge since 1570. When Milton composed his treatise, it reigned supreme in England; it was to maintain itself there until the end of the century. In 1620 when the *Mayflower* sailed away from the English coast, Locke was not born, Descartes had published nothing; it was Ramus whom the Pilgrim Fathers carried away with them. His logic was to build up the framework of all the sermons of New England. Roger Williams' opponent, John Cotton, was to write: 'We have

[1] Jacques Chevalier, *Histoire de la Pensée*, 1956, vol. II, p. 586.

in us essential wisdom, that is to say our reason, which is natural'. His grandson Cotton Mather in 1695 would put the 'great and famous martyr of France, Peter Ramus' above Aristotle. Milton's manual, in fact, was for a long time in use at Harvard. And if to-day, according to Merritt Y. Hughes,[1] all American students during a term or even a whole year, 'are increasingly tasting, swallowing, or chewing and digesting large Miltonic rations', it is largely because the principles of Ramus which have passed into American life can be read in full in Milton. There, too, Ramus is forgotten, but he is to be found again in *Areopagitica*, where Milton asserts so emphatically that every man has the duty, and therefore should have the right, to find his truth himself by his free choice. 'When God gave man reason', declares Milton, 'he gave him freedom to choose, for reason is but choosing.'[2] This is pure Ramus. Milton's God does not speak otherwise—

'When Will and Reason (Reason also is choice) . . .'[3]
And I will place within them as a guide
My Umpire *Conscience*, whom if they will hear,
Light after light well us'd, they shall attain. . . .[4]

At the beginning of 1673, when the King's Declaration of Indulgence was intensifying the uneasiness of the people, Milton intervened with his twenty-fifth pamphlet, sixteen pages entitled *Of True Religion, Heresy, Schism, Toleration, and the Growth of Popery*. The pamphlet did not name the printer but designated the author by his initials. The theory of it amounted to this—all those who base their belief solely on the Bible such as they understand it, are brothers and should form a front against Popery, which follows human traditions and adds to the Bible. Heresy is merely a choice; honest differences between Protestants are a matter of small importance. Popery, a deliberate deviation, is 'at this day in Christendom the only or the greatest heresy' (B. II, 510). Moreover, it is an enterprise of political domination. Lastly, it is idolatrous. Now God forbids idolatry, even in private. It follows that the magistrate, even when he does

---

[1] *John Milton, Complete Poems and Major Prose*, New York, 1957; p. vii.
[2] Bohn II, 74.   [3] *Paradise Lost* III, 108.   [4] Ibid., 194–6.

not look upon Catholics as politically dangerous, still has the duty to 'remove their idolatry, and all the furniture thereof, whether their idols or the mass' (515). As to persons and property, Christian charity orders us to respect them. Moreover, if we wish to stay the progress of Popery, let us 'amend our lives with all speed' (519).

Never would Roger Williams have contemplated forbidding anyone to adore God in his own house after his own manner. Circumstances must be taken into account; England was sick and feverish. Moreover, sclerosis had crept over Milton's piety with the years. There was also something more. The Quakers found it excellent that the Declaration should include Catholics. Any extension of liberty of conscience seemed to them good to give and good to take. But they had never played any part in politics; none of them had searched suspects or censured the press; their hands were clean.

In the course of this same year 1673, Milton republished not only his *Logic* of the previous year, but his collection of verse of 1645, adding about fifteen poems, but not his republican sonnets. L'Estrange would not have allowed it. The Italian eulogies were lovingly reproduced. After the poems came the treatise *Of Education*.

Thus, in these few months, the career of the poet-polemist-pedagogue was presented afresh to the new generation. At the year's close that generation rendered the poet homage that made him smile.

Dryden had undertaken to produce three plays a year at the King's Theatre, of which he was manager. He seldom succeeded in achieving this, but he worked hard. Since opera was the fashion he had, as we have seen, produced an operatic version of *The Tempest*. In those days when rhyming was also in fashion, he claimed, and proved, that he could rhyme richly any text whatever. He called this 'transversing'. Having decided to apply his talents to *Paradise Lost*—naturally, with the author's permission, one winter's day he called at Artillery Walk. Waller was with him, curious to see at last, and to hear, this strange poet, his junior by two years, of whom Dorset and Dryden spoke so highly. As for him he did not envisage the possibility of this Milton eclipsing every poet living and dead. Had he not written:

> Poets that lasting marble seek
> Must carve in Latin or in Greek;
> We write on sand. . . .

It should be noted that Dryden and Milton had no deep regard for each other. Milton said of Dryden: 'He is a rhymist but no poet'. Dryden declared in his turn: 'He writes in blank verse because he has not the gift of rhyme'.

Richardson has related from the reminiscences of an aged clergyman, Dr. Wright, what were the impressions of visitors at that time. He was approaching his end when Dr. Wright went to see him.

> He found him in a small house, he thinks but one room on a floor. In that up one pair of stairs, which was hung with a rusty green, he found John Milton, sitting in an elbow chair, black clothes, and neat enough, pale but not cadaverous, his hands and fingers gouty and with chalk-stones . . .[1]

Milton received his colleagues with his usual politeness, but his reply to Dryden was not without irony: 'It seems you have a mind to *tag* my points and you have my leave to tag 'em'.[2]

Dryden did not ask for more. It only took him a month to write his transversion *The State of Innocence, and Fall of Man: An Opera*.[3] Though it was not to be printed until 1677, copies were circulated immediately; they finally amounted to hundreds, for the poet laureate, royal historiographer and manager of the principal London theatre, was famous. The solitary and his close friends were tickled with Dryden's couplets in which the jingle of rhyme replaced the mighty Miltonic swell.

Since the heroic opera was so warmly received, why not republish the epic? Simmons offered a second edition 'revised and augmented by the author'. This time the pages were numbered, though the lines were not. The

---

[1] Masson VI, 679.
[2] Hanford, *John Milton, Englishman*, New York, 1949, p. 241.
[3] *John Dryden: A Bibliography*, by Hugh Macdonald, Oxford, 1939, No. 81a.

spelling and the punctuation were corrected in accordance
with a system elaborated by the poet,[1] the Books VII and X,
being longer than the others, were divided into two, and
the Argument was distributed between the twelve Books.
So much for the revision; as for the announcement 'augmented by the author', it was justified by the fact that
Milton, to smooth the breaks caused by the new divisions,
added three lines at the beginning of Book VIII and five
at the beginning of Book XII.

Two epistles in verse introduced the volume.[2] That by
Marvell was a methodical examination, adorned by a few
images:

> Thou singst with so much gravity and ease,
> And above humane flight dost soar aloft
> With Plume so strong, so equal, and so soft.
> The Bird nam'd from that Paradise you sing
> So never flaggs, but always keeps on Wing.

At the end came an effectual kick to Dryden:

> While the *Town-Bayes* writes all the while and spells,
> And like a Pack-horse tires without his Bells:
> Their Fancies like our Bushy-points appear,
> The Poets tag them, we for fashion wear . . .
> Thy Verse created like thy Theme sublime,
> In Number, Weight, and Measure, needs not Rhime.

We notice that this eulogy was rhymed. A modest poet
using a minor literary form must not venture into blank
verse.

Milton's two final publications came out in July 1674.
He had kept copies of letters written by him in Latin either
to friends, or to foreign Powers, and wanted to hand them
down to posterity. The government refused its *imprimatur*
for the official letters. The others appeared with seven
Cambridge lectures. The interest of these hundred and
fifty pages is almost solely biographical. They have been
quoted here more than once.

---

[1] Owing to Milton's blindness, the correction was imperfect, so that the text of
1674 is no more reliable than that of 1667.
[2] See above, p. 263.

The other publication was the translation into English of a Latin document of about fifteen pages, *A Declaration, or Letters-Patents (sic) for the Election of this present King of Poland, John the Third...*[1] The Polish Diet had sent these Letters to all the chancelleries in Europe. Milton considered that the English public could draw a lesson from them. This translation was therefore one more political gesture, the final one.

John III, in fact, was the renowned Sobieski. Years before, after conquering the Swedes, the Turks, the Tartars and the Cossacks, he had refused the crown. An incapable and cowardly king, Michael Koribut, had then surrendered provinces to the enemy. Sobieski had won new triumphs, and, finally, Michael being dead, he had allowed himself to be declared king by the unanimous Diet. His election dated from May 22nd, 1674, the *Letters Patent* had arrived in London in June; Milton's translation appeared in July. The Polish document contained a phrase which explains the haste of the old fighter: Poland had 'at length abolished ... that reproach cast upon her, ... "That none can be elected King of Poland, but such as are born out of Poland" ... and by a certain divine instinct, turned upon the high marshal of the Kingdom ... John Sobieski'.

How could one help comparing Sobieski and Cromwell, Michael Koribut and the Stuarts? How could one refrain from thinking also of the Stadtholder of the Low Countries, elected by the people for his heroism? As soon as the peace had been signed, a new Councillor, Danby, had sounded the Dutch with a view to a marriage between the prince and the eldest daughter of the Duke of York. The marriage was not to take place until 1678 and the couple did not reign in London until ten years later, but had not the author of *Lycidas* obscurely sensed the end of Laud? Milton liked to compare himself to Tiresias.

While some of his fellow-countrymen were reading his final appeal, Milton had an attack of gout which made him fear for his life. His brother was then a member of the London Bar, but spent the summers in Ipswich as a deputy

[1] Bohn III, 479 seqq., or Masson VI, 725 seqq.

judge. That summer, about July 20th, he came to say goodbye to the poet as usual. The latter told him in confidence that they would perhaps not see each other again, and that all his property was to go to his wife.

Through negligence, timidity, or a blind man's diffidence, Milton was to leave no other will than this declaration. His biographers have lost nothing thereby, for his daughters, after his death, protested before the Courts and the verbatim report of the investigation is rich in the detail of everyday life. The chief witness, Christopher, attested that his brother, who had often complained to him of the ingratitude of his children, that day had declared to him solemnly:

> Brother, the portion due to me from Mr. Powell, my former wife's father, I leave to the unkind children I had by her; but I have received no part of it: and my will and meaning is that they shall have no other benefit of my estate than the said portion and what I have besides done for them, they having been very undutiful to me. And all the residue of my estate I leave to the disposal of Elizabeth, my loving wife.[1]

Then the servant, Elizabeth Fisher, cited facts and remarks in support of Milton's displeasure. She testified that he had provided his daughters with a good means of livelihood by trade; she also deposed that a day or two after Mr. Christopher's visit, when her master and mistress were at table in the sick man's room, she had brought a dish prepared by her mistress of which Milton was very fond and that he had then said gaily to Mrs. Milton: 'God have mercy, Betty, I see thou wilt perform according to thy promise in providing me such dishes as I think fit whilst I live; and when I die, thou knowst that I have left thee all'.[1] Later she had heard him express himself in the same sense several times.

A sister of this Elizabeth Fisher affirmed that when she was with her in the Miltons' kitchen at the moment when the master and mistress were taking their meal there, she had heard Mr. Milton say to his wife: 'Make much of me as long as I live, thou knowest I have given thee all when I die at thy disposal'.[2] This incident occurred three months

---

[1] Masson VI, 727–8.   [2] Ibid., 731.

after Christopher's visit, that is, in the middle of October. The poet was as cheerful as usual and seemed fully restored to health.

A fortnight later a fresh attack obliged him to take to his bed. He died on November 8th, aged sixty-six all but one month, 'with so little pain or emotion', relates the Anonymous Witness, 'that the time of his expiring was not perceived by those in the room'.

It was this easy death that the Archangel Michael promised to Adam, provided he observed the golden rule—the rule of not too much:

> So maist thou live, till like ripe Fruit thou drop
> Into thy Mothers lap, or be with ease
> Gatherd, not harshly pluckt, for death mature . . .
>
> *P.L.* XI, 535-7

EPILOGUE

HE was buried near his father in the chancel of the church of St. Giles, which happened to be his parish. The celebrant was a friend, Dr. Annesley, cousin of the Earl of Anglesey.

The lawsuit as to the inheritance came on in December. When the Court rejected the nuncupative will, the prudent Betty, without waiting for arbitration, came to an understanding with her step-daughters. She made over one hundred pounds to each of them. The remainder, about seven hundred pounds, enabled her to live very modestly in her native Cheshire.

Must we continue? The biographer has done his work and is under no obligation to do so. Yet, even man's earthly life does not end with the grave. Indeed, most of the fruits of genius only ripen after the fall of the tree. It was to that law that Milton was alluding when he wrote—'A good book is the precious life-blood of a master-spirit, embalmed and treasured up on purpose to a life beyond life'. To retrace Milton's life beyond life would require the united efforts of an international team of scholars over a number of years. A few facts will at least indicate how vigorous has been Milton's survival and how singular. While the children of his body soon became 'heads without name no more remembered', the fruits of his mind have never ceased to arouse both admiration and hostility.

1679   His tombstone was removed to make room for two altar steps.

1683   Oxford and Cambridge condemned '27 propositions found in Milton, Knox and others'. The object of the dons was to reassure Charles II and his brother on the subject of the succession to the throne. The two universities declared—'Our princes hold their title not from the people, but from God. . . . The fundamental right of heriditary succession cannot be tampered with by any religion, any law, any fault or treason on the prince's part.'

1687   Winstanley, once a barber, declared in his *Lives of the most famous English Poets* that Milton's fame 'is gone out like a candle in a snuff, and his memory will always stink', because he had 'most impiously and villanously bely'd that blessed martyr King Charles the First' (Masson VI, 783).

1688   *Paradise Lost* passed into the hands of an enterprising editor, Tonson. He produced a *de luxe* edition, men of quality subscribed, among them Sir Edward Waller.

1692   The reply to Saumaise was published in English.

1693   Cambridge incorporated in its Latin dictionary, the source of all the Latin dictionaries in the realm, the manuscript *thesaurus* of Milton, in three folio volumes.

1694   Phillips published the official letters and the republican sonnets, with a biographical notice.

1697   Article on *Milton* in Bayle's *Dictionnaire*.

1698   Toland published the complete works in Amsterdam.

1709   The Dean of Westminster refused to allow in the abbey the epitaph of a poet,[1] in which Milton's name figured with honour.

1719   Addison discovered that one of Milton's daughters was still living. She was a Mrs. Deborah Clarke, widow of a weaver, who was teaching a few children. He gave her some guineas and promised her a pension, but he died that same year.

1727   Death of Deborah and of Mrs. Milton. Voltaire introduced Milton to the French.

1729   *Paradise Lost* published in French.

1737   A bust of Milton was placed in the Poets' Corner at Westminster.

1738   Complete works published in London by Birch.

1750   Lauder, by dint of forgeries, persuaded a large public that Milton was a wholesale plagiarist. Dr. Johnson discovered the poet's last descendant, Mrs. Foster, Deborah's daughter. She was keeping a grocer's shop in a side-street in the East End. Garrick, a former pupil of Dr. Johnson's, was in charge of Drury Lane. He gave a performance of *Comus* for the benefit of Mrs. Foster, who had to have explained to her what benefit performance meant. The richer by £130, she left Cock Lane to sell soap and candles in the pleasant village of Islington.

1790   The parochial authorities of St. Giles had the church repaired. They took advantage of this circumstance to open the poet's tomb, profane the leaden coffin, exhibit the bones for a shilling, and sell them piecemeal.

---

[1] John Philips (1676–1709), author of *The Splendid Shilling*. The epitaph read— 'Second to none but Milton'.

2A

We need go no further than this perfect example of a double destiny. The general public naively respected the biblical frescoes and their author but, to quote Péguy, 'les docteurs ont la mémoire longue'. Providentially, the piety of the crowd enabled 'the doctors' to purge St. Giles of a presence which weighed heavily upon them. At length, in 1790, the doctors could breathe; the material link was snapped between them and this '*anarque*', whose poisonous principles were triumphing on both shores of the Atlantic. His writings and his example had constantly enlightened and encouraged the American rebels. In 1789 they had just elected their first president, Washington, who applauded the fall of the Bastille. The sovereigns and the clergy were threatened. While Marie-Antoinette was reading *Paradise Regained* (her copy still exists) Mirabeau was translating the *Areopagitica* and Salaville, in his *Théorie de la Royauté*, was summing up the famous reply to Salmasius.

What is our final impression of the poet and polemist? In certain respects he repels us, in certain others he eludes us. His life at least shows us (and that is why it had to be written) the nobility and spiritual unity of his work, which is itself inseparable from his person. English people neglect him in times of calm, but call upon 'the supreme Englishman' in the hour of danger, as, for example, Wordsworth in 1802 or London in 1940. He remains one of the heroes of what Denis de Rougemont calls 'l'aventure occidentale de l'homme'. No one was more convinced than Milton that 'quest, unceasing quest, is our form of existence'.[1]

---

[1] *L'Aventure occidentale de l'homme*, Paris, 1957, ch. xii.

MILTON'S WRITINGS

POETRY   PROSE

1628 *Naturam non pati senium.*
1632 On Shakespeare.
1637 Comus.
1638 Lycidas.
1640 *Epitaphium Damonis.*

1641	Of Reformation . . . in England.
1641	Of Prelaticall Episcopacy.
1641	Animadversions . . .
1642	Reason of Church Government.
1642	Apology for Smectymnuus.
1643	Doctrine and Discipline of Divorce (repr. 1644, 1645).
1644	Of Education (repr. 1673).
1644	The Judgement of Martin Bucer concerning Divorce.
1644	Areopagitica.

1645 (old reckoning)
Poems both in English
and *Latin* (repr. 1673)

1645	Tetrachordon.
1645	Colasterion.
1649	Tenure of Kings and Magistrates (repr. 1650).
1649	Observations on . . . Irish rebels.
1649	Eikonoklastes (repr. 1650, tr. into French 1652 (old reckoning)).
1651	*Pro Populo Anglicano Defensio* . . . (repr. 1652, 1658).
1654	*Pro Populo Anglicano Defensio secunda.*
1655	*Pro se Defensio: Ad Mori Supplementum Responsio; Scriptum dom. Protectoris . . . contra Hispanos* . . .
1659	Of Civil Power in Eccles. Causes.
1659	How to remove Hirelings out of the Church.

1660 Ready and Easy Way to establish a free Commonwealth (repr. 1660).

1660 Present Means . . . (for Monk).

1660 Brief Notes on a late Sermon. (Collaboration in 'Mercurius Politicus', 1650–1660)

1667 Paradise Lost (repr. 1674).

1669 Latin grammar.

1670 History of Britain to the Conquest.

1671 Paradise Regained.

1671 Samson Agonistes.

1672 *Artis logicae . . . Petri Rami . . .* (repr. 1673).

1673 Poems of 1645, with additions.

1673 Of True Religion, Heresy, etc.

1674 R. Paradise Lost.

1674 *Epistolae familiares et Prolusiones.*

1674 Letters Patent for the Election of John III, King of Poland.

POSTHUMOUS PUBLICATIONS

1681 Character of the Long Parliament and Assembly of Westminster.

1682 A brief History of Moscovia.

1694 *Official letters* (Latin) and political sonnets.

1698 Letter to a Friend (written in 1659).

1825 *De Doctrina Christiana*, ms. of 735 pp. found in the archives of a ministry.

WARS AND PARLIAMENTS
FROM 1625 TO 1674

1625   Charles I (*b.* 1600) holds his First Parliament (one month). Abortive expedition against La Rochelle. Failure before Cadiz.

1626   Second Parliament (four months). Sir John Eliot and John Hampden imprisoned for refusal of a forced loan.

1627   Failure before La Rochelle.

1628   Third Parliament (March–June). Cromwell (*b.* 1599) there denounces Laud and other 'Papists'. Petition of Rights. Buckingham assassinated. New failure before La Rochelle.

1629   Recall of the Third Parliament (one month). Eliot imprisoned in the Tower for a speech. Cromwell retires to his lands.

1631   Cromwell refuses a knighthood.

1632   Death of Sir John Eliot in the Tower.

1633   The Puritans against the theatre. Laud appointed Archbishop of Canterbury.

1635   Ship-money extended to the whole kingdom.

1636   Ship-money being decreed permanent. Hampden refuses it.

1637   Hampden condemned. Writers penalized. Riot in Edinburgh.

1638   Scotland swears the Covenant and excommunicates its bishops.

1639   War 'of the bishops'; the Scots invade the North.

1640   Short Parliament (April; Cromwell represents Cambridge in it). Second 'bishops' war'. Long Parliament (Nov.). Strafford and Laud arrested. Cromwell demands that Parliament be convened every year.

1641   Parliament votes that it cannot be dissolved or adjourned except by itself[1] (May). Strafford executed. Cromwell and Vane demand the abolition of the episcopate. Ten bishops arrested. Massacre of Protestants in Ireland (Oct.). The Great Remonstrance (Nov.).

---

[1] It was this law that Bradshaw reminded Cromwell of on the occasion of the *coup d'Etat* in 1653. See above, p. 189.

1642 Civil War (August). Cromwell and sixty combatants formed by him rejoin the Parliamentary army. Essex beats Charles at Edgehill (Oct.). London repulses the royal army (Nov.).

1643 Cromwell promoted to colonel. Hampden killed (June). Victory of the 'Ironsides' at Gainsborough (July). The Parliament adheres to the Covenant (Sept.). Charles recruits Irishmen.

1644 Cromwell leader of the army of the West (Jan.). Charles beaten by Essex and Cromwell at Marston Moor (July). Essex and Manchester beaten, or fail to exploit their successes. Cromwell's complaint to Parliament (Dec.).

1645 The New Model organized. Execution of Laud. Presbyterian organization imposed on the Anglican Church. Fairfax General in command (Feb.), Cromwell his second (June). Royal army crushed at Naseby (June).

1646 Charles surrenders to the Scots (May). Oxford capitulates. Bishops' lands put up for sale.

1647 Charles handed over to Parliament (Jan.) and removed by the army (June), takes refuge in the Isle of Wight (Nov.) and negotiates with Scotland.

1648 Second Civil War (Feb.–Sept.). Scotland subdued. The army expels the Presbyterian members of Parliament (*Pride's Purge*, Dec.). The Rump (Independents) remains.

1649 Charles beheaded January 30th.

1649 Commonwealth (Feb.). Cromwell masters the Levellers and Ireland (Drogheda). Scotland rises.

1650 Cromwell returns from Ireland (May), replaces Fairfax at the head of the army (June) and beats the Scots at Dunbar (Sept. 3rd).

1651 Charles II, crowned in Scotland, defeated at Worcester (Sept. 3rd), takes refuge in France. Navigation Act.

1652 War on Holland (May).

1653 Cromwell expels the Rump (April). Convention known as 'Barebones Parliament' (July–Dec.). Protectorate begins.

1654 Protectorate. Alliance with Holland. First Parliament (irregular) opens in Sept.

1655   Parliament dissolved (Jan.). Major-generals. War with Spain.

1656   Second Parliament (irregular) meets in Sept.

1657   Cromwell refuses the Crown. The régime is modified.

1658   Dissolution of second Parliament (Feb.). The Dunes. Death of Cromwell (Sept.). His son Richard succeeds him. Third Parliament.

1659   Richard abdicates (April). The Rump is recalled and dismissed.

1660   Monk in London (Feb.). Recall of those excluded in 1648 (Feb.). Parliament-Convention (April).

1660   Charles II (May). Restoration. Trial of the regicides, including Cromwell, Bill of Indemnity.

1661   Cavalier Parliament (dissolved only in 1679). Corporation Act.

1662   Act of Uniformity. Acquisition of Bombay. Sale of Dunkirk. Quaker Act.

1664   Conventicle Act.

1665   War with Holland. Plague. Five Mile Act.

1666   Fire of London.

1667   Peace of Breda. Acquisition of New York. Fall of Clarendon.

1668   Triple Alliance (England, Holland, Sweden) against Louis XIV.

1670   Secret Treaty of Dover between Charles II and Louis XIV (May).

1672   Declaration of Indulgence. War with Holland.

1673   Declaration recalled. Test Act.

1674   Peace with Holland. Death of Milton.

PORTRAITS OF MILTON

WHEN the poet's widow went to establish herself in Nantwich, Cheshire, she took with her the portrait of Milton as a child, and another which dated from his Cambridge days.

On Mrs. Milton's death (1727), the first passed to Charles Stanhope. On the latter's death (1760), it was acquired by an American, Thomas Hollis, surnamed 'The Republican', a passionate admirer of the polemist. It can be seen to-day in the Pierpont Morgan Library in New York.

The portrait of the student passed into the hands of Onslow, the Speaker of the House of Commons. He was supposed to have burnt it (see Hanford), in order that he might no longer be importuned by the curious. But it had been engraved by Vertue in 1731 and also several times later by him and by others. It has come to light recently and hangs in the National Portrait Gallery.

A bust, in Christ's College, belonged in turn to Vertue, to the painter Sir Joshua Reynolds and to Hollis. It was probably made partly from a plaster cast taken about 1654.

Another bust, found in South Italy by a clergyman between 1880 and 1890, was acquired by the collector Emile Mond. An expert in Italian art, G. Loukomski, recognized in its workmanship the manner of the Neapolitans of the seventeenth century. The late Denis Saurat was its possessor, and he reproduced it in his *Milton, Man and Thinker*.

Faithorne (see above, p. 248) had first of all drawn Milton in pastel, but this preparatory study seems to have disappeared. Another pastel by Faithorne, quite probably the one which moved Deborah, was acquired in 1959, through the generosity of W. H. Scheide, for the Princeton University Library.

A SELECT BIBLIOGRAPHY

Compiled by R. W. GIBSON

FOR the numerous contributions to literary journals, etc., relating to Milton and his works refer to Annual Bibliography of English Language and Literature, vol. I (1921)—vol. XXXIV (1959). M.=John Milton.

1. COLLECTED EDITIONS AND ANTHOLOGIES:
   (a) Poetry and Prose
   (b) Poetry
   (c) Prose
2. SEPARATE PUBLICATIONS:
   (a) Poetry
   (b) Prose
3. REFERENCE WORKS AND BIBLIOGRAPHY
4. BIOGRAPHY
5. CRITICAL AND MISCELLANEOUS STUDIES

1. COLLECTED EDITIONS AND ANTHOLOGIES

(chronological arrangement of a series of groupings)

(a) POETRY AND PROSE

Works, in verse and prose, ed. by J. Mitford, 8 vols., 1851, *the Aldine edn., Latin text of prose, no translations.*

Student's Milton, ed. by F. A. Patterson, N.Y., 1930; revised, 1933, *complete poems and majority of the prose.*

Works, ed. by various hands, gen. editor—F. A. Patterson, 18 vols., N.Y., 1931–38, *Columbia University edn., with two volume index, modern spelling, the only complete edn. of Milton's works.*

Complete Poetry and selected prose, ed. by E. H. Visiak, 1952, *the Nonesuch Library.*

Portable Milton, ed. by D. Bush, 1949; re-issues to 1962.

Complete Poems and major prose, ed., with notes by M. Y. Hughes, N.Y., 1957.

(*b*) POETRY

Poems, both English and Latin, 1645; type facsimile, 1924; photo-facs. (English only), Noel Douglas replica, 1926; reprint, with essays by C. Brooks and J. E. Hardy, 1957.

Poems, etc. upon several occasions, with tractate of education, 1673; ed. by T. Warton 1785; revised edn., 1791.

Poetical Works, ed. by P. H(ume), 1695.

Poetical Works, with notes by various authors, ed. by T. Newton, 3 vols., 1749–52; many subsequent edns.

Poems, ed. by S. Johnson, 3 vols., 1779, *Works of English poets*.

Poetical Works, ed. by H. J. Todd, 6 vols., 1801; with additions and verbal index, 7 vols., 1809; several subsequent edns., *a variorum edn.*

Life and Poetical works, with notes by W. Cowper, ed. by W. Hayley, 4 vols., Chichester, 1810, *includes transln. of Andreini's Adamo.*

English Poems, ed. by R. C. Browne, notes by H. Bradley, 2 vols., Oxford, 1866, etc., *annotated edn.*

Poetical Works, ed. by D. Masson, 3 vols., 1874; revised edn., 1890; Golden Treasury series, 2 vols., 1874; One vol. Globe edn., 1877.

Cambridge Milton for schools, ed. by A. W. Verity, 10 vols., 1891–96, *Pitt Press Series, annotated edition.*

Complete Poetical Works, ed. by W. M. Moody, Boston, 1899; new edn., by E. K. Rand, 1924.

Poetical Works, ed. by H. C. Beeching, 1900; revised edn., 1938, *reprints from the first edns.*

English Poems, ed. by H. C. Beeching, 1900; revised 1938, 1941, *World's Classics, modern spelling.*

Poetical Works, ed. by W. Aldis Wright, 1903, *modernized text, with variant readings*; Poems, *Everyman's Library.*

Poetical Works, ed. by W. Raleigh, 1905.

Sonnets, with original notes and new biographical matter, ed. by J. S. Smart, 1921.

Poems, ed. by H. J. C. Grierson, 2 vols., 1925, *arranged in chronological order.*

Poems in English, with illustrations by William Blake, ed. by G. Keynes, 1926.

Latin Poems, ed. by W. Mackeller, Yale, 1930.

Minor Poems, ed. by W. J. Halliday, 1931, etc.

Poems, ed., with introd. and notes, by J. H. Hanford, N.Y., 1936, *chronologically arranged, modern spelling.*

Complete Poetical Works, a new text edn., with introd. and notes, ed. by H. F. Fletcher, Boston, 1941, *a revision of the Cambridge edn.*

Complete Poetical Works, reproduced in photographic facsimile, ed. by H. F. Fletcher, 4 vols., Urbana, 1943–48.

Poetical Works, ed. by H. Darbishire, 2 vols., 1952–55, *Oxford English texts*; Poems, 1961, *Oxford standard authors.*

Complete English Poems, ed. by J. Gawsworth, 1953, *illustrated edn.*

Dramatic Poems, ed. by G. & M. Bullough, 1958, 1960.

(*c*) PROSE

Complete collection of the historical, political and miscellaneous works (Published by J. Toland), 3 vols., 1694–98; ed. by T. Birch, 2 vols., 1738; enlarged, 1753.

Prose Works, with life, interspersed with translations by C. Symmons, 7 vols., 1806.

Prose Works, ed. by J. A. St. John, 5 vols., 1848–53, *Bohn Library edn., translns. only of the Latin Works, includes De doctrina Christiana.*

English Prose Writings, ed. by H. Morley, 1889, *Carisbrooke Library.*

Prose, selected by M. W. Wallace, 1925, etc., *World's Classics.*

Prose Writings, introd. by K. M. Burton, *Everyman's Library.*

Yale University edition of Prose, ed. by various hands, gen. editor—D. A. Wolfe, 7 vols., 1954–, *in progress; vols. I–III (1624–49) published.*

2. SEPARATE PUBLICATIONS

(alphabetical arrangement under the titles of the works)

(*a*) POETRY

Arcades, part of a masque, *in* Milton's Poems, 1645.

(Comus), A Maske presented at Ludlow Castle, 1637; ed. by H. J. Todd, 1798; ed. by O. Elton, 1893; facsimile, N.Y., 1903; with notes by Lady Egerton, 1910; ed. by D. Figgis, with Blake's Illustrations, 1926; ed. by E. H. Visiak, 1937.

Epitaph (An) on the admirable dramaticke poet, W. Shakespeare, first published in Shakespeare's Plays, 1632 (Second folio); also found in the folios of 1664, 1685, and Shakespeare's Poems, 1640.

Epitaphium Damonis, 1640; translated by W. W. Skeat, 1933; text, ed. by E. H. Visiak, with transln. by Skeat, 1935.

Lycidas *in* Justa Eduardo King naufrago (obsequies), 1638; reprinted, Dublin, 1835, etc.; Facsimile Text society, 1939.

Ode on the morning of Christ's nativity (1629); Daniel Press, 1894; with M.'s Hymn, Blake's illustrations, note by G. Keynes, 1923.

Paradise Lost, 1667; reprod. in exact facsimile, 1873, 1877; revised and augmented, 1674; ed. by R. Bentley, 1732; ed. by T. Newton, 2 vols., 1749; various other edns.

Paradise Regain'd, with Samson Agonistes, 1671; various other edns.

Samson Agonistes, 1688, 1695.

Some newly discovered stanzas on engraved scenes illustrating Ovid's Metamorphoses, by H. C. H. Candy, 1924.

(Sonnet to H. Lawes) *in* Choice Psalmes, 1648.

(Sonnet to Sir H. Vane) *in* [Sikes (G.)] The life and death of Sir Henry Vane, 1662.

(*b*) PROSE

Accedence commenc't grammar, 1669.

Animadversions upon the remonstrant's defence against Smectymnuus, 1641.

(Apology for Smectymnuus). An apology against a pamphlet . . . 1642.

Areopagitica, a speech for the liberty of unlicenc'd printing, 1644; ed. by J. W. Hale, Oxford, 1882; Noel Douglas facsimile, 1927; various other edns.

Artis logicae plenior institutio, 1672, 1673, 1678.

Brief History of Moscovia, 1682; ed. by R. R. Crawley, 1941.

Brief Notes upon a late sermon, 1660.

Character of the Long Parliament and assembly of Divines in mdcxli, omitted in his other works, 1681; reprinted in Harleian Misc., vol. 10, 1810.

Colasterion, a reply to A Nameless answer against the Doctrine and discipline of divorce, 1645.

Considerations touching the likeliest means to remove hirelings out of the Church, 1659; reprinted 1839.

De Doctrina Christiana, with transln. by C. Sumner, 2 vols., 1825.

Declaration (A) or letters patents of the election of this present King of Poland, John III., 1674, M.'s transln.

Doctrine (The) and discipline of divorce, 1643; revised edns., 1644, 1645.

Eikonoklastes, in answer to ... Eikon Basilike, 1649; much enlarged, 1650, 1690; other edns.

Epistolae familiares and Prolusiones, 1674; transl. by J. Hall, 1829; Private correspondence and Academic exercises, transl. by P. B. Tillyard, 1932.

History (The) of Britain, 1670; other edns.; ed. by F. Maseres, 1818.

Judgement (The) of Martin Bucer, concerning divorce ... now Englisht, 1644.

Literae Pseudo-Senatus Anglicani, 1676, 1690; Letters of State, 1649–59, with life, etc., 1694; ed. by H. Fernow, 1903.

Observations upon the articles of peace with the Irish rebels, 1649.

Of Education (1644); ed. by O. M. Ainsworth, Yale, 1930; other edns.

Of Prelatical episcopacy, 1641.

Of Reformation touching Church-discipline in England, 1641; ed. by W. T. Hale, Yale, 1916.

Of True religion, haeresie, schism, toleration, 1673; new edn. 1826.

Pro Populo Anglicano defensio, 1651; ed. correctior, 1658; A Defense of the people of England, transl. by J. Washington, 1692, 1695.

—— Defensio secunda, 1654; English translns. by R. Fellowes, 1806, and F. Wrangham, 1816.

Pro se defensio contra A. Morus, 1655.

Prolusions quaedam oratoriae, added to Epistolae, 1674.

Readie (The) and easie way to establish a free commonwealth, 1660; ed. by E. M. Clark, Yale, 1915.

Reason (The) for Church-government urg'd against prelaty, 1641.

Reply (A) to the answer, 1642.

Tenure (The) of Kings and Magistrates, 1649; ed. by W. T. Allison, N.Y., 1911.

Tetrachordon, expositions . . . which treat of mariage or nullities of mariage, 1645.
Treatise (A) of civil power in ecclesiastical causes, 1659.

3. REFERENCE WORKS AND BIBLIOGRAPHY

Bradshaw (J.) A Concordance to the poetical works, 1894.
British Museum. Catalogue of printed books, excerpt—Milton, 1892.
—— Facsimile of the autographs and documents, 1908.
Cann (C.) Scriptural and allegorical glossary to Paradise Lost, 1828.
Cleveland (C. D.) A Complete concordance to the poetical works, 1867.
Cooper (L.) A concordance of the Latin, Greek and Italian poems, Halle, 1923.
Fletcher (H.) Contributions to a bibliography, 1800–1930, Urbana, 1931, *addenda to Stevens Reference Guide.*
Gilbert (A. H.) A geographical dictionary, New Haven, 1919.
Grün (R. H.) Das Menschenbild M. in Paradise Lost, 1956.
Hanford (J. H.) M. handbook, 1926, etc., *the best general guide, with bibliography.*
Huckabay (C.) A Bibliographical supplement, 1929–57, Duquesne studies, 1960.
Le Comte (E. S.) A Milton dictionary, 1961.
Lockwood (L.) Lexicon to the English poetical works, N.Y., 1907.
Marsh (J. F.) On the engraved portraits and pretended portraits, 1860.
Oras (A.) M.'s editors and commentators, 1695–1801, 1931.
Osgood (G. G.) The classical mythology of English poems, N.Y., 1900; reprinted, Oxford, 1925, *dictionary of M.'s mythological allusions.*
Parker (W. R.) Contributions towards a bibliography *in* The Library, 4th series, XVI, 1935.
Prendergast (G. L.) A Complete concordance to the poetical works, Madras, 1857–59.
Retrospective Review, Vol. 14, pp. 282–305, contains a bibliographical account of M.'s Poetical works.
Sotheby (S. L.) Ramblings in the elucidation of the autograph, 1861.

Stevens (D. H.) Reference guide from 1800 to (1930), Chicago, 1930.

Thompson (E. N. S.) A Topical bibliography, Yale, 1916.

Williamson (G. C.). The portraits, prints and writings exhibited at Christ's College, Cambridge, 1908, *M.'s tercentenary*.

Wright (W. A.) Trinity College manuscript published in facsimile, 1899; published in part by F. A. Patterson, Facsimile Text society, 1933, *the MS. of M.'s minor poems*.

4. BIOGRAPHY

The life of Milton was first told to the public by Anthony Wood in *Fasti Oxonienses*, 1691–92. Hating the 'Phanatics' and having never known Milton, he distorted the facts and misconstrued the motives. 'Wood it was that poisoned the wells' (B. A. Wright). The favourable accounts of Edward Phillips and others, besides the irresistible popularity of *Paradise Lost*, seemed to have hushed calumny, when Dr. Johnson, while doing ample justice to Milton the artist, unmercifully belaboured the character of the man, a dichotomy still prevalent to-day. Hence two traditions, impartially represented in the present section and in Section 5.

Early biographies by Aubrey, Wood, E. Phillips, Toland, Richardson, and Ellwood, are collected in the *Student's Milton* ed. by Patterson (see Section 1. a). Helen Darbishire (below) included in her six early lives the anonymous memoir now attributed to Cyriac Skinner. M. Y. Hughes (1. a) reproduces Aubrey, Phillips and the anonymous witness.

For several generations every student of Milton has been chiefly indebted, directly or not, to Masson's Life of Milton (below). He remains the standard authority. Gaps have been filled and errors corrected by a host of searchers.

Allodoli (E.) M. e l'Italia, Prato, 1907.

Bailey (J.) M., 1915, etc., *Home University Library*.

[Blackburne (E.)] Remarks on Johnson's Life of M., added Tract of education, 1780.

Brown (E.) M.'s blindness, 1934.

Clark (D. L.) M. at St. Paul's School, N.Y., 1948.

Darbishire (H.) The early lives of M., 1932.

Diekhoff (J. S.) M. on himself, 1939, *collection of personal passages from his works*.

Dunster (C.) Considerations on M.'s early reading and the Prima Stamina in his Paradise Lost, 1800.

Ellwood (T.) The history of the life of M., 1714; ed. by C. G. Crump, 1900; ed. by S. Graveson, 1906.

Fletcher (H.) The intellectual development of M., 1956.

French (J. M.) M. in Chancery, new chapters in the lives of the poet and his father, 1939.

—— editor. Life records of M., 4 vols., New Brunswick, 1949-58.

Garnett (R.) Life of M., 1890, *bibliography of J. P. Anderson.*

Godwin (W.) Lives of E. and J. Phillips, 1815, *to which is added collections for the life of M., by J. Aubrey and E. Phillips.*

Hamilton (W. D.) Original papers illustrative of the life and writings of M., 1859, *Camden Society.*

Hanford (J. H.) M., Englishman, 1950.

—— The youth of M., in Studies in Shakespeare, M. and Donne, N.Y., 1925.

Hardeland (G.) M. Anschauungen von Staat, Kirche, Toleranz, 1934.

Hayley (W.) The life of M., added Conjectures on the origin of Paradise Lost, 1796.

Horwood (A. J.), editor. A commonplace book of M., 1786, Camden Society; revised edn., 1877; MS. reproduction, 1876.

Johnson (S.) Life of M., 1779, etc., *in his Lives of the English Poets.*

Keightley (T.) Life, opinions and writings of M., 1855.

Leach (A. F.) M., as schoolboy and schoolmaster, *British Academy pamphlet.*

Macaulay (R.) M., 1933, etc., *Great Lives.*

Macaulay (T. B.) Essay on M., 1825; ed. by J. Downie, 1960.

Marsh (J. F.) Papers connected with the affairs of M. and his family, 1851.

Masson (D.) The life of M., 7 vols., including index, 1859-94.

Morand (P.-P.) De Comus à Satan, l'oeuvre poétique de M. expliquée par sa vie, 1939.

—— The effects of his political life upon M., 1939.

Muir (K.) M., 1955; new edn., 1960, 1962.

Parker (W. R.) M.'s contemporary reputation, 1940, *with tentative list of printed allusions to M.,* 1641-74.

Pattison (M.) M., 1879, *English Men of Letters series.*

Peck (E.) New memoirs of the life and poetical works of M., 1740.

[Phillips (E.)] An account of the life of M., *added to* M.'s Letters of State, 1694.

Saillens (E.) M., poète combattant, 1959.
Schultz (H.) M. and forbidden knowledge, 1955.
Spaeth (S.) M.'s knowledge of music, 1913.
Svendsen (K.) M. and science, 1956.
Toland (J.) Amyntor, or a defence of M.'s life, 1699, 1761.
—— The life of M., 1699, 1761; reprinted, with Fenton's life, 1924.

5. MISCELLANEOUS AND CRITICAL STUDIES

Adams (R. M.) Ikon, M. and the modern critics, 1956, etc.
Addison (J.) Notes upon the twelve books of Paradise Lost, 1719; ed. by E. Arber, 1868.
Allen (D. C.) The harmonious vision, studies in M.'s poetry, 1954.
Bailey (M. L.) M. and Jakob Boehme, 1914.
Barker (A.) M. and the Puritan dilemma, 1942.
Blondel (J.) M., poète de la Bible dans le Paradis perdu, 2 vols., 1959.
Bowra (M.) From Virgil to M., 1945.
Bredvold (L. I.) M. and Bodin's Heptaplomeres, 1924.
Bridges (R.) M.'s prosody, 1893; revised edns., 1901, 1921.
Broadbent (J. B.) Comus and Samson Agonistes (critical study), 1961.
—— Some graver subject, essay on Paradise Lost, 1960.
Brunner (H.) M. persönliche und ideele Welt in ihrer Beziehung zum Aristokratismus, 1933.
Buff (F.) M.'s Paradise Lost in seinem Verhaeltnis zur Aeneide, Ilias und Odyssee, 1904.
Bush (D.) Paradise Lost in our time, some comments, 1945; reprints, 1948, 1957.
Chauvet (P.) La religion de M., 1909.
Coleridge (S. T.) Seven lectures on Shakespeare and M., 1856.
Cope (J. I.) The Metaphoric structure of Paradise Lost, 1962.
Daiches (D.) M., (critical study), 1957; revised impressions, 1959, 1961, 1963.
De Guerle (E.) M., sa vie et ses oeuvres, 1868.
Eliot (T. S.) M., 1947, *British Academy annual lecture on a master mind.*
Empson (W.) 'M. and Bentley', some versions of pastoral, 1935.
—— M.'s God, 1961.

Ferry (A.) M.'s epic voice, Harvard, 1963.
Fletcher (H.) M.'s Rabbinical readings, 1930.
—— M.'s Semitic studies and some manifestations of them in
    his poetry, 1926.
—— The use of the Bible in M.'s prose, 1929.

Gajsek (A.) M. und Caedmon, 1911.
Geoffroy (A.) Étude sur les pamphlets politiques et religieux
    de M., 1848.
Gilbert (A. H.) On the composition of Paradise Lost, 1947.
Gilman (W. M.) M.'s rhetoric, studies in his Defense of liberty,
    1939.
Grierson (H. J. C.) M. and Wordsworth, poets and prophets,
    1937, etc.

Hamilton (G. R.) Hero or fool? a study of M.'s Satan, 1944.
Harding (D. P.) The Club of Hercules, studies in the Classical
    background of Paradise Lost, 1962.
Hartwell (K.) Lactantius and M., 1929.
Havens (R. D.) The influence of M. on English poetry, 1922.
Herford (C.) 'Dante and M.', the post-war mind of Germany,
    1927.
Hübener (G.) Die stilistische Spannung in M.'s Paradise Lost,
    1913.
Hutchinson (F. E.) M. and the English mind, 1947, etc.

Kelley (M.) This great argument, 1941, *study of M.'s De Doctrina
    Christiana.*
Kermode (P.), editor. The living M., essays by various hands,
    1960.
Kirsten (R.) Studien ueber das Verhaeltnis von Cowley und M.,
    1899.
Knight (G. W.) Chariot of wrath, the message of M. to demo-
    cracy at war, 1942.
Krouse (F. M.) M.'s Samson and the Christian tradition, 1947.

Langdon (I.) M.'s theory of poetry and fine art, 1924.
Larson (M.) The modernity of M., 1937.
Lauder (W.) An essay on M.'s use and imitation of the moderns
    in his Paradise Lost, 1750.
Lewis (C. S.) A preface to 'Paradise Lost', 1942, etc.
Liljegren (S. B.) Studies in M., 1918.
Looten (C.) M., quelques aspects de son génie, 1953.

Marilla (E. L.) Central problem of 'Paradise Lost', 1953.
Masterman (J. H.) The age of M., 1897.

McColley (G.) Paradise Lost, account of its growth and major origins, 1940.
McLachlan (H.) The religious opinions of M., Locke and Newton, 1941.
Mohl (R.) Studies in Spenser, M., and the theory of monarchy, N.Y., 1949, 1962.
Muir (K.) M., 1955; 2nd revised edn., 1961, general guide.

Nelson (F. G.) The sublime Puritan, M. and the Victorians, 1963.

Orchard (T. N.) The astronomy of Paradise Lost, 1896; revised 1913.

Parker (W. R.) M.'s debt to Greek tragedy in 'Samson Agonistes' 1937.
Patrides (C. A.), editor. M.'s Lycidas, the tradition and the poem, 1961.
Peter (J.) A critique of Paradise Lost, 1960, 1961.
Pizzo (E.) M.'s Verlorenes Paradies im deutschen Urteile des 18. Jahrhunderts, 1914.
Pommerich (E.) M. Verhaeltnis zu Torquato Tasso, 1902.
Pope (E. M.) 'Paradise Regain'd', the tradition and the poem, 1947.
Prince (F. T.) The Italian element in M.'s verse, 1954, 1962.

Rajan (B.) Paradise Lost, and the seventeenth-century reader 1947, 1962.
Raleigh (Sir W. A.) M., 1900, treatment of the poet's art.
Ricks (C.) M.'s grand style, 1963.
Ross (M. M.) M.'s royalism, study of the conflict of symbol and idea in the poems, 1943.

Sampson (A.) Studies in M., 1913.
Saurat (D.) Blake and M., Bordeaux, 1920.
—— La pensée de M., 1920.
—— M. et le matérialisme chrétien en Angleterre, 1928.
—— M., man and thinker, N.Y., 1925; revised, 1944.
Schork (W.) Die Dramenpläne M., 1934.
Sewell (A.) A Study of M.'s Christian doctrine, 1939.
Sims (J. H.) The Bible in M.'s epics, 1962.
Smith (L. P.) M. and his modern critics, 1940.
Stein (A.) Answerable style, essays on Paradise Lost, 1953.
—— Heroic knowledge, an interpretation of Paradise Lost and Samson Agonistes, 1957.
Stern (A.) M. und der Calvinismus, 1872.
—— M. und seine Zeit, 1877–79.

Stevens (D. H.) M. papers, Chicago, 1927.
Stoll (E. E.) Poets and playwrights: Shakespeare, Jonson, Spenser, M., Minneapolis, 1930.
Summers (J. H.) Muse's method, an introd. to Paradise Lost, 1962.
Taylor (G. C.) M.'s use of Du Bartas, 1934.
Telleen (J.) M. dans la littérature française, 1904.
Thompson (E. N. S.) Essays on M., 1914.
Thorpe (J.), editor. M. criticism, selections from four centuries, 1951, etc.
Tillyard (E. M. W.) M., 1930, etc., *a treatment of M.'s literary development*.
—— M., 1952, *Writers and their works*, 26; reprinted, with additions to bibliography, 1962.
—— M.: l'Allegro and Il Penseroso, 1932, *E.A. pamphlet* 82.
—— The metaphysicals and M., 1956.
—— The Miltonic setting, past and present, 1938; last edn., 1961.
—— Studies in M., 1951.
Tuve (R.) Images and themes in five poems by M., Camb., Mass., 1957.
Visiak (E. H.) M. Agonistes, a metaphysical criticism, 1923.
—— Portent of M., 1958.
Vogt (K. F.) M. als Publizist, 1933.
Waldock (A. J. A.) Paradise Lost and its critics, 1947; reprinted 1962.
Warren (W. F.) The universe as pictured in Paradise Lost, 1915.
Watkins (W.) Anatomy of M.'s verse, 1955.
Werblowsky (R. J. Z.) Lucifer and Prometheus, 1952.
Whaler (J.) Counterpoint and symbol, an inquiry into the rhythm of M.'s epic style, Copenhagen, 1956.
Whiting (G. W.) M.'s literary milieu, 1939.
Wilde (H. O.) M.'s geistesgeschichtliche Bedeutung, 1933.
Wilkes (G. A.) The thesis of 'Paradise Lost', 1961.
Wolfe (D. M.) M. in the Puritan revolution, 1941, 1963.
Wood (L. A.) The form and origin of M.'s antitrinitarian conception, 1911.
Woodhall (M.) The epic of Paradise Lost, 1907.
Wright (B. A.) M.'s Paradise Lost (a re-assessment), 1962.

INDEX

Acts of Parliament: Corporation Act, 241; Conventicles Act, 253, 254, 293; Five Mile Act, 254; Act of General Pardon, Indemnity & Oblivion, 237, 241; Navigation Act, 177, 181; Quaker Act, 242, 243; Test Act, 336, 337; Act of Uniformity, 242, 243
Ad Patrem, 42, 43
Addison, J., 27, 265
Agar, Thomas, 78, 112
Anglesey, Earl of, Arthur, 230, 236, 241, 252, 300, 346
Anglicans, 22, 110, 136
Animadversions, 90, 95
Annesley, Dr. Samuel, 346
Apology for Smectymnuus, 18, 32, 33, 90, 91
Arcades, 47, 53
Areopagitica, 125–35, 145, 255, 339, 347
Aristotle, 19, 20, 25, 29, 143, 319, 325, 326, 327, 338
army, 191, 193, 221, 223, 224
Arnold, C., 200
At a Vacation Exercise, 26, 27
Aubrey, xv, xvi, 7, 8, 9, 10, 14, 23, 153, 186, 202, 216, 247, 248, 250, 294
Augustine, St., 51, 281
Avenge O Lord, 208

Bacon, Francis, 19, 25, 27, 119, 201, 204, 294
Bailey, J., 313, 314, 317
Baptists, xix, 145, 146
Barberini, Francesco, 76, 77, 78
Barebones, Praise-God, 183, 230
Baring, Maurice, 278
Barrow, Isaac, 263, 294
Beaumont, 295
Bentley, 44, 265, 266, 274, 275
Bible, xx, xxii, 106, 143, 148, 198, 217, 220, 267, 251, 328
Blake, Robert, 181, 183, 206–8
Blondel, vi, 317, 318
Bodin, 45
Boyle, Robert, 119, 124, 294
Bradshaw, John, 153, 154, 174, 175, 186, 188, 189, 192, 206, 219, 221, 223, 229, 240
Bridges, Robert, 274, 342
Brief Notes, 229
Brockhurst, Lord, 302
Browne, Thomas, 94
Browne, William, 35, 36, 37
Brownings, 40

Buckingham, Duke of, 12, 13, 22, 27, 41, 158, 294, 296
Buckingham, son, 301, 335
Buommattei, Father, 70, 72
Bunyan, John, 232, 294
Butler, Samuel, 244, 295

Calamy, Edmund, 89, 238, 239, 252
Calvin, xviii, xix, xx, 65, 142
Cambridge, xvi, xxii, 6, 16, 17, 18, 19, 23, 33, 44, 294, 346
Canu, Jean, 12
Carew, 35, 51, 136
Carissimi, 68
Casaubon, 6
Catherine de Braganza, 242
Catholics, xxii, 4, 110, 134
censorship, 125–35
Cezanne, 274
Chappell, 21, 23
Character of the Long Parliament, 300
Charles I, xvii, xix, 13, 21, 22, 27, 28, 56, 57, 79, 83, 101, 103, 111, 137–8, 150, 152, 153, 157, 198, 202, 229, 292
Charles II, 124, 135, 158, 159, 162, 200, 201, 210, 232, 233, 235, 237, 238, 239, 240–4, 256, 259, 292, 294, 295, 335, 336, 346
Chateaubriand, xv, 20, 94, 135, 153, 195, 240, 277, 279
Chaucer, 9, 296
Chillingworth, 95, 126n
Christian Doctrine (De Doctrina Christiana), 142, 147, 197, 216, 265, 279
Christina of Sweden, 161, 163, 188
Christ's College, Cambridge, 17
Civil Power, Treatise of, 220
Claypole, Lady Mary, 199, 215
Cleveland, 60, 137, 203
Coke, Sir Edward, 145, 173
Colasterion, 106, 127, 136
Coleridge, S. T., 314
Comenius, 118, 119, 121, 122
Comminges, Comte de, 247
Commonwealth, xxii, 124, 135, 144, 154, 155, 158, 171, 177, 181, 189, 198, 201, 206, 217–18, 221, 223, 226, 229
Comus, 48, 49, 50–3, 55, 56, 63, 163, 194, 290, 326, 328, 347
Constitutional Convention, 183
Copernicus, 286
Corneille, 34, 56, 60n, 65, 66, 99, 203, 296

367

370

INDEX

More (Morus), Alexander, 185, 186, 187, 196, 197, 206, 208, 242
More, Henry, 201
Moseley, 137
Muir, Professor Kenneth, 94, 291

Napoleon, 195
Nayler, 211, 249
Naseby, 112, 137
Needham, 172, 173, 179, 180, 208, 225, 228-31, 235, 244, 253
Newton, Isaac, 201, 294
New Model Army, 112, 127, 137, 178

Ode to Rous, 138
Ode to the Nativity, 30, 33, 141
Of Education, 119-24, 126, 340
Of Prelatical Episcopacy, 90
Of Reformation in England, 90, 94, 96
Of the tenure of Kings and Magistrates, 152
Of True Religion, Heresy, Schism, Tolerance and the Growth of Popery, 339
Oldenburg, xiii, 197, 201, 294
On May Morning, 33, 35
Ordinance for Printing (1643), 135
Overton, Robert, 193, 198, 206
Oxford, xxii, 4, 5, 144, 145, 201, 294, 346

Paget, Dr. Nathan, 249, 253
Palmer, 108, 111, 126
Parliament, 83, 101, 110, 111, 125, 128, 132, 135, 137, 138, 144, 148, 150, 177, 178, 180, 194, 206, 210, 211, 212, 213, 220, 221, 241, 253, 292; Barebones, 183, 199; Rump, 152, 154, 178, 183, 221, 222, 223, 224, 225, 226
Paradise Lost, v, viii, 27, 51, 69, 72, 98, 112, 113, 114, 115, 116, 117, 142, 169, 170, 197, 216, 217, 248, 251, 254, 259-91, 299, 301, 302, 304, 305, 315, 331, 340, 341, 342, 345
Paradise Regained, 303, 305-18, 328, 329
Pascal, 89, 95, 119, 130, 287, 288
Péguy, xiv, 87, 348
Penn, William, 206-7, 211
Penn, son, 211, 293
Pepys, Samuel, 244, 258, 294, 295
Personal Defense, 187, 208
Peters, Hugh, 235, 239, 240, 255
Petition of Rights, 27
Petrachus, 32
Pilgrim Fathers, 12, 338
Pindar, 40
Phillips, Edward, *see* Milton
plague, 253, 254, 255, 256, 304
Plain English, 228, 230
Plato 30, 33, 37

Platonic Idea as understood by Aristotle, 29
Pope, Alexander, 203, 236
Pory, 17, 238
Poussin, 54
Powells, *see* Milton
Powicke, Sir M., xix, xx
Presbyterians, xxii, 57, 106, 108, 110, 127, 131, 134, 150, 151, 152, 156, 180, 206, 293, 336
Pride, Colonel Thomas, 152, 178, 211, 220, 225
Prolusion, 20
Protector, Lord, 133, 184, 187, 195, 200, 206, 207, 211, 212, 216
Protectorate, 135, 193, 200, 204, 210, 219
Prynne, 55, 56, 57, 108, 229, 235
Puritans, xx-xxii, 5, 7, 11, 12, 22, 36, 89, 106
Pym, xx, 83, 84, 101
Pythagoras, 121

Quakers, 145, 292, 340

Rabelais, 123
Racine, Jean, 314, 319, 326n
Raleigh, Sir Walter, 11, 213
Ramus, Peter, 19, 337, 338, 339
Randolph, 39
Ranelagh, Earl of, 98
Ranelagh, Lady, 119, 124, 172, 201, 209, 252
Ready and Easy Way to Establish a Free Commonwealth, The, 225-6, 229-30, 232-3
Reason of Church Government, 56, 89, 90, 97
Regii Sanguinis, 176, 185
Richelieu, 21, 65, 159
Rochester, Lord, 295
Roos, Lord, 301
Roscommon, 295
Rossetti, 40
Rota, 201, 202, 225
Rous, J., 133, 136
Royal Society, 119, 204, 264, 294, 337

Sabellius, 9
Sacrobosco, 9, 123
Sadlier, Mrs., 173, 174, 175
St. Evremond, 203, 293
St. Lambert, 39
St. Paul, 14, 114, 116, 326
St. Paul's School, 8, 9, 10
Saintsbury, G., 51, 94
Samson Agonistes, 56, 166-7, 215, 303, 319-34
Saumaise, Dr. de, 71, 158, 159, 160, 161, 162, 163, 164, 168, 176, 186, 188, 196, 218, 237, 247, 299, 347, 348
Saurat, Denis, v, 143, 315, 319

Barbican

Jewin Street

Finsburie Field

S. Albons

Moor gate

Oatmeale

St. Paulus

Bread Street

R I V E

R. Walls along the Ri
S. Snow hill
T. Smith field
VVV. Cyt Walls

Bull
Bayting
Shakspere's
Play-house